Latin American Nations in World Politics

Foreign Relations of the Third World

Latin American Nations in World Politics

*edited by Heraldo Muñoz
and Joseph S. Tulchin*

Westview Press • Boulder and London

For Judy,

who has been over every step of the way with me

J.S.T.

The paper used in this publication meets the requirements of the American National Standard for Permanence of Paper for Printed Library Materials Z39.48-1984.

Foreign Relations of the Third World, No. 3

Published in 1984 in the United States of America by Westview Press, Inc., 5500 Central Avenue, Boulder, Colorado 80301; Frederick A. Praeger, Publisher

Library of Congress Cataloging in Publication Data
Main entry under title:
Latin American nations in world politics.
    (The foreign relations of the Third World series; v. 3)
    Includes index.
    1. Latin America—Foreign relations—1948– —
Addresses, essays, lectures. I. Muñoz, Heraldo.
II. Tulchin, Joseph S., 1939–   . III. Series.
F1414.2.L329   1984   327.8   84-7302
ISBN 0-86531-688-0
ISBN 0-86531-689-9 (pbk.)

Printed and bound in the United States of America

10   9   8   7   6   5   4   3   2

Contents

Preface

The study of foreign affairs in the last two centuries has been dominated by the great powers, just as they have exerted influence and control over relations among nations. Since the great powers for centuries have been located in Europe and North America, the study of international affairs has had a Eurocentric bias. That bias has affected the way in which people all over the world have discussed diplomacy and international politics: It has been apparent in setting the "rules of the game" for international politics and international law, in setting the agenda for negotiations in the forums of international agencies, and in setting the framework within which international affairs have been studied. That framework, like the dominant social-science paradigms concerning economic development, political modernization, and cultural change, legitimated the hierarchy of status in the world system in which the nations in the Third World were considered subordinate. Not only were developing nations weaker than developed nations, they also were inferior or subordinate as subjects for study. Their reality was to be understood in terms of their relationships to the great powers.

The intellectual subordination of Latin America was attacked first in the 1940s by the staff of the United Nations Economic Commission for Latin America (ECLA), under the leadership of the Argentine economist Raúl Prebisch, within the context of a search for an explanation for the region's economic subordination or underdevelopment. The outgrowth of that effort, known as dependency theory, served both to explain the persistence of Latin American underdevelopment and to provide a framework for the study of the region that was not merely a function of great power perceptions or models. Similar efforts have been made in the past twenty years in the analysis of politics, society, culture, and literature. All of these serve to highlight Latin American reality and, in one way or another, help to explain the region's position in world affairs. It is strange, then, to realize that very little has been accomplished from a Latin American perspective in the field of international relations.

In recent years there has appeared, both in the United States and in Latin America, a series of case studies of the external policies of Latin American nations. This work is essentially descriptive. Other lines of research have emphasized the diplomatic history of the region or of some particular countries or have studied the functional or geographic dimensions of the international relations of Latin America as a whole. (See the Research Bibliography.) Little, if any, of this work explicitly tests the dominant paradigms of the field with a view to exploring their appropriateness for the analysis of Latin American international relations.

To remedy this deficiency, scholars at the Instituto de Estudios Internacionales of the Universidad de Chile and the Institute of Latin American Studies of the University of North Carolina at Chapel Hill organized a conference at Viña del Mar, Chile, from September 20 to 23, 1982. The conference was supported by the National Science Foundation of the United States and the Comisión Nacional de Investigación Científica y Tecnológica of Chile. The Universidad de Chile provided generous hospitality during the conference and the Office of International Programs of the University of North Carolina at Chapel Hill provided funds for translating manuscripts and for preparing the manuscript for the press. Heraldo Muñoz, who was my collaborator in organizing the conference and in preparing the papers for publication, joins me at this opportunity to thank officials of both institutions for their encouragement and support.

The conference was designed to apply different theoretical models, developed in the United States as well as in Latin America, to the concrete study of the foreign policies of Latin American states. (I should note here that the book edited by Julio Cotler and Richard Fagen, *Latin America and the United States: The Changing Political Realities* [Stanford, Calif.: Stanford University Press, 1974], attempted in part to do something similar. But even though the volume included articles that applied decision-making models to the analysis of U.S.–Latin American relations and essays that utilized structural approaches, the chapters concentrated on inter-American relations in general and did not present varied theoretical alternatives for the study of Latin American foreign policies.) The central objective of the conference was not to describe those policies in greater detail, but—more ambitiously—to find systematic explanations for the external behavior of Latin American nations in the light of various theoretical approaches to the study of foreign policy. The organizing principle of the conference was sessions focusing on one of several theoretical models in which papers by Latin American and U.S. scholars were juxtaposed and in which the foreign relations of Latin American nations were discussed in comparative perspective. The following sessions were held: (1) theoretical models for the analysis of foreign policy, (2) perceptions and decision making in foreign policy, (3) power politics and diplomacy, (4) nongovernmental actors and foreign policy, (5) external dependency and foreign policy, (6) political regimes and foreign policy, and (7) external context and foreign policy.

Many papers at the conference brought out the intimate relationship between external factors and internal power groups in the formulation of foreign policy in any Latin American country, irrespective of the type of political regime in that country. Similarly, despite the desire for autonomous action, it was clear from many of the case studies that certain constraints, such as economic dependency and long-standing relationships with hegemonic powers, had greater influence on the formulation of foreign policy than regime type or specific economic development objectives. Further, alliances of political parties have had important roles to play in the foreign-policy behavior of several countries in the region. Finally, regime type was held to be a more significant factor in determining the manner in which policy is formulated than the definition of national foreign-policy objectives.

The conference participants concluded unanimously that the comparative mode adopted during the proceedings was an invaluable aid to enhancing our understanding of the foreign-policy behaviors of Latin American nations. The nature of the comparative mode, together with the intense, collegial atmosphere of the conference, made it easier and more exciting to revise the papers for publication. Heraldo Muñoz and I feel that this volume represents a step forward in the study of international relations in Latin America. We recognize, with a combination of pride and humility, that a great deal remains to be done. We will consider our efforts successful if we stimulate more and better work by our colleagues in this field.

Joseph S. Tulchin

1. The Analysis of Latin American Foreign Policies: Theoretical Perspectives

The last years have witnessed an increased scholarly interest in the field of Latin American foreign policies. This development is hardly surprising. For one thing, the region includes several important international actors. Cuba, one of those actors, was the main protagonist in one of the most dramatic international crises since World War II and at present is playing a crucial role in the Caribbean, Central America, and Africa. Brazil— which has been variously characterized as an NIC (New Industrializing Country), an upper-middle-class country, a regional power, or an emerging new world power—has a gross national product (GNP) that currently ranks among the ten highest of the world and already possesses a large industrial sector, comparable to that of several advanced European countries. In a less dramatic way than Cuba, Brazil has expanded its foreign relations significantly, establishing cultural and commercial links with Black Africa, selling military equipment to Middle East countries, and signing far-reaching agreements with West Germany for the transfer of full-cycle nuclear technology, in spite of strong U.S. opposition. Mexico's strategic importance as an oil producer need not be highlighted, and its increasingly crucial role in Central America and the Caribbean has been recognized not only by Washington but by Western Europe as well. And—to take the most dramatic example—another Latin American country, Argentina, launched an outright war against Great Britain, thus challenging one of the main European powers.

From a theoretical perspective, the analysis of Latin American foreign policies also seems especially promising. Whereas the region is one of the most homogeneous in the world,[1] its component countries still exhibit marked differences in terms of national capabilities, foreign-policy traditions and styles, political regimes, and external linkages, differences that make them most suited for comparative analysis. Finally, a long if not necessarily successful experience in foreign affairs and the existence of increasingly sophisticated foreign-policy establishments and decision-making processes in Latin America provide the researcher with a relative

1

abundance of data on the external behavior of a group of developing countries. Indeed, in light of these favorable conditions, what seems surprising is that only now is interest in Latin America becoming evident among students of international relations.

Although studies in the field of Latin American international relations have appeared steadily during the last two decades, the same cannot be said in the specific case of foreign-policy analysis.[2] In fact, in this latter field it is appropriate to speak of a "first wave" of studies that emerged in the 1970s. This initial wave undoubtedly represented a significant and much-needed contribution to the field, but, as often happens, it was of uneven coverage and quality. As expected, some countries have received more attention than others—Brazil, Mexico, Cuba, Venezuela, Argentina, and Chile. Although several case studies have been included in collective and purportedly comparative volumes, real cross-national studies are still conspicuously absent. Moreover, the differences between traditional diplomatic history and foreign-policy analysis have not always been evident in these works. With some exceptions, studies on Latin American foreign policies seem to fluctuate between the descriptive and prescriptive levels, typically including a historical overview, present trends, and a proposal for a better policy.[3] The prescriptive orientation is especially evident in those authors who argue that, with the exception of two or three cases (usually Brazil, Cuba, and sometimes Mexico or Venezuela), Latin American countries have no foreign policy at all, since their external behavior does not respond to a grand strategy or to a preconceived, articulate, and long-range plan for the attainment of certain national objectives.

Considering the previous dearth of sound foreign-policy descriptions and the distressing historical experience of Latin America in its dealings with the rest of the world (especially with its northern neighbor), descriptive and prescriptive studies are to be welcomed. However, there is still a need to elaborate explanatory and explicitly comparative studies in this field. This chapter attempts to demonstrate that there are many disparate elements available for such an effort, but that they have yet to be systematized and integrated into a coherent and comprehensive approach.

Where can we search for these theoretical perspectives that will allow us to explain at least part of Latin American foreign-policy behavior? In some academic circles both in Latin America and the United States, this question has been answered by postulating the need to look for a new, unique, and special approach that focuses exclusively on the reality of developing or Third World countries. In this chapter, it is assumed that this argument must be treated with caution. First, a minimum requirement for any general approach in the social sciences is a reasonable degree of universality, in the sense that the approach is applicable to more than a few cases. Second, the foreign-policy-making process of several Latin American countries is fairly complex and sophisticated, and there is no practical reason to give it a unique status. Third, it could well be argued that just as Latin American processes are very different from, say, North American ones, they are also far apart from those prevailing in other Third World regions, if only because the internal political and economic environments in which they function are also radically different.

On the other hand, this is not to deny that Latin American foreign policies operate within specific contexts and that certain variables could be more or less relevant to explain them. However, these differences, important as they are, do not allow us to exclude theoretical approaches from the outset for the simple reason that they were elaborated in, and for, the developed countries. Theoretical ethnocentrism is no less to be avoided in the Third World than in the United States. Furthermore, most conventional theoretical perspectives have something to offer to foreign-policy analysis in Latin America. Similarly, many of the reservations that some conventional perspectives deserve are equally as valid for Latin American countries as for the Western European ones.

In the field of comparative foreign policy, a theoretical perspective is described as a general orientation that "posits the importance of some specified and interrelated set of variables for explaining foreign policy behavior and that provides an explanatory logic relating the set of variables to foreign policy behavior."[4] It is the purpose of this chapter to sketch those theoretical perspectives that are most frequently employed in the analysis of Latin American foreign policies or, alternatively, those that seem more promising for this purpose.

Perhaps the best-known and most widely used classification of the variables considered to affect foreign-policy behavior is the one that distinguishes between external and internal factors. Even though most authors agree that both kinds of variables are relevant, they do not ascribe equal weight to them. In the case of Latin America, it is often assumed that the external behavior of the countries of the region is mainly a reflection and reaction to events located abroad. Be this as it may, the distinction between external and internal variables that influence foreign policy is still widely accepted, although the new forces of transnationalism tend to make them less clear-cut than they were in the past. In this chapter this basic distinction is maintained as an organizing device, without implying that the theoretical perspectives that will be grouped under each heading necessarily adopt a monocausal approach or are always mutually exclusive.

PERSPECTIVES ON EXTERNAL SOURCES
OF FOREIGN POLICY

Several well-known approaches in the fields of Latin American international relations and foreign policy coincide in highlighting those external variables that seem to place constraints on—yet might also offer new opportunities for—the region's role in the world. This tendency to emphasize external factors is especially evident in the case of Latin American scholars, but it is also gaining acceptance among U.S. and European analysts. The perspectives that stress external variables belong to very different intellectual traditions, ranging from traditional power-politics studies to systems analysis and from *dependencia* theory (to be defined later) to foreign-policy compliance testing. What these highly different approaches have in common is that they tend to concentrate on variables originating outside the nation-states of Latin America.

International System

Few Latin Americanists would disagree with the assertion that the international system shapes to a great extent the region's foreign behavior. In fact, it is almost commonplace to initiate any study on this topic with reference to the basic changes that have taken place within the global system and the ways in which these changes have affected individual or regional policies. This interest in systemic variables explains the relative abundance of works dealing with the historical evolution of the international system, its component units (states, regional and global international organizations, transnational corporations, other transnational entities, and so on), and the distribution of economic and political resources at this global systemic level.[5] Obviously, the underlying assumption in all of these studies is that Latin America is extremely sensitive to its external environment and that its behavior toward other nations tends to be a reaction to stimuli originating at this level.

International system variables often are assumed to have a particularly negative effect in Latin America. In the economic sphere these adverse conditions were analyzed in the 1950s by the structuralist approach, developed mainly by scholars associated with the United Nations Economic Commission for Latin America (ECLA or, in Spanish, Comisión Económica para América Latina—CEPAL). Initially, this approach placed special emphasis on the deteriorating prices of those primary export products on which Latin America was heavily dependent, in relation to rising prices of manufactured goods that had to be imported mainly from the developed countries. This long-term trend caused chronic balance-of-payments difficulties in the region and also contributed to the relatively slow growth rates of most countries. Subsequently, this analysis was extended to the impact on the late-developing periphery of other external variables, such as foreign direct investment, foreign financial reliance, and the scientific-technological gap.[6]

According to CEPAL, the negative effects caused by these systemic trends could be overcome through a strategy of industrialization based on import substitution, through the implementation of economic integration and of other regional cooperation agreements, through the promotion of manufactured and other nontraditional exports, and, of course, through the reform of the international economic order. It should be noted that almost all of these strategies impinge directly on the field of foreign policy.

At the political level, most specialists in the field of Latin American foreign policy focus on such international system variables as evolution from bipolarity to multipolarity, détente, recent changes in the distribution of resources in the global system, the energy crisis, and the declining role of the United States in the world. Helio Jaguaribe, a leading Latin American specialist in the field, has in several of his works concentrated on the changes experienced by the international economic, political, and military systems and their impact on the region. In particular, he has attempted to assess the degree of "permissibility" resulting from these changes, concluding that only the more viable countries of the region can attain a relatively high degree of autonomy.[7]

A somewhat different approach within this general perspective tends to view Latin America as a regional subsystem within the global system, characterized by the existence of a set of geographically proximate and frequently interacting states that share a sense of regional identity and are so perceived by external actors.[8] Various inferences are drawn from this very general proposition. Some are inclined to view Latin American foreign policies as basically identical, in the sense that their objectives and concrete policies show striking similarities. Others, while not denying that the countries of the region form a subsystem, also pay special attention to internal differences, stressing the varying roles played by powers such as Brazil, Mexico, Venezuela, Argentina, and Cuba within the regional and global spheres. Finally, there are scholars who have addressed themselves to the prospect of a common foreign policy on the part of all the countries of the region, assessing the favorable and adverse conditions for the achievement of this objective.[9]

In general, systemic approaches have offered valuable insights into the study of Latin American international relations, especially by demonstrating the region's sensitivity and vulnerability to external variables. However, by its very nature this approach can lead to a certain neglect of the widely different functions that individual countries perform within the system and of the diverging ways in which they react to the same external stimuli. Furthermore, international system analysis, if not combined with perspectives that also take into account internal variables, only gives a partial picture of Latin American foreign policies.

Power Politics

In an excellent review of the recent literature on inter-American relations, Jorge Domínguez identifies what he calls a "strategic" perspective in Latin America, which is characterized by its strategic, rational, and calculating orientation, by its rational and unified state actor assumption, and by its stress on international conflict.[10] First developed in the United States and Western Europe, this power-politics approach still enjoys enormous popularity in Latin America,[11] not only among more traditionalist scholars but also among some young, recently trained social scientists who typically combine it with other approaches, such as imperialism, dependency, and international system theory. Applications of the power-politics approach, in its "pure" form or in combination with the other perspectives, are especially evident in such Latin American journals as *Estrategia* (Argentina), *Foro Internacional* (Mexico), *Estudios Internacionales* (Chile), *Mundo Nuevo* (Venezuela), *Revista Argentina de Relaciones Internacionales*, and *Relaciones Internacionales* (Mexico).

In the power-politics approach the actions of other countries are often considered as the primary conditioning factors affecting foreign-policy decisions, and the capabilities or national attributes of the state—especially its military, material, and intellectual resources—are the predominant internal factors that impinge on concrete policies. Along these lines, nations can, and indeed must, act independently of internal social and political forces in the pursuit of their national interests, which are almost self-evident: physical protection of their territories and citizens, economic development and the general well-being of the population, regional balance of power, and so on. Even though foreign-policy options are influenced by distinct national capabilities, the skillful employ of these objective factors is equally important in the shaping of outcomes; accordingly, a country's position of lesser capability can be partially offset if its leaders utilize national resources efficiently. How and when this can be achieved is not very clear, but usually the approach stresses the need of an enlightened leadership and a unified and supportive national population.

Traditional balance-of-power analysis falls within this general description. It views Latin America as a typical scenario of regional competition, where countries like Brazil and Argentina attempt to maintain a fragile equilibrium in the Atlantic area, whereas Venezuela and Mexico are beginning to compete for the control of Central America and the Caribbean.[12] Similarly, competition between the greater powers of the region is said to affect the weaker and smaller countries such as Bolivia, Paraguay, Uruguay, and the Central American ones, whose economic and political systems are prone to penetration by their powerful neighbors.

Traditional power-politics perspectives have led to capability analysis, characterized by the comparison of such national attributes as size, geographic location, population, natural-resource endowments, industrial capacity, educational levels, scientific-technological development, and political stability. Even if all these variables are typically internal, capability analysis must be listed under the external-variable perspectives because what matters in this approach is its relative value vis-à-vis other countries, and not its intrinsic value. However, capability analysis, in Latin America as elsewhere, is often undertaken without a theoretical framework that specifies the conditions under which the available resources will be employed, or the relative weights assigned to each.[13]

Another current within the general power-politics perspective goes a step further: It views conflict in the region not only as an objective reality but also as a necessary and natural product of the coexistence of several states in Latin America. An extreme version of this perspective can be found in Latin America's geopolitical approaches, which tend to view states as organisms that develop, live, decay, and die according to rather precise life cycles and that struggle constantly in a wild scramble for survival.[14]

Dependency Perspectives

In comparative foreign-policy literature the concept "dependency" has had widely divergent meanings and implications, which at times have provoked rather confusing debates. In Latin America, and later also in other regions, this theoretical perspective has been utilized as a broad and general framework of analysis that attempts to describe and explain the region's economic underdevelopment and also its multiple repercussions in the sociopolitical sphere.[15] By means of an eminently totalizing, historical, and dialectical approach, *dependencia* (dependency theory) explains the failure of national development in Latin America in the light of the historical insertion of the region into the capitalist world system. Development and underdevelopment are seen not as different stages within a unilinear process through which all nations pass, but as partial and highly interrelated aspects of one global and simultaneous process, as two faces of the same phenomenon. According to this approach, the region's position in the international economic system and the ties that were historically established between the external and internal structures condition to a great extent the economic and political processes that take place in Latin American societies.

The mechanisms of dependency are multiple and tend to vary over time and from case to case; however there is consensus in stressing the crucial role played by internationalized elites or bridgeheads in the dependent societies that are closely associated with the core groups within the world economic system and that exert a dominant role both in the economic and political spheres of their own societies. Foreign penetration in dependent countries usually materializes through concrete linkages such as direct investments in the most strategic and dynamic sectors of the economy, asymmetrical trade relations, heavy financial reliance on sources based at—or controlled by—the developed countries, military cooperation and training programs, and specific cultural and educational mechanisms. These linkages, though, are not based merely on external forms of exploitation and coercion, "but are rooted in coincidences of interests between local dominant classes and international ones, and, on the other side, are challenged by local dominated groups or classes."[16] In consequence, underdevelopment is not simply the result of the impact of external variables on dependent societies, but of a complex set of interrelations that involve both external and internal factors. This is why the approach is usually described as holistic by its proponents.

This brief and certainly not original description of the *dependencia* approach does not give full justice to its level of theoretical refinement and obviously does not reflect the fundamental divergences that separate many of its practitioners, but perhaps it is sufficient to show that it is an approach to development theory (economic as well as political) and to international political economy. It is definitively not a theory of foreign policy. In fact, there are relatively few references to this subject in Latin American dependency writings, and the few that can be found are almost never expressed in terms of general relational propositions. To be sure, most authors who utilize this approach would be willing to recognize that economic class structures—which, as we have seen, are closely related to international structures—affect in the last analysis all political processes, including foreign policy, but this causal chain is too undetermined, mediated, and abstract to allow for precise relational hypotheses.

This last remark explains why several *dependencia* authors, when dealing with a subject like inter-American relations,[17] are willing to recognize that Latin American countries are now adopting foreign policies that are increasingly autonomous from the hegemonic power in the region. These societies continue to be characterized by a general situation of structural dependency, but the new realities of the international system and the relative autonomy of the state and its bureaucracy vis-à-vis the dominant classes allow for considerable independence in the field of foreign policy.[18] Accordingly, the foreign policy of a hegemonic power cannot be viewed as a mere instrument of the main transnational corporations seated in that country, nor can the foreign policy of a dependent state be automatically identified with the interests of the ruling social sectors. The relationships in this field are much more complex and include also important strategic, historical, and political elements.

In sum, authors who write within the Latin American *dependencia* tradition offer only the most general guidance to the specific study of foreign policy in the dependent countries. Theoretical and methodological reasons explain this omission. First, as Fagen puts it, "it is almost painfully obvious that simply analoging over into the study of international politics some of the main elements of the dependency perspective (developed primarily to represent economic relations and their consequences) was and is doomed to failure. . . . Politics are not 'dependent' on each other in the same sense as economics."[19] Second, the units of analysis employed by the *dependencia* approach do not lend themselves easily to comparative foreign-policy studies. Thus, *dependencia* theory usually focuses on the relationship between, on the one hand, a highly aggregate external unit, the global capitalist system, and, on the other, a highly disaggregate and fluid dependent society, composed of distinct class arrangements, alliances between local and external groups, and so forth. By contrast, foreign-policy analysis maintains a state-as-actor perspective. Third, *dependencia* theory does not consider foreign-policy behavior as a very significant indicator of dependency; thus, the fact that several Latin American countries exhibit an independent behavior at the United Nations (UN) and even dare to resist U.S. pressure in bilateral and multilateral negotiations does not say much about the structural economic dependency of these countries vis-à-vis the world economy or even the North American one. Finally, it should be emphasized that, in general, *dependencia* theory is not easily amenable to the "if and when" propositions that traditionally have been employed in comparative foreign-policy analysis. Rather, the approach has concentrated on specific and concrete situations of dependency, utilizing contextually bound hypotheses and data in the case of both internal and external variables.

External Reliance

Studies in this relatively new field of foreign-policy research have occasionally been associated with Latin American *dependencia* writings, especially in the United States. Although there are some links between both intellectual traditions, in the sense that they focus on international inequalities and the consequences that flow from them, they are in essence very different. To avoid confusing them, James Caporaso proposed, in a special issue of *International Organization* on the subject of dependent international relations, a distinction between "dependency" and "dependence." According to this distinction, "dependency" refers to the process of insertion of the lesser developed countries into the global capitalist system, while "dependence" refers to the external reliance of one nation-state on another.[20] I follow this distinction, although the concept "dependence" has been replaced by "foreign reliance," for the sake of clarity.

The external-reliance perspective seeks to explore and probe the consequences of asymmetrical economic relations between nation-states. Specifically, in the field of foreign policy, this perspective attempts to determine the relationship between economic external reliance and foreign behavior. This association has been suggested by the common belief that, within an asymmetrical relationship, the economically dominant country can exact favorable foreign-policy decisions from its dependent economic partner, by virtue of the power levers it has at its disposal. Accordingly, one could expect a high degree of compliance between the dominant and the dependent countries in their foreign behavior, provided that this compliance is highly valued by the dominant country.

Considering the region's high degree of economic reliance on the United States, as expressed in foreign-trade concentration, financial flows, direct investments, and aid programs, it is not surprising that the general foreign-reliance proposition has been tested in the specific case of Latin

America. The results of these empirical testings, though, have tended to indicate that there is no clear relation between economic external reliance and foreign-policy behavior. According to one study, for instance, "agreement with the U.S. position is not a positive function of the extent of a country's dependence."[21] Another work concluded that "the analyses here clearly support an argument that compliance by Latin American states in the form of voting agreement with the United States in the UN is unlikely to be associated consistently with trade dependence, power disparities, or distance from the United States."[22]

It is evident that countries that are economically very reliant on the United States have shown for a long time a noncompliant foreign behavior in relation to their main partner. Mexico is a good case in point. Argentina, for instance, was able to resist U.S. pressure during World War II and to continue its friendly relations with the Axis powers.[23] Mexico and Argentina are regional powers in Latin America and it may seem unlikely that the smaller and even more reliant countries of the region can follow a similar path. However, Panama, one of the most dependent countries in the region, has nevertheless adopted an independent foreign policy with regard to Central America and, at the same time, has been able to exact new and more favorable canal treaties from the United States.

PERSPECTIVES ON DOMESTIC SOURCES OF FOREIGN POLICY

Traditionally, internal variables that affect foreign-policy behavior in Latin America have received less attention than the external ones. In part, this may be the result of a relative underestimation of the importance of domestic factors in the foreign-policy decision-making process; but, for the most part, this omission stems from the scarcity of detailed case studies.

Obviously, it is problematic to identify purely domestic sources in a region where transnational actors of very different kinds have developed close ties with local groups. However, because these transnational forces act through local agents and their influence consequently is mediated, it is still possible to speak of internal variables. It is difficult to classify internal-variable perspectives for the simple reason that they tend to overlap to a great extent. However, varying degrees in emphasis allow us to distinguish four broad categories: regime orientation, decision making and domestic politics, bureaucratic politics, and leadership perspectives. Obviously, this classification is only tentative.

Regime Orientation

This perspective focuses on the structural characteristics and basic orientations of a society in the realms of both politics and economics, in order to assess their relevance to foreign-policy decision making. Three general variables that can be listed under this heading have received special attention in the case of Latin American foreign-policy studies.

The first one concentrates on the relationship between the form of political organization and the foreign policy of a given country. As could be expected, the primary distinction that is made in this area is between democratic and authoritarian regimes and points to the question of whether internal differences in regimes affect the type of foreign policy that is pursued.

In Latin America the relationship between political regime and foreign policy has been explored in a diachronic way, comparing the same country under different regimes. For instance, several authors have traced the main changes experienced by Brazilian foreign policy after the breakdown of the democratic regime in 1964, concluding that during the first years the new authoritarian regime completely reversed the policies of its predecessors and adopted a rather passive foreign policy, characterized by a narrow and highly ideological stance with respect to the rest of the world.[24] Contrast with prior policies was particularly evident because the last two democratic governments had attempted to pursue an activist and reformist foreign policy, oriented toward the establishment of new links with other countries and regions, especially in the Third World, and toward the adoption of a more independent policy vis-à-vis the United States. However, and this is particularly interesting, this reversal from an independent pro–Third World policy proved to be short-lived. Although the authoritarian regime remained essentially the same, in the early 1970s Brazil shifted again to an active foreign policy, characterized by pragmatism and adaptability to external changes.

The case of Chile, a country that experienced a particularly violent change of regime in 1973, has been studied from a similar perspective.[25] However, the Chilean case points to still another dimension of this relationship between political regime and foreign policy that merits attention. During a long period before the 1973 coup, the democratic nature of Chile's political regime not only influenced its foreign-policy processes and outcomes but also became in itself a national capability. Thus, the fact that prior to 1973 Chile was one of the few stable and relatively participatory democracies in a region plagued by chronic instability and dictatorial regimes gave it special prestige both in Latin America and the rest of the world and explains to a great extent why it was able to pursue a foreign policy somewhat disproportionate to its size and physical capabilities. This case of an international presence based more on prestige than on "objective" power assets can also be observed, to a lesser extent, in other smaller Latin American democracies, such as Costa Rica and Uruguay until the 1960s. It would be interesting to compare these cases with those countries of Europe, Africa, and Asia that have also included regime prestige as an important foreign-policy capability.

The second regime-orientation variable refers to the development strategy adopted by a country. Traditionally, in Latin America this variable has had a direct incidence in foreign-policy behavior, which seems understandable given the priority assigned to developmental goals in the region. As Coleman and Quirós Varela suggest, "For Latin America, where political leaders are judged by their ability to articulate goals for national economic transformation as well as for their ability to produce such changes, foreign policy-making is unavoidably very much a function of the requirements of development statecraft."[26] Thus, foreign policy is viewed not only in terms of its contribution to traditional economic objectives such as promotion of trade and procurement of financial assistance in favorable conditions but also as a means of manipulating international variables in a way favorable to developmental goals. This emphasis explains the important role played by foreign policy in Latin America in the nationalization of foreign-owned corporations that extract the countries' natural resources.

The close relationship between economic development strategy and foreign policy has been highlighted in case studies dealing with diverse Latin American countries. Mario Ojeda has shown that during a very long period Mexico's foreign policy assumed the role of "external promoter of the country's economic growth," projecting abroad an image of stability and progress for Mexico and acting in a way to obtain better treatment for its exports and new markets for its products.[27] Although Brazil has adopted a different development strategy than Mexico, its foreign policy is also generally viewed in terms of its possible contribution to the internal development strategy.[28] And, in the case of Chile, the adoption of an orthodox and extreme monetarist and outward-oriented economic model has also placed new requirements on its foreign policy.

The third regime-orientation variable focuses on the existence of a distinct national approach in a given country, which stems from a certain historical tradition that has permeated the state's external behavior. In some cases, this tradition contributes to the emergence of a conscious attitude of the foreign-policy establishment in order to perpetuate this legacy. Thus, although in general it could be argued that because of its immutability a foreign-policy tradition must be considered as a capability rather than as a regime-orientation variable, in the Latin American case this is not so evident. Historically, most countries of the region have experienced important alterations in their foreign behavior. Mexico, in spite of its remarkable political stability, shifted in the early 1970s from a passive, isolationist, and conventional foreign policy to an activist and expansive one. The fact that a recent book on Argentine foreign policy was entitled *Argentina's Foreign Policies*[29] illustrates the absence of a consistent and permanent foreign-policy tradition in its case. Even Brazil, the only Latin American country in which it is possible to speak of a certain foreign-policy tradition, has not been immune to important innovations in both style and substance.

Decision Making and Domestic Politics

This perspective is similar to the previous one in that it focuses on domestic sources of foreign policy. However, it differs from it in the sense that it tends more to disaggregate the internal setting, concentrating on participants, types of decision-making processes, and domestic influences that intervene in the foreign-policy area.

Considering the enormous power wielded by the presidency in almost all Latin American countries, many analysts are inclined to view foreign policy in the region as an essentially presidential and one-person decision process. Some authors even speak in this case of idiosyncratic politics. Although there have been some cases of one-man foreign-policy processes, for instance during the Duvalier ("Papa Doc") and Trujillo regimes in Haiti and the Dominican Republic,[30] in general it is erroneous to view the foreign-policy-making process in Latin America as a very simple and restricted process in which only two or three persons participate. For one thing, political systems in the region, democratic as well as authoritarian, include highly institutionalized bureaucracies and complex networks of interest groups that participate in the foreign-policy area. For another, relatively high levels of development according to Third World standards have imposed new demands upon what used to be traditional foreign-policy establishments.

The number of actors that participate in foreign-policy decisions varies from country to country and over time. In general governmental actors tend to be more numerous in the more developed countries such as Brazil, Mexico, Argentina, and Venezuela. Parliaments and political parties, where they exist, have a variable role in the foreign-policy decision-making process.[31] On several occasions, the pressure exerted by political parties on the executive has been sufficient to force it to adopt or reject a given course of action.[32] On the other hand, most Latin American parties have developed links with ideologically similar parties of other countries in Latin America and Europe. This is especially true in the case of the Christian Democrats, Social Democrats, and Communists, but it also holds for more indigenous parties such as the Peruvian Alianza Popular Revolucionaria Americana (APRA) or the Argentine Justicialistas.

Specific interest groups also have played an important role in foreign-policy making in Latin America. For instance, the powerful coffee growers association of Colombia, the Federación Nacional de Cafeteros, officially takes part in the administration of coffee policy both at the national and international levels.[33] In Venezuela, the Federación de Cámaras de Comercio (Fedecámaras), the national association of entrepreneurs, for several years blocked the country's participation in regional and subregional integration schemes because it perceived this participation as detrimental to the interests of local industry.[34]

Case studies on concrete foreign-policy decisions in Latin America have been rare. However, some scholars have done interesting studies in this field, concentrating especially on highly salient issues in the region that have involved the U.S. government and/or U.S. business interests. Several historical studies, for instance, have traced Latin American decisions and policies toward the United States and some other world powers.[35] More recent research has dealt with nationalization processes of U.S.-based multinational corporations and the conflicts or tensions that arose with Washington.[36]

Relationships between domestic politics and foreign policy in Latin America have been explored in several cases. Mexico has probably received most attention in this regard. In fact, there seems to be a consensus that interrelations between internal and external politics are particularly close in the Mexican case.[37] Against this general background it is hardly surprising that when President Luis Echeverría in the early 1970s initiated his "New Foreign Policy," many observers interpreted this change as a response to Mexico's internal economic and political crisis.

Mexico is certainly not a unique case in Latin America regarding the interplay between internal and external policies. Indeed, at times this relationship also has been particularly evident in very dissimilar countries of the region, such as Trinidad and Tobago, Jamaica, Bolivia, Panama, and Argentina. It would be interesting to analyze these cases from a comparative perspective, in order to assess the importance of this variable for the whole region.

Bureaucratic Politics

This perspective tends to view foreign policy as the outcome of interactive bargaining processes among diverse governmental agencies with different values, perceptions, and styles. Accordingly, foreign policy is seen not as the result of a rational, coherent, and purposeful process, but as the result of the pulling and hauling of rival agencies.[38] Obviously, this competition takes place within certain limits because there are external constraints and also common values shared by all participants.

This perspective has never been very popular among Latin Americanists, which seems understandable given the high levels of centralization and power concentration that characterize political systems in the region. It certainly would be a misrepresentation to view the region's external policies as the result of bureaucratic infighting.

However, the approach is still valuable. In the first place, some Latin American foreign bureaucracies are relatively complex. They include highly differentiated and specialized groups, each endowed with its own perceptions and interests. In the second place, even in those cases where only one sector of the bureaucracy seems to hold sway in important issues, this group need not necessarily be monolithic. Finally, there have been clear indications of bureaucratic fighting in some crucial foreign-policy decisions in Latin America. Mexico's recent decision not to join the General Agreement on Tariffs and Trade (GATT) is a good example.

In sum, even though the bureaucratic-politics perspective may not provide a complete explanation of Latin American foreign policies, it still can offer useful theoretical insights at more restricted levels.

Leadership

In a region that has been characterized by its personalist politics and charismatic leadership, one might expect a high number of foreign-policy studies concentrating on the personal traits of prominent leaders and their effects on foreign policy. Paradoxically, this has not been the case. And, for better or worse, psychohistory has no known followers among specialists in Latin American international relations.

However, leaving aside psychological explanations, several analysts are willing to stress the importance of leadership in the molding of Latin American foreign policy. Thus, the role of President Juan D. Perón in the shaping of Argentina's "Third Position" during the early 1950s has been sufficiently highlighted.[39] And, more recently, several observers of Mexican foreign policy have pointed to the influence of President Echeverría's personality in the formulation and conduct of Mexico's "New Foreign Policy."[40]

Another study combined bureaucratic politics and leadership perspectives to explain recent Cuban foreign policy. According to this approach, Cuba's external contradictions in the mid-1970s derived from the existence of three distinct foreign-policy tendencies: the pragmatic economic tendency, headed by Carlos Rafael Rodríguez; the revolutionary political tendency, headed by Fidel Castro; and the military mission tendency, headed by Raúl Castro and other officers of the Ministry of the Revolutionary Armed Forces.[41] The implication is that complex interactions between these tendencies explained important decisions and shifts in foreign policy.

Although outstanding leaders have played an important role in Latin American foreign policies, research relating the personal characteristics of those leaders to their external policies seems most unlikely for the near future. Structural forces, both at the international and domestic levels, are considered to have more explanatory potential in this area.

CONCLUSIONS

Even though the state of the literature on Latin American foreign policies is clearly not satisfactory, it would be unfair to describe it as hopeless. Whatever the validity of some individual perspectives, research on the subject is rising both quantitatively and qualitatively. And, encouragingly, the whole subject seems to be entering a more theoretical phase. The theoretical perspectives that have been described in this paper do not constitute mutually exclusive approaches. Rather, they tend to complement and enrich each other, casting light upon new dimensions and allowing for the reformulation of old ones. The picture that emerges is one of potential convergence between different emphases and concerns.

However, the road is not as easy as it might appear at first glance. Most of the perspectives are still incipient and, in some cases, they do not amount to more than two or three often implicit propositions based upon a case study or the experience of a single country during a specific time period. Moreover, not even the most conciliatory review could deny that there are incompatibilities between some perspectives. A purely systemic approach, for instance, inevitably leads to the neglect of domestic variables and gives only a partial picture of the foreign policy of a particular country. Conversely, a perspective that focuses exclusively on the interactions that take place within the bureaucracy is very likely to lose sight of important trends within the international system that restrict or expand options available to decision makers. Other perspectives are so confusing and inarticulate that one may question whether they are indeed perspectives. Many geopolitical writings belong to this category.

The preceding review suggests some future directions for research in the area of Latin American foreign policy. First, it is necessary to build conceptual schemes that may facilitate more theoretically oriented analyses. These schemes should be sufficiently broad to allow for multicausal explanations, but at the same time they should not be converted into mere listings of variables, without any suggestion of their relevance and mutual interaction patterns.

Second, a more explicit comparative methodology is needed in the area. This can be achieved through the application of a common theoretical framework to several Latin American countries, through collective projects involving several institutions, or, at least, through the presence of a comparative awareness in individual case studies. Quantitative cross-national comparisons also could be a useful complement in this regard, provided that they do not consist of the accumulation of endless lists of variables and indicators, without any reference to historical contexts and to internal qualitative differences.

Third, as several authors have suggested, issue-area analysis seems especially useful to advance our understanding in the field of foreign policy. As in other cases, Latin American countries tend to respond differently to various types of external stimuli. Thus, Ferris's classification of three relevant issue-areas in the region—military/strategic, economic development, and status/diplomatic—appears as a very appropriate point of departure for this mode of anlaysis.[42]

Finally, before we pretend to explain, we must determine exactly *what* we want to explain. If, as Kalleberg states, "comparison can only be made after classification has been completed,"[43] then we must certainly move in that direction. What differences in Latin American foreign behavior do we want to explain? Is it possible to speak of innovative and traditional foreign policies in the region? How do we differentiate an assertive from a passive external policy? Are there acquiescent, reformist, and radical countries in the region? Answers to these questions are not only theoretically relevant, but may help Latin American countries design new strategies to improve their participation in the international system.

ACKNOWLEDGMENTS

I wish to thank Maurice A. East, Larman C. Wilson, Heraldo Muñoz, and Kenneth M. Coleman for their helpful comments on an earlier draft of this chapter. I would also like to acknowledge the assistance of Mary Kay Loss in the preparation of the English version.

NOTES

1. Most authors dealing with the international relations of Latin America view the region as a unified entity and as a specific "system of actions." See, for instance, Louis J. Cantori and Steven L. Spiegel (eds.), *The International Politics of Regions: A Comparative Approach* (Englewood Cliffs, N.J.: Prentice-Hall, 1970) in which Latin America is considered to be a single subsystem, whereas Africa is divided into five such units and Asia into four.

2. Granting that the distinction between international relations and foreign-policy studies is not always clear, it is assumed that this difference is necessary and useful. Whereas international-relations studies focus on global interactive processes involving at least two different units within the international system, foreign-policy studies refer to those actions and objectives within a given country that are directed to its foreign environment. See Fred A. Sondermann, "The Linkage Between Foreign Policy and International Politics," in James N. Rosenau (ed.), *International Politics and Foreign Policy: A Reader in Research and Theory* (New York: Free Press, 1961), pp. 8–17.

3. Harold E. Davis, Larman C. Wilson, et al., *Latin American Foreign Policies* (Baltimore: Johns Hopkins University Press, 1975); G. Pope Atkins, *Latin America in the International System* (New York: The Free Press, 1977); and Elizabeth G. Ferris and Jennie K. Lincoln (eds.), *Latin American Foreign Policies: Global and Regional Dimensions* (Boulder, Colo.: Westview Press, 1981). A previous and more geographically restricted volume is Carlos A. Astiz (ed.), *Latin American International Politics: Ambitions, Capabilities, and the National Interests of Mexico, Brazil, and Argentina* (Notre Dame: University of Notre Dame Press, 1969).

4. Charles F. Hermann and Maurice A. East, "Introduction," in Maurice A. East, Stephen A. Salmore, and Charles F. Hermann (eds.), *Why Nations Act: Theoretical Perspectives for Comparative Foreign Policy Analysis* (Beverly Hills, Calif.: Sage, 1978), p. 22.

5. A pioneering effort in that direction was Gustavo Lagos, *International Stratification and Underdeveloped Countries* (Chapel Hill: University of North Carolina Press, 1963). Although from a different perspective, José A. Silva Michelena, *Política y Bloques de Poder*, 2d ed. (México, D.F.: Siglo XXI, 1979), also focused on the recent evolution of the international system and its impact on the Latin American countries.

6. For a good summary of CEPAL's approach see *El Pensamiento de la CEPAL* (Santiago: Ed. Universitaria, 1969). For a revised and up-to-date version of this

line of thought by its most outstanding representative, see Raúl Prebisch, "Notas sobre el desarrollo del capitalismo periférico," *Estudios Internacionales* 11 (43), July–September 1978, pp. 3–25; and "La periferia latinoamericana en el sistema global del capitalismo," *Revista de la CEPAL* (13), April 1981, pp. 163–171.

7. Helio Jaguaribe, *Political Development: A General Theory and a Latin American Case Study* (New York: Harper and Row, 1973), pp. 371–382; and Helio Jaguaribe, "Autonomía periférica y hegemonía céntrica," *Estudios Internacionales* 12 (46), April–June 1979, pp. 91–130.

8. Atkins, *Latin America*, pp. 10ff.

9. Luciano Tomassini, "Tendencias favorables o adversas a la formación de un sistema regional latinoamericano," *Estudios Internacionales* 8 (29), January–March 1975, pp. 3–46.

10. Jorge I. Domínguez, "Consensus and Divergence: the State of the Literature on Inter-American Relations in the 1970s," *Latin American Research Review* 13 (1), 1978, pp. 104–106. The next paragraphs owe much to Domínguez's description.

11. Hans J. Morgenthau's *Politics Among Nations* (New York: Knopf, 1978) is probably the most popular international-relations textbook in Latin American diplomatic and military academies and also in most of the region's universities. Two other widely used books are Raymond Aron, *Peace and War: A Theory of International Relations* (Garden City, N.Y.: Anchor Press, 1973); and Georg Schwarzenberger, *Power Politics: A Study of International Relations* (New York: F. A. Praeger, 1951). All of these works have been translated into Spanish.

12. Balance-of-power approaches to Latin American international relations can be found in Norman A. Bailey, *Latin America in World Politics* (New York: Walker, 1967), chap. 3; Robert N. Burr, *By Reason or Force: Chile and the Balancing of Power in South America* (Berkeley: University of California Press, 1967); Atkins, *Latin America*, chap. 8; and Alberto Sepúlveda, "La dinámica de equilibrio de poder en Sudamérica y sus proyecciones en las políticas exteriores de la región," in Walter Sánchez (ed.), *Las relaciones entre los países de América Latina* (Santiago: Ed. Universitaria, 1980), pp. 69–101.

13. James N. Rosenau, "Comparing Foreign Policies: Why, What, How," in James N. Rosenau (ed.), *Comparing Foreign Policies: Theories, Findings, and Methods* (New York: Sage, 1974), p. 13.

14. For a brief but very useful summary of these approaches, see John Child, "Geopolitical Thinking in Latin America," *Latin American Research Review* 14 (2), 1979, pp. 89–111, which includes an annotated bibliography.

15. It would be impossible to include here a bibliography of the *dependencia* literature. For the sake of brevity we refer to the writings of the most representative Latin American authors of the approach: Fernando H. Cardoso, Theotonio Dos Santos, Andre Gunder Frank, Sergio Bagú, Osvaldo Sunkel, Enzo Faletto, Helio Jaguaribe, and Aníbal Quijano. The list is not exhaustive and does not imply that all of these authors agree on most of the points with which they are concerned. Good reviews, introductions, or summaries of the approach can be found in Philip J. O'Brien, "A Critique of Latin American Theories of Dependency," in Ivar Oxaal, Tony Barnett, and David Booth (eds.), *Beyond the Sociology of Development: Economy and Society in Latin America and Africa* (London: Routledge and Kegan Paul, 1975), pp. 7–27; Ronald M. Chilcote and Joel Edelstein (eds.), *Latin America: The Struggle with Dependency and Beyond* (New York: John Wiley and Sons, 1974), especially the introduction; James A. Caporaso (ed.), "Dependence and Dependency in the Global System," *International Organization* 32 (1), Winter 1978; and Heraldo Muñoz, "Cambio y continuidad en el Debate

sobre la Dependencia y el Imperialismo," *Estudios Internacionales* 11 (44), October–December 1978, pp. 88–138, and his edited volume, *From Dependency to Development* (Boulder, Colo.: Westview Press, 1981).

16. Fernando H. Cardoso and Enzo Faletto, *Dependency and Development in Latin America* (Berkeley: University of California Press, 1979), p. xvi.

17. For a useful summary of the *dependencia* approaches to inter-American relations, see Domínguez, "Consensus and Divergence," pp. 100–108. It should be emphasized, however, that Domínguez refers mainly to international-relations approaches, whereas this chapter deals with the more specific field of foreign policy, in which *dependencia* writings have been scarce.

18. See, for example, Marcos Kaplan, "Commentary on Ianni," in Julio Cotler and Richard R. Fagen (eds.), *Latin America and the United States: The Changing Political Realities* (Stanford: Stanford University Press, 1974), pp. 52–66. See also the articles by Aníbal Quijano and Guillermo O'Donnell in the same volume.

19. Richard R. Fagen, "Studying Latin America Politics: Some Implications of a *Dependencia* Approach," *Latin American Research Review* 12 (2), 1977, p. 17.

20. James A. Caporaso, "Introduction to the Special Issue of *International Organization* on Dependence and Dependency in the Global System," *International Organization* 32 (1), Winter 1978, pp. 1–3.

21. Neil R. Richardson, *Foreign Policy and Economic Dependence* (Austin: University of Texas Press, 1978), p. 163. The study included a sample of twenty-three countries, of which only four were non–Latin American.

22. James Lee Ray, "Dependence, Political Compliance, and Economic Performance: Latin America and Eastern Europe," in Charles W. Kegley, Jr., and Pat McGowan (eds.), *The Political Economy of Foreign Policy Behavior*, Sage International Yearbook of Foreign Policy Studies (Beverly Hills, Calif.: Sage, 1981), p. 123.

23. See Michael J. Francis, *The Limits of Hegemony: United States Relations with Argentina and Chile During World War II* (Notre Dame: University of Notre Dame Press, 1977). On the persistence of Argentine resistance to the United States, see Joseph S. Tulchin, "Two to Tango: From Independence to the Falklands Crisis, Argentine and U.S. Foreign Policies Have Been out of Step," *Foreign Service Journal* 59 (9), October 1982, pp. 18–23.

24. See Wayne A. Selcher, "Brazil in the World: Multipolarity as Seen by a Peripheral ADC Middle Power," in Ferris and Lincoln, *Latin American Foreign Policies*, p. 98; and Brady B. Tyson, "Brazil," in Davis, Wilson, et al., *Latin American Foreign Policies*, pp. 221–236.

25. Heraldo Muñoz, "Las relaciones exteriores del gobierno militar chileno: Una interpretación económica-política" (Mimeographed, May 1981, Instituto de Estudios Internacionales); Manfred Wilhelmy, "Hacia un análisis de la Política Exterior chilena contemporánea," *Estudios Internacionales* 12 (48), October–December 1979, pp. 440–471.

26. Kenneth M. Coleman and Luis Quirós Varela, "Determinants of Latin American Foreign Policies: Bureaucratic Organizations and Development Strategies," in Ferris and Lincoln, *Latin American Foreign Policies*, p. 40.

27. Mario Ojeda, *Alcances y límites de la política exterior de México* (México, D.F.: El Colegio de México, 1976), p. 104.

28. Ronald M. Schneider, *Brazil: Foreign Policy of a Future World Power* (Boulder, Colo.: Westview Press, 1976), p. 40. See also Celso Lafer, *Comercio e Relações Internacionais* (São Paulo: Ed. Perspectiva, 1977); and Celso Lafer, "La

política exterior brasileña: Balance y perspectivas," *Estudios Internacionales* 13 (51), July–September 1980, pp. 309–327.

29. Edward S. Milenky, *Argentina's Foreign Policies* (Boulder, Colo.: Westview Press, 1978). See also Alberto Conil Paz and Gustavo Ferrari, *Argentina's Foreign Policy 1930–1962* (Notre Dame: University of Notre Dame Press, 1966).

30. Larman C. Wilson, "The Dominican Republic and Haiti," in Davis, Wilson, et al., *Latin American Foreign Policies*, p. 215.

31. Edy Kaufman, "Latin America," in Christopher Clapham (ed.), *Foreign Policy Making in Developing States: A Comparative Approach* (New York: Praeger, 1977), p. 152; and Harold Eugene Davis, "The Analysis of Latin American Foreign Policies," in Davis, Wilson, et al., *Latin American Foreign Policies*, p. 12.

32. F. Parkinson, *Latin America, the Cold War, and the World Powers, 1945–1973* (Beverly Hills, Calif.: Sage, 1974).

33. David Bushnell, "Colombia," in Davis, Wilson, et al., *Latin American Foreign Policies*, p. 410.

34. See Nelson Rodríguez, "Venezuela: Actores y agentes políticos internos del proceso de integración andina," in Raúl Atria and Iván Lavados (eds.), *Variables políticas de la integración andina* (Santiago: Ed. Nueva Universidad, 1974), pp. 154–187; and Carlos Portales, "Democracia y políticas de integración: El caso de Venezuela," in Manfred Wilhemy (ed.), *Sociedad, política, e integración en América Latina* (Santiago: Ed. Corporación de Investigaciones para el Desarrollo, 1982), pp. 149–168.

35. See Parkinson, *Latin America, the Cold War, and the World Powers*; Francis, *The Limits of Hegemony*; Stanley E. Hilton, *Brazil and the Great Powers 1930–1939* (Austin: University of Texas Press, 1974); and Joseph S. Tulchin, "The Argentine Proposal for Non-Belligerency, April 1940," *The Journal of Inter-American Studies* 11 (4), November 1969, pp. 571–604.

36. See, for instance, Theodore H. Moran, *Multinational Corporations and the Politics of Dependence: Copper in Chile* (Princeton: Princeton University Press, 1974); Charles T. Goodsell, *American Corporations and Peruvian Politics* (Cambridge: Harvard University Press, 1974); and Franklin Tugwell, *The Politics of Oil in Venezuela* (Stanford: Stanford University Press, 1975). For a less recent case, see Lorenzo Meyer, *México y Estados Unidos en el Conflicto Petrolero* (México, D.F.: El Colegio de México, 1968).

37. Olga Pellicer de Brody, "Mexico in the 1970s and Its Relations with the United States," in Cotler and Fagen, *Latin America and the United States*, pp. 316–317. See also her *México y la Revolución Cubana* (México, D.F.: El Colegio de México, 1972), which she describes as a study of the utilization of Mexico's foreign policy for purposes of domestic policy. Wolf Grabendorff, "Mexico's Foreign Policy—Indeed a Foreign Policy?" Review essay, *Journal of Inter-American Studies and World Affairs* 20 (1), February 1978, pp. 85–92.

38. See Graham T. Allison, *Essence of Decision: Explaining the Cuban Missile Crisis* (Boston: Little, Brown, 1971); and Morton M. Halperin, *Bureaucratic Politics and Foreign Policy* (Washington: The Brookings Institution, 1974). For a discussion of the bureaucratic politics approach in the context of U.S.–Latin American relations, see Cotler and Fagen, *Latin America and the United States*, especially the articles by Ernest May, Christopher Mitchell, Abraham Lowenthal, and their discussants.

39. On Argentina's foreign policy during the Peronist era, see Conil Paz and Ferrari, *Argentina's Foreign Policy*; Sergio Bagú, *Argentina en el mundo* (México, D.F.: Fondo de Cultura Económica, 1961); Harold F. Peterson, *Argentina and the*

United States 1810–1960 (New York: State University of New York Press, 1964); and Joseph S. Tulchin, "Foreign Policy," in M. Falcoff and R. H. Dolkart (eds.), *Prologue to Perón: Argentina in Depression and War, 1930–1943* (Berkeley: University of California Press, 1975), chap. 4.

40. Referring to Echeverría's foreign-policy initiatives and actions, one author asserted that at a certain point "it became difficult to discern to what extent many of his initiatives and acts responded to a State policy, and to what extent they responded rather to a personal prestige policy." Mario Ojeda, "El régimen de Echeverría y la nueva política exterior," *Trimestre Político* 2 (5), July–September 1976, p. 31. A similar point is stressed in Yoram Shapira, "La política exterior de México bajo el régimen de Echeverría: Retrospectiva," *Foro Internacional* 19 (1), July–September 1978, pp. 67ff. Robert D. Bond has offered a similar interpretation of Venezuela's foreign policy under Carlos Andrés Pérez: "Championing Third World demands clearly accords with President Pérez's desire to be viewed as a leader of international stature." Robert D. Bond, "Venezuela's Role in International Affairs," in Robert D. Bond (ed.), *Contemporary Venezuela and Its Role in International Affairs* (New York: New York University Press, 1977), p. 247. See also the article by John D. Martz in the same volume.

41. Edward González, "Institutionalization, Political Elites, and Foreign Policies," in Cole Blasier and Carmelo Mesa-Lago (eds.), *Cuba in the World* (Pittsburgh: University of Pittsburgh Press, 1979), pp. 3–36.

42. Elizabeth G. Ferris, "Toward a Theory for the Comparative Analysis of Latin American Foreign Policy," in Ferris and Lincoln, *Latin American Foreign Policies*, pp. 242–245. Another author who stresses the utility of the issue-area approach is Yale H. Ferguson, "Through Glasses Darkly: An Assessment of Various Theoretical Approaches to Inter-American Relations," *Journal of Inter-American Studies and World Affairs* 19 (1), February 1977, pp. 3–34.

43. Arthur L. Kalleberg, "The Logic of Comparison: A Methodological Note on the Comparative Study of Political Systems," *World Politics* 19 (1), October 1966, p. 75.

2. On Comparing Foreign Policies: Comments on van Klaveren

Chapter 1 by Alberto van Klaveren provides an excellent overview of a very extensive and growing bibliography on foreign policy in Latin America. The essence of van Klaveren's discussion is that there are both internal and external determinants of foreign policy. Factors internal to the "nation-state"[1] as well as forces external to it condition not only the goals that foreign-policy makers can choose to pursue but also, once goals have been decided on, the extent to which the desired ends can be attained. In this sense, foreign policy depends both on choice and on constraint. The choices may appear to be volitional and thereby domestic in nature, but both internal and external social forces compete to influence the choices made. Hence, even the act of choosing goals may be subject to international influences. The international environment, of course, imposes constraints on foreign-policy makers, as has been emphasized by the literature on *dependencia*. But not all constraints upon "the choosable" or upon "the attainable" stem from the international environment; some constraints are internal to the political or economic environment of the nation-state.[2]

Consequently, any comprehensive attempt to explain foreign-policy behaviors will force the analyst to deal with complex processes of causation involving determinants operating both inside the nation-state and in its external environment. Indeed, these determinants may interact with each other. In such interactive cases causal influence would be attributable to the juxtaposition of exposure to an international setting that imposes constraints on action or that makes certain actions more likely than others[3] with domestic circumstances that make more probable a specific response to the international constraints shared by others.[4] If such is the case, analysts who aspire to study Latin American foreign policy comparatively would do well to attend to the four concluding recommendations of van Klaveren. These were, once again:

1. the elaboration of conceptual frameworks that would facilitate theoretically grounded studies employing multicausal explanations,
2. the use of methodologies that are more explicitly comparative,

3. the use of sectoral analyses of foreign policy or analyses distinguishing between dimensions of foreign-policy action that differ from each other, and

4. the introduction of greater clarity about what it is precisely that one purports to explain or about "which dimensions of the external behavior of Latin America" are to be examined.

Each of these recommendations is worthy of attention if Latin American cases are to be used as a kind of surrogate laboratory for uncovering causal processes that operate in the making of foreign policy.[5]

Of the four suggestions offered by van Klaveren, the fourth one is perhaps the most important for individual investigators but also the most difficult to implement across a whole field of study. It is especially important to specify that which one wishes to explain. It is not sufficient to say, for example, that one wishes to study the evolution of Bolivian foreign policy over time. To make a theoretical contribution of interest to other scholars, one must not only specify what one means by *foreign policy*, but one must also suggest how foreign policy can vary—that is, one must specify the distinct values that foreign policy can entail or can assume over time.[6]

Without knowing the possible alternative values that might be represented in foreign policy, the reader cannot comprehend the full meaning of the foreign policy observed at any one point in time or the implications of changes observed over time. Obviously, when writing for other specialists or for advanced students, investigators often think it is justifiable to assume that readers will be astute observers of social processes and will be capable of imagining outcomes other than those we describe. However, when we fail to specify the values that foreign policy might assume (or, as van Klaveren says, when we fail to define specifically what we mean by foreign policy), we are likely to fail to construct theories that will explain the differential results of social processes. We will fail to do so because we will restrict our attention to the individual case that interests us most, without asking just how different that case is from other cases, or in what consists the difference, or how the apparent difference might best be explained.

Van Klaveren suggests implicitly, and I concur, that this is a very basic goal of theoretical thought: *Social theory exists to make sense of differential results.*[7] The foreign policies of Latin America interest us precisely because they are distinct and variable between countries and over time. In order to comprehend this variation it is necessary to impose a certain measure of intellectual order on the vast array of observable facts. The individual investigator does so in part by the very choice of a definition of foreign policy.[8] If the investigator does not make explicit his or her definition to other researchers or to the intended audience,[9] communication and comprehension can be impeded in a number of ways. The most important of these is clearly that others fail to see what is comparable between one case and another, as well as what is distinct. But, in addition, others may more easily discard the researcher's preferred interpretation of the data or may misuse the results of one investigation to lend superficial credence to interpretations of foreign policy that the original researcher never had in mind. Definitions are not mere formalities, then, insisted upon merely by philosophers or "rank empiricists."

If researchers truly want to participate in the construction of social theory, they ought to begin any study by defining foreign policy in terms that allow readers to comprehend the distinct values that the external behavior of states can manifest across cases and across time. The catalogue of alternative values need not be exhaustive, but collective progress in theory construction will not be made unless we all know what others assume the alternative outcomes might have been.

At the same time, this counsel of van Klaveren's is never going to carry us to a moment in which we will all be in agreement over the most useful definition of foreign policy. Here we need to consider personal values. Precisely because as human beings we have distinct values, as researchers we are going to be attracted to different aspects of foreign policy as "more interesting" or "more important to under-stand." There are no remedies for these differing values. Instead of launching into a useless debate over what ought be the one consensual definition of foreign policy, a definition at which we shall never arrive, we ought simply to begin more modestly by advising others what we mean when we use the term. It would be enough to say: "To me foreign policy means X, which implies that external behavior may take on the values of A, B, C . . . n." The best manner of confronting our different values is to confess how they influence us in conceiving the explanatory task; the most important way in which our values influence our conception of the explanatory task is quite probably in our definition of foreign policy itself.

The second dictum of van Klaveren also merits special attention; this has to do with the use of methodologies that are more explicitly comparative. In his summary of the extensive bibliography on Latin American foreign policies, van Klaveren mentions by way of illustration one type of study that is genuinely comparative—study of foreign policy in a single country both before and after a disjunctive change of political regime. I would concur with van Klaveren's commendation of this type of research. Such research employs comparison in the service of theory construction *because it allows us to identify the temporal manifestation of causal mechanisms.* The logic here is that if the character of a political regime in fact determines a portion of the variation in foreign policy, this influence ought to be detectable by examining the reorientations of foreign policy that follow a disjunctive regime change.[10] This approach exhibits some features of the logic of quasi experimentation.[11]

Quasi experimentation implies the examination of the effects of a stimulus that occurs naturally, in the sense of not being produced by the investigator. As a research technique, quasi-experimental designs encourage investigators to examine the effects of changes in conjunctural variables, such as a coup having taken place or other disjunctive and dramatic change, but limit the changes to those that are not subject to control by the investigator. Nonetheless, by careful case selection or by systematic data collection across time, researchers can investigate the effects of exposure to a "stimulus." The stimulus can be conceived as a "shock" or "external change" applied to a single system at a given point in time, after which effects can be observed, quantified, and compared with "measurements" taken before the shock was applied.[12]

Alternatively, genuinely comparative research designs may contrast the effects of stimuli that are "present" or "absent." Cases are selected so as to contrast situations where the stimulus is present with those where it is absent, while making the cases selected as similar as possible with regard to the values they exhibit on all other possible causal agents.[13] This classic method of comparison is used when there are too few cases to warrant a more elaborate approach involving multivariate statistical analyses.

Let me illustrate the possible applications of these more genuinely comparative research designs by taking a simple example from the literature reviewed by van Klaveren. If it is true, as van Klaveren suggests, that foreign-policy decisions and the external behaviors of states are conditioned both by internal and by external factors, it ought be possible to select cases for research that would maximize the theoretical lessons that we derive from our research efforts. Let us consider, for example, the simple hypothesis that external constraints determine that which can be done. Specifically, one might hypothesize that the typical balance-of-payments deficits of Latin American states would impede the degree of "foreign-policy activism" exhibited, with the corollary implication that freedom from balance-of-payments difficulties would permit latent tendencies toward foreign-policy activism to be revealed.[14] Operationally, this might be approached by the examination of petroleum booms and their consequences for foreign-policy activism. The focus of the initial hypothesis would be on the relationship of the state to the external environment.

We might, of course, compare petroleum-boom countries with non-petroleum-boom countries. But I propose another route. Let us differentiate between subtypes of petroleum booms, following our initial theoretical logic. Let us compare "manna from heaven" booms with "front-end" booms on the assumption that not all petroleum booms imply equal freedom from balance-of-payments constraints. If those who make foreign policy think along the lines of "We currently have a historic, largely unexpected, and probably nonrecurrent opportunity to invest resources in international projects," they will probably behave differently from foreign-policy makers who recognize that any long-range infusion of petroleum earnings must be balanced against the cost of short-term investments in production capacity.

It might be argued that the former situation, the "manna from heaven" setting, was approximated by Venezuela between 1973 and 1978 and that the latter situation, the "front-end" boom, was approximated by Mexico's experience in 1977–1981.[15] Now, assuming that we have correctly identified the difference between the two settings, our little theory would produce the expectation that the Venezuelans would have been much more the foreign-policy activists than would the Mexicans. The external situations of the two countries or, better said, the freedom that each would enjoy in the short term from balance-of-payments difficulties, were very different. Our theory is that the greater freedom from constraint enjoyed by the Venezuelan policymakers ought to lead to a different style of behavior from that exhibited by the Mexican policymakers.

I do not know if the results of a serious comparative study of the two cases would confirm this prediction or not. My impression is that the theory is much too simple—that the determinants of foreign-policy activism are multiple. It is also my impression that the degree of foreign-policy activism of Venezuelan President Carlos Andrés Pérez was high, but was more or less equaled by that of Mexico's Presidente José López Portillo. If presidential attention were taken as a operational indicator of national foreign-policy activism, a serious study might reveal that the two cases exhibited roughly equal values on the dependent variable. If so, we would then confront an interesting theoretical puzzle: The Mexicans did not behave as the theory predicted; their level of foreign-policy activism was higher than the one that the theory would have predicted. Such puzzles can be fortuitous for theory construction.

Since this theory of the influence of external constraints on foreign-policy behavior predicts certain differences, but the expected differences do not occur, I must conclude either that the initial theory was wholly inaccurate or that some other third variable intervenes to distort or to conceal the expected results. In the example at hand I may wish not to discard the initial theoretical premise but rather to focus on the intervening effects of other internal variables mentioned by van Klaveren—the quality of leadership, preferred development strategies, presidential ideologies, nature of the political regime, and so on. These are all variables internal to the nation-state. The basic point about the logic of quasi experimentation and explicit comparison can now be made. If we have selected our cases seriously according to an explicit logic of comparison, we can distinguish results that are theoretically "expected" from results that are theoretically "unexpected," and in doing so we can more rapidly rectify the deficiencies of the theoretical postulates from which we begin.

My own view of research is that, as investigators, we ought have no fear of beginning from a mistaken theoretical premise: This misfortune is inevitable, as inevitable as death. Theories are temporary instruments made to be refined. But we should avoid the temptation to continue studying what we know best, simply because it is convenient for us to do so and because our expertise will go unquestioned. If the comparative study of foreign policy is ever going to flourish, we shall have to follow the advice of van Klaveren and undertake studies that are genuinely comparative. To be genuinely comparative is to have a theory that guides one to make certain comparisons and not others. This implies conscious thought about what cases one ought to compare and why one compares them. To do that, one must define explicitly not only the dependent variable, foreign policy, but also the independent variable(s) as well. Ultimately, one must choose cases to be studied that can teach something about the relationship between presumed causal factors and the dependent variable. Theory and method must interact symbiotically in comparative research. Theory can be refined and enriched by comparative methods of inquiry, but intelligent comparison cannot even be undertaken without the explicit guidance of some initial theoretical postulates, however mistaken those postulates may later prove to be.

NOTES

1. This term is used loosely, for as Aníbal Pinto has observed, an essential characteristic of the Latin American experience with recent economic change has been the growth of a class of people who reside within the geographical boundaries of the state but whose interests and affective commitments are not necessarily strongly linked with other members of the "nation" that is presumed to coincide with the state. See his *Capitalismo Transnacional y Desintegración Nacional* (Buenos Aires: Editorial Nueva Visión, 1971). After this initial caveat, I shall use the term "nation-state" without quotation marks, having now advised readers that I am aware of imprecision in the concept.

2. Such as (1) those implied by the probable reaction of domestic political factions or social groups to foreign-policy initiatives that affect interests differentially, or (2) economic resource constraints on foreign undertakings.

3. These represent the contribution of *setting variables*, shared by many individual nation-states that are located in similar international environments, to the interaction effect. On the concept of a setting variable, see Adam Przeworski and Henry Teune, *The Logic of Comparative Social Inquiry* (New York: John Wiley and Sons, 1970), pp. 53–56.

4. These conditions represent the contribution of *attributes of the unit of analysis* (i.e., the nation-state) to the interaction effect. The interaction effects of which we speak would then involve the presence of both a setting variable or variables, which would tend to exhibit less variation across Latin American cases, and variables representing attributes of the nation-state, which would tend to exhibit considerable variation across cases in the Latin American region.

5. I take this to be the fundamental purpose of proposing to study foreign policy comparatively. The comparative study of foreign policy must belong to that tradition of explanation that is characterized as *nomothetic*, i.e., explanation that seeks to uncover general explanatory principles applicable to a variety of cases based on observable patterns of covariation across cases. Nomothetic explanations would attribute differential outcomes to the occurrence of variant values on specific independent or intervening variables. *Idiographic* explanation, by contrast, would treat outcomes of specific cases as situationally conditioned,

unique, and nonrepeatable instances that can best be comprehended only by a full understanding of the specificity of each individual case. Idiographic explanation, then, attaches no particular merit to comparing one case with others, but attaches great merit to what might be called the evolutionary logic of a situation. Nomothetic explanation is impossible without comparison. On nomothetic versus idiographic explanation, see Przeworski and Teune, *The Logic of Comparative Social Inquiry*, pp. 5–8. On the origin of the comparative method in the social sciences, see Arend Liphardt, "Comparative Politics and the Comparative Method," *American Political Science Review* 65, no. 3 (September 1971):682–693.

6. I have deliberately used the rather ambiguous word *values* because I wish to convey two meanings. First, for studies that aspire to be quantitative, it is essential to have an explicit operational definition of foreign policy (or of each of the multiple dimensions thereof) that would allow other observers to replicate one's own measurements. But for other studies that aspire merely to introduce qualitative distinctions among possible types of foreign-policy orientations, it is also equally important to distinguish between the various values (that is, desired ends) that either might be or are in fact given priority in packages of foreign-policy choices. For an attempt (surely less than fully successful) to do the latter, see Kenneth M. Coleman and Luis Quirós Varela, "Determinants of Latin American Foreign Policies: Bureaucratic Organizations and Development Strategies," in Elizabeth G. Ferris and Jennie K. Lincoln, *Latin American Foreign Policies: Global and Regional Dimensions* (Boulder, Colo.: Westview Press, 1981), esp. pp. 48–55.

7. Empirical social theory obviously exists to serve other functions: to reduce empirical complexity to manageable proportions by focusing on patterned relationships, to identify presumed causal processes, and so on. But among the functions of empirical theory is the one highlighted in the text. Normative theory, of course, exists to serve other purposes, such as the ranking of desired ends in terms of a hierarchy from most transcendent to least so and the elaboration of decision rules for choosing among competing values.

8. This might be seen in the article by Richard Fagen, "The Nicaraguan Crisis and the International Setting," prepared for the 1982 conference at Viña del Mar on Latin American foreign policies and subsequently published in *Monthly Review* 34, no. 6 (November 1982):1–16. In it Fagen analyzes the movement toward political closure in Nicaraguan society in some measure as foreign-policy action designed to cope with a hostile international environment. Normally, the elaboration of a national political formula would be seen by many analysts as "domestic action" and not as behavior properly construed as "foreign policy." Yet the definition implicitly adopted by Fagen suggests that foreign policy includes all attempts to cope with one's international environment, either in the form of attempts to influence that environment in a positive fashion so that the environment can be used to pursue national goals or in the form of attempts to render the environment less threatening to the pursuit of national goals. Others have also adopted such an implicit definition when analyzing revolutionary regimes; see Coleman and Quirós Varela, "Determinants of Latin American Foreign Policies," p. 54.

9. According to this criterion, both the Fagen and the Coleman-Quirós articles previously cited are properly subject to criticism. Neither contains a formal definition of foreign policy that makes explicit just how it is that "domestic political reorganization can be a dimension of 'foreign policy.'"

10. Given van Klaveren's summary of the literature, which tends to suggest that the Brazilian coup of 1964 produced a much less dramatic reorientation of foreign policy than did the Chilean coup of 1973, it becomes apparent that comparing such comparisons can lead one to refine theories even further. After discovering that some coups have substantial foreign-policy effects and others do not, the next question quickly becomes: What type of regime change is necessary to produce a dramatic reorientation of foreign policy?

11. The *locus classicus* is still Donald T. Campbell and Julian C. Stanley, *Experimental and Quasi-Experimental Designs for Research* (Chicago: Rand McNally, 1963). See also Eugene Webb, Donald T. Campbell, Richard Schwartz, and Lee Seechrist, *Unobtrusive Measures* (Chicago: Rand McNally, 1966).

12. Qualitative assessments can be undertaken, following the logic of quasi experimentation, just as easily as can quantitative assessments. For this reason, we use the word "measurement" loosely.

13. This is a design that dates back to James Mill, as discussed in Liphardt, "Comparative Politics and the Comparative Method." It has been called the most-similar-systems design by Przeworski and Teune, *The Logic of Comparative Social Inquiry.* The idea is that, via careful and very self-conscious case selection, attention is to be focused on the effects of one independent variable, while the potential effects of other variables known to be causally related to the dependent variable are to be removed. Such potentially confounding causal effects are eliminated by selecting cases where no virtual variation exists on certain independent variables, *but where variation does exist on the one independent variable that is the subject of the quasi experiment.*

14. This is not a hypothesis that I recommend that anyone take seriously; it is used *merely* for illustrative purposes. Also note that to investigate this hypothesis a specific operational definition of foreign policy-cum-activism would have to be adduced.

15. I ask readers to tolerate any empirical inaccuracies in the caricatures of the two settings and to assume that the descriptions were correct. The only point here is to illustrate the logic of inference, if a certain pattern of results were to be found.

3. The Formulation and Implementation of Brazilian Foreign Policy: Itamaraty and the New Actors

BRAZILIAN FOREIGN POLICY AND THE MYTH OF THE BARON

It is widely known that in politics, truth is what people believe rather than what happens. In this respect, the beliefs that exist about Brazilian foreign policy and its foreign service are of paramount importance. Latin American diplomats praise the virtues of the Brazilian foreign service. An Argentine and a Chilean diplomat told me they wished the Palacio San Martín and the Cancillería could work as efficiently as the Itamaraty (the Brazilian diplomatic service) did.[1] A former president of Bolivia wanted to create a diplomatic academy based on the model of the Instituto Rio Branco, the Brazilian school for diplomats.[2] However, the external image of efficiency and effectiveness of the Itamaraty is not shared as intensely within Brazil.

The whole operation of the Brazilian Foreign Service takes place under the aegis of the baron of Rio Branco, who maintained the use of his aristocratic title during republican times and was historically responsible for "consolidating Brazilian borders," as school children are taught in Brazil or, to use the term coined by Genaro Arriagada, for consolidating Brazil's position as a geopolitically "satisfied" country.[3] Without entering into a discussion about the actual deeds of the baron during his tenure as minister of foreign relations in the beginning of this century, the most important point about him in relation to the Brazilian diplomatic service is that he and the policies attributed to him are the major symbolic source of the esprit de corps of the Itamaraty. The originality of this situation is that, with the exception of the armed forces, no other Brazilian government agency or ministry has such a powerful historical symbol to help it act coherently and to face the uncertainties of bureaucratic competition in the present.[4]

Nowadays, the highest professional decoration a diplomat can be awarded is the Rio Branco medal, and the boldly modern building in which the Ministry of Foreign Relations is housed in Brasília is called Palácio Itamaraty. The diplomatic service itself is known as Itamaraty, the name of the former headquarters of the ministry in Rio de Janeiro. So, it is possible to say that the Brazilian diplomatic service operates around the image of the baron.

Ironically, during the tenure of the baron, the Brazilian diplomatic cadre was not professional. It was composed of elite youngsters, selected and approved by the baron, who implemented foreign policy according to their mentor. At that moment, the Brazilian diplomatic corps was not so different from what it was in other countries—a safe nest in which the elite youngsters could grow old. This remained basically the same until the Getulio Vargas years (1930–1945). Even though class patronage and nepotism were still rampant in the Itamaraty at that time, the difference rested in the class origins of recipients of patronage.

Vargas's attempts to modernize and rationalize Brazilian public administration were implemented by creation of the Departamento de Servicio Público (DASP). In accordance with the centralizing ethos of the time, all sectors of the bureaucracy were put under control of DASP.[5] It was in charge of recruitment, selection, admission, promotion, demotion, and retirement of civil servants. Somehow, DASP intended to copy the rationality of the British and French systems of elite training.[6] The rationality about to be introduced, however, was not looked upon with favor by the Itamaraty, whose members felt that the egalitarian-at-the-door ideology of the new system of selection would probably open the Itamaraty to the riff-raff, an unacceptable policy for such a stronghold of the elite. To circumvent the centralized admission system, the Itamaraty created and put under its own control the Instituto Rio Branco, a professional academy that was to be the only one of its kind for a long time in Brazilian civil service.

The entrance exam to the Rio Branco was considered to be very difficult, and indeed it was. In addition, however, it was biased in favor of the upper classes, because the type of knowledge demanded from the applicants was much more likely to be part of the "natural" stock of knowledge of upper-class students than of those with middle- or lower-class backgrounds. The bias also favored diplomats' offspring, since it involved foreign languages and other skills more easily acquired abroad than in Brazil.

After admission to the institute, the young future diplomats were trained for two years; upon graduation, they were automatically admitted into the diplomatic profession as third secretaries. Operated by the Itamaraty, the Instituto Rio Branco played the double function of training and socialization. Through the years the institute consolidated a reputation of an elite training center, and diplomats were considered to be very well trained for the standards of Brazilian civil service in general. As a matter of fact, it is possible to locate in recent Brazilian history an intense outward movement on the part of the Itamaraty with regard to other governmental agencies: The Ministry of Foreign Relations has been a regular supplier of elite cadre members to other governmental agencies. The reverse was not and is not true. There is no lateral entry whatsoever into the diplomatic career.[7]

These peculiar characteristics of the diplomatic service in Brazil have contributed to a strong esprit de corps among diplomats, who regard themselves as different from (and superior to) other bureaucrats. Partly because of that (and partly because of the high geographic mobility of diplomats), they have cultivated a strong sense of isolation from the rest of the bureaucracy, for which they have sometimes been mocked as the *jeunesse dorée*. The social origin, training, competence, isolation, and relative esotericism of the diplomats, associated with the fact that they constituted a homogeneous elite group, contributed to an insulation of the process of foreign-policy making (and especially implementation) from much, although not from all, politicking of the day.

On the one hand, this style of behavior of the diplomats isolated them internally; on the other, it had good effects externally. Professionalism became the trade mark of Itamaraty in its dealings with other bureaucratic agencies in Brazil and with foreign representatives, in Brazil and abroad. Professionalism and competence legitimated Itamaraty's performance. These characteristics proved to be very important, especially after 1964, when the Itamaraty remained to a large extent immune to external intervention, an exception in civilian bureaucracy. Since the government that took office then was conservative, a conservative career diplomat was found to occupy the ministry (Ambassador Vasco Leitão da Cunha, April 4, 1964–January 17, 1966). Only when things became too much even for a conservative career diplomat was a retired general appointed to the post (General Juracy Magalhães, January 17, 1966–March 15, 1967). The "immunity" of the Itamaraty was not complete, however. Several diplomats were purged on the grounds of leftism, corruption, or misbehavior, but the numbers were small compared to what took place in other agencies.[8] Also, no "replacements" were sent into Itamaraty, in comparison to what happened, for instance, in Argentina's and Chile's foreign services, where the Palacio San Martín and the Cancillería were occupied by professional soldiers after the military took over.[9] In Brazil the profession itself was left intact. No noncareer personnel—civilian or military—were admitted either temporarily or permanently to the cadre of diplomats.[10]

Finally, one feature of the Itamaraty that has become more pronounced recently is that of diplomats occupying positions in other governmental agencies. Just as an example, the current chief of the civilian household of the presidency has three advisers who are professional diplomats, the spokesman for the president is a professional diplomat, and diplomats have been assigned to the National Intelligence School. The president of the Brazilian Nuclear Authority (Nuclebrás) is a diplomat and so are advisers on international matters in several ministries.

In this sense, it is almost possible to say that in relation to the Ministry of Foreign Relations, the military government in Brazil has produced a movement contrary to the one that was to be expected. Instead of the ministry being occupied by military officers, as had happened in other countries and as happened in virtually all other ministries in Brazil, the movement has been reversed; it was the diplomats who increased their presence outside of their own professional realm. Aside from prejudices in favor of the diplomats, one factor that facilitated the respect of the military for the diplomats (which most military officers *do not* have for bureaucrats in other agencies) was the career structure of the diplomatic profession (very similar to that of professional soldiers) and the actual professional effectiveness of the diplomats.

The isolation of diplomats has gone hand in hand with the ever-increasing complexity of Brazil's foreign relations, especially with the introduction of new actors on the scene. This is the subject of the next section of this chapter.

FROM GRAND SCHEMES TO DAY-BY-DAY TRADE

When coffee accounted for the majority of the country's exports, Brazilian diplomats had little to do with commercial matters. Young diplomats from privileged backgrounds could dedicate themselves to the grand schemes of international politics (many times vicariously), or alternatively they could pursue literary and artistic careers, taking up diplomacy as a quasi hobby that provided for their financial support. There were a few diplomatic posts of real political importance; provided that these were covered by competent diplomats, the others were for the most part, symbolic representations. There was not much consular work to do since most Brazilians were second-class citizens and either did not travel or, when they did, did not deserve much protection abroad.[11]

During this period of export-led growth, exports were being taken care of by competitive agencies not subject to Itamaraty's authority. Coffee was dealt with by the Instituto Brasileiro do Café, sugar by the Instituto do Açúcar e do Álcool, and so on. These *autarquias* (autarkies) were subject to authority other than the Itamaraty, which played no role in their day-by-day operations. With commerce highly concentrated in a few products over which diplomats did not have authority, international politics was scarce.

The turning point can be placed around the beginning of the Juscelino Kubitschek administration (1956–1960), when the development plans implemented by the new president, although completely out of the political reach of the Itamaraty and involving almost no direct international aspects, were the first step in a change of outlook for diplomats and for other segments of the elite. The *ufanismo* (the boast) that had existed in the past started to take material shape with the acceleration of the process of import substitution: "Brazilian" Volkswagens and Jeeps started to run in city streets, Brasília was built, and inflation was rampant according to the relatively modest standards of the 1950s. However, not much was accomplished in terms of international relations, not even Kubitschek's grand scheme represented by the aborted Operação Pan-Americana.

The major Brazilian move in international politics came with the administration of Janio Quadros and with the so-called independent foreign policy of foreign relations minister Affonso Arinos de Melo Franco. Roughly speaking, this meant independence from the United States and a stronger orientation toward the Third World. A journal to celebrate this move, the *Política Externa Independente*, was almost as short lived as was the Quadros administration (Janaury 1961–August 1961).

After the overthrow of João Goulart (1961–1964) in 1964 all visible traces of the independent foreign policy (*política externa independente*) were erased. Despite that, two events that had taken place could not be undone. First, several cohorts of young candidates admitted to the Instituto Rio Branco had taken the exam and had joined the diplomatic career, motivated by the ideological premises of the *política externa independente*. Ambassador João Augusto de Araujo Castro, Goulart's minister of foreign relations during the last months of his administration (August 21, 1963–April 3, 1964), who was strongly nationalistic, cast a spell over the young diplomats and candidates to the diplomatic career. When Goulart fell and Araujo Castro was punished by appointment to Athens (1964–1966) and to Lima (1966–1967), the young diplomats who had joined Itamaraty motivated by the prospect of an independent foreign policy nevertheless did not quit the diplomatic service. They remained and started moving slowly up the professional ladder.[12]

The conservative orientation of the military government in foreign policy started to shift as time went by. During the tenure of President Arturo Costa e Silva, when Representative Magalhães Pinto (a professional politician) was minister and Ambassador Sergio Correa da Costa was secretary general of the ministry, Brazil refused to sign the Non-proliferation Treaty (NPT), thus leaving open the road for a nuclear policy that *might* include military use of nuclear energy. A young diplomat who was involved in these negotiations, Paulo Nogueira Batista, later became the president of Nuclebrás.[13]

During the late 1960s and early 1970s, several relevant changes took place in Brazil and in the world. The industrialization program pushed during the Kubitschek administration matured, and the need for a more aggressive export policy was felt, as a result partly of the need to pay the foreign debt and partly of the conservative position adopted by the successive governments with respect to income distribution. Aside from these changes in Brazil, elsewhere the process of decolonization was consolidated, the cold war eased,[14] new markets were opened, and Latin America was more eager for more independence from the U.S. In foreign policy, Itamaraty continued to carry the torch, but there was little time left over for other important tasks, especially those connected with the creation of markets. The then finance minister, Antonio Delfín Netto, a strong minister,[15] was aggressively entering the international arena and competing in an area in which the Itamaraty had, up until then, operated in a monopolistic fashion. The bureaucratic feud between Finance Minister Delfín Netto and Foreign Minister Gibson Barbosa reached such a point that both of them were called in by the president, who ordered them to put an end to the feud, at least in public terms. The finance minister was playing the game of the First World, and the Itamaraty was playing the game of the Third World.

A motto was spread in Itamaraty (by means of posters) that made a very imaginative and shrewd use of its negative image before the Brazilian public, that of being a nest of elite punks and a very traditional and conservative institution: *A melhor tradicão do Itamaraty é saber renovar-se* (the best tradition of Itamaraty is to know when to change). The motto was not sheer rhetoric; it did reflect several changes starting to occur, particularly a more activist policy toward the Third World. Parallel to this, inside Itamaraty the Departamento de Promociones Comerciales (DPC—Department of Commercial Promotion) was taking shape under the direction of Counselor Paulo Tarso Flexa de Lima. During those days DPC was a very modest department, and in a sense it was not regarded as an "honorable" one in the career, because after all diplomats did not like the idea of being considered "salesmen." Another development that occurred during this period was the professional maturation of what I call the generation of the independent foreign policy, those young diplomats who had joined the profession motivated by the promise of significant change during the Quadros administration. Members of this cohort already had started to reach the middle levels of their careers where they could have a stronger influence in actual policymaking.

The inauguration of the Geisel administration in 1974 and the appointment as foreign minister of Ambassador Antonio Francisco Azeredo da Silveira (a highly controversial and charismatic career diplomat) consolidated the changes. That was the moment for a period of creative foreign policy to blossom. There was already a structure for more aggressiveness in foreign sales; Angola became independent and its new government was recognized by Brazil despite U.S. opposition; a nuclear agreement was signed with West Germany, also despite U.S. opposition; and the blunders of the Carter administration caused Brazil to cancel its military agreements with the United States.

In his study of Chilean foreign policy, Heraldo Muñoz pointed out that after the overthrow of Salvador Allende and the adoption of the Chicago School of Economics as the Bible of the Pinochet regime, Chile gave total priority to the economic aspects of foreign policy.[16] This alternative was not, however, the result of a free choice. It was partly the result of the economic policy adopted by the regime, but it was also a result of the political isolation to which Chile was submitted after the 1973 coup.[17] Brazil never experienced such a situation. In the first place, it was not subjected to similar international political pressures after the fall of Goulart.[18] Second, as has been pointed out, the intervention in Itamaraty by nondiplomats was virtually nil.

Thus, even after the coup Brazilian foreign policy was not affected as it might have been by a new conservative government. Some compromises were necessary to satisfy the demands of the new power holders, such as severing diplomatic relations with Cuba and Hungary (whose legation was invaded by self-appointed revolutionaries), as well as interrupting a commercial mission from the People's Republic of China (whose members were taken as scapegoats and accused of planning a communist coup in Brazil). In addition, policy did shift toward a stronger emphasis on alignment with the United States, but not at the expense of other areas. The two major visible demonstrations of the conservative and pro-U.S. stance of the government were the statement by then Ambassador to Washington General Juracy Magalhães that "what was good for the U.S. was good for Brasil" and the sending of troops to the Inter-American Peace Force that intervened in Santo Domingo on behalf of the U.S. interests.

Aside from these concessions, which Itamaraty had to make because they were key issues for the military, the Foreign Relations Ministry kept control of foreign policy, with the independent-foreign-policy generation in recess, so to speak. During this period, however, several points became clear to Brazilian diplomats. The "diversification of dependence" was essential if Brazil was to acquire a higher status. This diversification had to take place in several directions: (1) it was necessary to be less dependent on the United States, (2) it was important to be less dependent on coffee, and (3) it was necessary to be more integrated with other areas of the world. The diplomats took care of doing just that, but slowly and discretely. It was their professionalism, their sense of historical continuity, and their capacity to project a future that allowed them to introduce the changes at a pace palatable to a government that was, in terms of international relations, far more conservative than were the diplomats, a government strongly influenced by the cold war ideology developed under the leadership of the United States after World War II.

Commercially speaking, it was necessary to get out of coffee, but something had to replace it, and at the time there was just not much. The import-substitution industrialization policy had accelerated during the Kubitschek administration and had started to provide the manufactured goods to be exported. Despite this, the problem was that the manufactured goods Brazil could produce could not compete successfully with manufactures from more developed countries. The way out was to try to open markets in less developed countries where the demands for quality were lower than in developed countries.

The results of these changes were significant. With respect to coffee, in 1954 it amounted to 53 percent of Brazilian exports; in 1973, 20.1 percent; and in 1975, 10.8 percent. While coffee went down, soybeans and sugar went up.[19] With respect to minerals, the role of iron ore was increased; more recently there have been plans to develop the bauxite reserves near São Luiz in a joint venture with Alcoa and Shell Oil.

The most important fact about this policy was that, with respect to exports to less developed countries, several political concessions had to be made. In Brazil's opening to Africa, the political price was to decrease the importance of relations with South Africa, which Brazil did, and to use as the bridgehead to Black Africa the former Portuguese colonies, under the assumption that by showing solidarity with them Brazil would conquer the hearts of other Black African countries. On the occasion of the independence of Angola, the Brazilian government was the first to recognize the revolutionary government, against the will of the United States. That was an unprecedented move on the part of Brazil, since it meant recognizing a Marxist government that had taken power by means of armed struggle.

The policy of gaining influence in Africa through the former Portuguese colonies has been a relatively successful one. Brazil's exports to other Black African countries have been increasing, not only in terms of manufactured goods but also in terms of technical assistance, construction work, culture (TV programs, movies, granting of fellowships), and, more recently, weapons. This policy has been officially called responsible pragmatism, although some more conservative sectors have christened it submissive opportunism. The important fact to be stressed is that, despite the ideological preferences of the military, the diplomats have managed to implement a foreign policy that is much less tied to political prejudices and will probably be far more productive in the long run.

The risk inherent in this option, in combination with Brazil's position in international rankings, is that of emphasizing what Wayne Selcher called the betweenness of Brazil's foreign policy.[20] This "betweenness" has caused Brazil to be accused of ambiguity in international relations. *Ambiguity* is linguistically correct, although Brazilian policymakers prefer not to accept its political usage. Since Brazil is not playing the game of competing for hegemony with anyone (as the Soviet Union and the United States have been doing), it can afford the luxury of a foreign policy that pursues its own interests without necessarily tying its positions to the ideology or to the interests of the United States. Despite the fact that such behavior may cause indignation in more conservative quarters in the United States (especially in the minds of those who perceive any move in one country's interest as a move against the United States), it reflects the fact that countries do mature and that a more independent foreign policy is part of the maturation process.

COMPETITIVE ACTORS: TRADE WAS THE NAME OF THE GAME

During the late 1960s and early 1970s, several bureaucratic agencies competed in the arena of foreign trade with the Itamaraty. Hypothetically speaking there were several possible outcomes to the competition.

1. Trade and foreign relations could have been separated, with one or several existing bureaucratic actors taking over. In the event of this outcome, CACEX (Export Office of the Central Bank of Brazil) or the Finance Ministry (or a hypothetical Ministry of Foreign Trade) could have reinforced its position, and Itamaraty would have lost much of its prestige.

2. Trade and foreign relations could have remained together with an external intervention in Itamaraty, that is, with a dramatic reshaping of the Chancery. This was what happened in Chile, where military officers were appointed to the Ministry of Foreign Relations, and a businessman, Hernán Cubillos, became chancellor. In order to counterbalance the excessive influence of the military, he called in the advisory committee to the minister, composed of former diplomats and academics.[21]

3. Itamaraty could have modernized itself and gone into commercial operations. This was what actually did occur. As already pointed out, despite the conflict between Gibson Barbosa (minister of foreign relations) and Delfín Netto (minister of finance) during the Medici administration, Counselor Paulo Tarso Flexa de Lima was slowly starting the Department of Commercial Promotion within Itamaraty.

DPC was the key actor in putting into effect the policy of establishing closer relations with less developed countries (which could absorb Brazilian services and manufactured goods) at the same time that the ministry supported them politically. To do this, Itamaraty acted as a bloc, facing the opposition of sectors in the military. During the Ernesto Geisel administration this was done with strong support from the president.[22]

The shifts resulting from these policies have been striking. In 1965, the United States absorbed 45 percent of Brazilian exports; today it absorbs less than 20 percent. In 1972, trade between Brazil and Nigeria amounted to $1 million; nowadays it is around $500 million.[23] From 1970 to 1979, the percentage of Brazilian exports to several regions of the world changed substantially: Exports to the United States dropped from 24.7 to 19.0; those to Western Europe dropped from 44.1 to 37.4; those to Latin America jumped from 11.1 to 15.2; those to Africa from 2.1 to 4.5; and those to the Middle East from 0.6 to 3.7. Selcher presented data on direct investment for December 1971 and December 1978, showing that, in percentage terms, direct investment in Brazil by all capitalist countries dropped, with the exception of West Germany (11.4 percent to 15.3 percent), Switzerland (6.5 percent to 11.9 percent), Japan (4.3 percent to 10.2 percent), and Sweden, Luxembourg, and the Low Countries, which showed small increases.[24] In addition to this shift from dependence on one good and shift of dependence from one country, Brazil has also diversified its agricultural production, becoming by 1981 second only to the United States as an exporter of agricultural products.[25]

The result of this diversification has been that, with an increase in the quantity of exports with the new markets, the number of internal competing actors in international operations has increased substantially, both within the bureaucracy and outside of it. In the past, as I pointed out, Itamaraty could comfortably maintain its position because not many actors were involved in the international arena. Nowadays, each new arena that opens means one new actor or a series of new actors competing, either with other actors for the attention of the Itamaraty for the fulfillment of its (or their) own interests or with the Itamaraty itself for the attention of other government agencies and offices, so as to capture a new slice of the international action.

Among these new types of actors are interest groups, state enterprises, and private corporations. Some examples of competiton can be cited. The State Federations of Industries and the National Confederation of Industries restricted their "international action" in the past to pressuring the government for import tax exemptions that would allow their associates to continue the import-substitution process. Nowadays, although this sort of pressure has not ceased to exist, its relative importance has decreased because Brazilian industry already has export problems. These involve, in many instances, government-to-government negotiations (such as the ones that have been increasingly taking place with the United States in regard to instant coffee, shoes, textiles, and, more recently, steel). So this is an important new role that Itamaraty is increasingly being called upon to play.

With respect to the involvement of government, there is also the situation created by the December 1981 trip to Cuba of Ruy Barreto, the president of the Federation of Commercial Associations. Barreto went to Cuba on a private commercial mission, and the government's reaction was cautious. On the one hand, the federation issued a communiqué stating that Barreto had *mentioned* his travel plans to officials in the presidential palace. The president, on his part, denied any involvement and stated that Barreto was traveling as a private citizen. Irrespective of the degree of communication existing between Barreto and the government, the fact is that just a few years ago the only Brazilian who would go to Cuba on a public mission would be an official of the outlawed Communist party. Nowadays what we see is that a very conservative businessman takes the lead in trying to reestablish commercial relations with Cuba, having in mind especially the interests of the business sector and ignoring to a large extent the interests of the government, of the Itamaraty, and of higher military officials.

The web of new actors performing internationally involves several state-owned enterprises whose vast business operations make it harder for Itamaraty to keep pace. The Brazilian Petroleum Corporation (Petrobrás), for one, has a monopoly of all oil imports into Brazil. This made it set up a large subsidiary, Interbrás (Brazilian National Telephone Company), a trading corporation that is basically in charge of exporting "packages" to countries from which Brazil imports oil. The Banco do Brasil, which already operates in import-export licensing as a state-owned bank, through CACEX set up another trading company of its own, COBEC, which owns warehouses in several places allegedly to store goods that may need to be exported to specific markets on a rush basis. In the weapons field the Army Ministry operates INBEL; its exports of weapons in many instances compete with private industries. Embraer (Empresas Militares Brasileiras Aéreas), the airplane manufacturing corporation operated by the Air Force Ministry, also operates internationally, selling both military and civilian aircraft. Many other state-owned corporations nowadays have international dealings such as exporting goods, technology, services, and know-how.

If we add to this all the private transnational and national corporations that deal in foreign markets, it is not difficult to see that the control of foreign relations has become a highly complicated matter involving the Foreign Relations Ministry (formally in charge of implementing the country's foreign policy), the Finance and Planning ministries, and the Central Bank (involved on the financial and economic sides of the operations). The Itamaraty, in a sense, is trying to control all these relatively independent actors in order to avoid incoherence and dissonance on the part of quasi-governmental actors, which might cause embarrassment or create problems for the implementation of foreign policy of the country as such.

The Itamaraty, as pointed out earlier, had an identity crisis during the early 1970s, when it had to face two challenges. First, it had to widen its capacity to control and coordinate other actors involved in the foreign arena. Second (and this was a condition sine qua non for the first), it had to develop a capacity to deal more effectively in commercial matters. It is possible to say that Itamaraty has managed, to a large extent, to face the challenge effectively. Nevertheless the problems are still of paramount importance.

One of the important and growing fields in which the Itamaraty has gained control has been arms sales for military use. An interministerial commission coordinated by Itamaraty monitors weapons sales and authorizes them according to the overall foreign policy of the country.[26] Of course, arms are very special kinds of products that allow for this kind of control and guidance on the part of the ministry without raising the protest from producers or dealers that would have been the case if the Itamaraty were trying to exercise similar control over the export of oranges, chicken, or what have you. In spite of this, this mixture of overseeing and helping may be the way for Itamaraty to manage to maintain control over the foreign policy in a situation in which all actors try to act as independently as possible.

Itamaraty already has gone a long way by creating a program to train nondiplomats in charge of commercial promotion, allowing diplomats to handle noncommercial duties while the commercial promoters "take care of sales." In the long run, however, there is a risk that the people in commercial promotion will not agree to be, so to speak, the "noncommissioned officers" of the foreign service. This is one of the most serious challenges that the diplomacy will have to face, trying to integrate as many people as possible into the process of foreign-policy making and implementation without losing control and without allowing the quality of the diplomatic service to deteriorate.

The Instituto Rio Branco, for its part, faces the problem of modernizing itself and its curriculum so as to adapt the training of the diplomats to the actual needs of foreign policy—commercial, political, and otherwise—balancing the curriculum so as to fulfill these conflicting demands without losing its effectiveness as a socialization agency.

CHALLENGES FOR THE FUTURE

The reforms through which Itamaraty will have to pass in the future will be determined by changes that can be predicted in the country's foreign policy. The key questions of Brazilian foreign policy seem to be how to manage more independence from the United States, while developing privileged relationships with another set of countries. As things stand now, although not adopting a Third World position, Brazil seems to be pretty much improving its position along the South-South axis, without necessarily losing its position in the North-South one. For how long this ambiguous position will be tenable is a question for the future.

Along the South-South axis, the most striking developments are the political investments being made by Brazil in Black Africa, starting by means of a highly preferential policy in relation to the former Portuguese colonies. A more recent development, which will perhaps be even more important, is the movement of what I call the Latin Americanization of Brazilian foreign policy. This development basically means a much greater attention being paid by Brazil to its continental neighbors. It is a new move because, in the past, Brazil largely conformed to a foreign policy "shaped" by the United States in the context of the cold war. This policy promoted the North-South axis, in detriment to the South-South one, even in relation to Brazil's own neighbors. If one takes presidential and ministerial visits as indicators of diplomatic intentions, it is possible to see that since President João Baptista Figueiredo took office in 1979, the number of visits at this level within South America has increased dramatically to a point never before reached in recent history. Accompanying these visits were the customary treaties of mutual cooperation, which are being implemented to the degree that Itamaraty is able to modernize itself and to use other actors to implement the operational provisions of the treaties (such as trade, technical assistance, and training).

Of course, Brazilian foreign relations will not limit themselves to Africa and South America. The focus on these two areas in the final part of this chapter was aimed at showing that these are the two geographic areas where Brazil is likely to become more militant in the foreseeable future. Other geographic areas, such as North America, Western and Eastern Europe, and Asia, are portions of the world with which Brazil will maintain relations, but in relative terms Africa and Latin America are the key ones.

The volatility of the political situation in Central America is one factor no analyst can avoid taking into consideration. From the Brazilian point of view, before the situations in El Salvador and Nicaragua had escalated, Central America and the Caribbean were two regions in which Brazil could have its influence increasingly felt, to the point of causing concern to Venezuelan officials who regard that area as their "turf." The resentment accumulated by former British colonies in the Caribbean turned those new nations potentially into countries with which Brazil could have very intense and very productive relationships. However, the Reagan administration policy of escalating its presence in Central America—by sending military advisers or by training Central American officers and soldiers—may have completely shifted the role that Brazil will play in the region.[27] Day by day Central America is becoming a bigger and bigger question mark in international politics. At this point it is virtually impossible to say anything with respect to the possible role Brazil may come to play in the area.

NOTES

1. Interviews, Buenos Aires and Santiago, April–May 1978.

2. Private conversation, Rio de Janeiro, September 1980.

3. Genaro Arriagada suggested that, from the historical point of view, it is possible to label countries as "geopolitically satisfied" and as "geopolitically frustrated." The criterion for the definition of frustration or satisfaction would be the amount of territory gained or lost during the history of that particular country. Arriagada's remarks were made during an oral presentation at the first meeting of the Asociación Chilena de Investigaciones para la Paz (ACHIP), held in Santiago, July 1–3, 1981. Using the concepts suggested by him, Brazil could be labeled as a "very satisfied" country from the geopolitical point of view. All through its history, Brazil has continually increased its territory westward of the Line of Tordesillas (the original dividing line between the lands of the Spanish and Portuguese crowns, which ran along a north-south axis approximately from Belém to Curitiba). Brazil has increased its territory over 200 percent.

4. See Alexandre de S.C. Barros, "A Formação das Elites e a Continuação da Construção do Estado Nacional Brasileiro," Dados 15 (1977), pp. 101–122.

5. See Alexandre de S.C. Barros, "O Estado Cartorial: An Attempt to Investigate the Political Role of Brazilian Bureaucracy," M.A. Thesis, University of Chicago, 1969.

6. The founder of DASP (a sort of U.S. General Services Administration or British Civil Service Department), Luiz Simões Lopes, was also the founder of the Getúlio Vargas Foundation, which had among its operations the now-defunct Escola de Nova Friburgo, a secondary school modeled after the British public schools with the explicit purpose of providing elite training.

7. Ambassadorial positions are an exception, because they are considered to be political appointments. In spite of that, the number of noncareer personnel in these positions has tended to decline sharply since 1945.

8. This is according to Marcus Figueiredo, who has done research on political punishments in Brazil, in a personal communication.

9. See Heraldo Muñoz, "Las Relaciones Exteriores del Gobierno Militar Chileno: Una Interpretación Economica Política," (mimeographed 1981).

10. See Alexandre de S.C. Barros, "The Brazilian Military: Professional Socialization, Political Performance, and State Building," Ph.D. Dissertation, University of Chicago, 1978. See especially chap. 4, "The Military in the Administration of the State," pp. 192–275.

11. On this issue see Alexandre de S.C. Barros, "A Caminho da Cidadania," Jornal da Tarde (São Paulo), October 18, 1978.

12. According to information provided in personal conversation by a professional diplomat who belongs to this generation, he knows only of one person who quit voluntarily because the política externa independente was over. Of course, it is impossible to know how many young people motivated by that policy did not join the diplomatic career for the same reason.

13. The positions of secretário-geral in Brazilian ministries were intended (at the time of their creation) to be like permanent secretaries in the British Civil Service. They were supposed to be professionals in charge of "coaching" politically appointed ministers. In all civilian ministries this did not materialize. The secretários-gerais have tended to be political appointees of the minister. Itamaraty was an exception. There, the secretário-geral has performed the intended function when the minister was a political appointee. When the minister was a professional diplomat, the political importance of the secretário-geral has been smaller.

14. See Alexandre de S.C. Barros, "The Diplomacy of National Security: South American International Relations in a 'Defrosting' World," in Ronald Hellman and H. J. Rosenbaum (eds.), Latin America: The Search for a New International Role (Beverly Hills, Calif.: Sage, 1975), pp. 131–150.

15. See Alexandre de S.C. Barros and Angelina C. Figueiredo, "Dissemination and Use of Social Sciences Research Among and by Policy Makers: Findings of a Brazilian Study," Interciencia 2, no. 2 (March–April 1977), pp. 38–75.

16. See Heraldo Muñoz, "Las Relaciones Exteriores."

17. The repressive policies of the Pinochet regime caused an interviewee to define Chile's position after the 1973 coup as that of "a sister with a bad reputation, i.e., you cannot deny that she's your sister but you try to ignore her acts and pray that people do not ask you whether she's your kin." Interview, May 1978.

18. Most of the international criticism of repressive policies took place between 1969 and 1974, during the tenure of the military junta and that of General Emilio Medici. Despite that, political repression never reached the levels it did in Argentina and Chile.

19. See Wayne Selcher, Brazil's Multilateral Relations: Between First and Third Worlds (Boulder, Colo.: Westview Press, 1978), p. 122.

20. Ibid.

21. See Heraldo Muñoz, "Las Relaciones Exteriores," p. 35.

22. Ambassador Antonio Francisco Azeredo da Silveira, lecture at the Instituto Universitario de Pesquisas do Rio de Janeiro, August 8, 1980.

23. Ambassador Paulo Tarso Flexa de Lima, interview, *Visão* 30, no. 50 (December 14, 1981).

24. Wayne Selcher, "O Brasil no Mundo," *Cultura* (Supplement to *O Estado de São Paulo*).

25. See "Brazil: Feeding the World," *Newsweek* (international edition) 99, no. 8 (February 22, 1982), p. 33.

26. Ambassador Azeredo da Silveira, lecture at IUPERJ, Rio de Janeiro, August 8, 1980.

27. See Beth Nissen, "America Is out of Options," *Newsweek* (international edition) 99, no. 8 (February 22, 1982), p. 9. See also pp. 6–8.

4. Politics, Bureaucracy, and Foreign Policy in Chile

The subject of this chapter is the effect on foreign policy of politics within the executive branch. Most of the research carried out until now in this general area of Chilean foreign relations has concentrated on two types of independent variables—variables at the level of the national system and the incidence of models and economic policies in foreign relations—at the macro level of analysis.[1] In this chapter the intention is to carry out an examination at the micro level, starting from the proposition that the behavior of a government in foreign policy cannot be explained only in terms of the regime and its policies, but requires also the consideration of structural units through which the government apparatus "filters" the general effects exercised by the variables of the political and economic macrosystems.

Concentration on the executive branch has clear justification. For more than half a century, the presidency of the republic has constituted the indisputable focus of national policy, as it had been formerly under very different circumstances during the period between the administrations of Diego Portales and José Manuel Balmaceda. In the executive branch converge the aspirations, demands, and pressures of individuals, groups, and parties that struggle to obtain a place for themselves and to attract on their behalf the power of the state, controlled by the president, both for collective and individual ends. The history of the Chilean politics in the past few decades has shown a constant growth in the number of matters submitted to governmental decision and an increase in the quantity and intensity of conflicts regarding alternative resolutions of such matters by the authorities.

The discussion of policies in the executive branch includes the bureaucracy of foreign relations, but the latter is considered only one part, and not the critical one. Even though it is necessary to recognize the importance of the bureaucratic politics approach developed by Graham Allison and others,[2] this constitutes an analytical tool that responds basically to the particularities of the United States and Western European reality, where the bureaucracy of foreign relations has, with some national differences, a significantly greater weight than in Chile. In those areas

45

it would be fitting to speak of a tendency toward the "bureaucratization of foreign policy," in which the bureaucratic actors are of crucial importance on political results, whereas in Chile it would be more appropriate to think in terms of a "politicization of the bureaucracy," without this having similar influence on the orientation of policies.

Obviously, this distinction must not obscure the relations between political and bureaucratic factors that, far from being excluded, form an integrated phenomenon that can only be unraveled for analytical purposes. In the careers of numerous actors, the political and bureaucratic elements combine, be it in a lone complex role or in various functions that an individual performs in his or her career. This fundamental fact, so different from the circulation between public and private roles characteristic of the United States or from the autonomy of bureaucratic careers peculiar to European systems, sets limits to the bureaucratic phenomenon and to its incidence in Chilean foreign policies.

It is also necessary to remember that the recruitment for bureaucratic positions depends decisively upon partisan political considerations, without excluding other considerations different from actual or potential merit in the performance of functions. Besides, the specialization or professional preparation required for appointment within the bureaucracy of foreign relations traditionally has been limited, one consideration being that the functionary should be trained principally on the job, a conception that only in the last decades has undergone a change.[3] Finally, the working of the bureaucracy constantly depends on political criteria: Functionaries tend to fit their activities into a political framework in order to avoid dysfunctional risks to the progress of their careers, as well as to maintain or increase their power in the organization (the latter is not, in reality, a phenomenon distinctive of a politicized bureaucracy).

There is no intention to ignore traditions, the "internal life," or "bureaucratic subcultures" of a ministry or other governmental organization. For an observer of administration, generally it is easy to identify or define the foreign-relations functionary in terms of a style that includes elements of diplomatic and juridical language, an emphasis on caution and discretion as functionary virtues, and an attachment to protocol formalities and the norms of official sociability. This style, with some changes, is common to governments of different political leanings, being maintained by informal horizontal and hierarchical controls and by súbtle internal mechanisms of co-optation, imitation, and sanction. However, there is no obstacle therein to the maintenance of the essentially subordinated nature of the bureaucracy regarding political actors. For these reasons, this chapter intends to encompass the political and bureaucratic roles in the generation of foreign policies within the executive. I analyze first the presidential role and the characteristics of presidents, so as then to address the study of the bureaucracy.

PRESIDENTIAL PARTICIPATION

The study of presidential participation in the formulation of foreign policy requires a distinction between the superior executive role of the president of the republic and the style or form of behavior of each of the individuals who has occupied that position.

The formal definition of the presidential role is its constitutional status. During the period under study—from 1946 to the present—we find two juridical frameworks of a contradictory tendency, which define in a different way presidential political options regarding foreign policy.

The first option corresponds to the Constitution of 1925. Notwithstanding its having conceded broad authority to the executive in order to conduct "political relations with foreign powers," it established important controls and limitations to presidential management of foreign policy.[4] This constituted a balance-of-power framework generally favorable to the executive, within which it tended to maintain a moderate behavior that served the purpose of preserving the free hand that Congress customarily gave it to carry out government views in international matters.

Starting in September 1973, the conduct of foreign policy fell into the hands of the military junta, an organ that in the beginning absorbed the functions of the executive and the Congress. Under the presidency of General Pinochet, which progressively differed from the junta although forming part of it until 1981, the elaboration and implementation of foreign policy fell upon the executive, with little intervention from the junta. The Constitution of 1980 contemplated the maintenance of the predominance of the executive branch. Thus the new text eliminates the requirement for senatorial approval of appointments of ambassadors and limits to a minimum the requirement for authorization for presidential travels abroad.[5]

The influence of the individual characteristics of presidents thus is evidenced only within the "margin of option" of an internal and international system that offers varied degrees of political opportunity to national leaders to project party conceptions and/or personal or group views into the international arena.[6] The distinctive feature of each president's foreign policy is to be seen precisely in the degree and form to which each president identifies and takes advantage of (or lets pass) political opportunities within the "margin" offered by the structural variables and in the degree to which he attempts to adapt to these or modify them with the goal of improving his position in the system.

For one thing, the presidents are distinguished by their more or less active inclinations in the field of foreign policy (which do not necessarily coincide with their general political views). Schematically, one could distinguish between *animateur* and referee chiefs of state. The first are characterized by their disposition to perform an active role in the elaboration and implementation of foreign policies. The referee presidents

Table 4.1. Typology of Presidential Orientation

	Orientation	
Style of Action	Pragmatic	Ideological
Animateur	Gabriel González Videla (1946–1952)	Eduardo Frei (1964–1970)
		Augusto Pinochet (1973–)
Referee	Carlos Ibáñez del Campo (1952–1958)	Salvador Allende (1970–1973)
	Jorge Alessandri Rodríguez (1958–1964)	

tend to give less priority to foreign affairs. Even though they do not necessarily lack international conceptions, they tend to limit their actions to reacting to the impulses originating from the presidential environment (principal party leaders, personal consultants, and more influential ministers) and lending their power to the selection of preferred alternatives.

A second distinction corresponds to the classic categories of pragmatic and ideological actors. A presidential actor shows ideological tendencies to the extent that, in order to orient his own behavior and that of his followers, he customarily uses concepts and propositions of a normative nature about political institutions and processes and the means and goals of political action. Whenever the presidential actor tends to dispense with such elements, it will be considered that he has a pragmatic orientation.

By combining these two distinctions, the descriptive hypothesis in Table 4.1 can be presented. What follows in this section is a justification for the classification of the presidents, with comments on their characteristics and their impact on the generation of policies.

In the presidency of Gabriel González Videla a personal interest of the chief of state in international affairs can be observed. González Videla had received some international political experience as ambassador to France and Brazil, which influenced his disposition to participate in foreign affairs. The diplomacy of his government was that of adaptation to the new circumstances of the cold war and especially to hegemonic direction by the United States. Nevertheless, González Videla skillfully exploited that small margin of international maneuver that the new bipolar international system offered him, without being guided by ideological prescriptions of his Radical party (which in any case were vague) more than in a rhetorical sense. Clearly, he was a president with a pragmatic tendency. The presidential initiative in new fields of foreign policy—affirmation of rights in the Antarctic, the declaration in 1947 and 1952 of new zones of maritime jurisdiction, increasing government revenues from the copper mining industry—show González Videla to be an *animateur*.[7] On the other hand, his policies showed a personalist stamp, a result of the temperament of the chief of state. The sudden, unforeseen, and emotional decisions of the president forced the bureaucracy to improvise, even in affairs of importance.[8]

The performance of President Carlos Ibáñez del Campo in foreign-policy matters constituted a clear case of pragmatic arbitration. The international policy did not much seem to interest the chief of state; probably he felt uneasy in this area.[9] His lack of personal conceptions in this field led him to accept the propositions of his various collaborators in international affairs,[10] without intending to alter greatly the general course of diplomacy determined to a large degree by the bipolar cold war situation. During his regime some innovative actions can be observed, such as those tending to improve hemispheric economic relations, but this utilization of the small margin of maneuver available must be attributed more to the efforts of some elements of the economic bureaucracy and party politics than to presidential initiative. The very bureaucracy of the Foreign Relations Ministry, to the degree that it succeeded in overcoming the instability of the period, was fortified by the passivity of Ibáñez and by ministerial rotation: The inexperience of many of the ministers led to the control of many affairs by career functionaries. But presidential arbitration, which was rather intermittent, ultimately showed its insufficiency and ineffectiveness: The disastrous management of border problems evidenced the organizational weakness of the Ibáñez government.

Even though ideological elements are found in the conservatism of President Jorge Alessandri Rodríguez, his political performance qualified him as a chief of state with a predominantly pragmatic orientation. Without ceasing to express frequent criticisms of the party system, Alessandri showed in practice his commitment to conventional rules of the contingent politics of the period. Maintaining his conservative viewpoints, he recognized the need and political convenience of including the Radical party in the government coalition after the right was not able to win sufficient seats in the parliamentary elections of 1961 to overrule eventual legislative vetoes in Congress. This step brought on changes in diverse aspects of government policy, including foreign policy.

Alessandri limited his role to arbitration, leaving the direction of foreign policy—a field to which he did not assign priority attention—in the hands of the respective ministers. In general, he succeeded in conciliating the interests within the government on the basis of minimal alterations of the status quo and of an emphasis on the legal aspects of problems. Thus, he justified in the name of Chilean adhesion to the rule of international law his pragmatic policy of denying support to the United States and its immediate followers on the problem of collective sanctions imposed on the Cuban government in the Organization of American States (OAS). This decision had significant conveniences in terms of internal politics.[11] On the subject of integration, he abandoned his initial opposition to the idea once he sensed that the initiatives that would lead to the agreement on the Treaty of Montevideo had the support of entrepreneurial interest groups that he himself had previously directed. Without giving importance to the political dimension of integration, he allowed the Radical party to cultivate its reformist and modernizing image through the advancement of this policy.[12]

Eduardo Frei was a president who distinguished himself by the close relationship that he established between ideological elaboration and government policy. He was, moreover, an *animateur* more than a referee between contradictory positions (in purely domestic affairs this probably was not the case). The ideological emphasis on foreign policy was especially marked in the first three years of the presidential period. Christian Democratic ideology, to a large extent expounded upon by Frei in numerous writings, contributed to establishing the principal themes of his diplomatic offensive, to structuring the perceptions of government, and to shaping a style of international action of a reformist type, with marked activism. Some important initiatives were the steps to accelerate the process of Latin American integration, the demands to reform the inter-American system, the efforts to tighten relations with Western Europe, and the opening of diplomatic relations with some socialist countries.[13]

However, the frustration of various of these initiatives, along with the deterioration of the internal political position of Christian Democracy, led Frei and his collaborators to reshape the orientation of their foreign policy. Frei continued to act as an *animateur,* but abandoned the unilateral tendency of diplomacy, emphasized the search for Latin American accords, and redefined the agenda. He sponsored new initiatives, such as Andean integration and regional negotiation of Latin America and the United States through the Comité Especial de Coordinación Latinoamericana (CECLA—Special Commission of Latin American Coordination).

Presidential activism did not dislocate the functioning of the foreign-relations bureaucracy, since Frei—contrary to what would be expected of an ideological *animateur*—did not try to concentrate the entire agenda in his hands. He left great political and operational latitude to the minister of foreign relations during the whole period, Gabriel Valdés. The latter conciliated the political needs of the government with bureaucratic routine through the co-optation of functionaries and through the management, together with Frei, of personal and party channels for the discussion of more important questions.

The era of ideological foreign policy continued under the government of Salvador Allende. In contrast to Frei, Allende was not in a commanding position in the context of the ideological elaboration of the Marxist left as a whole or of the Socialist party in particular. Rather he limited himself to support of ideological positions on the basis of the convergence of diverse tendencies within his party and to active development of linkages with the rest of the parties that assumed power in 1970.[14]

As a political actor, Allende was both a parliamentary expert, accustomed to the conventional political struggle, and a committed revolutionary with an ideological project of global change. The tensions inherent in the dual frame of reference of the Popular Unity coalition were the object of his tactical and ideological arbitration. But, as Arturo Valenzuela has argued, being "a superb politician, he was adept at resolving the day-to-day disputes that arose, but was unable to steer a clear course, either one provoking a clear and rapid confrontation, which he argued against, or one of moderation, which he advocated but could not consistently follow."[15]

This dilemma also affected the direction of foreign policy. Allende's inclinations and interests, centered on internal situations, and the ideological diagnosis of a dialectic type of his minister of foreign relations, Clodomiro Almeyda, coincided to place foreign policy on an instrumental plane, on which international behavior had to follow the priorities and demands of the internal situation. As Almeyda himself would write later, the intention was "to create external conditions in order to make feasible the development [of the] project of socialist transformations . . . " and "to contribute to strengthening in the international political arena those agents that struggle convergently for the transformation of a capitalist society into a socialist one at the world level." Attempting to reconcile both goals in practice, Almeyda asserted that "the principal and dominant form in which with the given conditions the contribution of the Chilean revolutionary movement to the Revolution as a whole had to be expressed was by working to construct socialism in one's own country."[16]

In the case of General Pinochet, his ideological positions originate from his geopolitical perspective. His central thesis is that of a relentless opposition between military government and international communism. This conception illustrates practically the entire international perspective with the partial exceptions of only two types of subjects: the relations with neighboring border countries—where the traditional logic of power politics dominates—and international economic relations. The growing importance of the latter in the last five years has reduced the ideological tone of foreign policy, but certainly has not eliminated it.

General Pinochet also has distinguished himself by his active direction of foreign policy. As Heraldo Muñoz has pointed out, important foreign-policy undertakings have originated directly from presidential initiatives, among them the normalization of relations with Bolivia and the subsequent negotiations on the cession of a sea outlet to that country and the hard line toward the United Nations commission for the study of the human-rights situation in Chile (Allana Commission). On numerous occasions the implementation of certain political initiatives has depended on direct presidential participation or that of his personal emissaries. All of these factors show Pinochet to be an ideological *animateur*.[17]

The preceding analysis suggests that the presidents and their political formulas constitute central elements that determine foreign policies.

Table 4.2. Categories of Participants in Bureacratic Politics

| | Policy Areas | | |
Actors	Internal	National	External
Political	Ministers, other politi-cal leaders	President of the Republic, principal political leaders	Foreign relations ministers, some ambassadors
Bureaucratic	Administrative Service heads	High officials of economic sector, military chiefs (civilian regime)	Ambassadors, functionaries of Foreign Relations Ministry

However, we have also stated that the executive operates within generally narrow political margins defined by the interaction of variables of the national and international political systems. The latter especially respond only in a marginal way to the attempts toward change that national agents may promote, in the direction of expanding the scope of foreign action.

In this context, presidential participation consists of the active development of initiatives (*animateurs*) or of the resolution among alternatives generated near the president (a referee). In both cases, the activity at the highest level of the executive branch can be oriented according to pragmatic or ideological criteria. In this way, distinct styles of presidential action are shaped and modalities characteristic of the relationship with bureaucratic actors are established. I will return to this point in the conclusion.

THE BUREAUCRACY

In this section I identify the categories of participants in bureaucratic politics, both in the Ministry of Foreign Relations and in other segments of bureaucracy. The processes particular to bureaucratic politics will be left to later analyses, preferably starting from case studies.[18]

The policy areas—internal, external, and "national"—will be distinguished at the levels of political and bureaucratic actors. The first comprises affairs typical of domestic politics, such as aspects of economic and social policy. The second entails the management of a great part of the foreign policy, especially in its more routine aspects. The third involves the recognition of the interdependence of all the political affairs of major importance, including the repercussions and requirements of internal policies and vice versa; this area, which obviously can only be differentiated from the others at an analytical level, is that of the "grand policy," where far-reaching decisions are made and the more significant reactions of actors that interact with the government within the country and international system are noted. Table 4.2 represents a combination of these distinctions.

The largest contingent of actors is found in the internal area. At the political level they are party leaders who have not reached positions of national power and at the bureaucratic level they are the majority of functionaries in charge of the direction of the state apparatus. The external and national areas are comparatively smaller, the first probably being smaller than the second.

National bureaucratic actors are of special importance. In contrast to functionaries in other areas, who must pass through the respective ministers, the national bureaucracy has direct access to the center of governmental political power. Its development responds to propositions of a technocratic character that begin to gain strength in governments of various political orientations as a result of the increasing state responsibilities in economic and social matters. The high officials of the Corporación de Fomento (CORFO) and of the principal public enterprises, the management personnel of the Central Bank, and the specialists in copper affairs make up some elements of the top layer of a growing technocracy. Some of its members serve throughout the different governments, occasionally at a ministerial level, which contributes to a consolidation of their influence. Their participation in the elaboration and implementation of foreign policies is due to the demands of development strategies, to the growing prominence of economic relations in the international agenda of the governments of the period, and to their globalizing definition of the problems. As Coleman and Quirós indicate, the participation of technocratic actors in foreign relations varies directly with the complexity of the development strategies.[19]

Also included in this category are the high military commands, whose interest and participation in foreign policy is more immediate than that of functionaries of the economic sector. In the last decade of civilian government there was a noticeable similarity between the structural position of the military and the national bureaucracy: Military officials have the benefit of access to higher levels of government and tend to define problems in an increasingly less sectorial manner, instead emphasizing their global dimensions, both internal and international. This signifies a clear expansion of military activity related to foreign policy. Transcending their limited character as "veto groups" interested in a few affairs such as border problems, the budget allocations for defense, and military assistance purchases, the armed forces adhere to comprehensive conceptions of national security and increase their participation in transnational military activities.[20]

In the external area, the principal political figures are the ministers of foreign relations. Some ministers have been politicians at the national level, but this has been the exception. Between November 1946 and September 1982, the position of minister of foreign relations has been filled thirty-two times by twenty-six individuals (some have served in the position more than once). More than 75 percent have been lawyers, with or without an active professional practice. This would indicate that juridical preparation—traditionally in close relationship with political activity—confers advantages for designation to the post. Without a doubt, this factor is related to the tendency, mentioned by diverse observers, toward a juridical or legalist style in Chilean foreign policy.[21] On the other hand, stress should be placed on the significant contrast that can be observed in this regard between ministers and presidents: Since 1946 only two lawyers have been head of state, González Videla and Frei.

Another important characteristic of ministers of foreign relations has been the marginal relationship that can be observed between the political careers of the ministers and a parliamentary career. Only five ministers were representatives or senators before and/or after serving in the ministry; on the other hand, nine of the ministers held ambassadorial positions. This tendency seems to indicate that the position of minister of foreign relations tends to "socialize" the person who serves in international activities and offers career alternatives regarding national contingent politics (the incorporation of various ministers into high-level functions in the international bureaucracy supports this interpretation).

The turnover of ministers has been relatively rapid. The average duration in the position is a little more than thirteen months, ranging from two days (José Serrano Palma in January 1956) to six years (Gabriel Valdés from 1964 to 1970). Of the thirty-two appointments, only thirteen have lasted for more than a year. This tendency has significantly limited the level of international experience of many ministers, which has strengthened the position of functionaries with greater influence in the ministry and stimulated dependence upon their advice and aid on the part of novice foreign ministers. During approximately five of the thirty-six years of the period, the ministers have been career functionaries, which obviously has fortified the position of professional diplomats.

The bureaucracy of the foreign (external) sector is constituted of functionaries of the Foreign Relations Ministry and ambassadors and other designated functionaries who are not situated among the political actors (even though the designations may have had that nature). The personnel of the Foreign Service in Santiago or in diplomatic missions abroad forms the nucleus of this bureaucracy. Other functionaries, attached to professional and technical groups, also belong to the category, but these are professionals who are specialists more than career diplomats.

The consolidation of the foreign-relations bureaucracy is relatively recent. It corresponds to the contemporary era in which the diplomatic service progressively lost its traditional character of being reserved in practice to individuals from families of greatest social prestige and political power.[22] Under Radical party governments, the composition of the diplomatic teams began to reflect new political and social realities; beginning in 1947, as a result of both internal pressures and the development of the international system of the postwar era, the teams increased in size. In the government of González Videla, the number of functionaries increased by 30 percent.[23] Under Ibáñez, the personnel growth was slower. Despite the efforts of some ministers, such as Oscar Fenner, to provide stability to the career, some forty functionaries were terminated and replaced by others designated for political reasons. Many lasted a few years in the ministry, after which some of those previously expelled returned.[24] Frei received from Alessandri a stabilized ministry, in which the functionary element that came in under Radical party governments continued to be very strong. Without the government intending to profoundly alter this situation, the Christian Democratic influence increased through the channels of advisers to Minister Valdés, a few functionaries freely designated, and regular career promotions.

Under Allende, the government relied in part on the Radical party contingent. At the same time it stimulated parallel channels to the ministry, above all SEREX, an organization in charge of foreign economic relations constituted on the basis of functionaries from the Central Bank. The most abrupt change in the ministry occurred in the first year of the military government, which proceeded to remove a large portion of the functionaries: according to one estimate, around fifty percent.[25] Among the causes of expulsion, the lack of political confidence in the functionaries was at least as important as the real or presumed Marxist leanings of some. To substitute for the functionaries removed from their positions, the government resorted to transfers and new destinations, both civilian and military, which significantly modified the internal reality of the Foreign Ministry.[26]

The functionaries with greatest prestige and influence in the ministry are general diplomats rather than specialists, who pass through the most varied positions in Chile and abroad without focusing their careers in terms of subjects, regions, or nation-states. If they develop some specialization, it is that of giving shape and a diplomatic discourse to political proposals elaborated in the respective circles of national political actors. In general, they do not enter into the determination of the content or substance of the policies, instead focusing their action on diplomatic management.

Only a minority of the top functionaries and advisers with aptitudes like those just described have chosen the development of some specialization, such as Antarctic affairs, United Nations, international cooperation, and so on. These specialists tend to be more creative in their vision than the generalists and are at the same time more independent, developing relationships outside of the strictly ministerial environment and influencing the substantive orientations of their fields of specialization under adequate political conditions.

Along with these categories of functionary and professional elite, there is in the ministry, as in all organizations, a majority of bureaucrats whose principal characteristic is the motivation of job security and promotion. Downs referred to these bureaucrats as "conservers" and "climbers," who maintain the inertial tendencies of the organization even in times of crisis, in which the majority tries to adapt to the political changes. Given that the ministry has been, as Cleaves noted, traditionally scarcely oriented toward innovation and highly limited in size and resources in comparison to more dynamic public entities, it has constituted an attractive environment for elements of a "conserver" type who identify themselves with its secular orientation, adapt their behavior to their own particular perception of the diplomatic tradition that the ministry embodies, and incorporate themselves at the same time into a career of great occupational prestige such as diplomacy.[27]

It is necessary to consider also some structural elements. The Foreign Ministry has a very simple organization; through distinct modernizing reforms it maintains a scheme that ensures a highly centralized direction. With few exceptions, the formation of "feudal" bureaucratic compartments is difficult since the gap between the directive levels of a political nature and the operatives is small. Besides, functionaries do not remain for long periods of time in a given division. The organizational emphasis is on routine affairs and support for task groups in charge of subjects of great complexity and transcendence, such as the papal mediation in the Beagle dispute with Argentina. These groups have a flexible organization and rely upon outside consultations as well as on administrative and political support. A positive contrast with past decades is observed in matters of this type: The investigation of the management of the Palena problem, provoked by the national Congress during the Ibáñez government, uncovered the fact that until then border problems were practically in a bureaucratic no-man's-land.[28]

The bureaucracy of international economic relations merits separate treatment. The growing importance of international economic relations within the whole of foreign policy of the last decades meant for the ministerial bureaucracy a challenge for which it was unprepared. The initiatives of Latin American integration, the fusion of foreign policy, multilateral economic relations, and "structural reformism" produced during the existence of the Alliance for Progress came about through partial changes. The Executive Secretariat for the Affairs of the Asociación Latinoamericana de Libre Comercio (ALALC) was created, under Frei an economist was designated to the staff of the under secretary of foreign relations, and importance was given to the Economic Advisory Committee of the minister. Allende, as has been stated, chose to remove from the ministry the treatment of international economic affairs. The military government, on the other hand, chose the road of augmenting the bureaucracy of international economic relations. Pro-Chile was established: An entity in charge of promoting nontraditional exports, it was initially located outside the ministry and later incorporated into it, in circumstances such that the progressive weakening of ALALC and the Chilean withdrawal from the Andean Group in 1976 left the aforementioned Executive Secretariat with few functions. Within the restructuring of the ministry in 1978 and 1979, this led to the creation of a new General Directorate of International Economic Relations, constituted through the fusion of the Institute for the Promotion of Exports Pro-Chile, the Executive Secretariat for the Affairs of ALALC, and Economic Directorate of the ministry. The General Directorate constitutes a specialized entity not incorporated into the Foreign Service, has its own budget and separate staff, and in the opinion of a former under secretary of foreign relations of the present government, represents a victory of the economic team over the traditional ministerial sectors.[29]

Perhaps the most significant fact in the bureaucratic landscape may be the proliferation of actors outside the Foreign Ministry, beginning with the presidency of the republic itself and including diverse ministries and agencies in the internal area. The growth of the presidential apparatus is still a new phenomenon. Under the last two civilian governments, the advisory functions at the highest level in the executive branch and the creation of the Oficina de Planeamiento (ODEPLAN—Office of National Planning) constituted the first signs of this tendency; however, ODEPLAN, in spite of its independence from the presidency of the republic, did not succeed in constituting a direct instrument of the head of state any more than other ministries or services of importance. In the military government, on the other hand, the creation of the Comité Asesor (COAS—Advisory Committee of the Military Junta) and the Presidential High Command, as well as the growth experienced by the General Secretariat of the Government, have converted the presidency and its immediate surroundings into an organizational body of considerable size and complexity. In the present system the gap between the presidential level and the bureaucracy has increased, and problems of communication between the immediate presidential environment (leading sector) and the regular government (led sector) have occurred.[30]

The legislative commissions that counsel the junta in the processing of projects of law constitute an element connected to this new bureaucracy. This element intervenes in some international affairs, especially in the approval of the treaties that are presented to it by the executive. The members of the junta have occasionally participated in bureaucratic politics. An example of the demand for participation is the claim for greater involvement in the cultural policies directed abroad, formulated by the cultural adviser to the junta in 1975.[31] A great number of sectorial actors interested in economic, social, cultural, and technical matters that have been progressively internationalized, within the general tendency of deepening international interdependencies, complete the bureaucratic picture.[32] The foreign relations of these actors develop through actions of ministerial representatives or other functionaries in specialized international organizations, as well as through contacts among equivalent functional units of governments and transnational relations with sources and/or recipients of information, technology, equipment, and consulting.

The Foreign Ministry, with varied degrees of presidential support, has attempted repeatedly to subject to its control and coordination these "foreign policies" of segments of the internal bureaucracy. In general these efforts have been frustrated by inadequate resources to address broad and complex matters whose technical details the actors of the other bureaucracies resist sharing as a part of their own power strategies in bureaucratic politics.

CONCLUSIONS

It is useful to distinguish between the orientation of foreign policy and the diplomacy destined to implement the policies. The orientation of policies originates from organized restricted political circles around the president of the republic, to whom the management of foreign relations formally corresponds, even though under the system of the Constitution of 1925 its international administration was subject to diverse controls. Presidential participation since 1946 has varied in terms of styles of relative activity or passivity (*animateur* and referee presidents), and in terms of pragmatic or ideological orientation. The general tendency of the period has been the increasing ideological content of foreign policies, even though pragmatic definitions retain relevance in terms of certain conjunctures or types of matters. The bureaucracy of the Ministry of Foreign Relations and other bureaucratic actors (national bureaucracy and parts of the internal bureaucracy) intervene in the implementation of the policies, even though in this aspect there is also presidential participation, especially in the case of chiefs of state of the *animateur* type (González Videla, Frei, Pinochet).

The relations between the presidential and ministerial levels vary according to what may be the management style of the executive branch and the state of the bureaucracy. The relation is less subject to tensions when the executive is a pragmatic referee and the Foreign Ministry is stable, as occurred in the government of Jorge Alessandri. This constellation favors the inertial and continuist tendencies represented by the Foreign Ministry, reducing the space for innovation and emphasizing the adaptative character of diplomacy. In the government of Alessandri, such tendencies prevailed while the political formula was clearly conservative, introducing innovative tendencies as a consequence of the change of the government coalition in 1961.

When the bureaucracy is found to be unstable, as happened in the government of Carlos Ibáñez del Campo, pragmatic arbitration tends to be ineffective in developing courses of political action. Functionaries dedicate their best efforts to defending their positions within the bureaucracy, and policy tends to be erratic or determined principally by variables of an external nature. Nonetheless, if along with functionary instability there is ministerial instability, the rotation of ministers can favor some career diplomats, who in such conditions make evident their indispensability in the management of affairs, even being able to influence the substantive orientation of some matters.

The direction of the pragmatic *animateur,* such as Gabriel González Videla, tends to demand a greater degree of response from the bureaucracy. Even though the margin of political options may be small, the *animateur* president tends to take new initiatives and to participate actively in their development. This can yield, as occurred in the case of González Videla, a diplomacy of a personalist tone, with the consequent difficulties for the bureaucracy, whose capacity to adapt tends to be left behind in the opportunism of political direction.

The relationship between ideological *animateur* and bureaucracy is highly problematic. The political leader tends to see in career diplomats elements that do not represent faithfully the truth of his position. They in turn are critical of the international approaches that they see to be lacking in realism (although bureaucratic realism is principally the adhesion to the status quo) and attest with preoccupation their growing separation from the circles of decision.

However, the management of the relationship permits variants. In the government of Eduardo Frei a crisis in the relations with the bureaucracy was not produced because the president did not try to alter profoundly the composition and functioning of the Foreign Ministry. He limited himself to resorting to the co-optation of functionaries and to creating confidence through the maintenance of only one minister in the post; at the same time, Frei reserved for nonbureaucratic channels the political deliberations of greatest importance. The present government, in contrast, chose to eliminate the functionaries defined as incompatible with its orientations, proceeding to submit the bureaucracy to direct military control. On these bases General Pinochet has actively given impulse to a foreign policy defined as ideological.

Lastly, ideological arbitration combines contradictory tendencies of fluidity at the level of coalitions with the schematism of the substantive definitions. The government of Allende demonstrated the unstable nature of this political style.

A comprehensive study of the Chilean international situation requires, of course, a consideration of both the governmental components and the political projects toward which their action aims. Here attention has been given to the first aspect; in the future the suggested hypotheses could be reviewed and broadened in the light of the content of the policies and the problems of their internal and external political feasibility.

NOTES

1. See the works of Heraldo Muñoz, "Las Relaciones Exteriores del Gobierno Militar Chileno: Un Análisis Político-Económico" (Santiago, Mimeographed, 1981); Carlos Portales, "Transnacionalización y Política Exterior Chilena," working paper 26, Facultad Latinoamericana de Ciencias Sociales (FLASCO), 1981; and

Manfred Wilhelmy, "Democracia, Autoritarismo, e Integración: El Caso Chileno," in the work I edited under the auspices of the Corporación de Investigaciones para el Desarrollo (CINDE), *Sociedad Política e Integración en América Latina* (Santiago: Ediciones CINDE, 1982), pp. 125–148.

2. Graham Allison, *Essence of Decision—Explaining the Cuban Missile Crisis* (Boston: Little, Brown, 1971); Abraham Lowenthal, "'Liberal,' 'Radical,' and 'Bureaucratic' Perspectives on U.S.–Latin American Policy: The Alliance for Progress in Retrospect," in Julio Cotler and Richard Fagen (eds.), *Latin America and the U.S.—Changing Political Realities* (Stanford: Stanford University Press, 1974), pp. 212–235.

3. Mario Barros, *El Ministerio de Relaciones Exteriores—Apuntes para una Historia Administrativa* (Santiago: n. p., 1973) goes into detail on these aspects.

4. Art. 72, No. 16 of the Political Constitution of the State of 1925.

5. Art. 32, No. 10 of the Constitution of 1980; Art. 25, par. 3 and Art. 49, No. 6.

6. For this reason, I do not agree with the hypothesis of James Rosenau, "Pre-Theories and Theories of Foreign Policy," in R. Barry Farrell (ed.), *Approaches to Comparative and International Politics* (Evanston, Ill.: Northwestern University Press, 1966), pp. 27–92, according to which personal political leadership is the element of greatest weight in the foreign policies of small developing states with open political systems.

7. On the copper policy see Theodore Moran, *Multinational Corporations and the Politics of Dependence: Copper in Chile* (Princeton: Princeton University Press, 1974), who states that the attempt by González Videla to establish a state monopoly on commercialization was the first step in overcoming the situation of Chilean dependence (p. 88).

8. In March 1948, "by a personal and direct order of the President of the Republic," the Chilean delegation to the United Nations denounced the coup d'etat in Czechoslovakia. Ministry of Foreign Relations, *Memoria correspondiente al año 1948* (Santiago: Imprenta Chile, 1949), p. 238.

9. Interviews with Alejandro Magnet and Oscar Pinochet de la Barra, July 6, 1982.

10. Interview with the former Foreign Minister Conrado Ríos Gallardo, March 11, 1980.

11. See Joaquín Fermandois, "Chile y la cuestión cubana, 1959–1964," monograph, 1981.

12. Minister of Foreign Relations Carlos Martínez Sotomayor considered that an innovative foreign policy constituted a central element of the new orientation that the political sector with which he identified was trying to promote within the Radical party. Interview, January 27, 1979.

13. More details in Manfred Wilhelmy, "Christian Democratic Ideology in Inter-American Politics: The Case of Chile, 1964–1970," in Morris Blackman and Ronald Hellman (eds.), *Terms of Conflict—Ideology in Latin American Politics* (Philadelphia: Institute for the Study of Human Institutions Press, 1977), pp. 129–160.

14. See Julio César Jobet, *El Partido Socialista de Chile*, 2 vols., 2d ed. (Santiago: Ediciones Prensa Latinoamericana, 1971), for an analysis of the positions held in each congress of the Socialist party.

15. Arturo Valenzuela, *The Breakdown of Democratic Regimes—Chile* (Baltimore: Johns Hopkins University Press, 1978), p. 68.

16. Clodomiro Almeyda, "La política exterior del gobierno de la Unidad Popular en Chile," in Federico Gil et al., *Chile 1970–1973: Lecciones de una Experiencia* (Madrid: Tecnos, 1977), pp. 92, 93.

17. On the direct participation of General Pinochet, see Muñoz, "Las Relaciónes Exteriores," p. 26 and chap. 3.

18. The concept of bureaucracy used in this work is that of Peter Cleaves, *Bureaucratic Politics and Administration in Chile* (Berkeley and Los Angeles: University of California Press, 1974), p. xvi. For the definition of bureaucratic politics, see I. M. Destler, *Presidents, Bureaucrats, and Foreign Policy* (Princeton: Princeton University Press, 1972), p. 52, which has been useful for this section.

19. Kenneth M. Coleman and Luis Quirós Varela, "Determinants of Latin American Foreign Policies: Bureaucratic Organization and Development Strategies," in Elizabeth G. Ferris and Jennie K. Lincoln (eds.), *Latin American Foreign Policies—Global and Regional Dimensions* (Boulder, Colo.: Westview Press, 1981), p. 44.

20. See Genaro Arriagada, *El Pensamiento Político de los Militares* (Santiago: Centro de Investigaciones Socioeconómicas de la Compania de Jesús en Chile, 1981); and Augusto Varas et al., *Chile, Democracia, Fuerzas Armadas* (Santiago: Facultad Latinoamericana de Ciencias Sociales (FLASCO), 1980).

21. The existence of this style as a key to understanding Chilean foreign policy is emphasized by Lawrence Littavin, "An Integrated Study of Chilean Foreign Policy," Ph. D. Thesis, New York University, New York, 1968.

22. In this respect, see the polemical comments of Mario Barros, *Historia Diplomática de Chile 1541–1938* (Barcelona: Ediciones Ariel, 1970), pp. 751, 752, 753. I do not agree with the position of Barros, who sees "a great spiritual mediocrity" resulting from this change.

23. Germán Urzúa and Anamaría García Barzelatto, *Diagnóstico de la Burocracia Chilena* (Santiago: Editorial Jurídica de Chile, 1971), p. 104.

24. Interview with former Ambassador Oscar Pinochet de la Barra, July 6, 1982. See Barros, *El Ministerio de Relaciones Exteriores*, p. 110, regarding the first decree on functionary stability, dictated in April 1953.

25. My own estimate is 35 percent, on the basis of a computation of decrees included in memoirs of the ministry of 1973 and 1974.

26. The actual structure of the Foreign Ministry originates in Decree Law 2101 (Decree Order 16.1.78), which authorized the executive to dictate the organic statute of the ministry and to determine its permanent personnel.

27. Anthony Downs, *Inside Bureaucracy*, quoted by Destler, *Presidents, Bureaucrats, and Foreign Policy*, p. 68. See the classification of the ministry between services least oriented toward innovation and least endowed, in Cleaves, *Bureaucratic Politics*, p. 11.

28. On this use, see Ministry of Foreign Relations, *Memoria correspondiente al año 1956* (Santiago: Imprenta Chile, 1959), pp. 291–310.

29. Interview with former Under Secretary Claudio Collados, June 29, 1982. See also Muñoz, "Las Relaciones Exteriores," p. 39.

30. On the relative weakness of ODEPLAN under Frei, see Cleaves, *Bureaucratic Politics*, pp. 99–100. COAS was in charge of the preparation of the document "Objetivo Nacional de Chile," on which importance was placed in the first years of the government. The Presidential High Command has intervened lately in aspects of the planning of foreign policy. *El Mercurio* of August 2, 1982, reports on a seminar on the matter. The existence of communication problems and the lack of coordination between security services and the Ministry

of Foreign Relations was given low-profile status by General Pinochet after the cancellation of his visit to the Philippines at the beginning of 1980. For a comparison with the United States, see Destler, *Presidents, Bureaucrats, and Foreign Policy*, p. 90.

31. See Ministry of Foreign Relations, *Memoria correspondiente al año 1975*, vol. 2 (Santiago: Imprenta Chile, 1976), pp. 1041–1043, in relation to these demands.

32. The most representative analysis of the effect of interdependencies in foreign relations is that of Edward Morse, "The Transformation of Foreign Policies: Modernization, Interdependence, and Externalization," *World Politics* 22, no. 3 (April 1970), pp. 371–392. Morse referred to the politics of the highly industrialized countries, but along general lines his thesis of a growing importance of economic and technical affairs in foreign relations is applicable to a case such as Chile. Attempts to centralize the sectorial management began with González Videla. See Ministry of Foreign Relations, *Memoria correspondiente al año 1950* (Santiago: Imprenta Chile, 1952).

5. Perceptions as Realities: The United States, Venezuela, and Cuba in the Caribbean

U.S. DIPLOMACY AND POLICY, 1980–1982

We are a long way from the days when the U.S. fleet was the dominant instrument of U.S. diplomacy and policy in the Caribbean, an area Alfred T. Mahan used to call "our Western Hemisphere Mediterranean." The time when U.S. battlewagons kept a permanent patrol before the Mexican ports of Tampico and Vera Cruz and the Cuban port of Havana is gone. It is inconceivable that any U.S. official would speak as did U.S. Secretary of State Philander Knox, who was apt to explain that those ships were meant to keep the Mexicans "in the salutory equilibrium, between a dangerous and exaggerated apprehension and a proper degree of wholesome fear."[1]

Not that U.S. material interests in the Caribbean have diminished; in fact, they are growing. From a geostrategic point one notes that some of the thirty-one "essential" U.S. foreign trade routes are in the Caribbean, and in the Caribbean the busiest routes all border Cuba, following the Windward Passage (between Cuba and Haiti) and the Straits of Florida (between Florida and Cuba).[2] Obviously, these routes are also crucial to the Latin American and Caribbean countries who have the United States as their main market. By the early 1970s, 55 percent of Caribbean exports and 43 percent of their imports were with the United States. In 1977, the assistant secretary of state for inter-American affairs calculated U.S. exports to the Caribbean at $2 billion and U.S. investments at $4.5 billion (excluding Puerto Rico). By 1982 those exports were $6.8 billion, investments stood at $5.65 billion, and U.S. imports from the area were $10 billion. In 1980, U.S. tourists there spent $1.1 billion. The heaviest investments have been in oil and bauxite. Two-thirds of the U.S. requirements of bauxite/aluminum come from the Caribbean; 25 percent of the petroleum imports as of 1980 are refined or transshipped in the Caribbean.[3]

And yet, despite this obvious U.S. economic interest in the area, the U.S. military presence—or at least visibility—has been in steady contraction. West Indian leaders who attempted to raise the rent on the U.S. bases on their territories and exact other benefits from the bases found the going rough in the 1970s and the Americans anything but responsive to their demands. "The problem with some of the islands," an American official told the press, "is that they have an exaggerated view of the value of the bases to us."[4]

The reality is that despite the sizable West Indian presence in the United States and the cultural and political ties that such a presence brought, the United States never included the West Indies in its Latin American policy; that policy centered on the Greater Antilles and Central America. Even during World War II when the "bases-for-destroyers" deal provided the United States with important bases in the area, there was no Caribbean policy. Despite the presence of the Vichy-loyal fleet on the French islands and the heightened U.S. awareness after the sinking of over four hundred ships by German U-boats, the United States never challenged the European presence in the area or attempted to substitute a policy of its own. That presence always had coexisted nicely with the Monroe Doctrine.

When the European withdrawal started in the 1960s, however, the search for a broader "Caribbean policy" began in earnest. The development of multiple, sovereign national systems and the traumatic experience of the Cuban Revolution (representing the first successful break with U.S. power in the area) speeded up the process. Even so, the development of a specifically Caribbean perspective as distinct from a hemispheric one has been problematic. The Eurocentric and Japan-oriented predisposition of top U.S. policymakers has always relegated Latin American policy to a secondary level; the Caribbean as such came in for even less attention. In fact, the search in the 1970s for a specifically Caribbean orientation in terms that fit the changing circumstances did not begin with the executive or the Department of State. It was pushed, rather, by Representative Dante B. Fascell of south Florida, whose state and specific constituency had vital Caribbean-oriented interests. As chairman of the House Sub-Committee on Inter-American Affairs, Fascell had long attempted to emphasize the significance of the Caribbean for U.S. policy. To Fascell there was a need to go beyond the concerns with Cuba, as the following extract from a 1972 hearing indicates:

Where would we get an overall briefing on conditions in the Caribbean not related to Cuban activities? I have been very nervous about what is going on in the Caribbean. We are talking now about millions of people, and a lot of governments. I have the distinct feeling that as far as the United States is concerned, first, we don't care, and, second, we are out. I just don't think that is good.[5]

In 1974, Fascell was happy to settle for the fact that the word "Caribbean" was now being used by the State Department.[6]

In congressional hearings following the Conference of Tlatelolco, Mexico, in 1974, the assistant secretary of state for inter-American affairs, Jack B. Kubisch, asserted that "there has been an important shift" in U.S. policy toward Latin America.[7] But Kubisch had to answer no when Representative Fascell asked whether the United States had made any commitments for additional funds for the region or intended to repeal any laws detrimental to the region's interests. In fact, Kubisch highlighted two dangers that resulted from this conference: (1) that unrealistic levels of expectation were created regarding what the U.S. people and Congress would be willing to do, and (2) that it might not be possible in an acceptable time frame "to translate many of these ideas and suggestions and proposals into a concrete program of action and results."[8]

The shift in diplomatic tone did, however, contribute to the eventual shift in policy that came with the Carter administration (1976–1980). President Jimmy Carter began to formulate measures very similar to those suggested by Representative Fascell in 1973: a concern with the Caribbean area that went beyond the purely military preoccupation with Cuba.

It was Fascell who in April 1973 enunciated the most complete outline of a desirable U.S. Caribbean policy. Making a distinction between a U.S. "policy of self-preservation" and a "true" Caribbean policy, Fascell's proposals were premised on the beliefs that "While military considerations remain important to U.S. policy they are not likely to become of overriding concern," and that given the dangers inherent in a relationship involving such disparities of power, "the United States should play a supporting and not a preponderant role in regional organizations."[9]

In fact, Fascell specifically recommended that the United States could and should stay out of the domestic affairs of the Caribbean. Intervention can only be legitimate, said Fascell, when there is a "clear and present danger to our survival." In September of that same year, Fascell's subcommittee began hearings on the Caribbean. The stress was very much on the need for a concerted multilateral approach to the area and to the policy changes recommended.

The Fascell approach, although new in its specific focus on the Caribbean, was in fact part of a wider public sentiment favoring change in inter-American relations in general in the early and mid-1970s. That the time was opportune for considering changes in the U.S.–Latin American/Caribbean relations was apparent to the drafters of the Linowitz Report.[10] They were encouraged, wrote Sol Linowitz, by signs of growing recognition in Washington, D.C., and other capitals of the need for change. Even though not addressing itself to the Caribbean specifically, the report reflected the changing general mood in certain influential circles that would have an impact on thinking about the Caribbean. Very significantly, the report recognized that extensive bilateral concessional assistance from the United States to Latin America is largely a thing of the past, and that the U.S. should cooperate with other Latin

American nations and multilateral development institutions in providing assistance. Three fundamental premises lay behind this multilateralism: (1) the need to respect diversity in ideology and economic/social organization, (2) the independent role of Latin American/Caribbean nations in international affairs, and (3) the global significance of the principal issues of U.S.–Latin American/Caribbean relations.

These premises coincided with Latin American sentiment. The 1973 General Assembly of the Organization of American States (OAS) established a special committee on restructuring the inter-American system. The November 1973 meeting in Bogotá of Latin American secretaries of state was preparatory to the February 1974 meeting in Mexico with Henry Kissinger. The OAS General Assembly was then invited to meet in Atlanta, Georgia, April 1974.

The official who opened this OAS General Assembly meeting in Atlanta was the then governor of Georgia, Jimmy Carter. The emphasis on multilateralism made its mark. Three years later, as president, Carter addressed the Permanent Council of the OAS, outlining a "new approach" to "Latin America and the Caribbean." That approach, said Carter, would be based on three elements: (1) a high regard for the "individuality and sovereignty" of each Latin American and Caribbean nation; (2) a respect for human rights ("You will find this country eager to stand beside those nations which respect human rights and promise democratic values"); and (3) a desire to press forward on the great issues that affect the relations between the developed and developing nations ("Your economic problems are also global in character and cannot be dealt with solely in regional terms").[11]

The Carter initiative, then, emerged out of the debate of the preceding years.[12] The approach would be multilateral: The International Monetary Fund (IMF), World Bank, General Agreement on Tariffs and Trade (GATT), the United Nations Commission on Trade and Development (UNCTAD), the Economic Commission for Latin America (ECLA), and Venezuela's chairmanship of the Paris conference on economic cooperation were all mentioned by Carter as elements of the new approach.

The Carter administration launched a diplomatic campaign more intense than any since John F. Kennedy's Alliance for Progress, and now the Caribbean was included. There were traveling emissaries— including Carter's wife, his secretary of state, his assistant secretaries of state for political affairs and inter-American affairs, and—very importantly—his ambassador to the United Nations, Andrew Young.[13] In part reflecting the significance of race in Caribbean international relations but mostly reflecting Caribbean wishes for a more concerted effort by the United States, Young had extraordinary diplomatic successes.[14] There were also significant changes in the diplomatic appointments to Caribbean posts and within the Department of State. A Caribbean Task Force was set up to develop blueprints for possible policy.[15]

Although the broad outlines indicated that the Kissinger notion of a multilateral approach to the area was embodied in the Carter proposals, there were important shifts in emphasis as to where vital U.S. interests lay. The concern with military security (especially Soviet naval activities) was not abandoned, but clearly the focus was no longer military. Assistant Secretary of State for Inter-American Affairs Terence Todman explained that "we no longer see the Caribbean in quite the same stark military security context that we once viewed it" and noted that the security concerns were now regarded as more political. Rather than the threat of foreign military bases at the U.S. doorstep, Todman spoke of "an even more troublesome prospect: proliferation of impoverished Third World states whose economic and political problems blend with our own."[16]

The emphasis, then, was on cooperation in definitions of problems and on multilateralism. Both necessarily meant that the United States was to adopt a supporting rather than a dominant role. Important in this context was the fact that although the United States had been holding bilateral discussions with many governments in the area, Venezuela, Costa Rica, and Trinidad and Tobago had been consulted the most and in turn had been supportive of this multilateralism. Carter chose his closest allies from among the democrats in the region.

The initiative was launched formally in Washington on December 15, 1977 at a conference at the World Bank on economic development in the Caribbean.[17] The United States was to be just one member of the Group for Cooperation in Economic Development that would begin to function in the spring of 1978. It appeared to be a popular arrangement among Caribbean leaders personally briefed by Ambassador Young.[18]

It is virtually axiomatic in political analysis that the powerful will tend to exercise a degree of influence consonant with the effects sought and with the tenacity of opposition present or anticipated. The Carter administration sought to influence Caribbean trends through an emphasis on human rights and on political and social pluralism and to do so in concert with other democracies inside and outside the area. They practiced what they preached, substantially reducing the flow of U.S. military equipment to Latin America at a time when the USSR was increasing its.

With this decline in weapons transfer went further reductions in U.S. military visibility. The number of U.S. military liaison officers serving in Latin America went from 532 in 1970 to 115 in 1980; the number of Latin American officers trained went from 3,700 to less than 1,700 during that same decade.[19]

There is evidence that by mid-1980 the Carter administration was reconsidering the central features of its policy: multilateralism and the virtual ban on military-security assistance. The massive exodus of Cuban refugees from Mariel that year plus the coup in Grenada in March 1979 had led to pressures for greater direct assistance, including military assistance.[20] This latter approach was very much favored by a growing conservative mood that perceived Cuban actions as out of control and it had strong support from academic and military figures in the United States. These writers argued that the North-South or rich-poor conflict Carter stressed had to be subordinated to this revival of the cold war. What was importrant was to keep the area "in line" and to avoid blows to U.S. prestige.[21] The view is a long standing one in the United States and continues to be widely held.

Nearly twenty years ago, Hanson W. Baldwin, military editor of the *New York Times*, admitted that "Cuba is not vital to us as a base," but concluded nevertheless that "its global importance is chiefly positional and political-psychological. . . ." Psychological factors usually are linked to the factor of prestige and all of these to the domino theory. "Revision of the treaty terms for Guantanamo," Baldwin asserted, "will inevitably lead to revisionism elsewhere—in Panama, in Trinidad, globally. . . . United States power and prestige are involved in Gitmo, whether we like it or not."[22]

The panelists' findings of the 1971 Caribbean conference held at the Center for Strategic and International Studies of Georgetown University provide an interesting early insight into the thinking of an intellectual group that would become politically influential after 1980. It saw the Soviet challenge—exercised by itself and through Cuba—as the overriding threat to U.S. interests in the area, one endowed with special significance by the presence of the Panama Canal, U.S. territories, and military bases. Aside from this very real military importance, to the members of this group the area was "of great symbolic and psychological significance." "Erosion of America's position in the Caribbean could adversely affect U.S. prestige" worldwide.[23]

Clearly, once the psychological and prestige dimensions of geopolitics are emphasized, then "objective" strategic and military factors become less significant. Arguments about shifts in military technology and in the alignment of conventional forces carry little weight in the face of what are essentially subjective and reputational variables. The panelists at the 1971 Georgetown conference made this clear in their conclusion that, in deciding how to respond to events in an area defined as vital (such as the Caribbean), what is of most importance is "not so much the reality of the situation" but whether the president and his advisers are convinced that the American public "believes" that vital U.S. interests are threatened. In other words, the perceptions to be considered are not only of those trained to evaluate such situations but indeed of the general public.[24]

It was precisely this approach to Caribbean affairs (and, indeed, these same scholars) that emerged victorious in November 1980. Even before the inauguration of President Ronald Reagan their views were widely circulated and affected policies from Haiti and Guatemala to Argentina. Although retaining elements of the Kissinger-Carter multilateralism, Reagan now declared the Caribbean "vital." With this definition came a new and more aggressive approach to the Soviet threat in which "consultation" with friendly nations appeared to replace outright multilateralism; human rights no longer seemed a prominent feature even rhetorically.[25]

CUBA: THE AUDACIOUS ACTOR

By far the greatest impetus to the formulation of U.S. diplomacy and policy in the Caribbean since 1959 has been the shifts in Cuban behavior. By 1982 seven U.S. presidents had had to deal with Fidel Castro, who—according to most analysts—is an independent actor on the world scene, in the Caribbean as in Africa.[26]

When Castro came to power in 1959, only Cuba, the Dominican Republic, and Haiti were independent insular countries in the region. By 1982, however, that situation had changed dramatically; there were now thirteen independent island states[27] and three mainland nations usually referred to as Caribbean.[28] Other states such as the Netherlands Antilles, Puerto Rico, and the French West Indies exercised nearly total internal autonomy and were very much actors in their own right in Caribbean international relations. None of these states, however, had the experience in foreign affairs that Fidel Castro and the Cuban Communist party had, certainly not in terms of the turbulent history of the Caribbean with its long-standing involvements across borders and seas.

By 1982 the Cubans had forged strong alliances with Grenada, Surinam, and Nicaragua; they had a massive banking and commercial operation in Panama; and they carried on a marriage of convenience with Guyana that gave them good access to the Movement of Nonaligned Nations. Their airlift capabilities extended far beyond the Caribbean, a fact demonstrated in 1975 and 1976 when they moved eleven thousand troops into Angola and later into Ethiopia and elsewhere in Africa. This supports the U.S. State Department assertion that Cuba has today a "substantial regional intervention capability."[29]

Yet by 1982 there was no evidence that Cuba actually posed a direct threat—military or otherwise—to any of the island states.[30] There was, however, ample evidence that there existed a widely held *perception* that Cuba was a threat in a broader sense because of its support for groups that did not accept the existing political constitutional order as legitimate. In fact, by the late 1970s the fears of Cuban ideas and actions were not only intense but also widespread. Had author K. S. Karol visited Cuba's installations in Jamaica then, he might not have laughed at stories of Cuban involvement as he did in the early 1960s. Rather than a dusty second-floor room, the Cuban mission in Kingston during the Michael Manley years (1972–1980) had become an impressive complex—complete with radio transmitting antennas similar to those of U.S. and British counterparts. The Cuban ambassador—not infrequently the center of political controversy—presided over an ever-increasing network of Cuban activities in health, education, construction, agriculture, tourism, sports, and—some maintained—politics. In international affairs the Manley government occasionally spoke of "party to party" relationships with Cuba, and their joint declarations had a strident and even revolutionary tone.

Even as Jamaica's elections of 1980 proved Cuba to be noninterventionist and Manley a solid democrat, the perceptions of the Cuban menace contributed to the massive victory of Edward Seaga's anticommunist Jamaican Labour party. The change in Jamaican official attitudes toward Cuba in 1980 was even more dramatic than the changes had been in the United States: The Cuban presence was terminated overnight.

It is important to note that West Indian suspicion of Cuba increased during the period of U.S. emphasis on multilateralism and downplaying of hostile and belligerent rhetoric. It was the result of a series of intra-Caribbean events, incidents played out by Caribbean actors themselves. Most important by far was Cuba's surreptitious use of Barbados to airlift some five thousand troops into Angola in 1975. It demonstrated Cuban audacity and Cuban logistical capabilities and at the same time showed how easily these small states could unknowingly be drawn into an East-West tangle. The airlift had a very negative effect on the relations among West Indian leaders; neither Michael Manley nor Forbes Burnham was overly concerned, but Eric Williams of Trinidad was particularly put out by the discovery of what an old Cuban hand called "this . . . sensational development in hemispheric history."[31]

It was in the context of this dramatic act by Cuba that West Indian apprehensions escalated when a coup d'etat toppled the government of Eric Gairy in Grenada in 1979. Cuba almost immediately had the only resident ambassador on the island, who soon presided over a growing Cuban presence. It seemed to replicate the situation in Guyana, where the Cuban mission took up nearly half a city block and where Cuba's multiple involvements had long been the talk of Georgetown. Some 15 Cuban doctors arrived; so did fishing trawlers and instructors. On November 18, 1979, Prime Minister Maurice Bishop told a rally that he expected 250 Cubans to start building a new international airport. Since he had just been in Canada seeking funds for a feasibility study for that same project, local and international surprise was understandable.

In 1980 an incident in the Bahamas out islands sent a chill through West Indian Cuba-watchers: A Cuban MiG aircraft sank one of the Bahamas' three gun boats and strafed the sailors while in the water. Cuban military helicopters later landed on Bahamian territory. Although the incident appeared to result from a genuine case of mistaken identity (the Bahamians were thought to be Cuban exiled "pirates") and apologies and reparations were eventually made, the harm was already done. A poll taken in the Bahamas showed that 85.9 percent believed that the attack had been deliberate and not a mistake and that 73.3 percent believed that Cuba still posed a threat to the islands.[32] As a writer in

Nassau put it, Cuba had attacked a "defenceless neighboring, friendly country." But even more important than this, he continued, it had attacked "a black developing nation at the same time that it purported to enjoy wide international prestige as a leader of the non-aligned movement."[33]

The 1980s were thus launched with a number of incidents that fed the growing perception of a Cuban threat in the area. All seemed to confirm the perception of a militarized and aggressive Cuba taking advantage of Carter's *apertura* (liberalization) toward multilateralism. Virtually anything emanating from Cuba or its ally, Grenada, elicited suspicion.

And yet, aside from the cases cited, how much of all this perceived Cuban involvement or subversion was real? Clearly in the 1970s there was at least a surface unity among the area's new and Cuba-leaning Marxist-Leninist groups. This could be seen, for instance, at the public launching of Jamaica's Communist party, Trevor Munroe's Workers Party of Jamaica (WPJ), formerly the Workers' Liberation League. In attendance were delegates from the Communist parties of the USSR, Britain, Canada, the United States, and Cuba; in attendance from the English-speaking Caribbean were representatives of the People's Progressive party and the Working Peoples Alliance, the Barbados Movement for National Liberation, Grenada's New Jewel Movement, St. Vincent's Liberation Movement, and the St. Lucia's Workers' Revolutionary Movement.

To see Cuban machinations behind this unity, however, is to ignore the long-standing ties between Caribbean radical groups—ties that predate the Cuban Revolution and that more often than not are the result of specific and independent decisions on each island.[34] Furthermore, the coups in Grenada and Surinam involved the overthrow of unpopular regimes by small groups of men lightly armed. Like the rest of the Caribbean, these were "open" systems where the only protection was the degree of legitimacy of the regime, a legitimacy they appeared to have lost. Both cases show that Cuba's role tended to be most effective in situations where regime legitimacy was eroded and a process of antagonism had the making of a broad-based social movement against the regime. The search seemed to be more for social redress and restoration of democracy and honesty than for sociopolitical revolution.[35]

Be that as it may, it would be a mistake to underrate the significance attached by Caribbean observers to the political and ideological role defined by the Cubans and the capacity (indeed, audacity) of their intelligence and diplomatic corps. Art, science, sports, music, and everything else are perceived as parts of this political thrust into the Caribbean. The Cubans take full advantage of the points gained by their popular and commendable anti–South African policies and actions. And this policy is implemented by a corps of diplomats well versed in Caribbean culture and psychology. Like the United States, Cuba plays the racial diplomatic game with verve and panache through the quite explicit and effective use of black Cubans as diplomats in the Caribbean. Although it is an island where less than 25 percent of the population is black and where few of these blacks had in the 1970s achieved important, high-level positions in the revolutionary government, Cuba has managed to be represented nearly exclusively by blacks in the Caribbean. It is not surprising therefore to note the number of West Indians who believed Cuba to be a black Caribbean state. But the Cubans, as distinct from the United States, have the advantage of using this racial angle with its popular appeal while also emphasizing class and class conflict as the basic units of struggle (which appeals to the small Marxist cadres). Such a strategy allows a fundamentally pragmatic approach to the complex politics of an area where issues of race and class interact in a bewildering fashion.[36]

The network of Cuban diplomatic and political involvements comes under the aegis of the Caribbean section of the Cuban Ministry of Foreign Affairs. Unlike so many of the U.S. diplomats sent to the area, the Cubans are professionals to be reckoned with. In Barbados (which has refused to allow a resident Cuban mission despite having had diplomatic relations since 1972) high government officials have a healthy respect for Cuban intelligence. They will note, for instance, that the man who heads the Caribbean desk in Havana was formerly posted in Guyana and before that was an important Directorio General de Inteligencia (DGI) agent[37] and that the Cuban ambassador to Jamaica during the late 1970s was also a high-level DGI officer, well briefed in Jamaican and Caribbean affairs.

Nevertheless, in island after island, radical, pro-Cuban parties have gone down to overwhelming defeat in campaigns in which their Cuban and Grenadian connections had been made an issue. Since pro-Cuban governments such as Grenada, Surinam, and Guyana were also authoritarian ones, the Cuban issue became much more than purely a foreign-policy matter; by the late 1970s it was central to the discussion of the type of society desired and the role that elections would play in making that decision.

A preliminary conclusion would be that Cuba overplayed its hand in its zeal to support and assist ideologically like-minded groups in the area.[38] The tenacious sense of independence and respect for nonintervention of the new nations of the region came into play in the face of Cuban diplomatic audacity. This same attitude was shown toward Venezuela, a country whose diplomacy—though much more circumspect than Cuba's—was still too presumptuous for some of these new leaders whose nationalism and defensiveness about their sovereignty had been brought close to the surface by events during the 1970s.[39]

PERCEPTIONS OF VENEZUELA'S ROLE

Since in politics the one thing that cannot exist is a vacuum, it stands to reason that the gradual withdrawal of the British and Dutch from the Caribbean would lead to a replacement by other forces. Certainly the United States and Cuba shifted their policies and diplomacy to fit the changing situation. So did Venezuela, and never more assertively than during the period of the early 1970s, when, as Demetrio Boesner noted, several factors contributed to a new Caribbean consciousness:[40]

- The dispute with Guyana had made Venezuela aware of how isolated it was in a Third World and nonwhite Caribbean.
- Venezuela's industrial bourgeoisie had begun to look overseas for markets.
- Cuba's attempts at turning the Andes into a Sierra Maestra had failed and a successful amnesty had brought the Venezuelan guerrillas into the political fold.
- The Caldera-Calvani idea of ideological pluralism in the area had been well received by the new Caribbean elites of the West Indies.

This last point showed a coincidence between Venezuela and an incipient U.S. attitude. According to Boesner, it was really Christian Democrat Rafael Caldera and his chancellor, Arístides Calvani, who initiated the Caribbean thrust. Boesner believed that they were audacious and decisive, in contrast to the social democratic Adecos (members of AD—Acción Democrática) who were too "easily influenced by Yankee 'liberals.'" Although such refined interpretations of Venezuelan national politics may be accurate, Boesner's partisan emphasis appears misplaced. The sources of Venezuela's concern with the Caribbean were geopolitical and as such traditionally elicited bipartisan support.

The Venezuelan "definition" of its role as a Caribbean actor is not so much a definition as it is a geopolitical claim that Venezuela is a Caribbean country through the "simple" fact that it has eleven hundred miles of coast on the Caribbean and seventy-two islands therein. By that accounting, Colombia, Central America, and Mexico are Caribbean countries and are so considered by Venezuela. Together with the islands (the archipelago), they form what Venezuela had called the Caribbean Basin much before that term came into use in the United States. And like all such geopolitical approaches, Venezuela's blends geographical reality with perceptions derived from historical and political thinking.

The writings of a major Venezuelan geographer, Rubén Carpio Castillo, reflected a keen consciousness of what is called Venezuela's Mar Interior.[41] This is the body of water lying between the coast and the chain of seventy-two Venezuelan islands that stretches from Los Monjes in the west to Islas Aves in the north and Los Testigos in the east and constitutes a total of 14,650 square miles of land—seven times that of Trinidad and Tobago. No other Latin American country has such a coastal configuration and certainly none has foreign-controlled islands as close to its coast as does Venezuela.[42]

Clearly Venezuela's main concern is with oil, whether it be inland, just offshore, or in the Continental Shelf.[43] But Venezuela has also become deeply concerned with its marine riches. Along with this concern go all the other concerns over environment of the modern world. Whether it is oil, fisheries, or ecological factors, in the final analysis it is geography and what Pascual Vanegas Filardo, a prominent Venezuelan geographer, called the "historical threats" to Venezuelan territorial integrity that agitate the Venezuelan military and civilian nationalists. In that vein he said, "The threats to our coast and sea are historical in character and the aggressive greed of the treaties, which were not fully successful in hiding such greed, led to the dismembering of the Netherlands Antilles and Trinidad. . . ."[44] It was this consciousness that led Venezuela to pressure a beleaguered Britain into ceding the island of Patos and concluding the Gulf of Paria Treaty in 1942, one of the first median-line, continental-shelf treaties in international law.

These geopolitical realities and perceptions were strong enough to force a regional vision and role on Venezuela. But shifts in the behavior of other Caribbean actors also contributed to an intensification of Venezuelan interest in the area. The increasing U.S. emphasis on multilateralism during the 1970s coincided with Marxist setbacks in the Latin American mainland generally and in Venezuela specifically. Both gave Venezuela the breathing space necessary to pursue a more active Caribbean foreign policy. Even though Venezuelan-Cuban relations were never fully cordial during the decade, there was a period of détente that Carlos Romero characterized as a type of "mini-max game" when relations were "mixed."[45] This started in 1973 and ended in 1979, more or less the same time during which U.S. and Caribbean relations with Cuba were improving. The year 1974 thus provided an interesting window into Venezuela's Caribbean actions and the area's response thereto.

The atmosphere was full of discussions of Venezuelan-Cuban trade, and older books such as Rubén Carpio Castillo's *México, Cuba, Venezuela: Triángulo Geopolítico del Caribe*[46] were pulled off the shelf and subjected to new analysis. To observers in the Caribbean, Venezuela appeared to be preparing for what was considered to be its new role. In 1974 two new foreign-policy bodies were created. The importance of the Advisory Commission on External Relations is attested to by its composition: former presidents (only those democratically elected), former ministers of external affairs (of democratic governments), the chief of staff of the armed forces, and the presidents of the Chamber of Deputies and of the Senate (each chamber to have two representatives who sit for five years). The commission's mandate was broad but included a specific role in territorial and frontier questions of land and sea.[47] The other newly created body was the National Council on Frontiers, which seemed to have the function of suggesting social and economic development *on both sides* of Venezuela's borders; it would be based in the chancellor's office and be composed of different state agencies that were concerned with all aspects of frontier development.[48] Both these bodies were designed to pull governmental, university, and private-sector talent together in a national effort in foreign affairs.

Similarly the investments in oceanographic and other scientific research indicated that the decision makers intended to come prepared to the anticipated negotiations, preparation that was also evident in the upgrading of the diplomatic corps. Finally, the nationalization of the oil industry and the surge in world oil prices beginning in 1974 provided the government with the means to marry policies to interests.

No one demonstrated the depth of this new consciousness more clearly than President Carlos Andrés Pérez, who pursued the Caribbean initiative of the previous government with even more vigor. In his inaugural address to the third United Nations Conference on the Law of the Sea in Caracas, 1974, Pérez was especially emphatic when explaining why it had taken Venezuela so long to develop such a consciousness of its maritime potential and wealth: "Venezuela cannot forget that in its past as a weak nation it had been the victim of the manoeuvres of great international interests."[49] He was quick to reassure his audience that such memories would not be used to nourish infertile feelings of vengeance or rancor but rather to make them "permanent and constructive lessons for the future."

The response to Venezuela in parts of the Commonwealth Caribbean demonstrated some of the same features of the later response to Cuban actions. Venezuelan-Trinidadian relations during this period of the mid-1970s are worth analyzing as a case of intra-Caribbean foreign-policy behavior. It involved strategic Trinidadian and Venezuelan geographic thinking on their respective maritime positions and a heavy dose of historical interpretations of past weaknesses of both countries, always a powerful source of prickly defensiveness.

It was Eric Williams, prime minister of Trinidad and by far the most knowledgeable stateman on Caribbean matters at the time, who provided the most elaborate interpretation of Venezuelan intentions. In what amounted to one of the most scathing attacks by one country on another in the Caribbean area during peacetime, Williams warned of Venezuela's "penetration" and "territorial ambitions" in the Caribbean, berated that country's "belated recognition of its Caribbean identity," and chastized his Caribbean Commercial (CARICOM) partners for falling for the new Venezuelan definition of the Caribbean (the Caribbean Basin) and for leading a "Caribbean Pilgrimage to Caracas."[50]

Trinidad's sources of friction with Venezuela were many: multilateral versus bilateral trade and arrangements between CARICOM members and Venezuela, especially as regarded bauxite and oil; differences regarding the law of the sea; objections to certain Venezuelan claims to islets in the Caribbean; Venezuelan loans; tourism initiative; and cultural "penetration" through scholarships. Fundamentally, however, Williams's fear was that the Caribbean and Latin American primary products were "jumping from the European and American frying pan into the South

American fire" and that the net result would be the recognition of Venezuela as "a new 'financial center' of the world."

The *facts* behind all this do not warrant the intensity of Williams's attack. There was not one indication of any Venezuelan military move of an offensive nature;[51] Venezuela had even refused to respond to Williams's call for help during the 1970 Black Power uprising on the island. All initiatives in the business area were joint-venture types with the Venezuelan government acting as guarantor. Venezuela had already begun to use its oil as a means of assistance, both multilaterally, through significant contributions to the Caribbean Development Bank, and bilaterally, through assistance such as that to the strapped Manley regime in Jamaica.[52]

If these news stories from the British islands had a ring of "small-island" paranoia to them, it was mild compared to what was going on in the press of the Netherlands Antilles. A report presented by Curazaleño international-relations expert Boeli Van Leeuwen to the parliamentary committee on the status of the Dutch islands created a sensation. Van Leeuwen claimed that there was a secret agreement between the Netherlands, Venezuela, and Royal Dutch Shell Oil Company on the future status of these islands. The report led the respectable *Beurs en Nieuwsberichten*[53] to headline the question: "Antilles: Sold and Betrayed?" Van Leeuwen's evidence was circumstantial if not outright unfounded, but the context of his report did provide grounds for serious speculation. So when in June 1974 the Dutch government announced that it was withdrawing its military protection from the oil refinery in Aruba and at the same time suggested that Dutch forces be replaced by Venezuelan troops, Arubanos must have recalled the Van Leeuwen report; they rejected the suggestion outright.

These events were occurring at a time, as we have noted, when the U.S. presence in the region was relatively low-key and U.S. statements about multilateralism (which became institutionalized with Carter, 1976–1980) appeared to cede the area as a Venezuelan sphere of influence. This interpretation soon led to new academic theories of Caribbean "middle powers" in an attempt to explain the behavior in the region of Venezuela, Brazil, and, to a lesser extent, Mexico.

But the fact is that what U.S. policy had done was merely to call attention to Venezuela. Venezuela really needed no U.S. encouragement: Its new oil wealth, its long-standing leadership role in the Organization of Petroleum Exporting Countries (OPEC), the bipartisan nature of its foreign policy, and its own perceptions of history and geopolitics made it quite an independent actor on the Caribbean stage. This in itself was threatening to some West Indians.

These *perceptions*, however, had as much to do with West Indian politics and historical consciousness as with Venezuelan action. The fear of Venezuelan capitalist expansion could not be divorced from the consistent anticapitalist rhetoric of West Indian leaders, including Eric

Williams,[54] nor could the latter disguise his frustrations at the inability of the CARICOM governments to formulate a set of cohesive policies toward the outside world, including Venezuela.[55] In the final analysis, what the events of this period indicate is that the nations in the Caribbean already had developed sensitivity toward any "unusual" actions by a neighbor outside of that neighbor's borders. Whether in relation to the United States, Cuba, or Venezuela, the heightened geopolitical thinking of these island societies was like exposed nerves responding to external—and even internal—factors with great rapidity if not always with great fanfare.

By 1979, Venezuelan-Cuban relations had deteriorated to the point of open verbal conflict and diplomatic confrontation, and by 1981 the situation Venezuela faced in the Caribbean was radically different from that faced during 1973–1979. Robert D. Bond attributed this change to three fundamental factors: Cuba's return to an active role in promoting insurgency, the new U.S. attempt to "reassert its traditional dominance over the Caribbean," and, finally, the collapse of the bipartisan nature of Venezuela's foreign policy.[56] This last factor had powerful international implications, since the Socialist International and the Christian Democratic International had taken opposing positions vis-à-vis the hottest partisan issue in Venezuelan foreign policy—the support for the Christian Democratic regime of Napoleón Duarte in El Salvador.

CONCLUSIONS

The Caribbean ministate reached the age of maturity in international relations during the decade of the 1970s. Any interpretation of Caribbean international dynamics today has to take the Caribbean actors into account in an attempt to explain perceptions and realities. And this raises one of the more intriguing questions about the dynamics of this decade: Why—given the existing perceptions that Cuba's foreign policy was vastly more aggressive than Venezuela's—was there no dramatic official Trinidadian outcry against Cuba similar to Williams's 1975 attack on Venezuela? The Jamaica Labour party (JLP) certainly has made Cuba an issue, but there has been no serious, in-depth analysis of Cuba's role, either from the political or private sector.

One explanation clearly has to be the role of cultural and racial concerns in the area. Once Fidel Castro had decided, as he said in 1976, that Cuba was not only a Latin American but also an Afro–Latin American nation, he was demonstrating a sensitivity toward the ethnic dimension in Caribbean international politics that had wide implications.[57] Venezuela, on the other hand, has consistently shown an inability to understand this ethnic factor. "The classes who determine Venezuela's internal and external policies," laments Demetrio Boesner, "have no consciousness of that reality." In fact, they have traditionally defined Venezuela as a "European" nation.[58]

This concern with race is not purely psychological; it relates to a fundamental dimension of West Indian ideology.[59] Nearly all the leaders of the new nations of the Caribbean came to power on platforms of social justice and condemnation of any form of racial discrimination. Even as conservative a government as Edward Seaga's of Jamaica has to reiterate periodically its traditional stand against South Africa. Cuban behavior in certain critical areas of international politics thus is not far removed from West Indian rhetoric. One such area is Cuban intervention in Angola, which is held to be a just response to South African involvement.[60] Even as they fear Cuban audacity in foreign policy, West Indians find it difficult to side with the U.S. propensity to make linkages between Cuba actions in Africa and in the Caribbean. As such, the Carter policy of multilateralism and pluralism tended to accommodate West Indian perceptions and needs more readily than does the post-1980 U.S. hard line, even as West Indians themselves appear to be shaping an anti-Marxist hard line of their own.[61]

Other than the observations already given, only very tentative conclusions can be derived from the analysis presented here. Rather than being purely secondary or derived versions of superpower rivalry, many of the conflicts and confrontations in the Caribbean are the result of independent Caribbean actors pursuing their perception of national interests as well as of their own survival in power in an area that has changed dramatically in the past twenty years. There are now some fifteen new actors with highly developed senses of national honor shaped by a very complex combination of traditional ideas of sovereignty as well as of racial and cultural solidarity on a global scale.

With few exceptions, they are more interested in a North-South dialogue than in the East-West confrontation. And yet neither these new actors nor the United States can escape some of the intricate and often intractible ironies or contradictions of the region. Only two can be mentioned here. Although these new actors publicly applauded the low military profile and multilateralism of the Carter years, they were privately apprehensive that a perception of U.S. weakness encouraged more powerful Caribbean actors to assert their interests at the expense of the smaller, weaker ones. Related to this is the fact that despite resenting the U.S. policy of linkages between events in the Caribbean and elsewhere, they themselves operate on the basis of linkages, especially as they relate to South Africa.

The upshot of all this is that there is no escaping the need for a specifically Caribbean focus on foreign policy (on both sides). It must, however, be one that places the Caribbean within the context of global international dynamics.

NOTES

1. Quoted in Howard F. Cline, *The United States and Mexico* (New York: Atheneum, 1963), p. 165.

2. U.S. Department of Commerce, *Essential U.S. Foreign Trade Routes* (Washington, D.C.: Government Printing Office, June 1975).

3. Ibid.; U.S. Department of Commerce, *U.S. Foreign Trade Statistics* (Washington, D.C.: Government Printing Office, 1983).

4. Don Bohning, *Miami Herald,* December 21, 1977, p. 28.

5. U.S. Congress, House Sub-Committee on Inter-American Affairs, *Hearings on Soviet Activities in Cuba,* pt. 3, September 26, 1972, pp. 24–25.

6. U.S. Congress, House Sub-Committee on Inter-American Affairs, *Hearings on a Western Hemisphere Relationship of Cooperation,* March 26, 1974, p. 14.

7. Ibid., app., pp. 2–8.

8. Ibid., p. 8.

9. Speech by Dante B. Fascell, American Assembly–University of Miami Conference on the Caribbean, Miami, Florida, April 28, 1973.

10. Commission on U.S.–Latin American Relations, *The Americas in a Changing World* (New York: Center for Inter-American Relations, 1974).

11. *Weekly Compilation of Presidential Documents* 13, no. 6 (Washington, D.C.: Government Printing Office, 1977), pp. 523–528.

12. It was a sign of the Caribbean leadership's keen interest in what Washington officialdom was thinking that in Trinidad the speech was carried in its entirety by the *Trinidad Guardian,* April 15, 1977, pp. 2, 6, 16.

13. An early and influential adviser was Philip C. Habib, whose first diplomatic posting had been in Trinidad, where he developed a good relationship with Prime Minister Eric Williams.

14. Andrew Young's trip was reported as follows by the *New York Times:* "'There really has been a change,' Mr. Young has been saying throughout the tour, and the responsiveness of the Caribbean leaders, . . . has seemed at times to be more than the visitors expected." (August 14, 1977, p. 15). "During the trip, hosts and guests sometimes seemed to be bursting with eagerness to cement the new relationships with praise." (August 18, 1977, p. 3).

15. I was appointed to the first task force sent to Barbados to explore trade, sports, and educational exchanges.

16. U.S. Congress, House Sub-Committee on the Inter-American Affairs, *Hearings on U.S. Policy Toward the Caribbean,* June 28, 1977, p. 30.

17. World Bank news release, December 15, 1977.

18. Note, for instance, the accounts of Andrew Young's efforts. On August 14, *New York Times* reported that Andrew Young had had earnest political talks with Caribbean leaders about "developing an overall Caribbean policy in which the U.S. would be a helpful partner but not a dominating presence." On August 18, 1977, *New York Times* carried the following account: "Andrew Young is bringing home an endorsement by Caribbean leaders of plans for a new regional partnership as a result of his 10-country mission for President Carter."

19. Major Noel Hidalgo, "Background of U.S. Military Training in Latin America," the *DISAM Journal* (Fall 1982), pp. 48–55.

20. A confidential report by Philip C. Habib still stressed social and economic conditions but emphasized that Cuba was using these as "targets of opportunity" and thus military assistance was called for (cf. *Washington Post,* June 15, 1980, pp. 1, 18).

21. Note that this discussion deals with perceptions and intentions, not with the full realization of these. This is important, for as Robert Pastor has noted, "the Carter Administration started with an interest in promoting economic

development . . . but eventually returned to a concern for national security."
Foreign Affairs 60, no. 5 (Summer 1982), p. 1042.

22. Hanson W. Baldwin, "A Military Perspective," in John Plank (ed.), *Cuba and the United States* (Washington, D.C.: Brookings Institution, 1967), p. 206. Interestingly, Raúl Castro is also quoted as saying "from a military point of view this base is not important . . . but it does constitute a cancer." (Cf. *Area Handbook for Cuba* [Washington, D.C.: Government Printing Office, 1971], p. 352.)

23. *Russia in the Caribbean*, pt. 1, *Panelists' Findings, Recommendations, and Comments* (Washington, D.C.: Georgetown University, Center for Strategic and International Studies, 1973), p. 5.

24. Ibid. There is some empirical evidence of such public perceptions about the Caribbean's strategic importance. In 1974 only 39 percent of the U.S. public felt that a Soviet invasion of Western Europe warranted the use of U.S. troops, but 54 percent approved of their use to keep the Panama Canal open. By 1978, when 92 percent of U.S. "leaders" would have used troops in Europe but only 49 percent would have in Panama, the public still saw Panama as more important by 58 percent to 54 percent. Cf. John E. Rielly (ed.), *American Public Opinion and U.S. Foreign Policy, 1979* (Chicago: Council on Foreign Relations, 1979). For an analysis of how this "soft-underbelly" perception has affected U.S. actions in the area, see A. P. Maingot, "National Sovereignty, Collective Security, and the Realities of Power in the Caribbean," in Roy Preiswerk (ed.), *Regionalism and the Commonwealth Caribbean* (Trinidad: Institute of International Relations, 1969), pp. 220–245. For a more general discussion of psychological factors in policy formulation, see Joseph S. Tulchin, "Inhibitions Affecting the Latin American Policy of the United States," *Ventures* 7, no. 2 (1967), pp. 68–80.

25. As if to emphasize the role of public opinion, U.S. Secretary of State Alexander Haig presented what he called this "new direction" on April 24, 1981, to the American Society of Newspaper Editors. Cf. U.S. Department of State, *Current Policy* no. 275.

26. Cf. Jorge Domínguez: "It [Cuba] is strikingly unconstrained by either fear of other African actors, of the Soviet Union, or of the United States." From "Political and Military Consequences of Cuban Policies in Africa," in Carmelo Mesa-Lago and June S. Belkin (eds.), *Cuba in Africa* (Pittsburgh: Center for Latin American Studies, 1982), p. 138. In the same volume see also the essay by William M. LeoGrande (pp. 15–20) and Chapter 11 by Enrique A. Baloyra in this book.

27. Cuba, Haiti, the Dominican Republic, Jamaica, Trinidad and Tobago, Barbados, Grenada, St. Vincent, St. Lucia, Dominica, Antigua, St. Kitts–Nevis, and the Bahamas.

28. Guyana, Surinam, Belize.

29. See the discussion of the study "Cuban Armed Forces and the Soviet Military Presence," in *New York Times*, August 22, 1982, p. 8. On the size of the Cuban armed forces, see John Keegan, *World Armies* (New York: Fact on File, 1979).

30. The one full-scale parliamentary investigation into subversive activities in Trinidad came up with little more than fears and apprehensions. Cf. *Report of the Commission of Enquiry into Subversive Activities in Trinidad and Tobago*, House Paper no. 2 (Port of Spain: Government Publishing House, 1965).

31. Herbert L. Matthews, *New York Times*, March 4, 1976, p. 31. Matthews believed that Angola was "as much Fidel Castro's policy as it was Moscow's" and characterized his old friend as a "Napoleon of the Caribbean."

32. *Image* magazine (Bahamas) (Summer 1980), p. 48.

33. Larry Smith, "The Flamingo Affair," *Image* (Summer 1980), pp. 48–53.

34. Cf. A. P. Maingot, "The Difficult Path to Socialism in the English-speaking Caribbean," in Richard Fagen (ed.), *The State and Capitalism in U.S.–Latin American Relations* (Stanford: Stanford University Press, 1979), pp. 254–301.

35. This antagonism seems to have as much to do with moral outrage and indignation as with class conflict. Cf. A. P. Maingot, "The Structure of Modern Conservative Societies," in Jan Black (ed.), *Latin America: A Multidisciplinary Introduction* (Boulder, Colo.: Westview Press, 1983).

36. For a fuller development of this theme, see A. P. Maingot, "Playing the Cuban Card," in Barry B. Levine (ed.), *The New Cuban Presence* (Boulder, Colo.: Westview Press, 1983).

37. Despite having diplomatic relations with Cuba, Prime Minister Eric Williams of Trinidad refused this particular Cuban a visa in early 1970 (personal information, Trinidad, 1974).

38. As if understanding this backlash, Castro's tone during his visit to Jamaica in October 1977 was moderate and conciliatory toward the anticommunist Jamaica Labour party (JLP); the latter, however, obviously had already seen the political benefits of anti-Cubanism and was not about to reciprocate.

39. Something of this sense can be gleaned from the address of Prime Minister Errol Barrow of Barbados upon his nation's admission to the OAS. "The Policy of non-intervention was first promulgated by the people of Barbados in 1651 . . . although our independence was formalized on the 30 of November, 1966, the people of Barbados have always regarded the declaration of 1651 as the corner stone of our independence. . . ." In Roy Preiswerk (ed.), *Documents on International Relations in the Caribbean* (St. Augustine, Trinidad: Institute of Social and Economic Research, University of the West Indies, 1970), p. 47.

40. Demetrio Boesner, *Venezuela en el Caribe: Presencia Cambiante* (Caracas: Monte Avila, 1978).

41. Cf. Rubén Carpio Castillo, *Fronteras Marítimas de Venezuela* (Caracas: Venediciones, 1974).

42. Venezuela shares land and sea and/or continental-shelf boundaries with Colombia, Trinidad, the Netherlands Antilles, the French Antilles, Dominica, and Guyana. The mix of national laws and the continued presence of metropolitan powers (France, Britain, and the Netherlands) all present Venezuela with an extraordinarily complex international panorama.

43. According to Salvador L. Dallanega P., Venezuela has two fundamental reasons for seeking closer ties with its Caribbean neighbors: (1) oil and mineral wealth shared on one geological formation, and (2) Brazilian hegemonic pretensions in this region. "Venezuela, América Latina, y Argentina," *Revista Argentina de Relaciones Internacionales* (January–April 1976), pp. 47–56.

44. "Fronteras marítimas de Venezuela," *El Universal*, June 24, 1974, p. 4. For even stronger calls to redress "a painful past," see articles by General (retd.) Aldolfo Ramírez Torres, *El Universal*, July 1, 1974, p. 5; Elias A. Sayegh, *El Universal*, July 13, 1974, pp. 1, 5.

45. Cf. Carlos Romero M., "Las relaciones entre Venezuela y Cuba desde la instauración de la revolución Cubana hasta principios de 1978" (Caracas, February 1980) and "Aproximación a la política del Caribe contemporaneo" (Caracas, 1980). Both are manuscripts in my possession.

46. Caracas: Imprenta Nacional, 1961.

47. *El Universal*, May 29, 1974, pp. 2–6.

48. *El Universal*, June 12, 1974, pp. 1–4.

49. *El Universal*, June 21, 1974, p. 1.

50. *Trinidad Guardian*, June 16, 18, 19, and 20, 1975.

51. Cf. Keegan, *World Armies*, p. 789. "Unlike the states with 'great power' aspirations in South America, particularly Brazil and Argentina, Venezuela does not feel it necessary to buy or attempt to manufacture large surface ships, advanced combat aircrafts or battle tanks."

52. In 1980 Williams compared the terms of the Venezuelan-Mexican oil facility to Trinidad's and was correct to note that the latter's was more generous for the smaller, less developed islands. His pique was evident: "Trinidad and Tobago's oil facility remains unnoticed, neither foreign press nor Jamaican press bothering about it." *Forged from the Love of Liberty: Selected Speeches of Dr. Eric Williams* (Port of Spain: Longman Caribbean, 1981), p. 446.

53. For a review of this and other aspects of the tensions, see "Caricom Problems over Venezuela," *West Indies Chronicle News* (May, June 1975).

54. In this Williams had some support from Venezuelan writers. Note, for instance, the conclusion of Demetrio Boesner: "If the capitalist factor should impose itself in Venezuela as the basic determinant of the national destiny and the political decisions, there might be a basis for certain fears that Venezuela might change into a new imperialist or sub-imperialist power in the Caribbean." "The Policy of Venezuela Towards the Caribbean," in Leslie F. Manigat (ed.), *The Caribbean Yearbook of International Relations, 1975* (Leyden: A. W. Sythoff, 1976), p. 463.

55. This is the conclusion of an excellent piece on the subject: Henry S. Gill, "Conflict in Trinidad and Tobago's Relations with Venezuela," in Manigat, *The Caribbean Yearbook*, pp. 465–491.

56. "Venezuela, the Caribbean Basin, and the Crisis in Central America" (MS, 1982, in my possession). After an excellent analysis Bond does conclude enigmatically by stating that a number of ". . . Venezuela's geopolitical and economic interests in the region are more potential than real." Perceptions in Venezuela—as we hope to have shown here—would not support Bond's conclusion.

57. Note Fidel Castro's words: "We are a Latin-African people—enemies of colonialism, neocolonialism, racism, apartheid, which Yankee imperialism aids and protects." Speech given in Havana, April 19, 1976.

58. Boesner, *Venezuela en el Caribe*, p. 92.

59. Cf. Locksley Edmundson and Peter Phillips, "The Commonwealth Caribbean and Africa: Aspects of Third World Racial Interactions, Linkages, and Challenges," in Basil A. Ince (ed.), *Contemporary International Relations of the Caribbean* (St. Augustine, Trinidad: Institute of International Relations, 1979), pp. 33–55.

60. This explanation appears to fit the African response, as William M. LeoGrande has explained. "Diplomatically, South Africa's troops made the difference . . . one of the most important and most consistently pro-western countries of sub-Sahara Africa, Nigeria explicitly praised Cuban and Soviet aid to the PRA [Partido Revolucionario Auténtico] in its struggle to defeat the South African intervention." "Cuban Policy in Africa," in Mesa-Lago and Belkin, *Cuba in Africa*, p. 25.

61. Symptomatic was the September 20, 1982, *secret* meeting of the prime ministers of St. Lucia, Dominica, and St. Vincent with the prime minister of Barbados to discuss regional security, which included the role of Grenada as one of the topics. United Press International (UPI), September 21, 1982.

6. The Role of Regional Powers in Central America: Mexico, Venezuela, Cuba, and Colombia

THE CHARACTER AND THE ROLE OF
REGIONAL POWERS IN THE THIRD WORLD

The discussion about the role of regional powers within the international system is of relatively recent origin, and generally accepted definitions about what constitutes a regional power are still lacking. For the purpose of this chapter it seems to be worthwhile to take into consideration not only a country's real ability to influence political developments in Central America but also the intention to do so. For that reason this chapter will include not only Mexico and Venezuela—whose regional-power status in the Latin American context is beyond doubt—but also Cuba and Colombia, which for very different reasons are usually not considered to be part of the select group of Latin America's regional powers. One of the reasons for their exclusion obviously is the lack of an autonomous power base, since Cuba's actions are often seen in the context of Soviet policies, and Colombia's policies are supposed to originate in Washington. Both allegations contain some half truths but cannot be validated in all of the respective attitudes and actions of Cuba and Colombia toward Central America or elsewhere. Given the concrete influence both countries exercise—or are likely to in the near future—in the region, it seems absolutely necessary to include them in the Central American regional-power group.

The same cannot be said about the other "accepted" regional powers of Latin America: Brazil and Argentina. Brazil's interest in Central America has waned in recent years, after some efforts at economic cooperation in the middle of the 1970s. Even on the diplomatic front Brazil has kept a very low profile with regard to one of the major international crises in recent Latin American history. Argentina has been much more active, especially with military advisers and transfers of weapons.[1] Its involvement in Central America has hardly been an expression of a national interest affected by the developments in Central America, but rather has made clear the intention of being useful to U.S.

83

global interests and has shown Argentina's willingness and ability to become a major strategic partner for the Reagan administration. Since the Malvinas crisis, this proxy position of Argentina in Central America has disappeared almost completely, whereas the other four actors are still very much involved.[2]

The internal prerequisites for regional-power status are to be found in a rather well developed level of national integration, the existence of economic means, and the ability of the foreign-policy elite of the given country to translate these economic possibilities into a coordinated use of foreign-policy instruments. Contrary to widespread opinion, the economic dimension is not necessarily the most important prerequisite for regional-power status. Mexico, before its oil boom, and certainly Cuba are good examples showing that other national capabilities— among them a consistency of ideological positions—can substitute for the economic dimension of foreign policy even over an extended period of time. Of great importance for the regional powers in the Third World is often the leading personality who is formulating the foreign policy of any given country. That is usually the head of state, as in the case of Fidel Castro, Luis Echeverría, and Carlos Andrés Pérez, but sometimes the foreign minister can assume a similar role, as in the case of Arístides Calvani of Venezuela. Their personal commitment and—in some cases— charismatic leadership constitutes an important element in the drive for regional-power status.[3]

Another unique feature of a regional power in the Third World is the emergence of its regional influence at the very moment when the country by many indicators is about to leave its typical Third World status behind. In this intermediate phase, often characterized in Latin America as "clase media de naciones,"[4] the regional powers seek out typical attributes and foreign-policy instruments of the established powers in the international system. They tend to make increasing use of bilateral treaties and will gradually establish foreign-aid programs on economic, military, technical, and educational levels. It is a characteristic element of such a new regional-power status that quite often the new instruments are not only used for furthering short-term or long-term national interests but in some cases are even applied to strengthen Third World solidarity.

For the analysis of the foreign-policy behavior of such regional powers it is of overriding importance to understand the context of their development within the international system. The rapid change of the international hierarchy since the oil shock of the early 1970s has made possible the rise of the "new influentials."[5] The increase of real negotiating power of some previously peripheral states because of their energy potential and/or their strategic location vis-à-vis the industrial powers reflects upon the increasing inability of the superpowers to pursue their global political and economic interests alone.

Another factor contributing to the rather sudden rise of some regional powers to international importance was the effects of détente on the international system, allowing greater foreign-policy autonomy and maneuverability of many Third World states. The effect of this development can be especially well observed in the case of the Central American crisis, where the superpowers find it increasingly difficult to stress "new" rigorous intrabloc behavior among their allies.

The relative decline of U.S. power in all its dimensions has to be seen as one of the most important prerequisites of regional-power development as such and especially around the Caribbean Basin. Whereas in 1965 the United States could intervene in the Dominican Republic against the will of Mexico and Cuba, efforts to find necessary support in the Organization of American States (OAS) to create a similar Inter-American Peace Force to prevent the success of the Sandinista revolution in 1979 was doomed from the very beginning. Mexico's and Venezuela's opposition to that effort made that very clear. The increased importance of the regional powers can best be illustrated by the fact that the United States now takes great care to find at least one, or if possible even more, of the regional powers to support its overt foreign-policy initiatives with regard to Central America.[6]

The notable absence of a regional conflict-regulating mechanism—such as the OAS might have provided in the 1950s or 1960s—has greatly enhanced the willingness of regional powers to mediate among contending forces within any given country in Central America as well as among some of the countries or between the United States and the postrevolutionary regime in Nicaragua. Such activities of regional powers in a geopolitical area hitherto dominated by a hegemonic power like the United States lead to a great plurality of international actors and interactions. They are characterized at the same time by a great variety of competing political, economic, and ideological forces from the countries that are interested in exercising political influence.

It would be shortsighted to see the role of regional powers in general and with regard to Central America in particular only as a positive development for regional stability. One of the serious problems that arise from the international posture of such regional powers is to be found in the extreme willingness to experiment with foreign-policy issues, which is characteristic for countries that have not previously enjoyed an important influence within any given international subsystem. Rather sudden changes of policies over a short period of time make the position of regional powers with regard to any given crisis situation difficult to calculate. This is even more so in those cases where expected or unexpected domestic-policy reversals lead to a change of foreign policy. It is also obvious that some of the regional powers are quite easily influenced externally whenever there arises an opportunity in which they can improve their own foreign-policy impact radically by an association with one of the established powers. Many observers have called Cuba's role in Africa a typical case of such a relationship,[7] but with regard to the Central American crisis, Venezuela at times has appeared to be not far from such a position and certainly Colombia has been seen as a country that has been very receptive to U.S. influence.

Given the great diversity of the national interests and capabilities of the four regional powers that are of importance to Central America, it is certainly a valid question if it makes sense to compare their policies in the region over a time span of four years, from 1979 to 1982.[8] The importance of such a comparison can only be measured with regard to the obvious community of interests that can be traced from the actions of all regional powers and the possible impact their common perceptions and objectives might have with regard to a slowly evolving new subregional system in the Caribbean Basin. Looking at the differences in their perceptions, one can possibly draw some conclusions about the viability of such a new subregional system—one that would not be dominated by the United States any more but could rather reflect a complicated scheme of burden sharing and power sharing between the regional powers and the United States.

THE OBJECTIVES AND THE ACTIVITIES OF REGIONAL POWERS IN CENTRAL AMERICA

To make valid comparisons of the foreign-policy postures of the regional powers in Central America, one can divide their objectives and activities into four different categories: (1) foreign-policy objectives, (2) perceptions of the Central American crisis, (3) levels of interaction with Central America, and (4) instruments used to achieve influence in Central America.

Mexico—A Regional Power Through Diplomacy

Mexico's foreign policy is characterized by two principal motivations: to react to the ever-present possibilities of incursions on its sovereignty by the United States and to stabilize its own political system by using a revolutionary foreign policy as an instrument to legitimate its overall policy against criticism from the left.[9] These motivations have contributed to a strengthening of the two main foreign-policy goals of Mexico: to uphold the principles of nonintervention and self-determination. It is as a product of its own historical experience that Mexico has developed a very strong stand on such issues even though its diplomacy has to a certain extent been rather reactive, managing most foreign-policy issues along the lines of a legalistic tradition.

The "revolutionary" character of its own political system and its self-perception as one of the principal anti–status quo powers in the Third World have led to a variety of actions that can be seen as forerunners to its present policy in Central America. The common denominator in all of those actions was obviously opposition against U.S. actions: in 1954 against the U.S. policy toward the Arbenz government in Guatemala; in 1962 against the U.S. policy to force the Latin American countries to break relations with Cuba; in 1965 against the unilateral U.S. intervention in the Dominican Republic, only later legitimated by the OAS; and in 1972 and 1973 against the U.S. destabilization policy in Chile. But this anti-U.S., prorevolutionary stand of Mexico's foreign policy is only one of its main features. Another is Mexico's perception as a self-styled "bridge builder" between the United States and other Latin American countries.[10] Taking its geographic position to be a form of geopolitical duty, Mexico has tried many times to mediate between the interests of the hegemonic power and those of the affected Latin American states. It is in that respect that Mexico's perceptions of the Central American crisis have to be seen as well. Failing to find some middle ground in such a vital area would therefore reflect upon the general foreign-policy capacity of Mexico.[11]

Until 1982 Mexico's engagement in Central America had been strengthened by its position as a new oil power. In 1979, when Mexico's involvement in Latin America had barely started, Mexico's oil reserves provided it with more "muscle" to pursue its foreign-policy aims.[12] But it would be premature to conclude that Mexico depended on its oil power to exercise a regional power's influence. Because of their historical understanding of revolutionary change in their own society, most Mexicans felt at ease with the changes under way in some Central American countries. Mexico's confidence in its own revolutionary political system was strong enough that revolutionary developments in neighboring countries were seen not as a dangerous development but rather as something that had to come about anyway and that would have to be dealt with in such a way that Mexico would be on good terms with the new elites rather than the old ones. What worried Mexican policymakers in the Central American crisis was not so much the outcome, but the turmoil created by increasing radicalization and militarization that might affect Mexican stability.

Mexico was one of the driving forces in the OAS against the establishment of an Inter-American Peace Force to be sent to Nicaragua; Mexico played the same role in the United Nations (UN) by sponsoring the General Assembly's resolution of December 16, 1981, which declared that there were no conditions for free elections in El Salvador and called for a negotiated political settlement. Two further diplomatic initiatives, seen as major peacekeeping efforts from the Mexican side, were the arrangement of a meeting between then U.S. Secretary of State Alexander Haig and Vicepremier Minister of Cuba Rafael Rodríguez in November 1981 in Mexico and the proposal for a comprehensive peace plan for the region outlined by José López Portillo in his speech in Managua on February 21, 1981.[13]

But beyond the bilateral and multilateral activities Mexico also used transnational mediation in its efforts to strengthen its influence upon the political developments in Central America. The organization used was a grouping of political parties founded in 1979, named Conferencia

Permanente de Partidos Políticos Latinoamericanos (COPPPAL), which was obviously an instrument by which the Mexican Partido Revolucionario Institucional (PRI) extended and formalized its international connections.[14] Through the help of COPPPAL, the Sandinista movement could be integrated into a "club" of other Latin American socialist, antiimperialist, or revolutionary parties, and the opposition forces in other Central American countries had a platform for international cooperation. COPPPAL was used not only for party contacts but also to supply financial, technical, and logistic aid to Central American opposition forces by allowing them to operate openly and actively in Mexico.

The major economic dimension of Mexico's influence in Central America has been the oil facility established in June 1980 by Mexico and Venezuela jointly to help nine Central American and Caribbean countries to cope with the high oil prices. It is not by accident that Mexico has, without any problems, included El Salvador in the group of recipient countries in Central America, although otherwise it has not met with much of Mexico's foreign-policy approval. That way Mexico could meet Venezuela's specific interest in strengthening the Christian Democratic party in El Salvador and at the same time demonstrate its evenhandedness with regard to Central American political developments.[15] Direct financing has also been made available, especially to Nicaragua.[16] Including the benefits from the oil facility, Mexico probably became the largest donor country to Nicaragua in 1981.

Looking at the relative importance of the different instruments used, it is obvious that diplomatic activities have been in the center of Mexico's policy as a regional power. But also its technical and economic help have been of such salience as to demonstrate Mexico's intention to become the major foreign-policy actor in Central America besides the United States.[17] Given the economic crisis of Mexico in 1982, it is quite obvious that the economic dimension of Mexico's involvement will decline. Its overall posture will nevertheless probably not be reduced considerably given the greater importance Mexico has always put on its political and diplomatic activities.

Venezuela—A Regional Power Through Wealth

The foreign-policy profile of Venezuela has always been characterized by one major asset: oil. For this very reason, the priorities of Venezuela's foreign-policy interests have not always been concentrated in Latin America. As one of the founding states of the Organization of Petroleum Exporting Countries (OPEC), Venezuela has been more interested in the relationships with other oil-producing countries and with its main oil customer, the United States. As a regional-power contender, Venezuela did not enter the scene until Rafael Caldera became president in March 1969. Since then, the Caribbean Basin obviously has been of growing importance for Venezuela's geopolitical and foreign-policy interests. Central America has been of some weight, but less so than the Andean states, to which Venezuela has provided economic and political leadership in the context of the Andean Pact.

Venezuela's perception of the Central American crisis has been very much influenced by party alignments and personal relationships.[18] The specific disgust that Social Democratic president Carlos Andrés Pérez felt for Anastasio Somoza contributed considerably to Venezuela's interest in helping the Sandinistas come to power in Nicaragua. On the other hand, his successor as president, Christian Democrat Luis Herrera Campins, has had very strong personal relations with Napoleón Duarte of El Salvador and therefore a stake in his political survival within the civil war in that country. Even though it would be far-fetched to analyze Venezuela's impact on the subregion along the lines of personal involvement, the strength of those feelings on the part of the country's presidents has certainly contributed to the ideological inconsistencies of Venezuela's position in Central America since 1979. Obviously, this has also reflected Venezuela's strong two-party system and the willingness of both parties to compete abroad and to provide leadership as well as aid to political groups of similar ideological inclination.[19]

The levels of interaction have been directly related to the ideological preferences of the parties in power. Much bilateral aid was available for Nicaragua during the Pérez presidency, but this changed rapidly during Luis Herrera Campins' government and was switched in part to El Salvador. The transnational relations between some Central American parties and their Venezuelan counterparts have not entirely reflected such shifts, since the Social Democratic Acción Democrática (AD) has kept a strong interest in the development of the Sandinista revolution even though there has been a change of emphasis within the party leadership.[20] Given Venezuela's economic possibilities, it was obvious that among its instruments employed to gain influence in Central America, financial aid was by far of greatest importance. The San José oil protocol has been the largest single effort, but direct financial aid also has been provided to various countries.[21]

The more independent line evolving in Venezuela's foreign policy since the Malvinas conflict, as demonstrated by Herrera Campins' visit to Managua on the third anniversary of the Sandinista revolution, must also be seen in the context of the 1983 elections in Venezuela. In addition, it shows in the failure of previous policies to foster the desired change in Central America.

Cuba—A Regional Power Through Ideology

Cuba's foreign-policy posture is basically a strategy for the survival of its revolution. Cuba, since its revolution, has been forced to turn to the other superpower to ensure its survival. This has colored all foreign-policy initiatives of the Castro regime. A main current of its foreign-policy is antiimperialism, understood as confronting the United States, which has refused recognition to its revolution, and offering internationalist help to other Third World countries. Cuba's effort to assume a role of Third World leadership has greatly increased its regional-power status, especially vis-à-vis other revolutionary movements and postrevolutionary countries.

The perception of the Central American crisis by the Cuban leadership has been quite consistent over a long period of time.[22] Contacts between Central American guerrilla groups and the Cubans go back to the early 1960s. Central American guerrilla leaders always had the opportunity to get training and, to a certain extent, material assistance, but mainly ideological help from Havana. Cuba's principal advice to the different guerrilla groups in Nicaragua, El Salvador, and Guatemala has been to find a unifying concept and leadership and to look for political alliances with other groups before trying to overthrow established governments. Since 1978 and 1979, assistance to such groups has been upgraded, but at the same time Cubans have made it very clear that a revolution in any of the Central American countries would have to be made by the country's own political forces and could only be aided from the outside.[23] Their own postrevolutionary problems have convinced the Cuban leadership that it is necessary to upgrade all types of aid to stabilize or to help to avoid destabilization in a country once the revolution has succeeded. The extraordinarily high level of military, educational, and even economic aid and the large numbers of advisers in Nicaragua are the best example for that strategy.

Cuba's involvement in El Salvador has been much more limited; it has consisted mainly of propagandistic and some logistic help to the guerrillas, as well as the facilitating of arms transfer, which has led to a very serious preoccupation on the part of the United States.[24] Cuba's own assessments—with regard to the chances that processes similar to that of Nicaragua could be evolving in El Salvador or Guatemala—are rather careful. Cuba, which obviously favors such changes, views them as long term in nature and is very much aware of the fact that, since the Nicaraguan revolution, the countervailing forces have gained ground since the Reagan administration came to power.

With regard to the policy instruments used in Central America, it is very difficult to find reliable data. Aside from the large numbers of doctors, teachers, and advisers on all levels of government working in Nicaragua, very little is known about the engagement in other countries. Most information is available only from U.S. sources and demonstrates a strong interest in blaming Cuba for the development of the Central American crisis. Cuba's role differs from that of any other regional power because it is seen by the United States and by some of the governments in Central America as a proxy of the Soviet Union and has therefore to move with extreme caution.

It is by no means clear that Cuba's interest lies in furthering virulent revolutionary changes. It advised its political friends in El Salvador to support the first junta of October 1979, and it has stressed over and over again in Nicaragua that the Sandinistas should not cut off relations with the United States or other Western countries because they would need help from and trade with the West to develop a viable new society. Indeed, Cuba's role in Central America might better be described as counseling restraint to revolutionary groups and the postrevolutionary government, since it is fully aware of the risks involved in further radicalization and militarization of the region.[25] A regional war endangering the survival of the Nicaraguan revolution would present the Cuban leadership with the critical choice between performing its "internationalist duties" and safeguarding its national security.

Colombia—A Regional Power Through Association

Colombia's foreign-policy profile traditionally has been very low.[26] Aside from some activity within the Andean Pact, Colombia has not shown much interest in foreign affairs in general, being until 1982 almost an unquestioning ally of the United States. Colombia's perception of the Central American crisis is shaped by three different factors:

1. It had to face over a long period of time the activities of different guerrilla groups. The type of revolutionary change that it is witnessing in Central America is therefore seen as a possible threat, especially in the context of the perceived "Cuban connection" of its own guerrilla forces.

2. Its relationship with Nicaragua, which was characterized in the final days of Somoza by a certain willingness to aid the Sandinistas and to participate in the Andean Pact initiatives to recognize the legitimacy of the Nicaraguan revolution, has been severely strained by the declaration of the Sandinista government in 1980 of its interest in reopening the discussion on sovereignty for the San Andrés Islands.

3. Its perception of Central America is directly related to its continuing interest in Panama, which was part of its territory until 1903. The Panama Canal is still considered one of the most important foreign-policy issues, and therefore anything that happens on the isthmus and in which Panama is remotely involved receives close attention.

The type of interaction that exists between Central America and Colombia has not reflected a great deal of foreign-policy concern so far. When the Nassau Group was conceived in 1981, even the United States left Colombia out of its original design of cooperative action with regional powers. The only demonstration of interest came when Colombia, together with Venezuela and the United States, became a guarantor country for the Comunidad Democrática Centroamericana (CDC—Central American Democratic Community).[27]

Colombia's inclusion in the group of the regional powers reflects partly the possibility of instrumentation by the United States and the increased leverage that comes with a position of such a political alignment and partly the willingness of the Betancur government to play a greater and more independent role from now on. Because of the previous close ideological identification with the Central American policies of the United States, Colombia's position as a regional power was not unlike Cuba's with regard to the autonomy of its decision making and the range of its policy options. Both certainly have national interests to pursue, but both owe—to a different degree—part of their impact upon the region to their superpower connections.

THE COMMUNITY OF INTERESTS
AND THE DIVERSITY OF OBJECTIVES

Comparing the activities of the four regional powers in Central America leads to rather strange results. Not only are two of the regional powers, Cuba and Colombia, relying on the two superpowers for at least part of their influence, but the other two regional powers, Mexico and Venezuela, are also using outside support—in this case transnational groups—as important means for achieving their desired regional position. This close interaction of subgovernmental transnational political organizations might have in the long run the greatest impact on political developments in Central America. Cuba can at least count on some of the small but usually active Communist parties and most guerrilla groups in the region, whereas Colombia is lacking any type of such an intrastate influence structure.

Assuming that the creation of a new type of political order in most Central American countries will take a long time, such rather limited and usually noneconomic, more technical and ideological influence might prove of greater impact than other forms of the state-to-state aid that depend not only on the actual economic capacity of any one of the four regional powers but also on their internal political power balance. The obvious disadvantage of such transnational relations is that they are much less calculable; more state-centered foreign policies—as in the case of Cuba and Mexico—demonstrate a higher degree of permanence.

So far all four of the regional powers have worked with a very different timing in the development and use of their policy instruments in Central America. It is almost impossible to evaluate their respective successes given the specific style of their foreign-policy behavior and the frequent absence of declared objectives. It seems hardly possible to distinguish between what is really aid and what constitutes an act of intervention in the region. No matter how much all regional actors talk about nonintervention, they all do intervene in a more or less open fashion—Cuba and Venezuela at times even in military matters—sometimes only to serve their own national interests, sometimes also to serve other countries' global interests. Given the importance of the Central American crisis for the East-West and North-South dimensions in the international system, the regional powers in the last four years have come to the same conclusion the United States has always taken for granted: Central America cannot be left alone to develop autonomously.[28]

All four regional powers share the conviction that the old order in Central America has outlived its time. They are all willing to work toward the estabishment of a new order, but do not agree about the nature of it. Cuba and Mexico are willing to aid or at least accept the development of one-party systems, whereas Venezuela and Colombia want a pluralistic new order to evolve in the region. This concept of a new order should not be seen only with regard to the internal order of postrevolutionary regimes in Central America, but also in a wider sense as a perspective of a new regional subsystem, which will be a great deal less influenced by the United States. The loosening of the U.S. hegemony in the subregion is a goal all regional powers are striving for, but they cannot agree on the ways and means in which this could be achieved.

For two of the regional powers, Mexico and Cuba, the anti-U.S. content of their policies in Central America seems to be of overriding importance. The other two are less outspoken and even appear to be supportive of some U.S. policies, depending on the priorities of the party in power. All four nations are aware of the relative decline of U.S. power and therefore want to use this opportunity to demonstrate their own foreign-policy capabilities. If indeed a new regional subsystem would develop, including not only Central America proper but possibly the entire Caribbean Basin, all four could gain immensely, since it would at the same time demonstrate a major setback for the superpowers' geopolitical control.

One of the strongest motivations for exercising influence in Central America originates from the competition between the different political and economic systems of the regional powers themselves. Nicaragua is an excellent case in point, because of the efforts of Cuba, Mexico, and—at times—Venezuela to convince the Sandinistas about the advantages of their respective political and economic systems. The way to do that is certainly not by the direct approach, but by the flow of human and/or financial resources, which is meant to demonstrate the built-in strength of any of the systems and to initiate a subtle process of imitation. Given the clear differences among the political systems of Cuba, Venezuela, and Mexico and the almost diametrically opposed development priorities resulting from the economic models of Cuba and Venezuela, it is easy to see how the regional powers' advice will differ for the Central American states. The severe economic crisis of 1982 will force Mexico to limit the transfer of resources but not its political resourcefulness in dealing with the region's crisis.

With regard to the internal dimensions, the community of interests among the regional powers becomes much more blurred. All four have to take into consideration the impact of their foreign-policy actions upon their internal balance of power, their economic performance, and their national security. Given the systemic political continuity of Cuba and Mexico, such considerations do not seem quite as evident as in the case of the democracies in Venezuela and Colombia, but they are by no means of less importance.

In the case of Mexico, the very clear function of a "progressive" foreign-policy posture for the co-optation and integration of left-leaning groups, whose demands cannot be met internally, is well known. An interpretation of Mexico's actions in Central America from that viewpoint alone is hardly convincing, but a strong argument can be made that especially in times of internal economic and social strife, the Mexican regime will rely upon an active, anti-U.S. foreign policy to demonstrate its revolutionary capacity. A similar line of thought seems to be suitable for Venezuela, whose two main parties have always tried to pacify their left wings with a nationalist, often anti-U.S. foreign policy. Such considerations have not been necessary for the two traditional Colombian parties, since until recently foreign policy in general has not been much of an issue for their followers. To what extent the Cuban leadership attempts to balance internal disenchantment with foreign-policy successes is very difficult to assess.

The economic dimension of the regional powers' interests seems to be rather insignificant. Mexico is the only one with some foreign investments in Central America, and Cuba would be the only one that could possibly profit from increased trade with the region in the case of further establishment of revolutionary regimes. Venezuela's and Colombia's economic interactions with these countries are marginal and will likely continue to be so.

The problems for the regional powers' own national security that evolve from their Central American policy are more a matter of perception than of measurable facts. Of all regional powers, Cuba feels the most affected and Venezuela the least. Given the general U.S. pressure against Cuba and the specific threats from the Reagan administration "to go to the source," it is no secret that Havana is most preoccupied with the possible retaliation by the United States in case of further revolutionary activity in Central America. It was for this very reason that Cuba wanted to cooperate with Mexico in an effort to find diplomatic solutions for the complicated political problems of El Salvador and of Nicaragua.[29] More than any other regional power Cuba has risked a great deal by assisting the guerrilla movements and the Sandinista government in Nicaragua.

For Mexico, the national-security implications are of an altogether different nature. Many U.S. analysts who like to see Mexico as the "last domino" in the Soviet-Cuban strategy to "roll up" Central America are preoccupied with the external threat Mexico's own sympathetic handling of the revolutionary movements in Central America might create.[30] The Mexicans themselves seem to be much less convinced that this will be their national-security problem—they are counting on their ability to deal with the new regimes as they have been able to deal with Cuba since its revolution. Their own reading of national-security problems originating from the Central American crisis is threefold: the wave of refugees, which has already reached Mexico and is steadily increasing; the danger that a regional war might break out, which would force Mexico to take sides officially or unofficially; and the effect the ongoing militarization of the region will have on their own military, whose political weight within the system has been rather reduced.[31]

For Colombia, the main concern is the "demonstration effect" that the revolution in Nicaragua and the civil war in El Salvador have had on its own guerrilla forces. The Turbay government tended to agree with the domino strategists in the United States, that there is not only a northern domino, Mexico, but also a southern one, Colombia, included in the Soviet-Cuban regional destablization design. Inasmuch as revolutionary developments in Central America can be stopped, Colombia counts on improving its own national-security situation.

After the successful political reintegration of the most prominent members of its former guerrilla groups, Venezuela sees no danger of a spillover effect from Central American revolutions. Its only security preoccupation would be the regionalization of a Central American war, in which Venezuelan troops might be asked to participate by one or another country.

Such a comparison of the different perceptions of the Central American crisis by the regional powers already shows the diversity of objectives among them. This can partly be explained by the short-term versus the long-term objectives of the four regional powers. Cuba and Mexico, again for systemic reasons, are much less preoccupied with the short-term effects of the crisis, since their foreign-policy planning is oriented toward long-term objectives. Venezuela and Colombia have less institutionalized foreign-policy processes and feel the immediate consequences upon their internal political systems. Closely interrelated are their positions on such central questions as the most promising methods for social change in Central America. The concepts of negotiations versus elections divide them along the same lines; Mexico and Cuba favor negotiations, whereas Venezuela and Colombia believe in elections as the most important measure to bring about the desired social change and some political stability in the region.

Another important diversity of objectives among them results from the entirely different threat perceptions held among them. Mexico and Cuba, for good historical reasons, see the main threat not only for their own autonomous development but also for Central America's future in U.S. policies. Venezuela and Colombia, on the other hand, are convinced that Cuba—and the Soviet Union—pose a serious threat to them as well as to the Central American countries. From such a position, it is understandable that Mexico would find it acceptable to see one or more socialist countries evolve after the Central American turmoil, since it sincerely believes in the possibility of integrating and not isolating such regimes in its own neighborhood, whereas Venezuela and Colombia feel that such a development might endanger the stability of a future regional subsystem.

THE PROJECTIONS OF POWER AND THE LIMITS OF INFLUENCE

The future impact of the regional powers will be measured not only by their "success" in influencing the outcomes of the Central American crisis but also by their ability to cooperate with one another. So far, only Mexico, Venezuela, and Colombia agree on each others' legitimate interests in Central America. Cuba's role is only sometimes accepted by Mexico and by Venezuela. Since the current role of the regional powers in the regional schemes inspired by the United States, such as the Caribbean Basin Initiative and the Central American Democratic Community, is by no means cooperative, it is difficult to imagine another division of labor between them as in 1978 and 1979 in their coordinated actions to facilitate the success of the Nicaraguan revolution.

The internationalization of the Central American crisis has led to the formation of three competing political tendencies:[32]

- *The status quo alliance:* United States, Colombia, the Christian Democratic World Union, Israel, and the governments of Guatemala, El Salvador, Honduras, and Costa Rica
- *The social-change alliance:* Mexico, the Socialist International, France, Panama, and Venezuela (since the Malvinas conflict)
- *The revolutionary-change alliance:* Cuba, the socialist countries, Libya, the Palestine Liberation Organization (PLO), Nicaragua, and the guerrilla movements

Since the leadership of the three tendencies is divided between the United States and two of the regional powers, the capability of the latter to form alliances among themselves becomes rather restricted. The situation is further complicated because different ideological groups from the same country—as in the case of Venezuela—participate in alliances whose policies toward Central America are mutually exclusive. The limits of influence are reached at the very moment when a national consensus over foreign policies in Central America cannot be reached anymore and/or instrumentation by one of the superpowers occurs.

There can be little doubt that any close identification of a regional power's policies toward Central America with one of the superpowers will in the long run lead to decreasing credibility, even though it increases the immediate impact upon current developments. A loss of credibility in the region can also occur for two additional reasons. One is the discontinuity of a policy posture—a problem that exists for Venezuela as well as for Colombia. The other is overcommitment, which leads to the suspicion of the establishment of a new patron-client relationship, a problem that Cuba seems to be faced with in Nicaragua.

The problem of to what extent a commitment to a new order in Central America should be made is closely related to the risks the regional powers are willing to take: internally, economically, and with regard to the alliance problems they might create by choosing sides in the Central American conflict. The latter problem reflects especially on the dependence situation of any of the countries. Cuba's risks in that respect are lower, because its positions seem to be widely accepted within the socialist countries. The other three are risking more in trying—at times—to formulate their own objectives, for which they will receive at best partial backing from some groups or countries in the West. They find it most difficult therefore to reconcile their First World ties with their Third World identity. If their initiatives fail, their regional-power status will suffer greatly. This is especially true for Mexico, which has no other foreign-policy area—aside from its bilateral relationship with the United States—of such vital importance to look after. It seems therefore very likely that Central America will be given top priority by Mexican policymakers almost regardless of other foreign-policy adjustments the government of Miguel de la Madrid might have to make in the context of reduced economic and political capabilities.[33]

During the 1970s, the two main external actors in the region were the United States and Cuba. Both developed a strong interest in cooperating with the two most important regional powers, Mexico and Venezuela, to advance their own influence. They both succeeded in doing so at times. Given their extreme positions with regard to the solutions advanced for the turmoil in Central America and the implications for the East-West conflict, it would appear highly unlikely that either one of them will have its way. Leaning toward a "third way" and pressuring for regional rather than global solutions of the crisis, Venezuela, Mexico, and to a lesser extent Colombia are in a prominent position to strengthen their role as regional powers and to evolve as major international actors in a possible future regional subsystem.

ACKNOWLEDGMENTS

This chapter has benefited greatly from the comments of Bruce Bagley, Enrique Baloyra, Esperanza Duran, Wayne A. Selcher, Helga Strasser, and Edward J. Williams. All errors or misconceptions are obviously mine.

NOTES

1. See "Argentina ofrece ayuda militar al gobierno Salvadoreño," *El Pais*, March 20, 1981; "Argentina Hovers on the Brink of Central American Adventure," *Latin America Weekly Report*, February 12, 1982, pp. 1–2.

2. About thirty-five Argentine advisers are still in Central America. For a detailed description of the Argentine role, see Christopher Dickey, "Argentine Defector Tells of Multinational Plots for Sandinistas' Ouster," *Washington Post,* December 2, 1982.

3. See the interesting approaches by Luis Maira, "The Policy of the Medium Sized Countries of Latin America with Regard to the English-speaking Caribbean: The Cases of Mexico, Venezuela and Cuba," paper prepared for the conference "Democracy and Development in the Caribbean," Center for Inter-American Relations, New York, May 6–8, 1979.

4. See Francisco Orrego Vicuña (ed.), *América Latina: Clase media de las naciones?* (Santiago: Universidad de Chile, 1979); and Wolf Grabendorff, "Perspectivas y polos de desarrollo en América Latina," *Estudios Internacionales* 13, no. 50 (April–June 1980), pp. 252–278.

5. For a conceptional framework of the role of regional powers in the Third World, see Raimo Väyrynen, "Economic and Military Position of the Regional Power Centers," *Journal of Peace Research* 16, no. 4 (1979), pp. 349–369.

6. For the origins of the Nassau Group, see *Estados Unidos, Perspectiva Latinoamericana* 6, no. 11 (November 1981), pp. 123–125. For the concept of the Comunidad Democrática Centroamericana (CDC), see "Central America: Few Cheers for Democracy," *Latin America Weekly Report,* January 29, 1982, pp. 2–4.

7. For a different assessment, see Wolf Grabendorff, "Cuba's Involvement in Africa: An Interpretation of Objectives, Reactions, and Limitations," *Journal of Interamerican Studies and World Affairs* 22, no. 1 (February 1980), pp. 3–29. For the best treatment of the issue, see Carmelo Mesa-Lago and June S. Belkin (eds.), *Cuba in Africa* (Pittsburgh: Center for Latin American Studies, 1982).

8. The comparison of Latin American regional powers—generally understood to comprise Mexico, Brazil, Venezuela, and Argentina—with regard to their specific regional policies has been done only recently. The pioneer work of Luis Maira, "The Policy of the Medium Sized Countries of Latin America," and the paper by Vaughan Lewis, "The Commonwealth Caribbean Countries, Diplomatic Decolonisation and Relocation: Relations with Hemispheric Middle Powers," Working Paper no. 96, Latin American Program, The Wilson Center, Washington, D.C., 1981, have been particularly helpful for my own research.

9. See Wolf Grabendorff, "Mexico's Foreign Policy—Indeed a Foreign Policy? Review Essay," *Journal of Interamerican Studies and World Affairs* 20, no. 1 (February 1978), pp. 85–92. Olga Pellicer de Brody states clearly: "Left-leaning diplomacy helps to maintain Mexico's political stability" in "Mexico's Position," *Foreign Policy,* no. 43 (Summer 1981), pp. 88–92.

10. So José López Portillo in his speech in Managua, February 21, 1982: "Los mexicanos queremos ser útiles, queremos conducto, enlace, comunicación entre quienes han dejado de hablarse o quienes nunca lo han hecho" (We Mexicans want to be helpful; we want to facilitate communication among those who have stopped speaking or never have spoken), *El Día,* February 22, 1982.

11. See the declaration by López Portillo, "Sexto Informe Presidencial," *Comercio Exterior* 32, no. 9 (September 1982), pp. 919–941.

12. "The historic coincidence of the Central American crisis with the appearance of the new petroleum wealth in Mexico has supplied the conditions for a new Mexican policy in the region," René Herrera Zuñiga and Mario Ojeda, "Mexican Foreign Policy and Central America," in Richard F. Feinberg (ed.), *Central America: International Dimensions of the Crisis* (New York: Holmes & Meir, 1982), pp. 160–186.

13. See López Portillo's speech in Managua, *El Día*, February 22, 1982; and Guadalupe Pacheco Méndez, "Centroamérica en la política exterior Mexicana 1981–1982," *Cuadernos Políticos*, no. 32 (April–June 1982), pp. 57–67.

14. For the history and intentions of COPPPAL see Neira Moreira, "La Conferencia de Oaxaca," *Cuadernos del Tercer Mundo*, no. 35 (December 1979–January 1980), pp. 7–17.

15. See Edward J. Williams, "Mexico's Central American Policy: Revolutionary and Prudential Dimensions," paper presented at the Annual Meeting of the Caribbean Studies Association, St. Thomas, May 26–30, 1981; and Bruce Bagley, "Mexico in the 1980's: A New Regional Power," *Current History* 80, no. 469 (November 1981), pp. 353–356, 386, 393–394.

16. For a detailed description of Mexican aid to Central America, see "La nueva dimensión de la política exterior de México," *Informe Relaciones México–Estados Unidos* 1, no. 1 (October 1981), pp. 111–124.

17. "En Centroamérica nuestra acción debe ser interrumpida, pluralista y con seguimientos adecuados. América Central ha sido de manera inevitable un área para la acción internacional inmediata de México. No es, pues, consequente, aceptar ningún cambio radical cerca de las fronteras de México sin que se escuche nuestra voz" (In Central America, our action must be smooth, multifaceted, and with adequate fellowship. Central America, inevitably, has been an area for immediate international action by Mexcio. It is not possible, therefore, to accept any radical change on our borders without having our voice heard), José Juan de Olloqui, "El diseño de la política exterior de México: Sus objectivos y dos casos específicos," *Informe Relaciones México–Estados Unidos* 1, no. 2 (February–June 1982), pp. 186–205.

18. See Robert D. Bond, "Venezuelan Policy in the Caribbean Basin," in Feinberg, *Central America*, pp. 187–200.

19. For the relationship between ideology and foreign policy, see Donald L. Heyman, "Ideology, Economic Power, and Regional Imperialism: The Determinants of Foreign Policy Under Venezuela's Christian Democrats," *Caribbean Studies* 18, no. 1-2 (April–July 1978), pp. 43–83; and Chapter 9 by John D. Martz.

20. For the background of the change of AD's policy in support of the Sandinistas, see "The Case of the Hidden Hand," *Latin America Weekly Report*, April 2, 1982, pp. 7–8.

21. Venezuela's support for Central American countries began with a meeting of Central American presidents invited by Carlos Andrés Pérez to Puerto Ordaz, December 13, 1974. See *La Política Internacional de Carlos Andrés Pérez*, vol. 1 (Caracas: Imprenta Nacional, 1980), pp. 173–176.

22. For Cuba's role in the Central American crisis, see W. Raymond Duncan, "Cuba in the Caribbean and Central America: Limits to Influence," paper prepared for the Annual Meeting of the Caribbean Studies Association, St. Thomas, May 26–30, 1982; Jiri Valenta, "Soviet and Cuban Responses to New Opportunities in Central America," in Feinberg, *Central America*, pp. 127–139; and Juan M. del Aguila, "Cuba's Foreign Policy in the Caribbean and Central America" in Elizabeth G. Ferris and Jennie K. Lincoln (eds.), *Latin American Foreign Policies: Global and Regional Dimensions* (Boulder, Colo.: Westview Press, 1981), pp. 211–221.

23. See William M. LeoGrande, "Cuba," in Robert Wesson (ed.), *Communism in Central America and the Caribbean* (Stanford: The Hoover Institution, 1982), pp. 31–51.

24. See U.S. Department of State, "El Salvador: Communist Interference and a Brief Background," *Department of State Bulletin* 81, no. 2048 (March 1981), pp. 1–11; and *Cuba's Renewed Support for Violence in Latin America*, Special Report no. 90 (Washington, D.C.: U.S. Department of State, Bureau of Public Affairs, December 14, 1981).

25. Cuba has not only counseled against radicalization in Nicaragua (see LeoGrande, "Cuba," p. 43), but also offered to talk directly with the United States about its role in the Central American crisis, as revealed by the former U.S. representative in Havana, Wayne S. Smith, *Washington Post*, September 5, 1982.

26. See Gerhard Drekonja Kornat, *Colombia: Política Exterior* (Bogotá: Universidad de los Andes, Fundación Friedrich Ebert de Colombia [FESCOL], La Editora Ltda., 1982). For a detailed discussion of the changes of Colombia's foreign-policy postures from the low-profile approach of President Julio Cesar Turbay Ayala to the activist stand of President Belisario Betancur, see Bruce M. Bagley, "Colombia in the Caribbean: America's Staunchest Ally?" (Washington, D.C.: School of Advanced International Studies, Johns Hopkins University, October 1982).

27. Some initiatives are described by Gerhard Drekonja Kornat, "Definiciones, contenidos, metas: Una comparación de la política caribeña de Colombia con las de México, Venezuela, y Brasil," paper presented at the International Conference about Colombia and the Caribbean, Universidad de los Andes, Bogotá, July 2–4, 1982, pp. 14–16.

28. This is the view expressed by Howard J. Wiarda, "The Central American Crisis: A Framework for Understanding," *American Enterprise Institute Foreign Policy and Defense Review* 4, no. 2 (1982), pp. 2–7.

29. See Wayne S. Smith, "Dateline Havana: Myopic Diplomacy," *Foreign Policy*, no. 48 (Fall 1982), pp. 157–174.

30. See especially Constantine Menges, *Current Mexican Foreign Policy and United States Interests* (Washington, D.C.: Hudson Institute, 1980); and Carlos Rangel, "Mexico and Other Dominoes," *Commentary* 71, no. 6 (June 1981), pp. 27–33.

31. See Olga Pellicer de Brody, "La seguridad nacional de México," *Cuadernos Políticos*, no. 27 (January–March 1981), pp. 23–34; and the perceptive analysis by Edward J. Williams, "Mexico's Central American Policy: National Security Considerations," paper presented at the 44th International Congress of Americanists, Manchester, England, September 1982.

32. See Wolf Grabendorff, "Mittelamerika als internationale Krisengregion," *Europa-Archiv* 37, no. 8 (April 25, 1982), pp. 247–258.

33. Miguel de la Madrid has already confirmed his intentions to continue the policy of his predecessor in Central America: "Nuestra destino como nación soberana e independiente esta ligado indisolublemente a lo que ocurra en toda la región. . . . Estamos dispuestas a contribuir a que no se postulen soluciones de fuerza o de violencia en la región y a que se resuelvan los conflictos del área mediante vias pacíficas, democráticas y legales" (Our destiny as an independent and sovereign nation is indissolubly linked to what transpires in the entire region. We are disposed to act to ensure that there are no solutions through violence or force and that all conflicts in the region are solved through peaceful, democratic, and legal means). See "La política exterior de México: 1982–1988," *PROA* 1, no. 3 (June/July 1982), pp. 12–16.

7. Recent Strategic Developments in South America's Southern Cone

CONTINENTAL TENDENCIES IN SOUTH AMERICA

The last decade witnessed consequential changes in the international relations among South American countries. The United States remained the single-most-important extraregional actor, yet its influence in South American affairs lessened because of competing national and transnational actors, official Washington's concentration on perceived threats in the rest of Latin America, growing local capabilities, and national assertiveness that tended to reject U.S. leadership. Japanese and West European economic involvement in South America increased, and even such conservative regimes as those of Chile and Argentina are now looking to the Soviet Union and China for trade and technical cooperation opportunities. In spite of the attempts of the Reagan administration to court Argentina and Chile as cold war allies, both of these governments remain willing to separate their support for domestic suppression of communists in Latin America from their intense economic dealings with Eastern Europe and China.[1]

Brazil's continental role has grown to clear primacy, but without arousing an anti-Brazilian anxiety among its neighbors. Brazil's very size will continue to compel a special concern on the part of its neighbors for the effects of its policies and actions. Yet President João Baptista Figueiredo's active and able Latin American summit diplomacy has been well received and has resulted in a network of cooperative agreements and official understandings that have largely dispelled earlier suspicions. As part of its Third World emphasis, Brasília has pursued policies that, as a side effect, have encouraged political and economic cooperation among South American countries. Argentine-Brazilian rapprochement in particular, dating from 1980, would, if continued, hold strong implications for the continental balance of power, which for decades has assumed rivalry between the two countries. Such an alliance could conceivably either counterbalance waning U.S. influence in the continent (in a way similar to the aims of the Mexico City–Caracas partnership in the Caribbean and Central America), spur regional economic integration, or (improbably) strive for a shared continental hegemony. At the very least, a major focus of tension will have been eased.

Both the Andean Pact and the Latin American Free Trade Association (LAFTA) failed to fulfill their economic purposes, with the latter replaced in 1980 by the Latin American Integration Association, which gives somewhat more favor to exceptions and bilateral complementary accords than did LAFTA. The formation of the Amazon Pact in 1978, although not an integrationist measure because of the small degree of sovereignty yielded up, highlighted the geopolitical significance of the occupation of the center of the continent, led by Brazil, with attendant possibilities for cooperation and conflict in a new arena.

The Malvinas war of early 1982 brought general world attention in a dramatic way to unsettled territorial conflicts, recent increased purchases and local manufacture of weaponry suitable for international war, and the addition of the South Atlantic to the effective geopolitical agenda of the continent. Like the 1978–1979 height of Chilean-Argentine tensions over the Beagle Channel and the 1981 Peruvian-Ecuadorian border skirmish, the Malvinas war demonstrated that with hopes of quick victory buoyed by new military hardware, civilian and military governments might take the opportunity to settle old territorial disputes or rivalries by threat or use of force. South American governments in their heterogeneity have cast aside former U.S. guidance in formulation of international-security doctrines in order to develop their own, thus creating a more complicated security relationship on the continent, without an apparent consensus and certainly without a conflict-resolution system of its own.

Although it might be superficially satisfying in the early 1980s to draw a North-South distinction between the "peaceful" democracies of the North and the "aggressive," geopolitically minded military governments of the Southern Cone, with the Brazilian *abertura* (liberalization) as a third model, such a regime distinction does not explain the skirmish between Peru and Ecuador. The strengthening of Venezuela's air force, for another example, appears ominous to Guyana and Colombia, both with border disputes with Venezuela. The emergence of a more autonomous international politics in South America could well be more, rather than less, likely to give play to the relevance of local tensions between governments of whatever type, particularly since both Washington and Moscow are now less credible external threats or causes for unity. Nor is Washington's policy a negating restraint on willingness to engage in conflict, as it once was.

THE SOUTHERN CONE SUBSYSTEM

The Southern Cone of South America is of the greatest importance in analyzing continental balance-of-power maneuvers in both political and military terms. This region has been identified as particularly conflict prone, because it is the setting for numerous frontier disputes, resource conflicts, and the two major axes of historical interstate rivalry on the continent (Chile-Argentina and Argentina-Brazil).[2] In terms of capability for organized violence should peaceful settlement fail, the Southern Cone defined in a larger sense (i.e., including Brazil) takes in much of the technologically sophisticated and upper-income sector of all of Latin America, as well as 49 percent of its population, 56 percent of its economic product, 42 percent of its arms imports, and 53 percent of its military expenditures in recent years.[3] Of the various possible geo-political divisions of South America—Southern Cone, Andean Region, Amazon Basin, River Plate Basin—the Southern Cone concept takes in the greatest number of significant actors that constitute a loose but active subsystem.[4]

Within the Southern Cone, the greatest influence has been exerted by Brazil, Argentina, and Chile, in that order, with Bolivia, Paraguay, and Uruguay serving as both buffer states and zones of competition between Argentina and Brazil. A rough index of the economic weight of each of the ABC powers (Argentina-Brazil-Chile) in the region and of regional interdependence in economic interaction can be deduced from the pattern of trade flows. Greater volumes of trade flows imply higher levels of economic cooperation. It would not be appropriate to infer political-influence relationships directly from commercial statistics, however, even though much of the diplomacy of the region is still concerned with fostering trade and other economic relationships. (It would be well to remember also that flows of legal trade do not reflect the considerable contraband trade, notoriously high in Bolivia and Paraguay.)

Table 7.1 shows the relative weight of the three larger states as a percentage of the total trade flow (exports plus imports) of each of the other five states in the subsystem, 1976–1980. Beyond Brazil's general predominance, the marginal position of Chile, and the lack of radical redirection of trade among the three largest states, several features stand out in the raw statistics and this proportional format. Southern Cone markets are considerably more important for Argentina than for Brazil, partly because of the latter's dependence on petroleum from other developing countries. There has been no significant change in the relative weight of Argentine-Brazilian trade in the global transactions of the pair, but they remain important markets to each other and contribute by far the largest bilateral flow by value in the region. Chilean-Argentine trade has declined markedly from the perspective of both partners, most likely as a result of the political tensions over the Beagle Channel dispute. During the period, Brazil rose from fourth place to third in Chile's trade picture, becoming its most important Latin American trading partner. This advance occurred more as a result of decreased Chilean trade with West Germany and Argentina than of a Chilean turn to Brazil as an economic option, as a conventional interpretation of ABC politics might lead one to expect.

Table 7.1.: The Trade Salience of Argentina-Brazil-Chile (the ABC Powers) in the Southern Cone, 1967–1980, as Percent of Total Trade Flow

Trade Salience of (A)	with (B)	1976	1977	1978	1979	1980
Argentina	Brazil	3.4%	3.5%	3.4%	4.9%	4.3%
	Chile	9.1	9.4	7.1	5.5	5.0
	Paraguay	15.4	14.8	12.7	17.1	21.8
	Uruguay	8.2	9.0	8.9	15.7	11.8
	Bolivia	18.8	16.1	13.4	13.3	18.6
Brazil	Argentina	11.4%	8.5%	9.0%	10.6%	9.9%
	Chile	8.4	8.8	9.4	9.3	8.7
	Paraguay	11.6	13.1	14.5	17.1	21.9
	Uruguay	14.3	14.1	15.2	18.7	17.7
	Bolivia	8.7	6.2	6.7	11.8	11.9
Chile	Argentina	4.7%	4.5%	3.7%	2.9%	2.5%
	Brazil	1.5	1.8	1.7	2.2	2.0
	Paraguay	2.5	2.1	2.9	1.4	1.9
	Uruguay	1.4	1.0	1.2	1.5	1.6
	Bolivia	1.8	2.2	2.9	2.5	4.0

$$\text{Trade Salience} = \frac{\text{B's exports \& imports to/from A}}{\text{B's total exports \& imports}}$$

Source: International Monetary Fund. *Direction of Trade Statistics Yearbook, 1982.* Washington, D.C.: IMF, 1982.

Southern Cone markets play the largest role in the trade of the three buffer states. Chile is a small commercial factor in those three countries, which have all increased the combined weight of Brazil and Argentina in their foreign trade picture. By 1980, 30 percent of Bolivia and Uruguay's trade was carried on with the two large countries, and 44 percent of Paraguay's trade, an intensification likely to continue at a moderate rate in all three cases, with an increase in Argentine-Brazilian commercial competiton. Over the period, Uruguay tended to favor Brazil as a commercial partner, Bolivia leaned toward Argentina, and Paraguay divided its trade nearly evenly.

Customary geopolitical interpretations hold that Chile and Brazil use their relationship, albeit discretely, to counterbalance the rivalry each one has with Argentina. In point of fact, Chile in recent years has been much more willing to play that sort of card than Brazil has, because Brazil prefers to avoid problems with Argentina in areas of the latter's highly nationalistic sensibilities, such as the Beagle Channel. Brazil's general policy is one of neutrality in others' border disputes. Argentina, on the other hand, was willing in the 1970s to use Spanish American concerns about historic Brazilian expansionism, its "geopolitical ambitions," or the alleged principle of "flexible borders" to counterbalance Brazil's growing continental predominance. Within this balance-of-political-power system, Argentine overtures to Andean Pact countries in the mid-1970s were claimed by many observers to be aimed at containing Brazil's influence. Brazil's subsequent proposal for an Amazon Pact was interpreted in part as a means to create a northern subcontinental grouping including Andean Pact members but not Argentina. Argentina would thus be limited to the Río de la Plata organization for subcontinental multilateral diplomacy while Brazil acted in both forums.

The three small buffer states, for their part, have characteristically maneuvered to avoid falling completely into the orbit of either Argentina or Brazil. Most observers of Southern Cone politics, nevertheless, feel that at present Bolivia leans toward Argentina, Paraguay is clearly in the Brazilian sphere, and Uruguay is about evenly balanced (with a light trade preference for Brazil). The economic activities of both Argentina and Brazil have increased greatly in all three states since about 1970. The most marked change has been the growth of Brazilian influence in eastern Paraguay as a consequence of the Brazilian-led construction of the Itaipu Dam, agricultural colonization of the region by large numbers of Brazilians, and smuggling of goods between Paraguay and Brazil.

ISSUES AT CONTENTION IN THE SOUTHERN CONE

The most contentious recent issues in the Southern Cone have involved a combination of territorial and resource matters that were interpreted by the parties involved as embodying principles and procedures tending to affect the outcome of future territory and resource claims. Thus the parties were willing to invest strategic and geopolitical significance in the acts and outcomes to a point well beyond the worth of the real estate itself, which is one of the hallmarks of national-security diplomacy. The as yet unresolved Beagle Channel and Malvinas Islands disputes, with Argentina on the offensive, have been the most volatile and ominous for the future of international relations in the Southern Cone. Both have been rallying cries and points of honor eliciting strong emotional reactions in Argentina and Chile. Because of its broader impact on the region, the Malvinas case will be examined separately.

Argentina-Chile

The Beagle Channel dispute ostensibly concerns possession of three small and barren islands (Picton, Nueva, and Lennox) at the eastern end of the channel, which links the Atlantic and Pacific oceans above Cape Horn.[5] The islands are now held by Chile but have been strenuously claimed by Argentina since boundary lines in the region were established rather imprecisely by treaty a century ago. The argument turns upon the delineation of where the Beagle Channel runs; the 1881 treaty used the channel as a boundary line, but it failed to stipulate the exact location of the channel among a number of islands. The strategic issues at stake in alternative cartographies are these.

1. Chile desires to confirm its status as an "Atlantic" power, with access free of Argentine maritime control. Such status would be conferred by extending a two-hundred-mile territorial or resource zone eastward from the Chilean-possessed southernmost tip of the continent, using the three islands as a starting point. Such a zone would not be blocked by an east-west line drawn along Argentina's southernmost border. Argentina, in turn, takes interpretations favoring a north-south line west of the islands that blocks free Chilean access to the Atlantic, alleging that the accepted tradition has always been that Chile is to be a South Pacific power and Argentina a South Atlantic one. Military control of the eastern end of the southernmost protected passage between the Atlantic and Pacific oceans is also an issue, particularly for Argentina, which has a port and naval base at Ushuaia, on the channel and west of the disputed islands. Global strategic analysis, which gives increasing significance to the South Atlantic and Antarctica and points up vulnerabilities in the Panama Canal, suggests higher stakes on the outcome now than when the controversy started to intensify in 1965.

2. Contending claims to Antarctica are drawn on the alternative bases of Chilean or Argentine possession of the islands and extend along lines of longitude southward from the accompanying two-hundred-mile maritime jurisdiction zones in each case. In effect, Chilean occupation of the islands cuts the Argentine claim to Antarctic land by about two-thirds and vice-versa, because of the presence of the Antarctic Peninsula in the disputed zone. Although the 1959 Antarctic Treaty (ratified in 1961) disallowed legitimacy of territorial claims for thirty years, the possibility of staking claims under a new regime after 1991 has been taken very seriously in both countries. National maps show the anticipated zones as explicit parts of the national territory. Both countries have sent scientific expeditions to the zones and maintain scientific stations there. Each country wishes to have its maritime access to these territories as free as possible from the maritime jurisdiction zone of the other. Recent Brazilian preparations for its initial Antarctic expedition have tended to heighten the worth of the issue for Santiago and Buenos Aires, although both capitals have offered assistance to Brazil's efforts.

3. Competing ocean resource claims, chiefly for krill and anticipated manganese nodules and petroleum deposits on the continental shelf, are inherent in the divergent cartographic versions based upon control of the islands. Both countries have begun exploitation of maritime resources in the disputed zone, occasioning tense incidents.

Solution of the matter is further complicated by its relationship to a number of ill-determined boundary points in the Andes and to the presence of numerous Chileans in southern Argentina, which nationalistic Argentines see as an assimilation problem. A history of rivalry for regional influence, geopolitical thinking by both military governments, and domestic political impacts in public opinion also militate against compromise. A 1902 Treaty of Arbitration relevant to the issue named Great Britain as binding arbitrator, but Argentina remains wary of what it sees as Great Britain's sympathies for Chile, perhaps because of its own dispute with Britain over the Malvinas.

In 1977, after a ten-year process initiated by Chile, the International Court of Justice (with the concurrence of the British Crown) awarded the three islands to Chile in a decision based solely on the legal merits of each case. The geopolitical implications of this award were much greater than those in most boundary disputes, with the advantages falling completely to Chile. (Compromise settlements are by far the most common results of referred boundary disputes.) Argentina in 1978 declared the International Court of Justice award to be null and void. Severely heightened tensions, air force and naval weapons imports, and military maneuvers and incidents on a prewar footing ensued, as Argentina pressured Chile to reopen the question and accede to Buenos Aires's interpretations in a bilateral negotiation format. Papal mediation began in 1979, which reduced the imminence of war. No generally acceptable judgment has been reached to date. Both countries resist the Vatican "sea of peace" proposal of sharing of the ocean resources, more at issue than the islands themselves. In early 1982, Argentina withdrew from the 1972 treaty that established a framework for peaceful settlement of frontier disputes between itself and Chile, as a signal to both the Vatican and Santiago.

Chile-Peru-Bolivia

In the War of the Pacific (1879–1883), Chile defeated Peru and Bolivia and took lands from both, now part of northern Chile. Peru and Bolivia both lost territory in the phosphate-rich Atacama Desert, but beyond this Bolivia lost its narrow corridor to the Pacific and became a landlocked state. Neither country has given up demands for revision of the settlement, and such demands are a stock item in the nationalism of each. As the centennial of the war approached, claims against Chile became more insistent in Lima and La Paz. Settlement between Bolivia and Chile in the form of a corridor to the sea for Bolivia along the Chilean-Peruvian border is complicated by a clause in the peace treaty giving Peru veto power over any disposition by Chile of land belonging to Peru before the war. But neither is Chile willing to concede such a corridor further south, because that would cut the national territory in two.

Intermittent arms purchases, threats by its northern neighbors, and ruptures of diplomatic relations have created a two-front security problem for Chile, with greatest concern during moments of political tension. Argentina sees in Peru and Bolivia useful allies for support on the Beagle question, worsening Chile's political position in the Southern Cone. In the clearest evidence of this, Argentine military officers were influential in supporting the 1980 coup by General Luis García Meza in Bolivia, both to prevent socialist Hernán Siles Suazo from being elected president and to assure that there would be a more reliable ally in La Paz should war with Chile occur over the Beagle Channel.[6] Chile typically attempts to reach out to Ecuador, Brazil, and the United States as counterweights. This compensation is made more difficult by the strongly negative international image of the Augusto Pinochet government, which lately has had to search for political support as far away as South Africa, South Korea, and (unsuccessfully) the Philippines.[7]

Argentina-Brazil

A number of issues are subsumed in the larger complex of Argentine-Brazilian rivalry, which so far has been carried on in a peaceful manner in spite of periods of intense disagreement. The key element of this equation is Argentina's reaction to Brazil's attainment of regional primacy and to its presumably permanently greater capabilities for initiatives and leadership. Argentina has been compelled by events to scale down its earlier credible hopes of continental paramountcy and to decide whether to conduct a strategy of opposition to Brazil or to accept the role of *socio menor* (minor partner), in the words of retired general and strategist Juan Guglialmelli.

A summary of the recent major issues involved in the evolution of the relationship includes these.

1. The first issue is competition for influence in South America and particularly in the three buffer states. A search for political sympathies and receptivities among neighbors has been a prominent part of the strategic political relationship between Buenos Aires and Brasília for decades, a discreet rivalry in which neither side would like to allow the other to gain too much advantage. Argentina reacts to Brazil's steady growth, as Brazil disavows attempts at leadership or hegemony and avoids any chance of isolation. Because Argentina is regularly handicapped by internal economic and political problems, the net advantage rather consistently belongs to Brazil, a characteristic most clearly observed in the greater Brazilian economic presence in the three small buffer states (above all, Paraguay).[8]

2. A second issue is the shared use of hydroelectric resources on the Paraná and Uruguay rivers and River Plate Basin development generally. Brazilian appropriation of a large share of the hydroelectric waterhead potential of the Paraná River in the construction of the Itaipu Dam, without giving Argentina what it felt was sufficient voice in the matter relative to its own plans, caused a major attrition in the relationship in the 1970s. The negotiated settlement among Brazil, Argentina, and Paraguay on hydroelectric project coordination on the Paraná River, signed in October 1979 after a decade of negotiations, dissipated a lot of suspicion and set up a propensity for consultation, which should

simplify the planning and execution of future binational and multinational projects in the River Plate Basin.

3. Trade problems are a third issue. Vis-à-vis Argentina, Brazil has considerable comparative economic advantage. Argentine business people have been critical of Brazil's export-subsidy program, charging that it unfairly benefits Brazilian products in the Argentine market. From time to time, Argentina has taxed imports from Brazil in retaliation against that country's export subsidies or import curbs. Reciprocity of concessions has been a constant issue. Another series of disputes has arisen from the occasional Argentine practice of closing its borders to Brazilian trucks transporting goods to Chile during periods of political tension between Buenos Aires and Santiago.

4. Policy differences based on regime dissimilarities are the basis of another issue. As the Brazilian political opening has progressed since 1979, conservative sectors of the Argentine military have been concerned about a possible strengthening of Brazil's political left, while Brazil's leaders have been uncomfortable with the authoritarian tone of Argentine government pronouncements. At the same time, disagreements on regional security issues have become more numerous. Argentina tried to strengthen the clandestine cooperation of security forces in the cause of an "anti-communist crusade" in the Southern Cone, but Brazil wanted to move away from association with the repressive apparatus of the more authoritarian regimes. Argentina initiated technical aid to anti-guerrilla government forces in Central America, whereas Brazil favored negotiations and elimination of all foreign influence in El Salvador's civil war and started a small aid program to the Sandinista government of Nicaragua. Recent Argentine governments have stressed the country's Western ties, anti-Marxism, and close relations with the United States, especially in strategic cooperation with the Reagan administration. Brazil has built its foreign policy on Third World relations and independence from Washington.

5. Yet another issue is that of activities in the South Atlantic and Antarctica. Because the activities of both countries in these areas are just beginning, disagreements are largely rhetorical. Although Brazil and Argentina have conducted joint annual bilateral naval exercises in the South Atlantic since 1978, they share very little during those maneuvers and differ on strategic preferences. Argentina, at least until the Malvinas war, found some attractiveness in the idea of a South Atlantic Treaty Organization (SATO), to include South Africa. Brazil finds the concept of a "zone of peace" in the South Atlantic to be preferable to militarization and to be advantageous to its Africa policy, as a way to dissociate itself from the controversial SATO notion. (In reality, neither navy has a major blue-water capability.) Regarding Antarctica, Argentina favors establishment of territorial claims based upon proximity and meridians extended southward from national borders, which places Brazil as a potential competitor. Brazil, in contrast, favors free access for all nations under

a *terra communis* legal formula, but is prepared to stake claims should that be allowed.

6. A sixth issue is nuclear matters. Much speculation and little hard evidence exist in the question of whether either Brazil or Argentina has the intention to build a nuclear weapon within the near future through diversion of civilian programs underway. It is generally conceded that Argentina is well ahead of Brazil in the technology required, but that both countries are at the technological threshold of nuclear-weapons production potential.[9] Given the present implausibility of a credible nuclear threat of significance against either country, the initial construction of nuclear weapons in the continent would not have a reasonable security justification or purpose. Stephen Gorman has argued persuasively that possession of nuclear weapons would greatly worsen the security position of both countries by raising the stakes but would fail to provide Argentina with a usable counterbalance to Brazil's greater economic, political, and military weight.[10] Still, nationalistic perceptions that nuclear weapons are a prerequisite for major-power status or national credibility in peace and war cannot be discounted as motivations for initial acquisition of nuclear capabilities even when nations are not threatened by a nuclear adversary.

These issues notwithstanding, the Argentine-Brazilian cooperation begun in May 1980 through a broad network of agreements (including nuclear and military) and a willingness to emphasize shared interests has survived several Argentine governments and the Malvinas war. High-level official consultations have become routine. Both sides give evidence of being committed to a continuation of the spirit of broad cooperation that transcends operational differences and divergent national interests in more limited areas. Judgment on the degree of transformation of the traditional relationship and its implications for continental trends will have to remain speculative, however, until more concrete results from the conciliation are achieved. On the face of the matter, much greater progress can be expected in the next several years in economic affairs than in political or military ones, and even here there are limits to economic complementarity. In the near term at least, both governments will be heavily absorbed in internal economic and political problems, so visions of a transnational integration of South America's most industrialized regions are certainly premature.

NATIONAL-SECURITY DIPLOMACY, GEOPOLITICS, AND MILITARY CAPABILITIES: AN ARMS RACE IN THE SOUTHERN CONE

The "low politics" of commercial issues and economic integration almost exclusively characterized South American international relations from World War II to the mid-1970s, making it one of the least international-conflict-prone regions in the developing world. The political violence that occurred was heavily attributable to domestic causes, although international overtones were occasionally present as both revolutionary and security forces became active in neighboring countries. Since about 1975, however, the Southern Cone regional subsystem has been increasingly affected by the adoption of a "high politics" diplomacy of national security.[11] With internal subversion defeated and their expanded political role still in serious question, the military-dominated governments in particular turned their formerly internally oriented national-security doctrines outward toward an agenda of largely territorial and resource issues that by definition involved conflict with the national interests of neighboring states claiming the same land, ocean area, or resource. Because in many cases the issues were cast in terms of national honor and economic well-being (possible legitimators for an authoritarian government), the stakes of disagreement were raised and compromise made more difficult. The level of national unity on touchstone questions of territorial claims contrasts strongly with the fragmentation of public opinion caused by controversial domestic questions so the temptation to use local disputes as patriotic symbols and rallying cries is always present.

The propensity of Southern Cone military establishments and civilian security agencies to interpret international-relations disputes in dogmatic and conflictual realpolitik terms of national prestige, fierce competition, expansion, the search for geopolitical advantage, preservation of core interests, zero-sum politics, and the need for firmness and perhaps force enhances the potential for crisis situations.[12] Topics that had earlier been settled through mutual inattention now appear more pressing in the context of higher levels of national development, territorial integration, popular expectations, external dependence, continental interaction, and cross-border migrations. Greater technological capabilities to exploit offshore resources have brought maritime sovereignty and claims to Antarctica to the military agenda as well as to the diplomatic agenda, with much the same insistence and logic as the more familiar territorial disputes. Along with these trends has gone an increase in military diplomacy among the Southern Cone states.

In a contagious reaction, when a significant regional power (in this case, any of the ABC countries) begins to frame its foreign-policy perceptions in this security-minded manner, there is greater pressure on other countries (or at least on its neighbors) to do the same out of a sense of threat. Higher potential for international conflict in the Southern Cone has been the consequence.

Along with a more international frame of reference for the mission of the armed forces went a capability need for more sophisticated weaponry, imported and locally manufactured. Even types of weapons inferior in quantity and quality to, say, those in circulation in the Middle East could serve well as compellers or deterrents in the Southern Cone, where a protracted local war is much less likely than a politically decisive border skirmish or a show of determination through repositioning of forces vis-à-vis a neighboring state. None of the countries in question ranks high on a world scale of military effort or ability to sustain a prolonged war, but the ABC powers do rank high among Third World states in capacity for domestic production of military equipment. Brazil and Argentina are gaining significant degrees of autonomy and diversification in arms supply and technical assistance and are undertaking ambitious sales programs to other Third World states, including some in South America.[13]

A comparative examination of the levels of military effort of the ABC powers from 1972 to 1981 provides some insight into trends indicative of threat perception or national preparations for the possible threat or use of force to support national goals.[14] Although Brazil's expenditures in constant dollars rose slightly until 1976 and then declined, Argentina's surpassed Brazil in that year and continued well above the Brazilian level and far above Chile's. Chilean outlays, greatly inferior early in the period, tended to rise, particularly after 1977, which coincided with more acute tensions over the Beagle question with Argentina. On all indicators of military expenditures per capita or as a percentage of gross domestic product (GDP), Brazil's ranking has characteristically been very low because its level of threat perception is low and its security focus is heavily internal. On the other hand, from 1972 to 1981 Argentina increased per capita expenditures and held nearly steady as a percentage of GDP. By all accounts Chile is quite vulnerable militarily because of its elongated shape, the antipodal location of the territorial threats far from its population center, and its quantitative inferiority vis-à-vis Argentina. Thus to keep pace it had to devote a larger share of its smaller economy and population to military purposes than did Argentina.

Although such data and the course of events cast much doubt on the existence of a systematic and reciprocal Brazil-Argentina arms race, the higher level of military effort in Argentina is clear. Beyond the traditional concern about Brazilian hegemony, only partially allayed by the understandings of 1980, the Argentine military, looking south, envisioned the possibility of armed force vis-à-vis Chile in the Beagle dispute and (as events proved) against Great Britain in the Malvinas controversy. (Two other "fronts" were concrete Argentine support for the 1980 García Meza coup in Bolivia and collaboration in antiguerrilla activity in Central America in 1982, both relatively low-outlay operations.) This frame of reference of varied possible conflicts yielded by far the highest levels of military expenditure per capita in Latin America, save for Cuba. The Chilean response can be seen principally as defensive of its internationally legitimated position in the Beagle case, apart from its ongoing concerns about Peruvian and Bolivian claims on sections of northern Chile. The result was an arms race dating from 1977, with large increases by both parties in the purchase of imported weapons.

THE EFFECTS OF THE MALVINAS WAR ON THE FUTURE OF THE STRATEGIC SITUATION IN THE SOUTHERN CONE

Beyond the more widely publicized effects of the April 2–June 14, 1982, Argentine-British war in the Malvinas on global strategic considerations, quite a few results of the engagement were felt in the Southern Cone itself. These can most accurately be analyzed as short-term (during the war) and long-term (postwar) consequences.

Short-term Consequences

Chile supported in principle the Argentine claim to the islands but had strong reservations about the use of force in view of its own dispute with Argentina in the Beagle Channel. Therefore Chile advocated a peaceful resolution of the conflict and declared neutrality regarding the war. It sent a naval squadron to the extreme southern region in defense of the Beagle Channel as commanding officers tried to judge the chances of an Argentine attack there, after a series of military incidents in recent months. Chile refused to give Great Britain the tactical support it requested on Chilean territory and sent naval units to help rescue the survivors of the sunken Argentine battleship *General Belgrano*. Although Chile did not stand to gain from a victorious and more belligerent Argentina, it would certainly lose from the longer-term consequences of open hostility and aiding Britain in its stronger neighbor's defeat. The most critical stand Santiago took was abstention (one of four members) on the resolution passed by the Organization of American States (OAS) supporting Argentine sovereignty over the islands. Chile's suspicion of Argentine intentions increased with the report that, if Great Britain had not resisted the Argentine occupation by force, Argentina had planned to seize next the three disputed islands in the Beagle Channel. During the war bellicose statements by President Leopoldo Galtieri in Buenos Aires on more vigorous assertion of territorial rights sharpened this fear and encouraged rumors. Chilean military officers were also concerned about the war's effect on Moscow's future role in the region, perhaps augmented by its significant technical military aid to Argentina. Some Argentine military officers criticized what they regarded as Chile's "false" neutrality, accused Chile of helping Great Britain, and voiced suspicions about a Chilean "stab in the back" in the form of seizure of disputed territory along the southern Andean frontier.

Brazil's government also supported Argentina's claims to sovereignty over the islands, but with strong private official condemnation of the use of force to seize them. Although Brazil was not physically involved or threatened, it had definite political and economic interests at stake and experienced considerable cross pressures and internal debate in developing policy. Government decision makers felt that the country was heavily at risk but with little other than symbolic means to affect the outcome. They were taken back first by the attack itself, then the extent of Argentine firepower, the force of Britain's response, and the abruptness of the pro-British policy switch of the United States. Their greatest security concern was either an aggressive Argentina jubilant and adventuristic in victory or a badly wounded Argentina thrown into turmoil, left-wing politics, or perhaps a revanchist attitude by defeat. Either case could conceivably increase Argentine pressure for a revision of the Itaipu-Corpus hydroelectric compromise, a favorite cause of the Argentine ultranationalists and a sensitive topic with the approaching starting date for the filling of the Itaipu Dam's impoundment.

In its preoccupation with the effects of Argentine volatility and instability, and with the impact of the status of the Brazil-Argentina link on the whole tenor of South American international relations, Brazil manifested once again its typical cautious prostability orientation. It was also highly sensitive to the war's disruptive effects on its trade with Argentina and to the potential of Argentine bankruptcy for restricting credit flows to developing countries with debt-repayment problems.

Brazilian opinion, public and official, was much less sympathetic to Argentina's cause than was opinion in most South American countries. Yet the military supported the foreign ministry lead out of consideration for broader values to be gained in protecting the overall relationship. Buenos Aires reciprocated by acknowledging Brazil's helpfulness on several occasions, which bodes well for continuation of the mutual understanding.

Argentina received little fervent South American support for its use of force, other than from Peru, Bolivia, and Venezuela, each with an eye to its own revisionist territorial claims. The first two of these affect Chile and relate partly to the Peru-Bolivia-Argentina pressure on that country. (Peru went so far as to send a naval task force to waters off the border with Chile during the early days of the crisis.) Lack of continental unity on the issue was notable, reflecting both a latent disdain for the widely perceived Argentine superiority complex and reservations about Argentina's military government and the use of force.

Long-term Effects

It is too early for a clear verdict, but a number of observations can be made concerning the probable longer-term effects of the Malvinas war on the Southern Cone. Latin Americans found out again where the United States will place its bets when its larger strategic interests are at stake. Systematic long-term anti-U.S. hostility from the affair is unlikely, because in sober reflection Latin American vital interests were more endangered than served by Argentine aggressiveness. The established drift toward greater Latin American political independence from the United States was further justified, however. Spanish American criticism of Great Britain and the United States, activating an old Anglo-Spanish rivalry, motivated discussion of more effective multilateral coordination of activities in a forum excluding the United States. This pique or sense of betrayal itself may not, with the passage of time, be the right type of motivation to bring about such integration. Less faith in multilateral action might well be a result, with more unilateral and bilateral activity.

There will definitely be less faith in the United States as a security partner and source of doctrine and more willingness to run counter to U.S. policy on political and security issues important to Washington. Military establishments in the Southern Cone, after studying the combat lessons of the war, were impressed by the vulnerability of Latin American countries to foreign suppliers' embargoes during armed conflict. They are thus likely to increase the drive for national production of more sophisticated weaponry and for the transfer of technology through coproduction with developed countries or more advanced local companies in Argentina and Brazil. (Electronic warfare and counterwarfare hardware will be heavily sought.) At the same time, the Rio Treaty lost all remaining credibility in Latin America as a mechanism for hemispheric response to a conflict in which there is no common and clear enemy, leaving the hemisphere with not even a paper plan for multilateral conflict resolution.

There is likely to be little "demonstration effect" of the war to encourage forceful solution of border disputes. Argentina's territorial conflict was unique in its tie to an extrahemispheric power; a war between Latin American countries would provoke more hemispheric disarray. The costs of the war to Argentina were also sobering to contemplate.

There is greater local concern over Argentine willingness to use force, its unpredictability, and its dependability as a partner. Argentina remains a geopolitically dissatisfied country. The Beagle and Malvinas issues have been thoroughly infused into domestic politics as the nucleus of the national identity, so they cannot easily be ignored. The speed and direction of Argentine rearmament after the war and the degree of support among military hard-liners to acquire nuclear weapons and a nuclear submarine will be closely gauged by neighboring countries. Conversely, there is now even less preoccupation about Brazil's behavior or fear about Brazil as a threat, because of its responsible diplomacy during the crisis. Argentina is undergoing a "Latin Americanization" of its foreign policy because of its distrust of Western Europe, but its political initiatives in South America will be hindered by the internal crisis and inability to plan ahead. This further opens the way for Brazilian diplomacy to play a constructive role as a moderating force in lowering Southern Cone tensions, aided by the continuation of good relations with Argentina. Chile especially would benefit from a Brazilian leading role. Santiago has been trying to use relations with Brazil to break out of its pariah position in Latin America ever since the visit of Brazilian president Figueiredo to the Chilean capital in October 1980—the first foreign head of state to visit since the 1973 coup.

Buenos Aires seems prepared to accept a long-term solution on the Malvinas. The way is therefore open for Vatican initiatives on the Beagle, since Argentina acceded again after the war to the 1972 arbitration treaty with Chile. Yet even in the best of circumstances, for some time the government in Buenos Aires will be insufficiently broad based to push the Beagle issue to negotiated resolution in the face of nationalistic opposition.

The Soviet Union and Cuba have become more acceptable to Argentina (both to government and public opinion) as economic partners because of their vocal support during the war. This could have positive results in Moscow's relations with the Argentine left. Greater Soviet naval attention to the South Atlantic is also possible, which would cause greater local tensions. At present, however, Soviet influences are likely to be limited to the economic realm, with military relationships improbable.

Chile gained in the short term from the military discredit of the Argentine army and the loss of many fighter planes from its air force, which had been greatly superior to Chile's. However, the Argentine navy remained intact, except for the loss of the *General Belgrano*, and this service branch would be highly important in a war in the Beagle Channel. There are those pessimists who believe that Argentina remains adamant on the Beagle and is only biding time to give precedence to the Malvinas issue and to put its government and armed forces in order. In weighing its defense needs Chile therefore will be pressured toward acceptance of a worst-case view and an increase of military spending, particularly in the air force and naval categories, because of the example of Argentine aggression. At the same time Santiago is taking a legal approach in using all possible occasions to reiterate its preference for peaceful and negotiated settlement of disputes, relying on International Court of Justice (ICJ) and papal support for its case.

In the initial stages of the war many Brazilian military officers were surprised by the firepower Argentina could muster and were made acutely aware of Brazil's defense liabilities. Newspapers and magazines speculated on the imminence of a massive armaments drive, largely in naval and air force categories, fueled by the navy minister's initial statements on the topic. With reflection, the military and the government came to the consensus that Argentina provoked the war with its arms race, brashness, and miscalculation, which did not imply that Brazil was also threatened by attack on its borders. For Brazil, the lessons of the war turned out to be an acceleration of conclusions or trends already underway, with common purposes of reducing foreign dependency and improving information flow and organization:

1. reaffirmation of the internal mission of the armed forces and of the role of capable diplomacy and moderation in preventing war

2. only a slight increase in military spending

3. slight acceleration of plans to create a more autonomous, inter-mediate-technology, national weapons manufacturing capability rather than to purchase fewer and more expensive sophisticated weapons abroad

4. improvement of the land and coastal air defense radar net

5. consideration of an integrated military command to mitigate inter-service rivalries

6. validation of military diversification away from the United States and toward Western Europe

7. opposition to a radical restructuring of the inter-American system

Argentina will remain the external frame of reference for the Brazilian military, but Brazil will not take flagrant advantage of Argentina's weakened condition or abandon the tacit bargaining that has prevented an arms race between the two. A reorientation of Brazil's national-security doctrine in an external direction to the extent of the adoption of a militant national-security diplomacy does not appear likely at present, but more attention will be paid to potential external threats as a result of the war. The Brazilian military still sees the country's chief security problems in the internal social and political effects of the foreign debt, high international interest rates, export problems, and petroleum prices. Military and nuclear cooperation with Argentina as foreseen in the 1980 treaties, however, have been made much more problematic. Economic cooperation opportunities are still promising in the longer run when Argentina's economy recovers. Brazil stands to be the chief benefactor if Argentina continues to diversify away from Western Europe, because Argentina needs Brazilian cooperation more after the war than before. The drive toward further accommodation is notable on both sides. In time the two countries may come to see each other less as rivals and more as partners, but a lot of traditional distrust and competitiveness must be overcome for that qualitative transformation to occur.

NOTES

1. Systematic analysis of this trend in Latin America as a whole is found in Robert Wesson, ed., *U.S. Influence in Latin America in the 1980s* (New York: Praeger, 1982).

2. Wolf Grabendorff, "Interstate Conflict Behavior and Regional Potential for Conflict in Latin America," Working Paper no. 116, Latin American Program, The Wilson Center, Smithsonian Institution, Washington, DC, 1982, p. 12.

3. For definitional purpose, the Southern Cone is taken here to include Chile, Argentina, Brazil, Bolivia, Paraguay, and Uruguay. Brazil is included because of the weight of its south and center-south in the economics and politics of the area and its position as Argentina's main rival. Statistical sources: Population

from Ruth Leger Sivard, *World Military and Social Expenditures, 1981* (Leesburg, VA: World Priorities, 1981); and the others from U.S. Arms Control and Disarmament Agency (USACDA), *World Military Expenditures and Arms Transfers, 1970–1979* (Washington, DC: USACDA, 1982). All statistics are for 1978.

4. A summary of a Southern Cone or "Southern Triangle" consensus on perceptions of international politics is found in Mariano Grondona, "South America Looks at Detente (Skeptically)," *Foreign Policy*, no. 26 (Spring 1977), pp. 184–203.

5. Analyses of the Beagle Channel issue are found in Stephen M. Gorman, "Present Threats to Peace in South America: The Territorial Dimensions of Conflict," *Inter-American Economic Affairs* 33, no. 1 (Summer 1979), pp. 53–58; Stephen M. Gorman, "The High Stakes of Geopolitics in Tierra del Fuego," *Parameters* 8, no. 2 (June 1978), pp. 45–56; and Jozef Goldblat and Victor Millan, "Militarization and Arms Control in Latin America," in Stockholm International Peace Research Institute, *World Armaments and Disarmament: SIPRI Yearbook, 1982* (Cambridge, MA: Oelgeschlager, Gunn, and Hain, Inc., 1982), pp. 408–411.

6. Kenneth F. Johnson, "Argentina: Pride and Weakness," in Wesson, *U.S. Influence in Latin America*, p. 51.

7. Heraldo Muñoz, "The International Relations of the Chilean Military Government: Elements for a Systematic Analysis," Working Paper no. 69, Latin American Program, The Wilson Center, Smithsonian Institution, Washington, DC, 1980, pp. 18–19, 24.

8. "Perceptions of Brazil in the Southern Cone," in Wayne A. Selcher, ed., *Brazil in the International System: The Rise of a Middle Power* (Boulder, CO: Westview Press, 1981), pp. 143–180.

9. Goldblat and Millan, "Militarization and Arms Control," p. 420.

10. Stephen M. Gorman, "Security, Influence, and Nuclear Weapons: The Case of Argentina and Brazil," *Parameters* 9, no. 1 (March 1979), pp. 52–65. Also see William H. Courtney, "Nuclear Choices for Friendly Rivals," in Joseph A. Yager, ed., *Nonproliferation and U.S. Foreign Policy* (Washington, DC: Brookings Institution, 1980), pp. 241–279.

11. Grabendorff, "Interstate Conflict Behavior," pp. 6–9, 13–16; and Alexandre de S.C. Barros, "The Diplomacy of National Security: South American International Relations in a Defrosting World," in Ronald G. Hellman and H. Jon Rosenbaum, eds., *Latin America: The Search for a New International Role* (New York: John Wiley and Sons, 1975), pp. 131–150.

12. The application of geopolitical interpretations to international disputes in the Southern Cone is reviewed in Howard T. Pittman, "Geopolitics and Foreign Policy in Argentina, Brazil, and Chile," in Elizabeth G. Ferris and Jennie K. Lincoln, eds., *Latin American Foreign Policies: Global and Regional Dimensions* (Boulder, CO: Westview Press, 1981), pp. 165–178.

13. See Clovis Brigagão, "The Case of Brazil: Fortress or Paper Curtain?" *Impact of Science on Society* 31, no. 1 (1981), pp. 17–31; and Edward S. Milenky, "Arms Production and National Security in Argentina," *Journal of Interamerican Studies and World Affairs* 22, no. 3 (August 1980), pp. 267–288.

14. For information on arms expenditures, see Stockholm International Peace Research Institute, *World Armaments and Disarmament: SIPRI Yearbook, 1982*, pp. 145, 153; and U.S. Arms Control and Disarmament Agency, *World Military Expenditures*, pp. 49–53.

8. The Malvinas Conflict: Analyzing the Argentine Military Regime's Decision-Making Process

INTRODUCTION

The purpose of this chapter is to present some reflections on the decision-making process of the Argentine military government in relation to the South Atlantic conflict, which may serve as a contribution to a more exhaustive study in the future, providing that the corresponding information is accessible. The aim at this time, therefore, is to organize certain elements around a conceptual point of reference, without attempting to deal with the subject in a more systematic fashion. It is of importance to analyze the decision-making process of the military regime in this case, since, in addition to the opportunity this provides for the application of theoretical instruments related to the consideration of internal factors in the formulation and implementation of foreign policy, it also involves recognition of the impact of the Malvinas conflict on the national and international scene.[1]

In the Malvinas conflict an authoritarian regime decided to recover the islands by force, excluding from the process the organizations and leaders representing the political domain. The outcome of the process, which was limited to a large extent to the top level of the armed forces, was a military defeat, the death of hundreds of British military personnel and Argentines, and the intensification of the political, economic, and social crisis that the Argentine society was undergoing. These two facts enhance the importance of this analysis for those who maintain that democracy must be restored and that the possibilities of a repetition of this type of situation in the future must be reduced to a minimum.

APPROACH AND THEORETICAL ELEMENTS

For this chapter it was considered advisable to use theoretical approaches based on the role of internal factors in the formulation and implementation of foreign policy. The characteristics of the political regime in power, the concentration of the decision-making process in a very limited number of actors (most of whom belong to only one type of organization, the armed forces), the exploitation of a national cause to get support and internal political legitimation for the regime, the particular world visions of the leaders and the problems of competition among them and among their respective organizations (e.g., the president, the commanders in chief, members of the military junta, and the respective forces)—all these factors suggest that emphasis should be placed on the internal variables, without losing sight of the influence of external factors.

At the micro level of analysis,[2] naturally the influences inside the nation-state are considered to be important in the formulation and implementation of foreign policy. With regard to contributions to microlevel approaches, the two main sources are the theoreticians of behavioral sciences and the academicians who acquire experience as they come and go in government offices (the in-and-outers) and who subsequently give a realistic account of the governmental process.[3] In view of my familiarity with the world visions and the internal decision-making process of the armed forces, and bearing in mind my periods of activity in various sectors of bureaucracy, I have logically depended more on the second source. My experience in that area has led me to make an eclectic use (perhaps a disorderly one) of different theoretical approaches based on internal variables.

As Alberto van Klaveren rightly pointed out in Chapter 1, those approaches that focus on internal variables elude a clear and well-defined classification. The variables tend to overlap and intermingle, the only means of distinguishing between them often being mere degrees of emphasis or nuances that give a highly subjective content to the classification. In principle, they can be divided into four major groups: orientation of the regime, decision-making process and internal policy, bureaucratic policy, and leadership.[4]

However, these approaches are considered to be insufficient to encompass adequately all aspects of the decision-making process. It therefore appears necessary to take into account the orientation of the regime and the close connections between the decision-making process and internal policy.

As for the approaches favoring external variables, note should be taken of the use of the "power policy" approach, with its idea of the state as a rational and unified actor, which emphasizes the use of force as an instrument to satisfy interests in different fields.[5] This becomes the paradigm of the military leaders who made the decision to occupy the Malvinas. Their decision-making process takes place within an alliance of social forces and a political and social structure that differ greatly from the democratic government elected in 1973 and overthrown in March 1976. The "national project" attempted following the military coup is based on a different concept of Argentine national interest. This implies substantive changes in Argentina's position vis-à-vis the rest of the world, based on world visions and dominant values different from those prevailing in the previous period. It is necessary, therefore, to bear in mind the orientation of the regime and the impact of certain forms of political organization, as well as the development model imposed.

It is in this context that any eventual changes in the actors, the relevant processes for the formulation and implementation of foreign policy, the channels used, and the interests at stake will be studied.

POLITICAL REGIMES AND FORMS OF INSERTION INTO THE INTERNATIONAL SYSTEM

The 1970s and the beginning of the 1980s witnessed two successive projects—distinct in nature—for Argentina's insertion into the international system: (1) that of 1973 to 1976, under successive Peronist presidencies, and (2) the so-called Process of National Reorganization following the military coup of March 1976. Under the command of different generals (Jorge Rafael Videla, Roberto Viola, Leopoldo Galtieri, and Cristino Nicolaides) the latter regime was in power when the Malvinas events occurred in April 1982. The characteristics of both models reveal the lines of continuity and the points of discontinuity in their foreign policy. This is the context within which the particular policies relating to the Malvinas are to be considered.

The Peronist Project

The Peronist administrations placed emphasis (to a greater or lesser degree, depending on the specific cases studied) on a project of insertion into the international system that sought to achieve greater independence in decision making and greater autonomy of action, by means of closer and permanent ties with Latin America; the maintenance of a more distant attitude and, at times, one of manifest opposition vis-à-vis the United States; and the establishment and intensification of cooperative relations with the developing countries. Nevertheless, following a line of basic continuity of Argentine foreign policy, they attached great importance to cultural, political, and economic links with Western Europe, usually as a manner of compensating for the attitudes assumed vis-à-vis the United States. This, however, did not usually imply any yielding to Great Britain in the case of the Malvinas. The Peronist political project sought to transfer the populist characteristics of internal social reform, one of its features, to the broader community of the international system. World reorganization (which included satisfying the interests of the developing countries in all areas) had to be evolutionary, avoiding as far as possible the use of violence. In its application, the project claimed to be pragmatic and adaptable to the changes occurring within the external framework.

Within this context, and bearing in mind its direct connection with other critical problems (the Beagle Channel, the Antarctic), the restitution of the Malvinas required a significant enhancement of bargaining power with Great Britain, based on overall growth for Argentina; the greatest possible legitimacy for the recognition of Argentina's rights to the islands; and limitation of any eventual support that London might receive from the great industrial powers of the West. For purposes of dissuasion, contention, and prestige and in support of negotiations, an eventual exhibition of elements of force was envisaged, but not its direct use on a large scale as a preventive measure.

The Process of National Reorganization

When the armed forces took over in March 1976, a political, economic, and social model was launched that claimed to achieve a profound transformation of Argentine society and its situation vis-à-vis the rest of the world. The economic project attempted to reorganize the economic and social sector as a whole, in such fashion as to adapt the process of capital accumulation to what it understood to be a more efficient utilization of comparative advantages, with a view to maximizing its possibilities of insertion into the international capitalist system. This implied the intention to consolidate the agricultural sector and certain financial and industrial groups of national origin.

One essential aspect of the model, which claimed to exploit the comparative advantages of the agricultural sector, was the creation and development of an important local financial market, closely connected with international financial capital. In order that it be economically viable, the project required the endorsement and cooperation of the traditional Argentine export poles—Western Europe and the United States—and that of international financial centers, particularly New York and London. The foreign economic policy therefore had to contribute to meeting these requirements and to determining conditions—a fact that was to influence the manner in which other matters of foreign policy were dealt with, including the case of the Malvinas.

With regard to the development of natural resources, the project implied an abrupt change in the policy concerning the exploitation of hydrocarbons. Up to that time, every effort had been made for the latter to remain as far as possible under the monopoly of the state-owned company, Yacimientos Petrolíferos Fiscales (YPF). In following years there was a considerable opening up toward the transnational corporations and toward new national groups engaged in oil and gas exploration and development activities. This led the government to organize a system of "risk contracts" by means of which bidding was instituted for exploration areas covering part of the continental shelf of the Patagonian Atlantic and Tierra del Fuego.[6]

As far as trade was concerned, the project promoted a diversification of markets, in which a privileged place was allotted to the Soviet Union (Argentina's exports to the Soviet Union increased from 5.7 percent of total exports during the period 1975–1979 to 33.7 percent in 1981). However, any type of connection was avoided that might eventually lead, according to military criteria, to potential Soviet penetrations of any kind in Argentina.

With regard to the Malvinas, the fear existed, shared by some of the top-ranking officers who bore the responsibility of handling strategic matters, that the North Atlantic Treaty Organization (NATO) might attempt to extend its jurisdiction to the South Atlantic and that Great Britain might fortify the islands and offer them to that organization as a suitable base for that purpose. The military leaders would have wished Argentina to be the country that, by obtaining control over the islands, would play an important role in the region's western defense system, thereby consolidating its prestige and "legitimizing" its possession of these archipelagoes.

The aim of this foreign-policy project was to achieve an active incorporation into the strategic, economic, and political subsystem of the Western industrialized countries. Emphasizing its character of "emerging intermediate power," Argentina hoped to modify its position in the international hierarchy. That implied, in general, the need to choose a way to obtain greater power and prestige on the basis of an "automatic alignment" in the field of strategy and a "subordinate link" in the economic sector.

THE EXTERNAL FRAMEWORK

The political and strategic orientation of the new model of insertion of Argentina into the world system was clearly stated by the military leadership. The ideology of the defense of the "Western and Christian world" against that "communist aggression," while it reflected continuity of the general orientation maintained by previous military regimes, at this stage, attained levels of singular aberration in the world view of the decision makers.

Following a cool period, due to the human-rights policy of Carter's government, relations with Washington improved rapidly with the arrival of the Reagan Administration. It was a question of developing close collaboration first with the United States in the political-strategic field and second with Western Europe, although in this case emphasis was placed on financial, commercial, and technological aspects.

The aim was to insert Argentina into the Western strategic system and assign it an important role by means of active participation in the North American security system for Latin America, with Central America as a privileged area. To this had to be added, according to this approach, the role that fell naturally to Argentina in the defense of the South Atlantic. This included the intention—long cherished by the navy and by some senior army officers—to establish an agreement with the Republic of South Africa and with countries of the Latin American area of the South Atlantic—the South Atlantic Treaty Organization (SATO)—for the security of the oceanic area situated between the southern cones of

Africa and Latin America, in view of what was felt to be a process of continuous communist expansion.[7]

The guiding paradigm offered a bipolar and highly conflictive concept of the distribution and competition for power on a world scale. It maintained concepts, criteria, and processes that dated back to the 1950s to the period of the cold war, carrying with them an overwhelming load of ideological schematism.

In the conceptual view of the decision makers, the inclusion of heterodox elements was not prejudicial to the central ideological axis to which they adhered (the struggle between "good" and "evil" represented by the East-West confrontation). Such an inclusion applied the rules of the game, of the system in force, in terms of their own interests. Within the context of this ideological discourse, the course of foreign policy becomes intelligible. Thus, for example, it was apparently possible to reconcile: (1) an active, although moderate, defense of certain Third World principles and reclamations with respect to the new international economic order; (2) the firm intention of the military leaders, during the greater part of the period, to break away from the group of nonaligned countries; (3) the rejection of the idea of considering Argentina conceptually as a Third World country; and (4) the enthusiastic and open participation of military advisers, the supply of war material, and financing in the internal conflicts of Central America, aimed at destabilizing the new revolutionary governments and supporting the authoritarian and repressive regimes.

The inflexibility of the prevailing ideological concepts, which were the result of and an internalization of the thesis of the "enemy within" and of the inculcation, through the doctrine of the U.S. armed forces, of the importance of the campaign against the Soviet Union, was accompanied by a provincial view of world events and a notably distorted idea of the country's own capacity. Some of these characteristics were due to the remoteness of the power centers, the country's relative marginality vis-à-vis the latter, and, to a large extent, the deficient cultural and political backgrounds and low degree of socialization of the majority of the officers of the armed forces.

Another reason, according to a U.S. military leader and political scientist, is that in the absence of real and serious external dangers, the military actor usually tends to universalize the communist threat to the "Western and Christian world" and seeks a role for his country in opposing said threat.[8]

THE INTERNAL FRAMEWORK

The function of the armed forces in society is, from the internal point of view, to act as an element of cohesion; from the external point of view, it is to act as an armed body to protect the society. Based on these functions, the real role of the armed forces depends, to a large extent, on the world view within which their thinking is framed and the interests that guide their action.

In the case of Argentina, the political process can be understood as competition between different social groups for the control of political and economic resources, without reaching the point of forming a block of alliances capable of completely imposing their hegemony. Up to the middle of 1966 (General Onganía's coup) the military, at critical moments, performed the function of temporarily imposing hegemonies and of taking authoritarian measures to assemble the social groups around some type of national project. The idea was to restrict (or exclude) political and economic participation of the groups that were considered to be "dangerous," protecting the interests of the dominant minority segment. Once order was reestablished and the threatening sectors had been "controlled," the armed forces returned to their barracks.[9]

With the coup known as the Argentine Revolution (1966–1973), a different stage began as regards the role the armed forces assigned to themselves in society. The change—which was tremendously intensified during the process of National Reorganization (1976–1983)—consisted of the replacement of the role of agent of arbitration between different social groups with that of agent of transformation of society.

The aim of overthrowing the constitutional government, on March 24, 1976, was to eliminate the predominance of Peronism and of the trade-union sector in the political sphere, in addition to eliminating the radical left-wing groups. The purpose was to solve the problems of an "inefficient" democracy, advancing—"without deadlines"—toward a hierarchical, orderly democracy, free of "Marxist subversion" and uncontrolled "Peronist demagogical populism."

As one of the military ideologists stated, the cause of the coup was not the need to battle against the guerrilla, since

> there was nothing to prevent eliminating subversion under a constitutional government. In March 1976, the Armed Forces overthrew a government which was submerged in its own chaos, its corruption and its absolute inability to govern the country from the political, economic and social point of view. . . . The justification of the taking over of power by the armed forces in 1976 was to close a historical cycle, as was stated even in the text of certain laws. . . .

Thus "the Armed Forces restored the nation's security and recovered their role as bastion of the Republic."[10]

The idea (supposedly definitely this time) was to get out of the impasse and impose a model that would place Argentina in a position consonant with the new situation of world capitalism. An economic reinsertion of Argentina would enable it to exploit its comparative advantages as an agricultural and livestock exporter and also, in the future, as an energy exporter and to finally join sides, in the strategic field, with the forces that were battling against "international Marxism."

"The war between the free world and Marxism headed by Moscow, is also fought on the battlefield of our continent."[11]

THE MALVINAS CRISIS

Internal Factors

The main internal factors were: (1) the transfer of priority from the Beagle case to that of the Malvinas; (2) the rapid and acute deterioration of the internal politico-economic situation; and (3) the possibility of using the Malvinas as a heroic feat that would legitimate the military regime, purging it of its repressive policy, the violation of human rights, the acts of corruption committed, and the serious economic deterioration resulting from its administration.

With regard to the modification in the situation of the conflict that would probably have to be settled by warlike means, several elements influenced the military assessment. One was the possibility of the presence of Chile in the South Atlantic—and an eventual closer link with Great Britain—in the event of a settlement unfavorable to Argentina in the Beagle dispute. Another was the fear that London might grant some form of autonomy to the inhabitants of the Malvinas or negotiate with the United States the establishment of military bases in those islands.

The manifestations against the regime during the weeks prior to the invasion, and particularly the strike of March 30, caused a sudden loss of political space for the government, rapidly increasing its vulnerability in a context of serious economic crisis and social unrest. This appears to have been one of the factors that most influenced the decision to invade immediately, since everything leads one to assume that the decision to invade the islands some time between August and October 1982 had already been adopted between December and February of that year.[12]

Finally, one element pointing to suggestive links between a segment of the military leadership and the crucial decision to recover the Malvinas emerges with the identification of those superior officers who took the most active part and assumed leadership in the operation. It was precisely those leaders of the armed forces—including the president himself—to whom the reports of Amnesty International and other sources referred as military people deeply involved in the process of the "war against internal subversion" (the outcome of which was the death and disappearance of over 20,000 people) who played the main roles in the decision-making process and commanded the Malvinas operation.

These military leaders were deeply concerned by the possibility of a transfer of power to the civil society, which would lead to investigations and trials and which might reveal their responsibility in the repressive measures. The intention of the military to "compensate" for their previous behavior in the government by recovering territories that constituted a national objective fully shared by the Argentine society, clearly emerges from the public declarations made by high-ranking officers of the armed forces. Some of them were of the opinion that it would even be possible to recover political control of the process and channel it toward an electoral solution suitable to their ends. General Galtieri's intentions were recognized in a newspaper report published after the defeat of the Argentine forces, which stated "if everything had gone as planned, Galtieri's idea was to call for gradual elections: Parliament and Presidency of the Nation, for which he would have posed his candidature with the certainty of an easy triumph. . . ."[13]

External Factors

There is already evidence that the Argentine military leaders were very mistaken in their assessment of the situation with respect to three essential aspects: the reaction of the United States, the reaction of Great Britain, and the support to be expected from the world community in international forums.

The president himself, General Galtieri, publicly acknowledged that a military reaction was not expected from the British, and, in the event there was such a reaction, it was expected to be extremely moderate and designed only to reinforce London's negotiation strategy. The military strategists were even less able to foresee the stand that the United States was finally to take in favor of Great Britain.[14]

In addition to an obviously elementary ignorance of the relative weight of Great Britain and Argentina in Washington's global plan of strategic alliances and of the depth of the cultural, political, ideological, and economic links with Great Britain, two types of factors seem to have contributed to the mistakes of the military leaders in their estimation of the probable U.S. response: (1) the situation of "privileged friendship" with the Reagan administration, as seen by the military regime, and (2) the previous feelers that had been put out with that administration. The first interpretation is based on what was considered to be an enormous contribution made by Argentina to the United States in Central America, in keeping with the strategy of containment of the revolutionary governments of the area as defined by the U.S. administration. Although there are no precise data on the subject, reports obtained in Buenos Aires, the United States, and Central America suggest that the participation of the military and paramilitary was significantly greater than that indicated in the international press, both as regards the number of participants and the variety of actions undertaken by them.

On the other hand, the "surprise" of the military government at what it considered to be a "betrayal" on the part of the U.S. government appears to be the result of: (1) assumptions as to implicit commitments contracted by the United States vis-à-vis the regime, in exchange for the collaboration provided by the latter in Central America and on obligations stemming from the Tratado Interamericano de Asistencia

Recíproca (TIAR); and (2) contacts and conversations that might have referred to these matters indirectly and that took place with eminent, high-ranking military and civilian personages in the Reagan Administration (among others, Ambassador Jeane Kirkpatrick and the under secretary for Latin American affairs, Thomas Enders). It is a fact, for example, that with the exception of a limited group of members of Congress, practically no feelers were put out or approaches made to the legislature. On the other hand, a large number of the contacts made by the Argentine military diplomats in Washington were with persons belonging to the so-called South African lobby.[15]

The prior assessment made in Buenos Aires of the support that Argentina could expect from the international forums capable of dealing with the problem and of the positions and measures that would be adopted by the industrialized countries of the West revealed a high degree of incompetence. One of the worst mistakes was the one concerning the results it was expected would be obtained in the United Nations Security Council when it considered the question of the Malvinas, which was to lead to Resolution 502.[16]

ATTITUDES AND POSITIONS ADOPTED BY THE POLITICAL LEADERS

This subject, in view of its complexity and importance, warrants an in-depth and exhaustive analysis. However, it is of interest to note here certain elements, in view of their effects on the interactions between the "civil society" and the "military actor."

In February 1982, a coordinating mechanism of the political parties, called the Multipartidaria, published a project for Argentina based on an agreement on national objectives and policies. With reference to the islands, "the immediate restitution of the Malvinas" was demanded. According to the information available, the political leaders had no previous information on the decision to recover the islands by force of arms. They were officially informed of this at a meeting with the minister of the interior when the Malvinas were already under control.

In general terms, the armed forces enjoyed the support of the political leaders. With the exception of severe criticism from the Movimiento de Integración y Desarrollo (MID), some personages of the center-right parties, a limited number of Peronist trade-union leaders, and the Intransigencia sector of the Peronist party, the party leaders at first not only gave their tacit consent but also their active collaboration. This took the form of missions abroad, undertaken by eminent political figures, to gain the support of the Latin American countries for the Argentine position and to "explain" to European countries and to the United States the reasons that had led to the military occupation of the islands. Likewise, the party leaders were invited to the formal establishment of Argentine authorities in the Malvinas.

The explanation offered by some political leaders with regard to this behavior was based on two causes. One was that the recovery of the islands constituted a "national cause," and as such the action taken by the regime deserved support. Another was that if support were not forthcoming, the political parties would lose face vis-à-vis their respective clients, since the latter had spontaneously and categorically approved the occupation of the Malvinas (although that did not mean they approved the military regime's actions in other problem areas such as disappearance, economic crisis, and corruption).[17] To put it briefly, the politicians estimated that if they opposed or refused to collaborate, they would lose their leadership capacity and prepare the ground for the support of the "military party" by the masses. Finally, there appears to have been confidence in the military's ability to retain the islands or to successfully negotiate their restitution by Great Britain.

The support initially given to the military operation decreased as the moment of defeat approached, while there was a withdrawal from the official positions and a gradual increase in criticism from such groups as the sector of the Unión Cívica Radical headed by Raúl Alfonsín, the Movimiento de Izquierda Revolucionaria (MIR), and the Peronist Intransigencia group.

The attitude of the civilian leaders indicates the inability of the political class to respond autonomously in the face of unexpected critical events. Likewise, it reveals their enormous professional limitations, since their attitudes were not exactly those of statesmen. To this is added their dramatic lack of knowledge of international affairs. Except for a few very rare cases, not only did they not realize the negative consequences of the decisions being made, but to a certain extent they shared the world view of the military leaders.

During the attempts at negotiation to settle the conflict between Argentina and Great Britain, very few politicians raised their voices to support or to demand the adoption of this course of action. Actually, the majority of those who in one way or another maintained that the conflict should cease were the leaders of the financial and entrepreneurial sectors most closely connected with transnational capital, for the obvious reason that the conflict affected their interests. The desire "not to be left out of the game" (even though they were actually playing a marginal role), to keep or to gain positions in the short run, drastically limited the realizations of the existing alternatives and tended to supply routine responses (e.g., follow whoever has leadership at the time) to new and complex situations.

CONCLUSIONS

The various elements presented in this chapter point out the importance of an in-depth analysis of the following factors:

1. The role played by the world view, ideological factors, and cor-
   porative and personal interests in the decision-making process of
   an authoritarian regime
2. The particular characteristics of the decision-making mechanism
   of this type of regime (for instance, the "shared veto")
3. The reiterated recourse to an international conflict to overcome a
   critical internal situation, attempting, by this means, to legitimate
   the military regime
4. The extent and depth to which the society's political decision-
   making space is occupied by the armed forces under a military
   regime
5. The significant reduction of the universe of alternatives that can
   be identified for the adoption of decisions with this type of regime
6. The gradual internationalization in the civil society of the military
   actor's world visions and patterns of thought, that is to say, the
   gradual coercive imposition of a national political subculture as
   the focal point of foreign policy
7. The differences existing between the behavior of democratic regimes
   and that of authoritarian ones in the field of foreign affairs
8. The effects on the foreign policy of the modifications of the regime
   (development model, actors, interactions, and relative power of
   each one) of the "hegemonic block" in that society

Within the context of the aforementioned points, the importance of
the international process and the possibilities afforded by the application
of the bureaucratic policy approach are evident. In this case there is no
unitary actor, but a certain number of actors who have to solve or
counteract different internal and international problems that are inter-
connected. Within this framework, the actors do not act according to a
consistent series of strategic objectives, but in terms of various concepts
of national security, personal interests, and interests of the organizations
to which they belong.

The decision-making process observed here does not consist of a
calm, balanced, and rational choice from among a set of alternatives,
taking all the factors into account. Instead it takes the form of an activity
that, on the basis of a given situation (usually very confused), considers
immediate alternatives in a process characterized by struggles, oscillations,
and frequently changing courses.[18]

Thus the bureaucratic-politics approach offers suggestions that proved
to materialize in the decision-making process related to the Malvinas.
Some of these are that organizational interests are often dominated by
the desire to maintain the autonomy of the organization and by the
competition for the obtainment of certain missions (e.g., conflicts between
the Air Force and Naval Aviation regarding the assignment of responsibilities and strategic tasks and tactics), that the majority of the actors
adopt a short-term approach, and that the structure of decisions is such

that it is difficult to supervise them. Other suggestions are that a considerable margin of action is left as regards which subordinates are to be involved and which specific actions are to be adopted; that the idea of the "national interest" and of the problems and priorities of "national security" involves attitudes, images, and values shared by the actors participating in the decision-making process; and that many of the participants tend to "interpret" the actions of other nations in such fashion as to adapt them to their previous images, instead of examining the facts objectively.

NOTES

1. The conflict between Great Britain and Argentina includes not only the Malvinas but also the archipelagoes of the Georgias and the South Sandwich Islands. For reasons of brevity, I shall refer to all of them with the term Malvinas Islands. The examination of internal and external factors is the subject of my study, "El conflicto de las islas Malvinas: Su papel en la política exterior argentina y en el contexto mundial," in *Estudios Internacionales*, no. 60 (October–December 1982), pp. 361–409. The effect of the conflict on the political process in Argentina and on the armed forces in Latin America was treated in an article by me in *Foro Internacional* (1983). The international aspects of the conflict are dealt with in *The Official History of the War* (London: Latin American Newsletter, 1983).

2. J. David Singer, "The Level of Analysis Problem in International Relations" in Klaus Knorr and Sidney Verba, eds., *The International System: Theoretical Essays* (Princeton: Princeton University Press, 1961), pp. 77–79.

3. See Bradford Westerfield, "Aproximaciones al estudio de la toma de decisiones de política exterior en Estados Unidos," *Estados Unidos: Perspectiva Latinoamericana*, no. 10 (México: Centro de investigaciones y docencia económicas [CIDE], 2d semester 1981), p. 19.

4. See ibid., p. 17; and Robert O. Keohane and Joseph Nye, *Power and Interdependence: World Politics in Transition* (Boston: Little Brown, 1977), pp. 30–31.

5. On the military regime, see Ricardo Sidicaro, "Argentine: La longue crise du gouvernement militaire," *Etudes* (Paris), June 1982; Raúl Green, "Argentine 1976–1981, Croissance et decandence d'un projet: Le capital national dans le processus economique," *Document de Travail*, no. 3 (Paris: Centre du Travail de America Latina [CETRAL], 1982), p. 11; *Evaluación Económica de la Argentina: Abril de 1976–Dicembre de 1980* (Buenos Aires: República Argentina, Ministerio de Economía, 1981); "Mensaje del Dr. Martínez de Hoz al concluir su gestión como Ministro de Economía," *Información Económica Argentina*, no. 115 (Buenos Aires: Ministerio de Economía, March 1981); "Política Industrial 1976–1980," *Información Económica Argentina*, no. 114 (Buenos Aires: Ministerio de Economía, February 1981).

6. The legal constraints governing oil exploration were eased in Law 21.278, Contratos de Riesgos. See "La expansión productiva de petróleo y gas entre 1976 y 1981," *Información Económica Argentina*, no. 114 (Buenos Aires: Ministerio de Economía, February 1981).

7. See Luis Maira, "La política latinoamericana de la Administración Reagan: Del discurso armonioso a las primeras dificultades," and Carlos J. Moneta, "El

papel de los Estados Unidos en la década del 80 en las relaciones entre América Latina y Africa Negra: Factores político-estratégicos" in *La política internacional de los años 80: Una perspectiva latinoamericana,* Helio Jaguaribe, ed. (Buenos Aires: Editorial de Belgrano, 1982). Also, see Carlos J. Moneta, "Aspectos conflictivos de las relaciones Afro-latinoamericanas: Las vinculaciones políticas, económicas, y militares de la República Sudafricana con los paises del Atlántico Sur latinoamericano" in C. J. Moneta, ed., *Geopolítica y Política del Poder en el Atlántico Sur* (Buenos Aires: Editorial Pleamar, 1983), pp. 130–137; and for a military perspective, Rear Admiral Luis Maria Mendia, "El Atlántico Sur," *Futurables,* no. 13 (1982), p. 59.

8. Charles D. Corbett, *The Latin American Military as a Socio-political Force: Case Study of Bolivia and Argentine,* Monographs in International Affairs (Coral Gables, Fla.: Center for Advanced International Studies, University of Miami, 1972), p. 13.

9. Roberto Russell and Teresa Carballal, "Democracia y autoritarismo en Argentina: Los problemas estructurales del sistema político y su incidencia en la redemocratización," paper delivered at the Seminar on Sistema Político y Redemocratización, Viña del Mar, Chile, April 1983.

10. General Ramón G. Díaz Bessone, "Sentido y justificación de las Fuerzas Armadas en el gobierno," *Futurables,* no. 13 (1982), pp. 8–9.

11. Carlos J. Moneta, "El factor energético en la política internacional de América Latina," *Gaceta Internacional* (Caracas) 1, no. 2 (October–December 1983); quote from Díaz Bessone, "Sentido y justificación," p. 13.

12. This chronology is based upon private interviews of senior military figures conducted by me in 1982.

13. Moneta, "El conflicto de las islas Malvinas"; for Galtieri's declaration, see Néstor J. Montenegro and Eduardo Aliverti, *Los Nombres de la Derrota* (Buenos Aires: Ediciones Nemont, 1982), p. 23.

14. See "Galtieri: Argentina seguirá combatiendo," *El Nacional* (Caracas), June 16, 1982, pp. A-8.

15. See Montenegro and Aliverti, *Los Nombres de la Derrota,* pp. 24–25.

16. On the coverage of United Nations Resolution 502, see *La Nación,* April 7, 1983, p. 16.

17. Based on private interviews with leaders of the Multipartidaria.

18. See Graham T. Allison and Morton H. Halperin, "Política Burocrática: Un paradigma y algunas implicaciones de política," *La toma de Decisiones hacia América Latina, Cuadernos Semestrales. Estados Unidos. Perspectiva Latinoamericana,* no. 10 (México, D.F.: Centro de investigaciones y docencia económicas [CIDE], 1981), p. 221.

9. Venezuelan Foreign Policy and the Role of Political Parties

Political truisms—at once banal and informative—are a mark of all political systems, whatever their character. Among those that readily come to mind for Venezuela, at least three have direct bearing on our topic. First, it is said that the day after national elections, the campaign starts for the next contest five years distant. Second, the public is unconcerned with foreign policy and bases its political preferences on a judgment of bread-and-butter economic issues. And third, every Venezuelan president devotes too much time to international relations and too little to domestic needs. One does not need to be a scholar of spectacular talent or insight to appreciate that although the first may be sui generis for the land of Simón Bolívar, the other two are familiar characteristics of most democracies, whether from the Third World or the Western industrial capitalist states. In combination, they help to frame the context for consideration of the role of political parties in the formulation and implementation of Venezuelan foreign policy. Moreover, they are further underlined by the profound pervasiveness of the party system throughout that body politic.

An examination of Venezuela over the past quarter century—the post-Pérez Jiménez era of bourgeois liberal democracy and state capitalism—suggests several themes that have recurred throughout the period. These can be summarized in the following form: (1) there has been a steadily rising level of foreign-policy activism throughout the period, from Rómulo Betancourt through Luis Herrera Campins;[1] (2) there has been a broad and generalized consensus on most major foreign-policy issues among the so-called Establishment elites of the two hegemonic parties, the Christian Democratic Party of Venezuela (COPEI) and the social democratic Acción Democrática (AD); (3) most basic criticisms have come from the political left and have largely failed to influence government policies; (4) each president has attempted, in varying degrees, to place his personal stamp on the foreign policies of his administration; and (5) despite a growing sense of independent self-confidence on the part of Venezuelan policymakers, external influences emanating from the Great Power rivalry between international capitalism and socialism have often been powerful determinants of Venezuelan thinking. In addition, it will be explained later that the degree of Establishment consensus was increasingly questioned for the first time with the approach of the 1983 elections and anticipation of a new government beginning in March 1984.

GOVERNMENTS, PARTIES, AND FOREIGN POLICY

Venezuela's first administration during the democratic era was a multiparty coalition under Rómulo Betancourt of Acción Democrática, then the dominant party.[2] Under the terms of the 1958 Pact of Punto Fijo, the AD had joined with COPEI and the Unión Republicana Democrática (URD) of Jóvito Villalba to pledge a mutual defense of democratic processes, respect for elections, restraint upon partisanship, and a collaborative government.[3] When Villalba withdrew the URD from the alliance in mid-1960 after disagreement over policy toward revolutionary Cuba—the major exception to foreign-policy consensus among political elites during this period—the two remaining parties continued in tandem. In Venezuelan political argot this was the famed *guanábana*—that tropical custard-apple delicacy whose colors of white and green matched those of the AD and COPEI respectively. Although Betancourt was a preeminently dominant civilian *caudillo* (personalistic political boss) and the AD controlled the majority of important government posts (including the foreign ministry through a pro-AD independent), the participation of COPEI was crucial to the survival of the democratic system.

The intermingling of domestic and international forces was pronounced at both polar extremes. Unrepentant rightist military leaders launched barracks uprisings against the regime, while Rafael Leónidas Trujillo of the Dominican Republic masterminded the assassination attempt that left Betancourt's hands scarred from burns and his physical equilibrium damaged for the last twenty years of his life. At the same time, domestic revolutionaries on the left, inspired and nourished by Fidel Castro, mounted first rural, then urban campaigns of violence against the constitutional government. As a consequence, the hallmark of foreign policy became the so-called Betancourt Doctrine, which adopted an equally uncompromising posture toward dictatorships of both left and right. This demanded the withholding of diplomatic recognition from illegitimate regimes—a policy first enunciated by the AD in statements of party principles years earlier.[4]

This was accompanied by the staunch anticommunism of both Betancourt and his party, which also dated far back to the early history of the man and the movement.[5] The presumed rivalry between the Venezuelan and the Cuban developmental models for Latin America was also personified by the larger-than-life figures of Betancourt and Castro, and the Venezuelan president took direct and personal command of foreign policy. It was the Caracas government that led the diplomatic offensive against Cuba to ultimately gain its suspension from the Organization of American States and, for a time, its isolation from the hemispheric family of nations. At the same time, the prodemocratic reformist and anti-Marxist community of interests between Caracas and Washington drew Venezuela and the United States into close diplomatic proximity, a fact enhanced by the warmth of friendship and mutual admiration that grew up between Betancourt and John F. Kennedy.

Although there were elements of the Venezuelan polity that disputed the official antagonism toward Havana—most notably the URD for characteristically opportunistic reasons—there was a strong consensus on the major outlines of foreign policy. Even for those otherwise disinterested in foreign affairs, the indiscriminate recklessness of Fidelista revolutionaries in their campaign of violence persuaded most Venezuelans of the validity of Betancourt's approach. This went largely unchanged from 1964 to 1969 under the government of Raúl Leoni, Betancourt's old friend and colleague from Acción Democrática. Once again a coalition administration was formed, although to Betancourt's deep distress, the AD-COPEI *guanábana* was not reconstituted by his successor. Instead, the Amplia Base alliance brought none other than the URD into government, accompanied by the newly organized Frente Nacional Democrático (FND) of the author and essayist Arturo Uslar Pietri. It was a jerry-built coalition erected largely for domestic reasons, which, however, survived most of Leoni's term. The direction of foreign affairs throughout the term remained in the hands of the president and his party.

Leoni's policies essentially maintained and extended those initiated by Betancourt. For one, the Betancourt Doctrine was continued. In honoring this cornerstone of AD thought, Leoni explained: "We maintain our principles, often alone, such as the repudiation of government by force and [opposing] the usurpation of governments by violence."[6] As did his predecessor, Raúl Leoni subordinated subregional to hemispheric-wide policy. Movement toward participation in the Andean Pact was halting, although Venezuela did eventually join the Latin American Free Trade Association (LAFTA) in 1966.[7] Meanwhile, Venezuelan energies were directed largely at attempting to heal the wounds of earlier civil violence, while building on the economic revival begun by Betancourt in correcting the mismanagement and corruption of the dictatorship. If foreign affairs did not receive high priority, this would change after 1969 when, for the first time in national history, a government defeated at the elections acquiesced in turning over power to the opposition. Rafael Caldera and COPEI, elected narrowly with 29 percent of the vote, undertook an administration free from formal alliances. It was under Caldera, in effect, that Venezuela began to assume greater importance in hemispheric affairs.

The new president, whose intellectual career and political writings had extended the Christian Democratic concept of social justice from the domestic to the international sphere,[8] became a vigorous participant in foreign affairs. Translating his notion of international social justice into what was termed "ideological pluralism," Caldera in his March 1969 inaugural address insisted upon "the establishment of relations with countries of political organization and ideology different from ours, for their presence in the world and their influence on economic relations cannot be ignored."[9] Diplomatic ties were progressively renewed with a number of countries, including the Soviet Union in March 1970. An approach to Cuba was also underway by the close of the administration. Under Caldera, Venezuela also overrode the opposition of domestic business and commercial elites to join the Andean Pact, while discourse with Colombia attempted to resolve the territorial dispute over the Gulf of Venezuela.

As I wrote elsewhere, "the administration cast its shadow across national boundaries through the personal stature and statesmanship of Rafael Caldera."[10] He was skillfully assisted by Foreign Minister Arístides Calvani, a longtime Christian Democratic intellectual and ideologue with particular expertise in international affairs. A more independent stance was adopted toward the United States, with whom relations had worsened owing to the intransigence of the latter concerning petroleum policy and tariffs.[11] Both bemused and alarmed by perceptions of Brazilian expansionism, there were even thoughts of mobilizing a Spanish-speaking continental alliance against Itamaraty. In February 1973 Caldera visited six South American capitals, preaching the gospel of ideological pluralism while exchanging *abrazos* (embraces) with such diverse chiefs of state as Guillermo Rodríguez Lara, Juan Velasco Alvarado, Salvador Allende, and Hugo Banzer. These efforts ultimately proved to be more cosmetic than practical, as before the close of his term Caldera met Brazilian President Emilio Garrastazu Medici at the border town of Santa Elena de Uairén to renew claims of mutual interest and sympathy. By March 1974, it was clear that the outgoing president had greatly enhanced Venezuela's hemispheric presence, as much through symbolism and personal prestige as from concrete policies. And notwithstanding his reversal of the AD's once-hallowed Betancourt Doctrine, foreign policy was of only secondary electoral interest during the 1973 campaign.

Again fought largely on domestic issues, the battle between COPEI and Acción Democrática resulted in a triumphant sweep and return to power for the latter in the person of Betancourt's one-time protégé, Carlos Andrés Pérez. Charismatic and controversial, Pérez soon undertook yet further efforts to project Venezuelan interests abroad. He was later to leave office accompanied by complaints that he should have devoted more time and attention to municipal services at home and less to the niceties of peripatetic visits to other chiefs of state. Even during the campaign Pérez had declared that the Betancourt Doctrine, while valid for an earlier period, was no longer applicable to international realities.[12] He consequently maintained the Caldera approach to diplomatic recognition and soon negotiated a renewal of ties with Havana. His position enhanced by the flood of *petrobolívares* (the currency earned by oil exports) that had been produced by the vertiginous rise of petroleum price from 1973-1974 and thereafter, Carlos Andrés Pérez undertook an extension of Venezuelan foreign engagements.

Years before the Mexicans were to join the enterprise, Venezuela announced at a December 1974 meeting in Puerto Ordaz with Central American chiefs of state the inauguration of a program of deferred payments on oil purchases. Both Central American and Caribbean nations were enabled to cut their expenditures virtually in half, with the remainder presumably going to other developmental purchases. Pérez also attended meetings of chiefs of state of the Organization of Petroleum Exporting Countries (OPEC), toured the hemisphere incessantly, and sought a position of Third World leadership. Speaking of petroleum and energy problems, he asserted that "we countries of the Third World . . . cannot accept the fact that prices of our raw materials are manipulated in the great financial centers of the world."[13] In time he would, join with Mexican president Luis Echeverría to found the Sistema Económico Latinoamericano (SELA), the seat for which was established in Caracas.

Under Pérez, again without serious domestic opposition, Venezuela moved more forcefully into the Caribbean. And while the Caribbean presence was growing and Pérez's travels continued, Venezuela was also providing moral and material support to Sandinista revolutionaries in Nicaragua, seeking further understanding with Havana, advising Panama's Omar Torrijos in his negotiations with the United States over the canal treaties, and courting Jimmy Carter to the point that the U.S. president termed Pérez "my number one adviser on Latin America."[14] These and many other activities marked the Pérez administration as among the most publicly vigorous and active in foreign affairs during the democratic era—for better or for worse.

It fell to COPEI's Luis Herrera Campins, who received 46 percent of the vote and was the victor over the AD's Luis Piñerúa Ordaz (who received 43 percent), to carry forward the Venezuelan cause after March 1979.[15] Few were surprised when the new chief of state soon found himself, whether deliberately or accidentally, deeply involved in foreign affairs and traveling as frequently as had Carlos Andrés Pérez before him.

A WEAKENING BIPARTISAN CONSENSUS: THE HERRERA YEARS

The basic core of *copeyano* (COPEI) ideological beliefs and views toward foreign policy—to be cited in the next section—endured through the years under Luis Herrera Campins. At the same time, however, there were perceptible shifts within the context of domestic politics and the COPEI-AD rivalry. Almost from the outset, the course of events in El

Salvador and Nicaragua, compounded by changing perceptions of Cuban policy, contributed to a lack of consensus between the Christian Democrats and their Social Democratic opponents. A second factor weakening the previous level of agreement came from internal differences within each of the two parties, most especially in the case of Acción Democrática. Added to this was a third and totally unanticipated event, the Malvinas war between Argentina and Great Britain. The confluence of these developments not only produced a reexamination of foreign-policy perspectives by the Herrera administration from mid-1982 on but also promised further partisan debate in the forthcoming campaign leading to the December 1983 elections.

During the first years of his term, President Herrera often appeared to be pursuing policies quite close to those of the United States and especially of the Reagan administration. This reflected at least three major considerations for the government: a strong and outspoken anticommunist attitude; ideological and personal ties to the hemispheric Christian Democratic movement; and a continuing desire for a position of prominence in regional affairs. Over the issue of communist conspiracy and subversion, the administration soon came into sharp conflict with Havana, provoked by a dispute over would-be Cuban exiles seeking refuge in Venezuela's embassy as well as by purported support for leftist revolutionaries in Central America. Relations with the Castro government were tense and strained until after the Malvinas conflict, whereas Venezuela negotiated the purchase of 24 F-16 aircraft from the United States. For critics, this was but further evidence of Herrera's willingness to become a surrogate for the interests of the Reagan administration in Central America and the Caribbean. Yet the charge failed to take into account a host of other factors; it similarly ignored differences between Caracas and Washington.

In embattled Central America, there were differences as well as agreements between Venezuela and the United States. These were relatively clear in the case of revolutionary Nicaragua. Although not sharing the early and sustained enthusiasm of Carlos Andrés Pérez toward the Sandinista government, Venezuela under Luis Herrera retained hopes that a pluralist system might evolve. Initial efforts by Caracas to employ aid as a means of securing benefits for Nicaraguan Christian Democrats were unsuccessful, and the level of cordiality between Caracas and Managua diminished somewhat. At the same time, however, Venezuela continued to hope that Nicaragua might be encouraged to move toward a more representative political system. It was felt that democratic pluralism might yet be possible. Venezuela also insisted upon this approach in its efforts to influence U.S. official perceptions following the inauguration of Ronald Reagan.

As Herrera told Reagan during an exchange of presidential toasts at the White House on November 17, 1981, "We have stretched out our hand to Nicaragua as Latin America awaits its conversion to democracy.

. . . As long as there remains any rational hope for a pluralistic society to be achieved there, we shall maintain our attitude of cooperation."[16] This intention—more a wish than a policy in the eyes of government critics—was restated on July 19, 1982, when Herrera attended ceremonies commemorating the third anniversary of the revolution in Masaya. Again urging the cause of pluralism, he pleaded with the Sandinistas that "On this day, Nicaragua is confronting its conscience."[17] As the authoritarian cast of the revolutionary government appeared to be solidifying by the close of 1982 and early 1983, Venezuela muted somewhat its public declarations, while continuing to monitor the situation both carefully and anxiously.

In the case of El Salvador, the superficial similarities between Venezuelan and U.S. policy were more evident, although there too the nations' policies were not invariably parallel. The ideological ties emanating from hemispheric Christian Democracy were of crucial relevance. This was an overriding consideration prior to March 1982 elections, during the time when José Napoleón Duarte served as head of the provisional government in San Salvador. A prominent Christian Democrat who had spent his 1972–1979 exile years in Venezuela following the annulment of his presidential victory at the polls by the Salvadoran military, Duarte was a personal friend as well as ideological brother of COPEI and of Herrera. Thus Venezuela, while lamenting the civil strife in El Salvador, insisted upon the importance of holding elections as a means of moving toward stability. When the voting led to the winning of power by rightist elements under Roberto D'Aubuisson and the departure of Duarte from government, the Herrera administration stepped back to undertake a reassessment, one that by the close of 1982 did not appear fully resolved. It continued to hope that revolutionary insurgency might be reduced in magnitude and, moreover, that Christian Democracy might eventually remain in a position of authority in El Salvador.

The course of events in these Central American countries helped to encourage a reassessment of perspectives and priorities on the part of the Herrera administration. This paled in significance, however, when compared with the powerful impact of the war in the South Atlantic. The initial landing of Argentine troops on the Malvinas Islands in early April produced cautious government statements supporting the use of diplomacy to resolve disputes, while politicians not burdened with official responsibilities were generally enthusiastic over what was regarded as a recapture of sovereign territory from an ancient colonial power. When the subsequent British task force sailed south into combat, however, the government became more explicitly sympathetic to Buenos Aires. Once the diplomatic travels of Alexander Haig proved unavailing and the United States declared its backing of the British, anti-U.S. feeling swept the government as well as the public. From that point on, as the record amply demonstrates, Venezuela became one of the staunchest defenders of Argentina.

Further rethinking of Venezuelan foreign policy continued in the wake of the South Atlantic war, with the Herrera government moving toward a more autonomous and independently "Latin American" posture. Relations with Cuba also began to shift. Cabinet-level exchanges took place in Havana, including discussions of the Nonaligned Movement, of which Cuba is an influential member. In July Foreign Minister José Alberto Zambrano spoke of renewed dialogue with Havana. "If Cuba wishes to overcome difficulties and again find the position it formerly occupied, . . . Venuzuela will not obstruct such an important political decision."[18] The next few months saw tangible evidence of a thaw in the relationship between the two nations, notwithstanding some signs of caution in Caracas.

Post-Malvinas policy reviews within the Herrera administration were also sensitive to a reexamination of ideological issues. Although the basic Christian Democratic thrust was unchallenged, it was also recognized that in the short run the picture had become somewhat cloudy. There was a recognition that the situation in Nicaragua was problematic, and that in any event local Christian Democrats were not a factor. The departure of Duarte from El Salvador also represented, at the very least, a temporary setback. In Costa Rica, the conclusion of Rodrigo Carazo Odio's term had brought the accession to power of Luis Alberto Monge and the Partido de Liberación Nacional (PLN), long-time Social Democratic colleagues of Acción Democrática. The earlier rise to power of Edward Seaga in Jamaica, who was strongly supported by Herrera, also lost some luster as economic conditions on the island remained sadly depressed.

In August 1982, amid his administration's ongoing review of foreign policy, Herrera met in Santo Domingo with the chiefs of state of Costa Rica, Belize, and the Dominican Republic and a Nicaraguan junta member. With nary a friendly Christian Democratic face in sight, Herrera joined in signing a document pledging a mutual commitment to national self-determination, ideological pluralism, and the avoidance of force as a means of resolving international conflicts. Back home in Venezuela, domestic debate was centering increasingly on partisan exchange linked to the unfolding electoral campaign.

Yet even as this was occurring, the administration was also engaged in continuing efforts to deal with the historic boundary dispute with Guyana over the Essequibo. Even before the Malvinas raised a speculative specter over the possible use of force, the controversy had gained renewed currency among both political elites and the Venezuelan public. A controversial and disputed settlement in 1895 had awarded a large chunk of territory to the British. The complexities of that arbitral award and the questionable circumstances around it go far beyond the scope of this chapter;[19] suffice it to say that there are defensible bases for Venezuelan claims to 130,000 square miles of land west of the Essequibo River. Venezuela had initially renewed discussion of the matter in 1962 during the Betancourt years, as then British Guiana moved toward independence from Great Britain. This led in time to the 1966 signing of the Geneva Accord between the newly independent Guyana and representatives of the Leoni government. It then fell to the Caldera administration to carry forward the negotiations, which produced the 1970 Protocol of Port-of-Spain and thereby froze the situation for twelve years. Even that agreement ran afoul of strident nationalistic critics in Venezuela, accompanied by opportunistic interference and opposition from Acción Democrática. The document was ultimately withheld from the Venezuelan Congress, where the outcome of the vote was doubtful.

The dispute lay fallow during the Pérez years, but was then revived by his successor. When Herrera and Guyanese prime minister Forbes Burnham met in April 1981 in Caracas, talks proved less than constructive. The two men had difficulty in establishing personal rapport, and Burnham upon his return home promptly announced that he would not yield "one millimeter" of territory. Herrera responded that he was uninterested in either renewing the protocol or extending the freeze. Shortly thereafter a group of fifty Venezuelan civilians, led by Herrera's minister of youth, temporarily crossed into the disputed territory and called for military occupation. As the situation gradually cooled—although Herrera rejected demands to censure his contentious lieutenant—both Foreign Minister Zambrano and Organization of American States (OAS) ambassador Hilarión Cardozo traveled extensively in both Latin America and Western Europe seeking diplomatic support for its claims. When the protocol officially lapsed on June 18, 1982, Zambrano told reporters that "Our claim is not now against the British empire . . . but we are concerned with a former British colony which, morally, is not responsible for the usurpation of which we were the object at the hands of the British empire."[20]

According to the Geneva Accord, there were three months after the lapsing of the protocol for the two governments to choose a means of peaceful settlement. Otherwise the conflict was to be referred to an international organ; this Venezuela had consistently opposed, preferring the bilateral venue for negotiations. As the matter continued to simmer, voices of immoderation arose in Venezuela. For one, former Defense Minister General Luis Enrique Rangel said "We ought to order the invasion of Essequibo today, tomorrow, or in fifteen days, but without further delay."[21] The foreign minister himself conceded the spread of such views as reflecting revived Venezuelan xenophobia as a consequence of events in the South Atlantic. Yet the government and most political leaders insisted upon denials of aggressive intentions. In mid-1982 Luis Herrera told interviewers that "Venezuela wants a peaceful solution, an honorable, intelligent, and satisfactory solution."[22]

There could have been further manifestations of shifting foreign-policy perspectives during the final months of the Herrera government, but it was apparent by the close of 1982 that the focus of attention was shifting to the campaign arena, with major decisions awaiting the elections and the formation of the next government. Before speculating about such possibilities, it is important first to review the ideologies and policy inclinations of Venezuelan political parties as they bear upon foreign affairs.

IDEOLOGIES AND PARTY INTERESTS

Of Venezuela's two dominant parties, COPEI has been more strongly influenced by, and more responsive to, ideological principles and philosophical tenets. The cornerstone has long been the thought and writing of Rafael Caldera,[23] a fact which did not change fundamentally under Herrera despite the rivalry and hostility between the two men.[24] Caldera's conception of "international social justice" as a logical extension of Christian Democratic thought bears directly on foreign-policy perspectives. Both internationally as well as domestically, in words penned two decades ago, Caldera viewed social justice as obligating the stronger toward the weaker, demanding from the richer commitment to the poorer. Such duties exist apart from mechanistic calculation and from the mathematics of communitarian justice. Thus, there is "a social justice which establishes inequality of duties to reestablish fundamental equality among men; that social justice, which exists in the same of human solidarity, imposes whatever is necessary for the common good."[25]

Such was the basis for the "ideological pluralism" of the Caldera foreign policy; it was reflected in the views of COPEI's unsuccessful 1973 candidate Lorenzo Fernández and echoed later by Luis Herrera, who for years was a major COPEI participant in both international and regional congresses of Christian Democrats. As stated in COPEI's basic program as early as 1948, moreover, there was a firm commitment to "international political economy based on the principles of cooperation, of free access to the sources of wealth for all people, of freedom of the seas, and of the application of the principles of social justice involving the defense of the weakest in the field of international economic relations."[26] As we have seen, the first *copeyano* administration saw Rafael Caldera applying ideological pluralism in the reestablishment of relations with both rightist dictatorships and socialist regimes. He also viewed Andean economic integration as consistent with ideological principles and, with some support from the AD, took Venezuela into the Andean community. In the same spirit, the Caldera administration directed greater attention than its predecessors to the Caribbean Basin.

When the party regained the presidency in 1979, political circumstances provided it for a time with greater opportunity for championing the cause of Christian Democracy on a regional basis. Thus policies toward El Salvador, Nicaragua, and Jamaica after Seaga's defeat of Michael Manley and collaboration with Ecuador's Christian Democratic president Osvaldo Hurtado[27] were linked to basic party ideological predispositions.

The frequent unofficial visits to Duarte in San Salvador by Arístides Calvani—at least nominally in the latter's role as secretary general of Organización Demócrata Cristiana de América (ODCA)—were an obvious manifestation of ideological ties. Yet it would be misleading to maintain that either Caldera or Herrera was unduly constrained in his policies by ideological blinders. In some instances foreign-policy decisions were strongly influenced by such considerations, but at other times ideology was merely helpful in rationalizing or systematizing decisions already made. In foreign as well as domestic policymaking, COPEI has traditionally blended practical political realism and careful calculation with its basic ideological orientations. Especially in foreign policy, this has produced a level of consistency found rather less regularly with Acción Democrática.

In turning to the AD, then, we find ideological considerations a less crucial factor in the determination of foreign policy. As already suggested, the best-known *adeco* (AD) principle was its support of democracy as reflected in opposition to militarism and unconstitutional regimes, embodied in the Betancourt Doctrine. Yet this was pragmatic as well as principled[28] and, when circumstances changed, was cast aside by Carlos Andrés Pérez—without, it might be noted, vocal protest from Betancourt himself. Significantly, although the AD has a series of lengthy party publications and policy statements devoted to such topics as labor, industry, oil, agriculture, and the like, there has been no such individual treatment of international affairs. The two major international objectives of the AD can generally be identified as, first, advocacy of political democracy and independence and, second, an emphasis on Latin American solidarity.[29] Clearly, neither constitutes an unmistakable ideological principle from which concrete policy might logically follow in predictable directions. Both reflect the domestic as well as hemispheric political context from which the AD emerged four decades ago and no longer serve to provide a meaningful distinction from rival party organizations.

To be sure, Acción Democrática has long shared fraternal bonds with such parties as Peru's Alianza Popular Revolucionaria Americana (APRA) and the PLN in Costa Rica—buttressed by close personal friendship among many of the party founders, including Betancourt, the now-deceased *aprista* (APRA member) Víctor Raúl Haya de la Torre, Costa Rica's José Figueres, and the late Luis Muñoz Marín of Puerto Rico.[30] Yet only within the past few years has the AD seemingly accepted the label of Social Democratic, a development energetically promoted by Carlos Andrés Pérez (most notably since he left office in 1979). Motivated at least in part by a desire to remain in the public eye and a determination to strengthen his standing within the party, Pérez has become perhaps the single-most-influential Latin American leader in the Socialist International. Certainly he has been the most visible—attending meetings, issuing declarations, traveling to Nicaragua and elsewhere, while sharing in the movement's leadership with Willy Brandt, the former West German chancellor who currently presides over the Socialist International.

In the summer of 1979 the movement held its annual conference in Caracas, with the sessions chaired by AD party president Gonzalo Barrios; Rómulo Betancourt himself appeared to cast his blessings on the meeting. In a September 1980 gathering of the Latin American Caribbean branch of the Socialist International, Pérez chaired the conference. It issued a communiqué condemning the Bolivian *golpe de estado* (coup d'etat) declaring solidarity with Michael Manley's People's National party (PNP) in Jamaica, and attacking authoritarian repression in Haiti, Paraguay, and Uruguay. At the same time, Acción Democrática was not entirely comfortable in this participation. It had serious questions about the Sandinista regime in Nicaragua despite the enthusiasm of Pérez, who was a widely lionized guest during earlier celebrations in Managua of the overthrow of the Anastasio Somoza dynasty.

Moreover, the strong identification of Pérez with the international Social Democratic connection has clouded the official party posture, given the continuing *adeco* party infighting and the presence of strong anti-*carlosandresista* elements (those opposed to Carlos Andrés Pérez). It is worth noting that a planned meeting of the Socialist International in Caracas scheduled for February 1982 was moved elsewhere when Acción Democrática, with the approval of Costa Rican and Dominican representatives, opposed the projected participation of Sandinista representatives. Both Gonzalo Barrios and Pérez himself opposed alleged Nicaraguan actions and inclinations "contrary to the principle of democratic pluralism."[31] Thus it would be a mistake to exaggerate the Social Democratic theme, although neither should it be forgotten nor discounted. It is a moot point whether the Acción Democrática return to Miraflores Palace in March 1984 will be a significant element in the future shaping and elaboration of Venezuelan foreign policy. Practical considerations, linked with internal party politics, will be more decisive than ideological concepts.

It is important to bear in mind that just as COPEI and Acción Democrática share many basic convictions in the realm of domestic policy, there has also been a commonality of values in international policy. To be sure, we have suggested that the consensus has been increasingly buffeted by the winds of rebellion, insurgency, and instability in the Caribbean Basin in the last few years. At the same time, it should be stressed that whatever the pragmatic or programmatic differences between the two great parties, they are as one in pursuing hemispheric unity while ardently defending the cause of political democracy. Concerning the former, hear first the words of then President Carlos Andrés Pérez in 1976: "The history of all our countries confirms and reaffirms the conclusion that we cannot develop or progress without uniting. The fortune of each and every one of us cannot be a matter of indifference to the others."[32] Now the voice of President Luis Herrera Campins: "Latin America, in spite of conflicts in its political life, does not forget that the special vocation of its people obliges them to march toward liberty and democracy—the only manner in which man can live fully in justice and dignity."[33]

Among the more recent public manifestations of such attitudes was the September 11, 1980, declaration of several Latin American chiefs of state (Venezuela, Costa Rica, Panama, Colombia, and Ecuador) enshrining the observation of human rights and the consolidation of hemispheric democracy. The words of Herrera reflected equally the outlook of COPEI and of Acción Democrática on such fundamental issues: "The despotism and the violence organized in portions of our continent where liberty had previously flamed, can only postpone *sine die* the democratic normalization of countries of humans. . . ."[34]

Of the remaining Venezuelan parties, little need be said in this context. For one thing, they have not held power or influenced foreign-policy decisions. For another, there has been a characteristic fragmentation and disunity of the political left.[35]

THE PARTIES AND THE FUTURE OF FOREIGN POLICY

Although the electoral campaign did not officially begin until the spring of 1983, it was known for many months before that the major contenders would be former president and COPEI founder Rafael Caldera for the Christian Democrats and Jaime Lusinchi for Acción Democrática. It was equally clear that the hegemonic power of the two parties assured that no other candidate or party could win. Social scientists know that domestic politics are inextricably interwoven into the fabric of foreign policy. Thus, in writing this chapter a year prior to election day, a few speculative remarks about the present priorities and outlook of the two parties may be in order. With COPEI and Acción Democrática looking toward a new administration and the fuller unfolding of the decade of the 1980s, past patterns remain important in projecting a future profile of Venezuelan foreign policy.

If one is to focus on political personality, the case of Rafael Caldera presents an earlier track record to guide judgments and expectations. Caldera is vastly experienced in foreign affairs both as scholar and statesman and can be expected to place his personal imprimatur on foreign policy while assuming a major hemispheric role. He will be vigorously nationalistic and independent. Although not seeking open conflict with Washington, he will not hesitate to differ should the situation dictate. The pronounced, often unsubtle anticommunist fervor of the early Herrera years is unlikely to be manifested. Caldera will in no sense diminish Venezuela's projection of its democratic vocation, but rather will blend ideology with pragmatism and an acute sense of international and regional realities. Equally importantly, Venezuelan foreign policy under another Caldera government will decidedly and unequivocally mirror the ideas and leadership of one man—Rafael

Caldera. In addition, the expertise and experience of the *copeyano* foreign-policy cadre will assure a skillful implementation of decisions.

With the opposition, more can be learned from examining Acción Democrática than from its candidate, whose experience in foreign affairs is not extensive. The AD, by no means the handmaiden of U.S. interests during its periods in government, has customarily been more comfortable than COPEI in its dealings with Washington. Its Social Democratic inclinations will not be exuberantly personified by Jaime Lusinchi as they were with Pérez, and policies will be dominated by practical realities. Those in the party with international experience who are closest to Lusinchi—as, for example, former Foreign Minister Simón Alberto Consalvi—are eminently practical men. The same is true of such foreign-policy veterans as Marcos Falcón Briceño, Ramón Escovar Salom, Enrique Tejera París, and others. A Lusinchi administration would generally be a team effort manned by *adeco* leaders, with the chief of state a less dominant personality than Rafael Caldera for COPEI.

Granted the rethinking of Venezuelan foreign-policy priorities and commitments following the Malvinas fighting, there is somewhat greater uncertainty over configurations in the near future than would have been customary in post-1958 Venezuela. To be sure, there will be continued advocacy of democratic values and principles, an opposition to Marxism, an enduring presence in the Caribbean Basin, and the exercise of leadership in hemispheric affairs. There will be both competition and collaboration with the Mexicans; ties with Colombia may be more proper than warm, given the still-unresolved border dispute between Caracas and Bogotá. Reasonable interchange with Washington will not deter expressions of independence, especially during the lifetime of the Reagan administration, which holds many perceptions of the Caribbean broadly rejected by Venezuelan elites of both major parties. This mirrors policy realities, differing national interests, and a widespread Venezuelan perception of U.S. party politics that was articulated by the late Rómulo Betancourt with characteristic bite on the eve of 1980 elections in the United States. As he put it, "There is a difference between Carter and Reagan which we . . . readily appreciate. Whenever the Republican Party has governed the United States, the White House and the Department of State have favored dictatorial regimes."[36]

Under the umbrella of multilateralism, Venezuelan policy will continue to be shaped by specific conditions in a number of countries. Even though the 1984–1989 stewardship of foreign affairs is the responsibility of the AD, a broadly shared perception of national interest will be articulated and interpreted through a sensitivity to hard practical realities. The greater ideological coherence found in COPEI may induce a greater depth of consistency in the application of foreign policy, but the responsiveness to new or altered conditions will endure, regardless of the party in power. Furthermore, the high level of civic politicization in Venezuela will assure the continuing centrality of the two historic party rivals as the government perceives and interacts with hemispheric and global powers. The weight of Venezuelan foreign policy will remain an important dimension of inter-American affairs. As I contended elsewhere, at the very least Venezuela will continue to be "an important and influential actor in the international affairs of Latin America and, barring a collapse of its present political system, will . . . speak out on behalf of the historic ideals of freedom and human rights."[37]

NOTES

1. For a discussion that includes the Pérez years, see John D. Martz, "Venezuelan Foreign Policy Toward Latin America," in Robert D. Bond (ed.), *Contemporary Venezuela and Its Role in International Affairs* (New York: New York University Press, for the Council on Foreign Relations, 1977), pp. 156–195.

2. Three essays that portray regional perspectives during the Betancourt administration appear in Rubén Carpio Castillo, *México, Cuba, Venezuela: Triángulo Geopolítico del Caribe* (Caracas: Imprenta Nacional, 1961).

3. For discussion of the tripartite agreement in a work that stresses the collaborative approach of party elites, see Daniel H. Levine, *Conflict and Political Change in Venezuela* (Princeton: Princeton University Press, 1973), especially pp. 42–44.

4. Detailed analysis of these AD "theses" appears in John D. Martz, *Acción Democrática: Evolution of a Modern Political Party in Venezuela* (Princeton: Princeton University Press, 1966), pp. 224–253.

5. Definitive accounts have been given by both Betancourt and his unofficial biographer. See Rómulo Betancourt, *Venezuela, Política, y Petróleo*, 2d ed. (Caracas: Editorial Senderos, 1967); also Robert J. Alexander, *Rómulo Betancourt and the Transformation of Venezuela* (New Brunswick, N.J.: Transaction Books, 1982).

6. For an English version of Leoni's full statement, see *Venezuela Up-to-date*, no. 12 (Winter 1968–1969), p. 8.

7. A contemporary treatment appears in Robert P. Clark, Jr., "Economic Integration and the Political Process: Linkage Politics in Venezuela," and also in Antonio Alamo B., "Economic Integration in Latin America and the Case of Venezuela," both in Philip B. Taylor, Jr. (ed.), *Venezuela: 1969; Analysis of Progress* (Houston: University of Houston, Office of International Affairs, 1971), pp. 216–237 and 237–249 respectively.

8. A review of Christian Democratic thought and of Caldera's contributions is found in Miguel Jorrín and John D. Martz, *Latin-American Political Thought and Ideology* (Chapel Hill: University of North Carolina Press, 1970), pp. 405–428.

9. Rafael Caldera, *Discurso a la Nación* (Caracas: Imprenta Nacional, 1969).

10. Martz, "Venezuelan Foreign Policy Toward Latin America," p. 162.

11. An overview that elucidates foreign-policy perspectives at the time is Charles J. Ameringer, "The Foreign Policy of Venezuelan Democracy," in John D. Martz and David J. Myers (eds.), *Venezuela: The Democratic Experience* (New York: Praeger Publishers, 1977), pp. 335–359.

12. John D. Martz and Enrique A. Baloyra, *Electoral Mobilization and Public Opinion: The Venezuelan Campaign of 1973* (Chapel Hill: University of North Carolina Press, 1976), pp. 149–150.

13. "Interview with President Pérez: What the Third World Wants," *Business Week*, October 13, 1975.

14. Cited in John D. Martz, "Ideology and Oil: Venezuela in the Circum-Caribbean," in E. Michael Erisman and John D. Martz (eds.), *Colossus Challenged: The Struggle for Caribbean Influence* (Boulder, Colo.: Westview Press, 1982), p. 125.

15. Essays concerning the 1978 elections are collected in Howard Penniman (ed.), *Venezuela at the Polls* (Washington, D.C.: American Enterprise Institute, 1980).

16. *Venezuela Up-to-date*, no. 22–24 (Winter 1981–1982), p. 8.

17. *Washington Post*, July 20, 1982, p. A-18.

18. *SIC* (Caracas), no. 447 (July–August 1982), p. 325.

19. A brief historical sketch appears in Stephen G. Rabe, *The Road to OPEC: United States Relations with Venezuela, 1919–1976* (Austin: University of Texas Press, 1982), pp. 7–8.

20. *Times of the Americas*, July 7, 1982, p. 9.

21. *Latin American Times* 4, no. 41 (August 1982), p. 10.

22. *Times of the Americas*, July 7, 1982, p. 9.

23. A selective listing of Caldera's voluminous writings accompanies the analysis of Jorrín and Martz, *Latin-American Political Thought*. Also see Rafael Caldera, *Especificidad de la democracia cristiana*, 2d ed (Barcelona: Editorial Nova Terra, 1983) and *Ideario: la democracia cristiana en América Latina* (Barcelona: Ediciones Ariel, S.A., 1970).

24. Useful discussions recently published from a 1962 seminar are accessible in Víctor Giménez Landínez et al., *Los copeyanos* (Caracas: Ediciones Centauro, 1982).

25. Rafael Caldera, *El Bloque Latinoamericano* (Santiago: Editorial del Pacífico, 1961), pp. 25–26.

26. As cited and elaborated upon in Donald L. Herman, *Christian Democracy in Venezuela* (Chapel Hill: University of North Carolina Press, 1980), pp. 172 ff.

27. One of the few extensive surveys of Ecuadorean political history, written a few years before his presidency, is Osvaldo Hurtado, *El poder político en el Ecuador*, 2d ed. (Quito: Universidad Católica del Ecuador, 1977). A later English translation by Nick Mills, which includes a postscript by then Vice-President Hurtado, was published by the University of New Mexico Press in 1980.

28. Both ideological and practical geneses of the attitude are carefully traced and developed for what were then termed the *aprista*-type parties in Charles J. Ameringer, *The Democratic Left in Exile: The Antidictatorial Struggle in the Caribbean, 1945–1959* (Coral Gables, Fla.: University of Miami Press, 1974).

29. Martz, *Acción Democrática*, pp. 250–252.

30. Treatment of Social Democratic thought is found in Jorrín and Martz, *Latin-American Political Thought*, pp. 316–386.

31. *Times of the Americas*, September 29, 1982, p. 9.

32. *Resumen* (Caracas), May 16, 1976, p. 14.

33. Luis Herrera Campins, "National Press Club Address," *Venezuela Up-to-date*, no. 22–24 (Winter 1981–1982), p. 12.

34. *SIC* (Caracas), no. 428 (September–October 1980), p. 370.

35. The stark ideological protest to Soviet action was powerfully argued in Teodoro Petkoff, *Checoslovaquia: El socialismo como problem* (Caracas: n.p., 1969). Among his many later works, a characteristic statement is Petkoff's *Socialismo para Venezuela?* (Caracas: Editorial Fuentes, 1972).

36. *El Nacional* (Caracas), October 31, 1980, p. D-1.

37. Martz, "Venezuelan Foreign Policy Toward Latin America," p. 195.

10. The International Policy of the Socialist Party and Foreign Relations of Chile

INTRODUCTION

It is a well-known fact that a country's foreign policy is the product of a complex interrelation of external and internal factors. Among these can be counted the role played by various nongovernmental agencies like the church, business, labor unions, and political parties. In Chile's case, the role that nongovernmental agencies play in its foreign policy has been virtually ignored in the specialized literature.

This chapter examines the relationship between the Socialist party (SP) and Chilean foreign policy and deals, at the same time, with the evolution of international thought within the party. The study of the Socialist party's international policy and of its influence on Chile's foreign relations seems important for several reasons. In the first place, international policy has been a fundamental element in the Socialist party outlook since its foundation. This orientation has, in fact, helped preserve its historical identity with respect to other parties, particularly with respect to the Communist party (CP). In the second place, the Socialist party has occasionally participated in government coalitions. It therefore seems relevant to analyze the extent to which the party's views of world reality influenced its conduct in the government and the formulation of the country's foreign policy. Finally, and in connection with the first point, the fact that a party of the left has a well-defined international policy has obvious domestic implications. In fact, a study of this phenomenon could help to clarify the nature of socialism in Chile and its possible future development.

The central proposition of this chapter is that the international policy of the SP has tended to concentrate midway between populism and doctrinaire socialism. Precisely in the balancing of these two ideological poles might be said to reside the originality and special character of Chilean socialism and of its international policy. In any case, I maintain that, despite the oscillations experienced by socialist international policy, it is possible to discern in it the more or less constant presence, over time, of particular principles or dimensions that may be said to constitute the basic nucleus of the international orientation of the SP.

In turn, the international policy of the SP must ultimately be understood as the expression or product of two fundamental factors: the nature of the Socialist party and the historical relationship between Chilean socialism and communism. With regard to the first factor, the character of the Socialist party can be defined succinctly as "national" and "popular."[1] The national and popular character of the SP would tend to explain not only the behavior of Chilean socialism on the domestic front but also its policy of nonalignment in the area of international politics, its emphasis on analyzing world realities from a Chilean standpoint as well as in terms of national priorities, and its opposition to the politics of blocs. The popular dimension of the SP, reinforced by the coexistence within the party of representative groups from different sectors of the society, could be seen as the original source of the populism, the integrationist Latin Americanism, and the Indo-Americanism of the Socialist party's international policy.

The adversarial streak that has characterized the relationship between socialism and communism in Chile since the 1930s tends to explain also the conduct of the SP in the area of international relations. In fact, from the very founding of the SP in 1933, the Socialists defined an autonomous foreign policy for Chilean socialism and for the country, in contrast to the pro-Soviet orientation of the Chilean CP. From this conflictive relationship between socialism and communism could be said to derive a fundamental dimension of the international policy of the SP, symbolized in its reluctance to participate in internationals, in its search for experiences and lessons derived from socialist countries outside of the Soviet orbit, and in its insistence on an autonomous and antiimperialist foreign policy for both the country and the party. In a certain sense, this aspect of socialist foreign policy could be seen as the "reactive" element that can also be observed in the overall behavior of the SP. That is to say, given the heterogeneous base of Chilean socialism, its "self-consciousness" is acquired, partly, through a "rejection of others," in this case, of the CP and its international policy.

As a corollary of what has been said above, my claim here is that, despite the variations in the international policy of the SP, when Chilean socialism did take part in coalition governments and had access to the decision-making process in the area of foreign policy, it adopted a policy of "principled pragmatism"[2] based on the central aspects of the international orientation that historically characterized the party. That is, whenever the Socialist party took on government responsibilities, and even when it found itself momentarily approaching one of the poles previously mentioned, the party's international thinking tended to relocate itself at a point equidistant between populism and doctrinaire socialism and to commit itself to a flexible national foreign policy free of abrupt breaks in continuity and consistency. This tendency might well be explained by the predominance within the SP of the most permanent features of its international thought derived from the nature of the party as well as from its leaders, by the relationship obtaining between the SP and the CP, by the fact that the SP had to reconcile its own policies with those of the other parties involved in government coalitions, and, lastly, by the limitations imposed by both regional and global realities.

THE EVOLUTION OF THE INTERNATIONAL POLICY OF THE SP

When the Socialist party was founded on April 19, 1933, one of its basic concerns was the need to advance an autonomous foreign policy. The adoption of an independent international policy was, on the one hand, a reaction against the aligned international position of the Chilean Communist party, which followed the dictates of the Soviet-oriented South American section of the Comintern (Third International), and, on the other, an outcome of the nationalist–Latin Americanist thought predominant among the various groups that constituted the Socialist party.

All of the groups that formed the SP in 1933 shared, despite their differences, a fundamental common vision of international reality, a perception of Chile as the point of departure of any political analysis, and a profound distrust of recommendations coming from abroad. In essence, the international line that the new party adopted stressed the need to oppose all types of imperialism and the necessity to foster Latin-Americanism—as opposed to Pan-Americanism—and regional integration.

Perhaps the central theme of socialist thought on international affairs during the period of Latin American nationalism of the SP was that of regional integration. This preoccupation emerged in the discussion on imperialism and was highly influenced by the linkages that the SP developed with Latin American populist movements like the Alianza Popular Revolucionaria Americana (APRA) of Peru, Acción Democrática (AD) of Venezuela, and the Partido Revolucionario Institucional (PRI) of Mexico.

In the view of the SP, economic nationalism and resistance to foreign penetration were indispensable elements to ensure long-range development in Chile. Considering the underdevelopment and dependency experienced by the countries of the region, it became necessary to stimulate the unification of Latin American nations and the pursuit of common goals based on shared interests vis-à-vis the developed powers. Unlike other parties of the left, the international policy of the SP was founded on the premise that the process of worldwide exploitation involved not only social classes but also nation-states; hence the need for regional cooperation and integration. The Socialist thesis, posed in 1933, of struggling for the establishment of a Federation of Socialist Republics in Latin America must be understood in this framework.[3]

During 1955 and 1956 several leaders of the SP visited Yugoslavia and met with Tito. The cordial relationship that developed between the SP and Yugoslavia contributed, in turn, to the deterioration of ties between Chilean Socialists and Communists, particularly when in 1958 the Communist Party of the Soviet Union broke relations with Yugoslavia. Thus, throughout 1958 and 1959 a sharp debate occurred between Chilean Communists who condemned the Socialist stand on Yugoslavia as "a third position which masked a rabid anticommunism" and Socialists who reaffirmed their support of Yugoslav socialism and its nonaligned policy and even translated into Spanish several key texts authored by Yugoslavian socialists.[4]

The Socialist interest in the Yugoslav model led the SP to expand contacts with many countries of Asia and Africa that were achieving independence and that shared the objectives of following an autonomous socialist development road and a nonaligned foreign policy.

The SP participated in the various Asian socialist conferences held throughout the 1950s and maintained privileged relationships with, among others, the Algerian independence movement and later with the independent state of Algeria. During this period, the nonaligned position of the SP was challenged by the Sino-Soviet dispute. Nonetheless, Chilean Socialists opted not to get involved in that conflict and stated their rejection of any effort to hegemonize socialist movements at the world level.[5] In the 1960s the influence of the Yugoslav experience in the international position of the SP declined and was replaced by the transcendental impact of the Cuban Revolution.

Although in general terms the posture of nonalignment continued, progressively the SP began to implement policies highly congruent with those of Cuban socialism. Never before had a foreign experience exercised the degree of influence on the orientations of the SP as did Cuba in the 1960s. The explanation of this phenomenon is consistent with the historical tradition of Chilean socialism. For the SP, the Cuban Revolution symbolized and synthesized the essential tenets of party thought on international affairs. In short, Cuba constituted a nationalist, antiimperialist, popular, anticapitalist, and Latin-Americanist experience. Unlike Yugoslavia, the Cuban case represented a process with which Chile and Chilean Socialists could identify fully—that is, politically, culturally, geographically, historically, and economically; unlike the various nationalist-populist experiments in Latin America, Cuba was to build socialism from below and not as the imposition of foreign troops, within the Western hemisphere and merely ninety miles away from the United States.

The Cuban experience also affected the notions on transition to socialism that prevailed within the SP. Consequently, some sectors of the SP assimilated tactical and strategic lines of the Cuban Revolution. The special relationship that developed between Chilean socialism and Cuba signified that the SP permanently supported the Cuban government in its confrontation with Washington and struggled to impede the isolation of Havana from the Latin American community.

In this context, the international policy of the SP radicalized and turned less flexible. During this period the Socialists condemned the Latin American Free Trade Association (LAFTA) as an instrument oriented to serve the interests of the United States and opposed the creation of the Andean Pact, which was seen largely as a scheme that would facilitate the expansion of transnational capitalism in the region.

The military coup of September 11, 1973, which overthrew the government of Salvador Allende, in its aftermath produced a profound breakdown of the social, economic, cultural, and political structures of Chile, including the party system. The Socialist party experienced perhaps the most severe crisis in its history. It entailed the division of the party into several factions and at the same time the development of a debate about the previous practices of Chilean socialism and an intellectual search for theoretical renovation as well as an effort to recoup the rich historical tradition of the SP. In fact, the retrieval of some of the basic consensual principles of Chilean socialism, particularly its nonaligned, Latin-Americanist perspective, contributed to the reemergence of the international attitude of the SP and to the process of reunification of the party.

In the evolution of the SP's international policy, there seems to have been an accumulation and superimposition of experiences rather than a linear process of neat substitutions of one current for another. These experiences, far from having been discarded by totally new realities, have gone on to form an amalgam of principles that has tended to endure over time. There are six of these international principles.

Antiimperialism. The SP has tended to oppose any type of imperialism and colonial domination. As a result, it has supported the right of nations to self-determination and particularly the efforts to construct autonomous and democratic socialism.

Nationalist Perspectives. The SP has maintained that the analysis of international realities must be carried out from a Chilean perspective, with national interests and priorities in mind. This point has been constantly emphasized in discussions with the Chilean CP.

Nonalignment. As a corollary of the preceding principle, Chilean socialism has generally avoided any involvement with particular coalitions or groups of countries and has permanently rejected the idea of formally becoming part of an international.

Opposition to the Politics of Blocs. In the eyes of the SP the emphasis some countries place on the maintenance of blocs and on international military confrontation tends to obscure the political importance of social classes and groups. Consequently, the SP has affirmed the need to reduce military spending in favor of economic development, and it has opposed military pacts.

Latin-Americanism and Third Worldism. To attain the objectives of national development, Chilean socialism has favored economic, cultural, and political integration of the region. This latter view has resulted in an attitude of reticence toward the concepts of Pan-Americanism and Inter-Americanism and of support for the idea of encouraging cooperative organisms proper to Latin America. As a subproduct of this principle, there has been an affirmation of the need to develop closer ties with the popular movements of Asia and Africa.

Protection of National Resources. As a result of its nationalistic orientation, the SP has consistently expressed the urgent need to defend national resources, both on land and in the ocean, and the need to exploit these for the benefit of the countries where they are found. At the same time, the national control of these resources, as well as their efficient exploitation, has been viewed as an essential factor in the process of industrialization.

THE SOCIALIST PARTY IN CHILEAN FOREIGN POLICY

Two cases will be used in order to evaluate the impact of the Socialist party's international policy on Chile's foreign relations: first, the period covered by the governments of Pedro Aguirre Cerda and Juan Antonio Ríos in relation to World War II; second, the period of the Unidad Popular (1970–1973). These two cases seem to be particularly relevant because in both periods Chilean socialism was part of the government and had access to the decision-making process in the area of foreign policy. It is important to clarify that it is not my intention here to analyze Chilean foreign policy during the periods in question, but only the role played in it by the Socialist party.

The Government of the Popular Front
and of Juan A. Ríos and World War II

The victory of the Popular Front in the 1938 elections meant the entrance of the SP into the government for the first time since the founding of the party. The SP's team of ministers was made up of Oscar Schnake in Development, Rolando Merino in Lands and Settlement, and Salvador Allende in Public Health.

During this period the SP's performance was essentially conditioned by its relationship with the Communists and by the course of events in World War II. The beginning of World War II in September 1939, in addition to the prior advance of fascism in Europe, led the SP to relegate its opposition to "international capitalism" to second place in favor of active resistance to the expansionism of Nazi Germany. The signing of the Molotov–Von Ribbentrop Nonaggression and Mutual Aid Pact between the USSR and Germany considerably increased Socialist resistance to the Nazi offensive. Together with other factors, it served to weaken the ties between the Socialists and Communists and erode the Popular Front.

The political and economic exigencies of World War II then led the Socialists—as well as the APRA in Peru who up to then had firmly opposed North American imperialism and foreign penetration—to adopt a positive stance toward the United States. In July 1940, President Pedro Aguirre Cerda designated Socialist minister Oscar Schnake as head of the Chilean delegation to the Inter-American Conference in Havana, which was held to confront the problems already being faced by the countries of Latin America as a result of the war. Schnake and the Socialists maintained that the defense of the nations of the continent and of their national resources was possible only if economic cooperation among all the American nations, as well as close antitotalitarian political unity, could be achieved. With this concern in mind, the SP convoked, in October 1940, the First Congress of Democratic and Popular Parties in Latin America. The congress was held in Santiago and was attended by, among others, Rómulo Betancourt of Venezuela. The purpose of the congress was to discuss the situation of the continent in light of the war. In 1941 the SP recommended calling an Economic Conference of Latin American Governments, an idea that did not prosper.

At the conclusion of the Havana Conference of July 1940, Schnake traveled to the United States with the purpose of obtaining financial aid to cover the deficits in the Chilean economy and to negotiate the sale of saltpeter and copper. The minister of development obtained what he had set out to get, including a loan of five million dollars to cover the existing currency deficit. He returned to Chile praising the high standard of living and political democracy enjoyed by the people of the United States.[6]

In the meantime, the Chilean Communist party had assumed an attitude of growing hostility toward the United States as its participation in what the CP called the "imperialist war"[7] became more imminent. Chilean Communists opposed the Havana conference and recommended that the Chilean representatives resist the "imperialist plans of the United States for the region." Afterward, the CP harshly attacked Schnake's conduct at the meeting and his mission to Washington. For its part, the SP pointed to the importance of the agreements negotiated by the minister of development, agreements the Socialists envisioned as the only available option for maintaining an acceptable standard for the Chilean people in times of austerity and crisis. At the same time, the SP denounced the CP as an obstacle to cooperation between Chile and the United States, criticizing the Communist policy of "tolerance of Fascism" in line with the interests of the Soviet Union.[8]

Toward the beginning of December 1940, relations between the SP and the CP had deteriorated to such a degree that the president of the Radical party felt obliged to intervene in order to bring about a "cessation of hostilities." However, on his return from Washington on December 15, Schnake made a violent speech against the CP and presented the Popular Front with an ultimatum: Either the Communists must be excluded from the alliance or the SP would withdraw. The remaining member parties of the front ignored the ultimatum; as a result, the SP left the coalition in January 1941.[9] The Socialist ministers subsequently relinquished their government posts. However, after the elections of March 1941, in which the SP participated independently, the Socialists again began to take part in the government.

Pedro Aguirre Cerda died at the end of November 1941; President Juan Antonio Ríos, who had been elected by a coalition of radicals, liberals, and Socialists, took office on April 1, 1942. Again the Socialists became part of the presidential cabinet, although a split began to develop between a group within the party that favored continuing in the Ríos government and one that argued for leaving the government in order to unite and renew the party. However, there was ample consensus regarding international policy.

By the time of the Eighth General Congress of the SP, held in March 1942, the United States had already entered the war, principally as a result of the Japanese attack on Pearl Harbor in December 1941. At that same congress the SP approved a resolution favoring Chile's breaking with the Axis powers because, according to the resolution, "this would aid coordinated action with other Latin American countries and with the United States in the defense and expansion of democracy and in the securing of effective economic assistance."[10] From then on the SP constantly pressed Ríos to abandon his neutralist position and to break all ties with the Axis powers. In this sense, the SP's objectives coincided with those of the U.S. Embassy in Santiago. Moreover, at that point the Chilean CP had changed its position; as a result of Hitler's attack on the USSR in June 1941 in violation of the Soviet-German mutual nonaggression pact of 1939, it now favored breaking with the Axis powers.

In July 1942 the possibility was raised in Washington of giving economic aid, with private funding from U.S. newspapers, to that part of the Chilean media that favored breaking with the Axis powers. At the same time, the U.S. ambassador in Santiago suggested the possibility of providing assistance to the daily La Crítica, which most strongly supported the idea of breaking with the Axis powers and which was going through serious financial difficulties.[11] However, perhaps because the newspaper was controlled by the SP, Washington finally decided not to grant the proposed financial assistance.

Nevertheless, the U.S. government maintained friendly contacts with the SP in connection with the idea of severing relations with Axis powers. At least in internal communications, and later publicly, Washington recognized the positive role the SP played during the period. At a certain point Nelson Rockefeller and an aide to Lord Mountbatten held personal interviews with Salvador Allende, Oscar Schnake, and other Socialist leaders, as well as with some liberal leftist leaders, to discuss common strategies tending to favor the position of the Allies in Chile.[12] Claude G. Bowers, U.S. ambassador to Chile at that time, maintains in his memoirs that the Socialist members of the National Congress were the most numerous and open partisans of breaking diplomatic ties with the Axis powers. He throws into relief as well the political significance of the anti-Axis stand of Oscar Schnake.[13] Also, on behalf of the Socialists, Marmaduke Grove assured the U.S. Embassy on several occasions that his party, more than any other, firmly supported the Allied cause.

Finally, in January 1943, the Ríos government broke diplomatic and economic ties with the Axis powers. Later on it capitulated to additional pressures imposed by the United States and declared war against Japan (in February 1945).

What were the reasons for the SP's insistence that Chile suspend relations with the Axis powers? It appears to have been the result of several factors. In the first place, the Socialists had been deeply affected by the position taken by the Chilean CP when, because of the Molotov–Von Ribbentrop pact, it had ceased its opposition to Nazi expansion in Europe. Consequently, the SP sought to make perfectly clear the pro-Soviet nature of the position taken by Chilean communism, since it was only after the USSR was directly attacked by Germany that the CP joined the local political forces in demanding the severing of relations with the Axis. In other words, by means of its militant stance *against* the Axis and *for* the breaking of relations, the SP tried to demonstrate the "erratic and dependent" nature of the international policies of Chilean communism and in the process to weaken communism's base of support in favor of socialism. In the words of Humberto Mendoza, the Socialist position in support of the Allies responded to a need to "gain the confidence of the proletariat for the Socialist Party through a clear and consistent international policy."[14]

Second, the SP supported the severing of relations with the Axis as the only pragmatic option that, in a period of generalized crisis, could assure Chile the financial and commercial support of the United States, support that was necessary to guarantee the economic and political future of the country. This is to say, at that particular time, the Chilean Socialist party's pragmatism and nationalism tended to override the other political priorities of Chilean socialism.

In the third place, the SP saw an eventual military victory by the Axis as the beginning of the end of the international labor movement and as the "destruction of every achievement made by the working classes and by society itself."[15] According to the Socialists, an Allied victory at least provided for the preservation of democracy and opened up a series of new political opportunities, especially in light of the differences of opinion that might well emerge among the victorious nations.

Finally, several of the Socialist leaders felt a genuine personal sympathy toward the United States and the Allied cause. Marmaduke Grove, for example, greatly admired President Franklin Roosevelt and his political and social program of the New Deal. Union leader Bernardo Ibañez, who was secretary general of the SP in 1943, had visited the United States on innumerable occasions at the invitation of the AFL-CIO and had even obtained the support of the State Department and the American Federation of Labor–Congress of Industrial Organizations (AFL-CIO) during the period when the Chilean labor movement found itself divided between Socialists and Communists. And Schnake himself, as was previously mentioned, admired the economic prosperity and the electoral democracy that existed in the United States. Taken together then, the elements mentioned tend to explain the position taken by the SP, both inside and outside the government, with regard to the most important international event of the late 1930s and mid-1940s.

The Socialist Party and the Foreign Policy of the Unidad Popular (UP)

The Socialist party played the role of the protagonist in both the formulation and the carrying out of the international policies of the coalition government of Salvador Allende, the Unidad Popular. But it is important to emphasize the great difference between the concrete contributions made by the SP to the foreign-policy section of the Basic Government Program of the Unidad Popular and what was actually accomplished by the Socialists who took charge of the government's foreign policy.

While the Unidad Popular's program was being developed, the SP submitted several proposals regarding international policy. In fact, according to one account of the meetings held to discuss the program, the international section was practically the exclusive responsibility of the Socialists.[16]

The SP representatives made it clear that foreign policy would be "aimed at affirming Chile's full political and economic autonomy"; that Chile would maintain relations with all the nations of the world "without regard to their ideological and political stance"; that it would develop ties of friendship with Latin American nations, as well as with countries on other continents; that it would attempt to resolve lingering border problems; and that it would defend the principle of national self-determination for all peoples and the rights of nations to control their own primary resources. In addition, the Socialists proposed reinforcing "relations, exchanges, and friendship with the Socialist countries" and supporting the Cuban Revolution and the Vietnamese people in the face of U.S. intervention. The most controversial aspects of the Socialist proposals were essentially three: first, the idea that there should be an "international policy of peoples, not of Ministries of Foreign Affairs," accompanied by the suggestion that Chilean diplomacy should "do away with all forms of bureaucracy and paralysis"; second, the conviction that the Organization of American States (OAS) had to be denounced as a "tool and agent of North American Imperialism," with the accompanying suggestion that there was a need to "create an organization that would be truly representative of the Latin American nations"; and finally, the view that it was "indispensable to revise, denounce, or reject, as the case required," all treaties or agreements that limited the nation's sovereignty, specifically reciprocal-aid treaties, mutual-assistance pacts, and other pacts made by Chile with the United States.[17]

When the Unidad Popular came to power, the SP in effect took over the foreign-policy operations of the nation. Responsibility for the direction of the Ministry of Foreign Relations went to Clodomiro Almeyda. It is important to note that only two ministers, Clodomiro Almeyda and Orlando Letelier, both of them Socialists, held the foreign relations post, whereas more than ten cabinet crises shook the rest of the ministries. That is to say, during the period in question there was a high degree of continuity in the management of Chilean foreign affairs.

With the exception of the three controversial aspects of the program already mentioned (all of which tended to reflect a leaning toward doctrinaire socialism, under the powerful influence of the Cuban experience, on the part of the SP's international policy), the remaining proposals were perfectly consistent with the long-standing postulates of Chilean socialism in the area of international affairs and with the character of the SP. Consequently, because they were elements shared by other political forces in the coalition and even by some outside the coalition, these international proposals were put into practice without delay, although somewhat eclectically.[18]

In accordance with the proposition that diplomatic relations should be maintained with all nations regardless of their ideological and political inclinations, the Allende government reestablished diplomatic ties with Cuba and went on to establish relations with other nations that had not previously had diplomatic ties with Chile: the People's Republic of China, North Korea, North Vietnam, the German Democratic Republic, and Albania. The Allende government's relations with Cuba were especially cordial and could be said to constitute a "special relation," a product of the so-called Cuban period through which the SP was passing at that point and especially of the personal friendship that existed between Castro and Allende and other Socialists. Only a few days after the new government came to power, the Chilean Foreign Office reestablished relations with Havana. A year later, during November and December 1971, the Cuban prime minister visited Chile as an official guest. Subsequently, President Allende visited the Caribbean island, at which time he received a number of expressions of support, both political and economic. In contrast to the ties between Chile and Cuba, the Allende government's relations with communist governments—those in Europe, for example—lacked the vitality and comprehensiveness of relations with Cuba and were limited mainly to the commercial and financial area.[19]

In line with the traditional Latin-Americanism of the SP, the foreign policy of the Unidad Popular was particularly active at the regional level. When Almeyda took over as chancellor, he implemented the so-called doctrine of ideological pluralism as the "basic foundation of a peaceful and constructive Latin American coexistence."[20] This doctrine, which was announced in April 1971 on the occasion of the signing of a joint declaration by Chile and Colombia, was the foundation of the cordial relations Chile developed with Peru, Ecuador, Colombia, Argentina, Mexico, and other countries in the area. Between August 24 and September 4, 1971, Allende visited Peru, Ecuador, and Colombia and used the opportunity to sign agreements with each of these countries. A little later he did the same with Venezuela.

The Allende government's policy on regional economic integration was notably more pragmatic and positive than the official position taken by the SP in the 1960s. The earlier policy had tended to oppose the existing integration plans on the grounds that they supposedly offered an expanded market favorable to the interests of corporations in developed countries. But the Andean Common Market's December 1970 approval, with Chile's support, of Decision 24 regarding the Common Andean Regulation for the Treatment of Foreign Capital and the political and cultural importance the Allende government gave to regional—and especially subregional—integration resulted in an official political attitude and commitment favorable to integration plans. However, especially in the last months of the government of the Unidad Popular, because of the serious economic problems facing the nation, the government invoked the safeguard clauses included in the integration agreements and pulled out of the common system as far as intraregional commerce was concerned. This was a move that undoubtedly tended to weaken Chile's participation in Latin American economic integration.[21]

Relations between the Allende government and the government of Luis Echeverría in Mexico reached a very high level, a situation fostered by an exchange of presidential visits during which Allende and Echeverría were able to establish parallels, centered in economic nationalism, between the histories of their respective countries. The personal friendship established between the two presidents would explain in part the economic assistance Mexico gave Chile during the most difficult moments of the Chilean economic crisis.

Ties between Chile and Argentina visibly improved during this period. Despite the fundamental political and ideological differences between the government of Salvador Allende and that of General Alejandro Lanusse, it was agreed during those years that Her Britannic Majesty would formally assume the role of arbiter in the Beagle controversy, and a new General Treaty on Judicial Solution of Controversies was negotiated to replace the one dating from 1902. During this time there was, in addition, a significant increase in bilateral commerce, and on several occasions Buenos Aires even granted short-term credit to adjust the Chilean balance of payments. When the Peronistas came to power in May 1973, the contacts between Chile and Argentina increased even more. In fact, during those months the Chilean Foreign Office endorsed, and was involved in the drafting of, the text issued by the Movement of Nonaligned Nations recognizing Argentine sovereignty over the Malvinas Islands, a recognition that Buenos Aires had demanded as a precondition for its entry into the Nonaligned Movement.

As was to be expected, and in accordance with the long-standing emphasis of Chilean socialism on its posture of international nonalignment, Allende's government formally joined the Movement of Nonaligned Nations in 1971 and actively participated in its various undertakings. Also, as is well known, the Ministry of Foreign Relations at that time played a rather important role in the North-South dialogue. The fact that the Third Conference of UNCTAD was held in Santiago in April 1972 was in itself a sign of the priority given by the government to economic nationalism and the defense of national resources, as well as the need for ties with the Third World and the establishment of a new international economic order.

In this context, the Foreign Office proceeded to exchange ambassadors or to establish embassies with Guyana, Zambia, and Libya and to establish diplomatic ties with Nigeria, Guinea, the Popular Republic of the Congo, Madagascar, and Tanzania. The SP's traditional interest in Algeria, even before its independence, facilitated the development of friendly relations between Santiago and Algiers. Allende visited the North African nation and met President Houari Boumedienne. Learning of the economic problems facing the Chilean government, Boumedienne promised to provide petroleum to Chile without requiring immediate payment. In a similar way, the Chilean Foreign Office obtained the backing of the members of the Comisión Internacional de Paises Exportadores de Cobre (CIPEC—Association of Copper Producing Nations)—Zaire, Zambia, and Peru—against the Kennecott Copper Corporation, which was involved in a move to impose an embargo on exportation of Chilean copper abroad.[22] Explicit support on this issue came as well from the Conference of Ministers of Nonaligned Nations in August 1972 and from Latin American and African coordinating organizations.

As can be seen, in large part the Allende government implemented the international proposals contained in the Unidad Popular program, which in turn gave voice principally, if not exclusively, to the international views of the SP. However, the three most controversial aspects of the program—though within the proverbial antiimperialism of the SP— were restrained and modified. That is, in the most delicate matters the political pendulum returned to a point equidistant from the two poles of populism and doctrinaire socialism. This fact reflected, on the one hand, the rather pragmatic nature of Chilean socialism and, on the other, the difficulties being faced abroad. Equally influential in the situation was the personal stamp that Allende and Almeyda gave to the conduct of Chilean foreign policy, which relied on the active collaboration of career diplomats in the Foreign Office.

The proposal made in the Unidad Popular's program regarding the need to denounce the OAS as "a tool of North American imperialism" and suggesting the establishment of an alternative Latin American organization was never put into effect in its original meaning. Assuming a more pragmatic stance, the Allende government limited itself instead to a moderate version of the traditional Socialist rejection of Pan-Americanism and the idea of the supposedly mutual interests of the United States and Latin America, which had already been questioned by the Consenso de Viña in 1969. The government thus criticized the structure and global orientation of the OAS and proposed ways of restructuring the inter-American system.

In the opinion of the Chilean Foreign Office, this system, to make sense, would have to take the shape of an "international forum for the bilateral discussion and resolution of problems." Such a forum would allow the United States to "establish a dialogue with Latin America as a whole." This required, in its turn, "prior agreement or accord on the part of the countries of Latin America."[23] In 1973 Chancellor Almeyda emphatically explained that Chile was not contemplating withdrawing from the OAS and that it was not asking that the United States be excluded from membership, only that the organization be revamped.

Chilean proposals regarding suggested changes in the philosophy and structure of the OAS were officially announced at the meeting of that organization's General Assembly held in San José, Costa Rica, in April 1971. Two years later the Allende government specifically suggested, with the backing of Peru and Argentina, that a distinctly Latin American organization be added to the inter-American system, one having its headquarters in Latin America. This would allow for the coordination of common positions to be discussed and negotiated at a later date with the United States. In addition, in June 1973 Chile and Venezuela proposed, at the Conference of the Special Committee on the Reorganization of the Inter-American Systems in Lima, a complete revision of the procedures of the Banco Interamericano de Desarrollo (BID— Inter-American Development Bank) because they did not achieve the objectives for which they had been created. However, given the hemispheric context at that time, the Chilean proposals did not go far. Ironically, the same ideas were embodied in part in the Sistema Económico Latinoamericano (SELA), founded in 1975, and have acquired even greater importance since the Malvinas war.

The program proposal that considered it "indispensable to revise, denounce, or reject the reciprocal assistance treaties, the mutual aid pacts, and other pacts made by Chile with the United States" was never put into practice either. In fact, the Allende government announced the need to introduce "modifications" only into the Inter-American Treaty of Reciprocal Assistance (TIAR). By way of contrast, while official political and economic relations between the United States and Chile progressively deteriorated during those years, military ties remained unchanged. Even though the SP had criticized the Inter-American Defense Exercises (UNITAS) operations involving the armed forces of the two nations before the Unidad Popular came to power, under the Allende government these operations continued to be held, without any "show of public protest."[24] Contrary to what was done by other Latin American governments (such as Peru under Juan Velasco Alvarado and Francisco Morales Bermúdez and Argentina under Jorge Rafael Videla and his successors), Allende's government did not establish active military relations with the USSR. Finally, despite the fact that during the period Chile tended to diversify its sources of military supplies by buying from Western Europe, many U.S. loans were granted to enable Chile to purchase arms from the United States and to develop the logistic capabilities of the Chilean armed forces.

The Allende government's stance toward the United States was particularly cautious and could be characterized as guided by what has been called principled pragmatism. Even at the most critical moments in the relationship between the two countries, following attempts by a number of transnational companies and by the Nixon administration itself to "destabilize" the Chilean government, Allende, in his speech before the United Nations in 1972, abstained from any specific reference to the part played by the United States in Chile. Similarly, the Chilean government continued to permit the Peace Corps and other organizations with ties to the U.S. government to operate in Chile and continued to honor the financial obligations that Chile had contracted with U.S. businesses.[25]

Finally, the paragraph in the program that advocated an "international policy of peoples rather than of Ministries of Foreign Affairs" and that proposed "doing away with all forms of bureaucracy and paralysis" in Chilean diplomacy was never implemented. In fact, the Ministry of Foreign Affairs and professional diplomacy were in no way superseded; on the contrary, Chancellor Almeyda relied in great measure on the experience of seasoned and prestigious career diplomats. Even if some Socialists—and especially those groups outside of the government coalition—expressed their disenchantment with the government's cautious management of foreign policy[26] and considered certain foreign-affairs proposals to have been thwarted, there was a consensus in the SP as to the successful management of foreign affairs by the president of the Republic and by the Ministry of Foreign Affairs, management that followed in every case the basic principles of Socialist international policy.

CONCLUSIONS

The evidence presented in this chapter suggests that the international policy of the SP has, in fact, oscillated between two poles: populism and doctrinaire socialism. These fluctuations have been manifested in, for instance, the movement of the SP from a position of support for Latin American nationalism in the 1940s to its most recent position of apparent renewal and reaffirmation of certain basic international roots. In between the two stances there were periods of Titoism and Cubanization. Despite the fluctuations seen in Socialist international policy, however, it is possible to detect the more or less constant presence, over time, of certain principles that could be said to constitute the basic core of the SP's orientation. At the same time, and in the last analysis, the SP's international policy seems to be the product of two fundamental factors that have already been explored: the nature or character of the SP and the historical relationship between Chilean socialism and communism.

As for the two cases previously analyzed that had to do with the impact of the SP's international orientation on the foreign policy of Chile, it is evident that, when Chilean socialism participated in governing coalitions and had access to the decision-making process in foreign affairs, it adopted a posture of principled pragmatism based on the central postulates of the party's long-standing international policy. That is, whenever the party came to power, even if at that moment it happened to be near one of the two poles, its thinking on international matters tended to relocate itself at a point of equilibrium between populism and doctrinaire socialism and to be translated into a flexible state policy without sharp breaks in continuity. The explanation for this tendency could be said to reside in the following: the dominant role played in the SP by the most enduring lines of its international thinking as derived from the nature of the party and its leadership, the relationship existing between the SP and the CP, the requirement that the SP reconcile its own positions with those of the other parties involved in particular governing coalitions, and finally, the limitations imposed on the SP by hemispheric and global events.

NOTES

1. Enzo Faletto, "Algunas características de la base social del partido Socialista y del partido Comunista: 1958–1973," working paper 97, Facultad Latinoamerícana de Ciencias Sociales (FLACSO), September 1980.

2. The concept of "principled pragmatism" is utilized by Carlos Fortín in his article on the foreign policy of the Allende government, "Principled Pragmatism in the Face of External Pressure: The Foreign Policy of the Allende Government," in Ronald G. Hellman and H. Jon Rosenbaum (eds.), *Latin America: The Search for a New International Role* (New York: John Wiley and Sons, 1975), pp. 217–245.

3. Partido Socialista "Declaración de Principios," cited in Fernando Casanueva and Manuel Fernández, *El Partido Socialista y Lucha de Clases en Chile* (Santiago: Quinantú, 1973), p. 102.

4. Statement quoted in Ernest Halperin, *Nationalism and Communism in Chile* (Cambridge: The Massachusetts Institute of Technology Press, 1965), p. 137;

and see Julio César Jobet, *El Partido Socialista de Chile*, vol. 1 (Santiago: Ediciones Prensa Latinoamericana, 1971), pp. 180–184.

5. See Partido Socialista, "Política Internacional: Informe y Conclusiones," *Boletín del Comité Central*, no. 1, February 1964, p. 12.

6. See Paul W. Drake, *Socialism and Populism in Chile: 1932–1952* (Urbana: University of Illinois Press, 1978), p. 176.

7. See Andrew Barnard, "Chilean Communists, Radical Presidents, and Chilean Relations with the United States, 1940–1947," *Journal of Latin American Studies* 13, no. 2 (1981), p. 351.

8. See Drake, *Socialism and Populism in Chile*, p. 246.

9. See Jobet, *El Partido Socialista de Chile*, pp. 150–151; and Barnard, "Chilean Communists," p. 351.

10. Cited in Jobet, *El Partido Socialista de Chile*, p. 167.

11. Regarding this incident, see Michael J. Francis, *The Limits of Hegemony: United States Relations with Argentina and Chile During World War II* (Notre Dame: University of Notre Dame Press, 1977), pp. 113–114.

12. Conversations with one of those attending the meeting.

13. Claude G. Bowers, *Misión en Chile: 1939–1953* (Santiago: Editorial del Pacífico, 1957), p. 115.

14. Humberto Mendoza, *¿Y Ahora?* (Santiago: Imprenta Cultural, 1942), p. 289.

15. Jobet, *El Partido Socialista de Chile*, p. 167. See also Mendoza, *¿Y Ahora?* pp. 285, 168.

16. See Eduardo Labarca G., *Chile al Rojo* (Santiago: Ediciones de la Universidad Técnica del Estado, 1971), p. 220.

17. See "Programa Básico de Gobierno de la Unidad Popular," in Leopoldo González A. et al., *Teoría y Praxis Internacional del Gobierno de Allende* (México: Universidad Nacional Autónoma de México, 1974), pp. 87–89. The most moderate aspects of the program are those referring to the Middle East, where the "search for a peaceful solution based on the interests of the Arab and the Jewish peoples" was proposed, and those referring to Latin American integration, where—despite the notion that integration should occur on the basis of "economies free from dependency and exploitation"—it was affirmed that the new government would carry out "an active policy of bilateral agreements on those matters that were of interest to Chilean development."

18. For a description and analysis of the various foreign-policy measures undertaken by the Allende government see, by way of introduction, Clodomiro Almeyda, "La Política Exterior del Gobierno de la Unidad Popular in Chile," in Federico Gil, Ricardo Lagos, and Henry Landsberger (eds.), *Chile: 1970–1973* (Madrid: Tecnos, 1977), pp. 88–115; Edy Kaufman, "La Política Exterior de la Unidad Popular Chilena," *Foro Internacional* 18, no. 2 (October–December 1976), pp. 244–274; Fortín, "Principled Pragmatism"; and González et al., *Teoría y Praxis Internacional*.

19. Concerning this aspect, see Joseph Nogee and John Sloan, "Allende's Chile and the Soviet Union: A Policy Lesson for Latin American Nations Seeking Autonomy," *Journal of Interamerican Studies and World Affairs* 21, no. 3 (August 1979), pp. 339–368.

20. Almeyda, "La Política Exterior del Gobierno de la Unidad Popular," p. 99.

21. Concerning this subject, see ibid., pp. 100–101; and Manfred Wilhelmy "Democracia, Autoritarismo, e Integración: El Caso Chileno," in M. Wilhelmy,

Sociedad, Política, e Integración en América Latina (Santiago: Ediciones CINDE, 1982), pp. 139–141.

22. With regard to this matter, in September 1972 the Chilean Chamber of Deputies agreed, by unanimous consent of all the political groups represented in it, "to express its most energetic repudiation of the maneuvers of the Kennecott Copper Corporation" designed to achieve an embargo of Chilean copper sent abroad to be traded (see *El Mercurio*, September 15, 1972, p. 13).

23. Almeyda, "La Política Exterior del Gobierno de la Unidad Popular," p. 104.

24. Kaufman, "La Política Exterior de la Unidad Popular Chilena," p. 259.

25. For a more detailed analysis of the policy of principled pragmatism the Allende government used in its dealings with Washington, see Fortín, "Principled Pragmatism," especially pp. 231–241.

26. See, for example, a criticism from the left of the Unidad Popular that appeared in *Punto Final*, no. 166, December 12, 1972, p. 15.

11. Internationalism and the Limits of Autonomy: Cuba's Foreign Relations

INTRODUCTION

This chapter deals with the topic of Cuba's foreign policy during the 1980s, using the period between December 1980 and August 1982 as a reference. The main characteristics of that policy emerge clearly during this period and are representative of early years even though the years 1980–1982 were heavily tinged by the high degree of tension and conflict in the relations between Cuba and the United States.

My starting point will be the chapter devoted to foreign policy in the principal report presented to the Second Congress of the Cuban Communist party (CCP) by President Fidel Castro on December 17, 1980. I will also discuss Cuba's conduct of foreign relations in terms of the blueprint used by the Cubans themselves, a plan that merges two classifications: one based on geographic areas and the other on types of economic systems and areas influenced by the superpowers. Finally, I will formulate some hypotheses about the immediate future.

As a preface to the subject I might mention that Cuba formally views normal relations between countries—those based on mutual respect, recognition of national sovereignty, and nonintervention—as a historic necessity. As Fidel Castro asserted in his report to the Second Congress of the CCP (December 17, 1980), Cuba is and will continue to be socialist—a friend of the Soviet Union and the socialist countries—and that it will remain an internationalist nation and will not sacrifice these principles in exchange for normal relations with the United States.

This posture closely resembles the one held by other socialist countries. However, it includes a component of projection of power and influence abroad seemingly out of proportion to the resources of a small nation. The continuity of this policy dates back to April 16, 1961, when the socialist nature of the revolution was proclaimed on the eve of the Bay of Pigs battle—an extremely critical period for the survival of the regime. In the mid-1970s that policy implied closer cooperation with the Soviets. Efforts to create Cuba's own sphere of influence were rewarded, in the late 1970s, with Cuba's election as president of the Movement of Nonaligned Nations (NAM).

Cuban international activism is intimately linked to the nature of the regime and its continuity. This creates confusion among those who insist on viewing such initiatives as completely subordinated to Soviet directives. I will argue that the coincidence with the USSR's goals colors but does not negate Cuba's interest in establishing international ties for its own purposes. The relatively successful implementation of this policy has given Cuba vast international influence, which in turn has exacerbated the conflict level with its principal adversary.

NONNEGOTIABLE PRINCIPLES

The primary goal of any country's foreign policy is to further its own national interests. In Cuba's case, the foremost foreign-policy objective is to guarantee the irreversibility of the revolution and thus the survival of the regime. Although this point is self-evident, the corollary to this principle calls for a detailed examination. It implies that Cuba commits itself to defend governments and regimes engaged in anticolonial, antiimperialist, and national liberation conflicts.

Cuban revolutionaries see the United States as their foremost enemy. To survive the thrusts of that foe—openly belligerent by the time the Moncada program had been fulfilled (April 16, 1961)—Cuba formalized what in fact already existed: the socialist nature of the revolution, that is, those changes effected up to that time. Having crossed that Rubicon, Cuba has been unable to accommodate its foreign policy to the United States or to the Cuban community abroad. Cubans on the island consider this to be the prime contradiction of their foreign policy.

The regime has manipulated this contradiction to boost its legitimacy, developing a militant, radical style presented as the only dignified, effective posture capable of withstanding U.S. assaults. An important corollary of this domestic stance is the international projection, designed to prevent a political, diplomatic, and economic isolation that would weaken the regime. Thus Cuba's potential vulnerability, the result of its proximity to the United States, became a spur to banish U.S. influence from the domestic scene and also to prevent strangulation for lack of markets, sources of capital goods, financing and raw materials, and bilateral and multilateral contacts with other nations. The confrontation with the United States led to serious instability and a great void; the effort to correct these problems had to be equally great.

In a previous study, devoted exclusively to analyzing different aspects of this fundamental contradiction, I concluded that it would be extremely difficult to evolve a "normal relationship" between the United States and the exiled Cuban community, on the one hand, and the current regime, on the other, given the latter's style, history, and basis for legitimacy.[1] Two subsequent developments bear out this contention. One was the incident at the Peruvian Embassy in Havana, which led to the massive exodus of 125,000 Cubans through the port of Mariel. The other was the election of Ronald Reagan as president of the United States.

The rekindling of militant revolutionary fervor and the high level of mobilization currently evident in Cuba began during the Carter administration. It is part of a strategy utilized by the regime in 1980 that accomplished several objectives. First, it calmed the discontent of many revolutionaries with the visit to Cuba in 1979 and early 1980 of more than 100,000 Cubans living abroad. Second, it led to recovery from the blow caused by the flight of more than 10,000 persons to the Embassy of Peru when President Castro said anyone who wished to could leave. It also provided an escape hatch for many who did not identify with the revolutionary process but were left outside the Peruvian Embassy.

In effect, the attempted "normalization" of relations between Cuba and the United States and the Cuban community abroad brought on an internal malaise for Cuba. Elements of that normalization effort had included formalization of relations beginning in 1977, the December 1978 accords for the liberation of political prisoners, visits to Cuba under the Family Reunification program, and a climate of relaxed tensions. In this relaxed context the Cuban government reacted to the incident at the Peruvian Embassy by refusing to honor the right of asylum, asserting that political repression did not exist in Cuba, and by launching a mobilization campaign reminiscent of the hard times of the 1960s. The regime reacted as if its own survival were at stake—not because of the threat of an armed invasion, but against the destabilizing effect of a bilateral effort to bring about "normality."

The "normality" brought on by the confrontation with the Reagan administration spared the regime from having to reconcile a friendship with its principal enemy with the basis of its legitimacy. Cuba reaffirmed its principles as it stood face-to-face with a more manageable enemy.

To summarize: Cuba sees its relations with the United States as the principal contradiction of its foreign policy because of irreconcilable differences between two antagonistic social systems. However, Cuba does not believe this justifies the extreme hostility toward Cuba of successive U.S. administrations, hostility that Fidel Castro interpreted in the foreign-policy section of his report to the Second Congress of the CCP (December 17, 1980) as an unfulfilled desire to destroy the revolution. Cuba cannot lower its guard toward the United States, whether through contact with the consumer society or in the face of the Yankee military threat. Cuba cannot tolerate a relationship that directly or indirectly undermines the legitimacy of the regime. We must keep in mind that the reaction is practically identical to one kind of threat (consumerism penetration and some degree of society opening) or another (fiery rhetoric from Secretary of State Alexander Haig, military maneuvers in the Caribbean, and the creation of a special U.S. military command). In my opinion, it is easier for the Cuban regime to deal with a confrontation than with a process of détente whose outcome is not easily predictable. In short, Cuba entered the 1980s on a war footing *against a lifestyle* to which Cuba has sought an alternative for twenty-three years. Herein lies the Cuban regime's radicalism—something much deeper than mere ideology.

We could paraphrase the "great communicator" by adding that who does not understand this does not understand the Cuban Revolution. As Castro himself put it in his address at the twentieth anniversary of the Bay of Pigs victory (April 19, 1981), "We are very conscious of the Bay of Pigs experience. No one will catch our country with its guard lowered or unaware . . . also mistaken are those who imagine that socialism in our Fatherland may weaken, that we may soften or be destroyed from within. . . ." Therefore, the primary principle of state policy that Cuba's foreign relations must implement is to preserve the integrity and ideological coherence of the regime.

A second principle that links the regime's continuity with its foreign activism is close collaboration with the Soviet Union and its allies. This is reflected in Article 12, section (f) of the 1976 Constitution of the Republic of Cuba and forms part of the Cuban Communist party platform. In his Principal Report to the Second Congress of the CCP, President Fidel Castro reiterated this principle. Shortly thereafter, in his address before the 26th Congress of the USSR's Communist party (published in *Bohemia* on February 27, 1981, p. 51), Castro stated that he regarded as decisive the role of the Soviet Union in the struggle against imperialists and colonialists. He reminded a somewhat reluctant audience of this and cited Cuban-Soviet relations as an example of a fraternal and respectful friendship. He concluded by adding, "We are and will continue always to be friends of a generous people who have helped us so much. . . ."

The chroniclers of the Cuban Revolution have accumulated sufficient evidence to confirm the difficulties that marked the beginning and development of those relations during the initial fifteen years of the revolution.[2] The relationship reflects what perhaps has been the principal *internal* contradiction of the regime, caught between a nationalist revolutionary tradition spanning more than one hundred years and represented by Fidel Castro and a hegemonic bureaucratic orthodoxy monopolized by the Soviet Union. Apparently, a quite viable synthesis has provided a means to manage this contradiction since the start of the institutionalization process. However, this cannot completely conceal the relatively antagonistic elements of both traditions nor should it lead us to overlook its implications for matters of symmetry in Cuban-Soviet relations.

It is important to underscore, moreover, that current cooperation between the two countries in aiding revolutionary and national-liberation movements is quite recent. Those who argue that Cuba has been

commissioned to do the Soviets' "dirty work" in the Third World seem
to ignore Cuba's record of militant internationalism. For Cuba this has
been a policy of state; much of the friction between Cuba and the
Soviet Union during the 1960s responded to serious differences of
opinion regarding the praxis of power taking. Therefore, if there were
any policy changes, they were made by the Soviet Union. The situation
resembles, although reversed, Cuba's relationship with the United States.
To counteract U.S. hostility, Cuba did not renounce the friendship of
the Soviet sphere, thus protecting itself from the economic embargo and
lessening the economic pitfalls on the road to socialism. In dealing with
the Soviet Union, Cuba—mainly in its self-interest—unfurled the banners
of militant internationalist solidarity to maintain its own sphere of
influence within the international system and in both cases to strengthen
itself ideologically and diplomatically vis-à-vis the Soviet Union.

We cannot expect the Cubans, under current conditions, to proclaim
this aloud. But prior episodes should not be forgotten; we should be
able to read between the lines. For example, Fidel Castro's report to
the CCP's First Congress of December 1975 (as reproduced in his
December 17, 1980, report to the Second Congress) read in part: "The
Communist Party of Cuba considers itself a modest but reliable de-
tachment of the international communist movement. . . . Our party
participates in this program in an *independent fashion* but, at the same
time, with complete *loyalty to the common cause,* joined with communists
from other countries (My emphasis)."

Obviously, the circumstances of 1982 are not exactly the same as
those Cuba faced in 1967, when Fidel Castro had to admit that "Cuba
stands alone." I suggest that the Organisation de Solidarité des Peuples
d'Afrique, d'Asie et d'Amerique Latina (OSPAAAL), the Organización
Latinoamericana de Sindicatos (OLAS), and Cuban efforts during the
1960s fertilized the ground, as Nelson Valdés demonstrated convincingly
for the African case.[3] The *modus operandi* has changed: from guerrilla
outbreaks to army units, from subversive incursions to formal agreements
with one of the parties to different local conflicts. The Soviet change
has come in providing supplies and advisers, extending the line of
operations from the Middle East to sub-Saharan Africa. But not even
this coincidence of effort, carried out during a period of U.S. retrenchment
following Vietnam and against highly unpopular enemies, nor the obvious
differences in power between Cuba and the Soviet Union, demonstrate
per se that Cuba does not pursue its own interests in the Third World.

In summary, the group surrounding Fidel Castro appears to support
three principles that serve as main guidelines for Cuba's foreign policy.
These principles are enshrined in the Cuban constitution of 1976, woven
into the platform of the CCP, and alluded to constantly in the leadership's
foreign-policy speeches and presentations. The principles are: (1) rejection
of any sort of relationship that might erode the legitimacy and coherence
of the regime, (2) close collaboration with the Soviet Union while

following an independent line, and (3) promotion of a militant internationalism in order to maintain a sphere of Cuban influence in the international system and the communist movement.

I will briefly analyze the practical application of these principles in Cuba's foreign policy. The discussion will suggest to what point these principles may or may not be negotiable.

MULTILATERALISM

Cuba's image of the world's problems is quite somber. The Cubans foresee an escalation of the cold war as a result of a more aggressive U.S. policy that includes reopening issues supposedly resolved by the Strategic Arms Limitation Talks (SALT II), an attempt to secure strategic arms superiority, the use of third parties to provoke regional tensions, constant harassment of Cuba, and the intention to destroy national-liberation movements and portray them as terrorist. Coinciding with this view is a global economic crisis aggravated by the fiscal and monetary policies of the Reagan administration. This crisis, which also affects the socialist nations, severely punishes Third World countries, caught in the worst economic problems of their history. The link between these two currents is ominous because the Cubans argue that "without development there is no peace." That translates into malaise in the Third World and crises of domestic domination accompanied by grave tensions that push the capitalist nations into policies that are more selfish economically and more aggressive militarily.

Fidel Castro repeated this analytical projection on many occasions during 1981 and 1982, including his long exposition to the 68th conference of the Interparliamentary Union (September 15, 1981) and his words spoken at the opening session of the Tenth Congress of the World Federation of Trade Unions (February 10, 1982). The latter speech constituted the central theme of the position taken by Cuba's foreign minister, Isidoro Malmierca, at the gathering of the Coordination Bureau of the Nonaligned Movement in June 1982. Therefore, certain consistency and theoretical refinement are evident behind the Cuban vision of the world's problems in the 1980s.

This view contains a strong component of Manichaeanism, which postulates that imperialism is society's worst enemy and that socialism can spread without wars of aggression. This, combined with the historical differences between Cuba and the United States, pushes Cuba into a position of constant and global confrontation with U.S. positions. It also suggests a broad but not immutable coincidence of views with the Soviet Union regarding world problems. Cuba's role as NAM president has helped Cuban initiatives. The Cubans have cleverly exploited their position to extend and strengthen contacts by championing popular causes.

In the Middle East, the Cubans consider the United States directly responsible for Israeli aggression against Lebanon and Iraq. No sooner had the June 1982 invasion taken place than President Castro contacted the heads of state of the NAM, the president of the United Nations (UN) General Assembly, the UN secretary general, and the UN Security Council president to request a condemnation of the Israeli aggression. Cuba's foreign ministry can respond to local crises very quickly, issuing pronouncements and communiqués that faithfully reflect Cuban foreign policy.

In the South African case, the Cubans support the Southwest African Peoples Organization (SWAPO), Angola's Movimiento para la Liberación de Angola (MPLA) regime, and the front-line states that have borders with the South Africans; they reject the proposal for a Cuban troop withdrawal from Angola in exchange for a South African military retreat from Namibia. The Cubans won NAM support for these initiatives as well as a declaration issued by the New Delhi ministerial conference in February 1981 endorsing movements of national liberation. The Cubans also mobilized their African contacts to lay the groundwork against the simultaneous-withdrawal plan. This proposal was denounced in a series of bilateral accords between Cuba and Angola, Mozambique, Guinea-Bissau, the Saharans, and the People's Republic of the Congo, concluded between the spring and summer of 1982. The process culminated September 4, 1982, when the chiefs of state of the front-line nations, meeting in Lusaka, issued a communiqué that backed the presence of Cuban troops, rejected the simultaneous-withdrawal proposal, supported SWAPO, and demanded compliance with UN Resolution 435/78.

Cuban activism tilled fertile soil in this case. The Cubans took up the cause against unpopular regimes such as Israel and South Africa, which seemed to be allied with the United States, and charged them with advancing imperialist interests in the region. Nevertheless, Cuba's accomplishments in Africa are neither permanent nor invulnerable. The Cubans have had to turn against their own previous policy in Ethiopia, where they had supported the Eritreans. They were expelled from Somalia and became involved in a conflict identified with a cause not broadly perceived as correct. The attempt to establish the Saharan Arab Democratic Republic in the former Morocco touched off a controversy that almost led to the cancellation of the 1982 African Unity Organization summit scheduled for Tripoli. A number of African states support Morocco's aspirations to annex the territory, while others, like Cuba, back the Polisario Front.

In contrast with its stance of reserved support for the Soviet invasion of Czechoslovakia in 1968, Cuba's government has been much more forceful—but less convincing—in its efforts to place the Afghan crisis within the framework of imperialist provocations in the Middle East. This is one of the peccadilloes the NAM might forgive Cuba at the moment, particularly in view of Cuban efforts to mediate the Iran-Iraq dispute. Nonetheless, it does tarnish Cuban legitimacy, spotlights the close Cuban-Soviet relationship, and casts doubts on Cuba's nonaligned status. In short, we could say that Cuban activism in multilateral initiatives is predicated on constant confrontation with "imperialist" aggressions, although not in the immediate area. This holds Cuba to a determined line that could clash with the interests of other medium-sized powers of the NAM in the future, given the underlying contradictions in what the Cubans call the "struggle" for peace.

The economic side of Cuba's multilateralism is much less effective. In the first place, Cuba is locked into a predetermined economic system that establishes the principal parameters of Cuban foreign economic policy. Cuba can speak with certain authority about its contribution in this field because, for example, Cuba has sent more of its doctors to work in Third World countries than has the World Health Organization. Cuban state-owned companies undertake construction and infrastructure development projects in many countries based on their ability to pay. But the Cuban model cannot be made to fit every situation,[4] nor is the East European Common Market (COMECON) in a position to offer Third World countries terms of trade similar to those offered to Cuba. Cuba may have stood the old Marxist parable on its head, proffering that socialism is the best road to development, but economic reality says something else.

Second, most of the economic problems of the less developed nations—at least the more urgent ones—spring from international economic imbalances. Their solution is not easy, regardless of extant domestic economic models. Third, the Cubans seem to prefer a strategy of confrontation that will not dilute the interpretation of international economic relations with language that is too technical. The Cubans believe that underdevelopment and exploitation cannot be separated, and the latter will not disappear on its own. Besides, the NIEO (New International Economic Order) concept is too tied to the strategies of the North-South dialogue—from which Cuba has been substantially removed, as at Cancún in 1981—and not far enough from the theory of the two imperialisms, which Cuba rejects.

Fourth, the Cuban position offers no viable alternative because it suggests change toward a mode of production requiring domestic political confrontation and inclusion in an economic area burdened by its own problems as well as those affecting all nations. The specific alternatives presented by the Cubans are no more than *desiderata* expressed by Fidel Castro to Third World economists and participants in the 68th Conference of the Interparliamentary Union: an end to inequality in commerce, to exported inflation, to protectionism, and to unfair exploitation of the resources of the sea; an increase in financial aid to underdeveloped countries (by $300 billion during this decade—a proposition endorsed by the NAM ministerial conference in 1981); a shift of arms purchases funds to foreign-aid use; debt cancellation for the more underdeveloped nations; relief from foreign debt; and abolishment of economic inequality. These proposals are neither more nor less realistic than those advanced within NIEO and suggest that the world economic crisis has impacted Cuba as well, despite the country's affiliation with COMECON.

Finally, Cuba frets about economic relations between COMECON and the capitalist world and expects the foreign economic policy of the Reagan administration to have destabilizing effects.

As we shall see, the Cubans are heavily burdened by the crisis and by these attempts at economic aggression. They find themselves compelled to stand in line to renegotiate their foreign debt with the capitalist area.

THE IMMEDIATE AREA

A comparison of the foreign-policy chapters in Fidel Castro's reports to the two CCP congresses held to date reveals a dramatic change in perspective and interpretation of the problems troubling a geographic area that encompasses the full repertory of relations at the disposal of Cuban diplomacy. At the time of the first congress, in December 1975, the prime architect of Cuba's foreign policy reported that Latin America simply was not ready for revolutions. Cuba's was the only revolution in power. A diplomatic offensive was underway to restore relations with some Latin American countries. Traditional ties were being preserved with Mexico, and efforts were underway to guide and promote a quite successful policy of rapprochement with the English-speaking Caribbean. Relations with the United States were going through a series of ups and downs.

By December 1980, Cuba had lost an important ally with the defeat of Michael Manley. Cuba prepared for the inauguration of Ronald Reagan and a series of confrontations with the United States over the Central American problem. But two new revolutionary governments had come to power to form a new alliance with Cuba in its immediate area and to mark an apparently important milestone for change. In his principal report to the Second Congress (December 17, 1980), the first secretary reported to the CCP about ". . . a readiness of the masses to struggle which has reached unprecedented levels. . . . The fact that national liberation revolutionary movements with strong social content are on the rise . . . indicates that the system of imperialism and oligarchic domination in this region is falling into a deepening crisis."

I will summarize the role of Cuba in national revolutionary movements, the Cuban-American confrontation in the region, multilateral efforts to resolve the crisis, and scenario changes during 1980–1982.

Let me begin by affirming that Cuba's strategists fully understand the geopolitical differences between their immediate area and Africa. They contemplate no use of regular units of the Revolutionary Armed Forces for any sort of operation in the Caribbean or Central America, other than possible logistical support missions to Nicaragua and Grenada.

Direct Cuban military intervention in, for example, El Salvador or Guatemala, such as occurred in Africa, is very unlikely. Such actions would only be used in response to an extreme situation in which Cuba would have to concentrate all its military power at home to defend itself against a direct U.S. military aggression. Consequently, the first principle would have priority over the third: There is no militant internationalism at the expense of the regime's survival. Nevertheless, the Cuban presence in Nicaragua and Grenada also leads to the process of polarization that appears to be emerging in the region.

Cuba clearly offered sanctuary and logistical support to the Sandinistas and the Salvadorean guerrillas. But the amount of this aid has been exaggerated by those who attribute to Cuba an efficiency beyond the scope even of the superpowers. Moreover, Cuba's role in Nicaragua is well defined and serves to secure a process of transition toward a socialist regime. Although it appears that Cuban influence has been directed toward helping the Sandinistas avoid the errors committed in Cuba as well as toward moderating the pace of the process, the problem is that there also seems to be a process of power concentration and formation of a hegemonic authority based on control by the armed forces. Nothing could be more ominous.[5]

Regarding El Salvador, Cuba's formal position was to support the initiative of Mexican president José Luis López Portillo and generally to seek a peaceful solution to the conflict. In this regard, the Cubans assign great importance to the role of the social democrats and speak of the broadest possible framework for cooperation. The Cubans, however, regard as inseparable the conflicts of their immediate area and those of the international scene generally.

This bears a resemblance to the Reagan administration's perception of East-West tensions in a local situation. I mention this because, at heart, the Cubans perceive the principal world contradiction as being between imperialism and socialism. Nevertheless, the Cubans have sought to use this opportunity to negotiate with the Americans. So far, the Reagan administration appears to have rejected three such offers, according to a top official who retired from the American diplomatic service recently.

Furthermore, I would underscore that Cuba lacks the capacity to dictate results or the outcome of these processes of change in its immediate area. Moreover, these processes constantly shift the correlations of power, whether by temporary or permanent removal of key leaders and players— Manley, Torrijos, Duarte, Roldós, to mention but a few—or by substantial changes of circumstances, such as Duarte's defeat and the Malvinas war affecting Venezuela's position in El Salvador, an attempted rapprochement with Cuba by Costa Rica through the "private" visit of ex-president José Figueres, or a hardening of the Honduran position and possibly Panama's, now guided by a new "strong man," General Rubén Darío Paredes of the National Guard.

The Reagan administration's Caribbean Basin Initiative has been ridiculed by the Cubans. They believe that the United States in truth cannot offer markets and that the area's ills cannot be healed with larger doses of precisely what causes their ailment: foreign investment, low tariffs, and so on. This view contrasts with Cuba's effort to attract direct foreign investment from some nonhegemonic capitalist countries. But the straw that broke the camel's back was "Radio Martí," an idea to create a sort of Radio Free Europe beamed at Cuba. In a not too subtle reaction to the project, the Cubans transmitted all night on the frequency assigned to Radio Martí, the same one used by radio station WHO of Des Moines, Iowa. The project has still not been finalized and appears to be another chapter of discord in a relationship fraught with misdirection and bitterness.

In sum, prospects are not as black as predicted by the Manichaean perceptions of Cuba and the United States: Cuba cannot decide the matter with its military aid, nor can the United States dictate its own solution. The optimistic formula would favor a policy of complete demilitarization of the region accompanied by open frontiers for ideological pluralism. This, however, appears as implausible as Fidel Castro's world economic propositions.

THE REST OF LATIN AMERICA

In his report to the Second Congress of the CCP, Castro also emphasized a current detectable among the countries of greater industrial development, particularly Mexico and Brazil, which are seeking to escape U.S. domination and assume an independent position. Argentina was added to the list following the Malvinas war.

Mexico's president, Miguel de la Madrid, visited Cuba in June 1981 while he was the minister of planning and budget. It is unlikely that Mexico will change its policy toward Cuba despite its overwhelming economic problems. That visit served to seal several technical cooperation accords that reinforced other bilateral agreements between the two countries signed in March of the same year. Mexico handled as tactfully as possible Reagan's veto of Cuban participation in the Cancún conference. Following a cordial weekend meeting between Castro and López Portillo in Cozumel, Mexico affirmed Cuba's right to attend the Cancún conference, while expressing appreciation for the Cuban decision to withdraw. Cuba, meanwhile, absolved Mexico of all responsibility for Cuba's exclusion from the conference but reserved the right to interpret the event.

In the case of Brazil, which Cuba sees as a natural future opponent of the United States, the absence of diplomatic relations did not preclude a degree of cooperation in the area of multilateral sugar policy. While in office, President João Baptista Figueiredo allowed greater freedom to travel to Cuba and to establish cultural contacts. In January 1982 a private commercial mission visited the island. The Cubans offered preferential treatment for Brazilian goods, a courtesy extended only to Mexico and Argentina. The Cubans showed interest in undertaking joint projects with Brazil in Third World areas, where the experience of both countries in civil engineering and infrastructure development could be used to advantage. Given Itamaraty's pragmatism, this prospect does not seem too remote, nor does the possibility of better relations with Cuba. But the level of future cooperation with Cuba will be determined by Brazil's process of transition.

The Malvinas offered Cuba the opportunity to strengthen its ties with the only Southern Cone nation with which it had relations. Argentina played an important role, during the second round of Peronism, in "unblocking" commercial relations with Cuba by securing a relaxation of the trading-with-the-enemy law and allowing some affiliates of U.S. firms to sell motor vehicles to Cuba. The Cubans seized on the Anglo-Argentine conflict to reciprocate. The usually moderate Carlos Rafael Rodríguez told French Foreign Minister Claude Cheysson in May 1982 that Cuba was prepared to give Argentina all possible assistance, including military. Cuba and Argentina ratified an agreement in June during the visit to Havana of Argentine foreign minister Nicanor Costa Méndez to present his government's position before the meeting of the Movement of Nonaligned Nations Coordination Bureau.

On that occasion the Cubans demonstrated their diplomatic skills by convincing many English-speaking NAM members that the Malvinas/Falklands case was not like Belize or Guyana. The Cubans succeeded in getting the meeting to issue a declaration condemning Great Britain and the United States and supporting Argentina. A high-level Cuban mission visited Buenos Aires in August 1982 seeking to expand trade and undertake joint ventures. But once again, the form and depth of future relations were clouded by a domestic situation in flux.

Cuba's relationship with authoritarian regimes in Latin America follows the pattern established in dealing with African governments. Apparently this is not as threatening to Cuba as having a cordial relationship with its main enemy. In South America, Cuba also has close relations with Guyana and backs a quite controversial regime considered responsible for the death of Walter Rodney, an authentic leader of the Guyanese left and a deserving intellectual. This relationship flowered during a period of tension between Cuba and Venezuela, the outcome of a drawn-out judicial process against four persons charged with dynamiting a Cubana de Aviación aircraft. The plane was destroyed over Barbados, killing all aboard. After the Malvinas affair, Venezuela began redirecting its policy guidelines and initiated a rapprochement with Cuba. A Venezuelan minister of state, Luis Alberto Machado, traveled to Cuba on an official mission in June 1982. He called for a normalization of relations between the two nations. Current speculation suggests that Venezuela might ask Cuba to mediate the dispute with Guyana.

This Cuban flexibility contrasts with the rigidity that chilled relations, or led to outright breaks, with several Latin American countries over the right-of-asylum issue. This position had cost Cuba the withdrawal of Ambassador César Rondón Lovera, before the Barbados plane crisis, and the withdrawal of personnel from the Ecuadorean Embassy in February 1981. This was in addition to the uproar sparked by the episode at the Peruvian Embassy, which climaxed with the 1980 Mariel exodus of 125,000 people. In September 1981 those people had to return home when the government absolutely refused to let them leave the country. It should be noted that with the exception of Colombia, no South American country severed relations with Cuba because of violent incidents associated with efforts to enter their embassies. The Ecuadoreans said officially in October 1981 that they were not interested in joining a campaign to isolate Cuba. Nor did the Peruvians, who resolved their crisis discreetly, break relations.

What emerges as established principle is that Cuba will not honor the traditional practice of right to asylum because it would be forced to admit the existence of political persecution in Cuba. This is a policy of state in keeping with the principle already identified. The Cubans will not yield on this matter, which will therefore continue to be a source of friction in the future for those Latin American states that have relations with Cuba.

THE ECONOMY AND THE CAPITALIST AREA

Early in the 1980s, as Cuban loans with strong-currency creditors began to mature, the Cuban government started to signal its willingness to adopt relatively pragmatic steps to resolve its balance-of-payments and foreign-debt problems with capitalist-area nations. Both the 1976 constitution and the CCP platform sanction these relations, principally with Canada, Japan, Great Britain, Spain, and, more recently, the nations of the Middle East's Organization of the Arab Petroleum Exporting Countries (OAPEC). The tactic Cuba followed initially could be termed a "Mexican solution" because it sought to stabilize the balance of payments with tourism income and direct foreign-capital investments. Cuba's total debt with the capitalist area was calculated at three billion dollars by 1982. About half of this amount was subscribed with private institutions.[6]

Decree Law 50, issued February 15, 1982, was the most notable initiative taken to provide new and generous incentives for foreign investment. Among its provisions: up to 49 percent (in some cases, even more) of the capital of a company could be subscribed by foreigners; *total* repatriation of profits; tax holidays on dividends, gross earnings, and executives' salaries; freedom to select personnel; authorization to import components if unavailable locally on competitive terms; and labor-management relations—including salaries—managed by the government. The decree's announcement was accompanied by a Cuban campaign designed to alert commercial missions of capitalist countries of Cuba's investment opportunities. A regular session of the National Assembly of the Organs of Popular Power approved the decree in June 1982.

A National Bank of Cuba mission that visited Paris in March 1982 apparently opened talks on the possibility of renegotiating the foreign debt. Cuba's situation was deteriorating. One reason was the deepening world economic crisis. For example, in an October 24, 1981, speech before the Comité de Defensa de la Revolución (CDR), Castro noted that every one-cent drop in the free market price of sugar meant a seventy-million-dollar loss for Cuba. Another reason was the discreet but firm pressure the Reagan administration applied on capitalist-area bankers to block credits intended for Cuba. These pressures obstructed at least two Cuban attempts to negotiate new loans during 1981.[7] Arguments used against the Cuban requests included the poor state of Cuba's economy as well as the uncertainty regarding use of the loans, which were not linked to any development project. Most probably the Cuban government may have been trying to arrange an implicit renegotiation of its debt by contracting new obligations to cover previous ones.

The Cubans accused Reagan of trying to strangle Cuba economically. As Castro proclaimed in several speeches, Cuba would not submit in this manner and was prepared to resist a total blockade. In October 1981 Castro vowed that Cuba would meet its financial obligations because it was vital to the national interest. The Cubans also complained of growing difficulties encountered in marketing their nickel because of U.S. pressures. There was also a series of incidents in which Cuban diplomats were expelled from the United States, under accusation of violating the trade-with-the-enemy law. Carlos Rafael Rodríguez reaffirmed Cuba's determination to fulfill its commitments in August 1982. But early in September the National Bank of Cuba telexed word to its principal creditors of its desire to renegotiate the debt. Cuba's proposal was accompanied by extensive statistical documentation—more than seventy pages—that explained in detail the country's financial situation. The Cuban plan included a grace period of three years, a ten-year moratorium to liquidate existing balances, and uninterrupted payment of all interest.

Perhaps most problematic for the regime is how to reconcile a pragmatic policy for solving the external-sector difficulties of the Cuban economy with a renewed militant emphasis designed to meet the political confrontation of the United States. The challenge thus is to reconcile economic pragmatism with the militant internationalism that has characterized Cuban foreign policy since 1960. Undoubtedly this represents a serious contradiction that affects the prime principle of the foreign policy of the Cuban state and will be difficult to handle.

CONCLUSIONS

The five years between the first and second congresses of the CCP saw a series of important changes both in the domestic context where Cuban foreign policy is made and in the arena where it is implemented. By hewing with considerable rigidity to three state-policy principles, the Cuban government exacerbates and deepens its confrontations with an administration inclined to view social systems in a global context. The political benefits Cuba has derived and continues to derive from espousing antiimperialist causes will allow Cuba to maintain its prestige among Third World nations. But this will not give Cubans greater freedom of action when it comes to facing economic problems that affect all systems. The growing collaboration between Cuba and the Soviet orbit will increase even more, given the lack of viable alternatives and the climate of political tension. Cuba might find some relief in its immediate area, but this would call into play the finest skills of its diplomacy.

Despite these difficulties, Cuba will maintain an activist stance internationally for reasons already mentioned: to avoid becoming isolated and to counterbalance a growing dependence on the Soviets. Cuba will continue to count on a highly qualified and motivated diplomatic staff capable of executing, within limits, the directives it receives. Consequently, Cuban diplomacy will not crumble under the present crises. Sacrifices will be made in other areas, but not here, because the regime will continue to use its foreign policy to strengthen its legitimacy at home and abroad.

Precisely because of these circumstances, any attempt to force Cuba to negotiate its return to the Western fold would be doomed to failure. The Cubans have demonstrated convincingly their strong aversion to such pressures and their ability to remain active on the international scene with a minimum of resources. Cuba might take advantage of this situation to redirect its trade somewhat more toward Latin America, seeking financing from Arab states interested in pressuring the United States into an acceptable Middle East solution. Cuba could also stimulate the slow pace of its commerce with traditional clients. Multilateral initiatives such as the Sistema Económico Latinoamericano (SELA) could be taken out of the closet and recharged to the level intended during the past decade. Cuba's relations with Brazil, Mexico, and Argentina could be decisive during the 1980s.

Cuba seems prepared to resist a South African push in Angola. So far this has been avoided, but Cuba's enemies might attempt it to puncture Cuban militarism and to humiliate the regime. It is a serious and real danger. Cuba probably will not try to escalate the Moroccan-Saharan conflict nor spur it to unfold following the Angolan example. In Central America, Cuba's policy will continue to provide solidarity and support for the guerrillas and strategic aid for the defense of Nicaragua and Grenada. The Symms Amendment, recently introduced and vehemently denounced by the Cubans, seems to offer nothing new other than energetic posturing during an election year in the United States.

If history is a trustworthy guide, the United States will miss a good chance to place the Cuban question in a context of negotiation and tension reduction in the immediate area. The Reagan administration gives no signs of wishing to shift from hard-line policy to serious negotiations, particularly at this time. Should Reagan win reelection— breaking the prevailing pattern of one-term presidents since Richard Nixon's resignation—while distancing himself from the extreme right, he could capitalize on the disorganization and internal quarreling of the Democrats to seize the U.S. political center and govern more freely during a second term. Were all these things to happen, it still remains to be seen if a broader, more positive outlook would guide U.S. foreign-policy making. Reagan would have little incentive or need to mount a broad negotiation aimed at finding a solution for the immediate area. Such an approach would include demilitarization, a peace treaty, ideological and political pluralism, economic interdependence without protectionism, and free movement within the subscriber nations. I am not certain that Cuba would accept all of these conditions.

Finally, Cuba will have to start paying its debt to the socialist bloc during 1984. The symbolic value of Cuba is too great for the Soviets to impose intolerable costs. Nevertheless, Cuba's dependency problem will deepen. Although it is reasonable to speak of the sovietization of the Cuban economy, the argument that Cuba already is a Soviet satellite still cannot be totally defended. Militant as they are, the Cubans see in the crises of Hungary (1956), Czechoslovakia (1968), and Poland (1970, 1981) good reasons for orthodoxy. However, the absence of common frontiers with the socialist area continues to serve as an important divide between Cuban and Eastern European communism. Cuba appears firmly anchored within that orbit and the revolution, by all accounts, seems irreversible. However, the problems of the 1980s may well introduce certain important changes in Cuba's very unique brand of foreign policy.

NOTES

1. Enrique Baloyra, "The Madness of the Method," in John D. Martz and Lars Schoultz (eds.), *Latin America, the United States, and the Inter-American System* (Boulder, Colo.: Westview Press, 1980), pp. 133–139.

2. For example, see K. S. Karol, *Guerrillas in Power* (New York: Hill and Wang, 1970), pp. 191–216, 249–283, 360–381, 468–476; and Andrés Suárez, *Cuba: Castroism and Communism* (Cambridge and London: Massachusetts Institute of Technology Press, 1967), pp. 114–184.

3. Nelson P. Valdés, "Revolutionary Solidarity in Angola," in Cole Blasier and Carmelo Mesa-Lago (eds.), *Cuba in the World* (Pittsburgh: University of Pittsburgh Press, 1979), pp. 87–96.

4. For more details, see Archibald Ritter, "The Transferability of Cuba's Revolutionary Development Models," in Blasier and Mesa-Lago, *Cuba in the World*.

5. For the Reagan administration's interpretation of this aid see U.S. State Department, *Communist Interference in El Salvador* (Washington, D.C.: U.S. Government Printing Office, February 23, 1981). For a detailed critique of the content and the analysis of the evidence presented in that special report, see "White Paper on El Salvador is Faulty," *Washington Post*, June 9, 1981, pp. A1, A14; and "Apparent Errors Cloud U.S. 'White Paper' on El Salvador," *Wall Street Journal*, June 8, 1981, pp. 1, 10. See also the text of Eric Nepomuceno's interview with Edén Pastora, "Eu acabo com tudo isso," in *Veja*, August 11, 1982, pp. 3–8.

6. For an analysis of this debt, see Ernesto Betancourt and Wilson Dizzard III, *Castro and the Bankers* (Washington, D.C.: The Cuban American National Foundation, 1982), pp. 8–10.

7. Ibid., pp. 5–6.

DOCUMENTARY SOURCES

Fidel Castro, "Principal Report Read Before the Second Congress of the Cuban Communist Party," Havana, December 17, 1980; *Granma, Resumen Semanal*, December 28, 1980:6–16.

————. "Without Development There Is No Peace: Fidel's Message to the Ministerial Conference of the Non-Aligned on the Occasion of the Twentieth Anniversary of the Movement," February 4, 1981; *Bohemia*, February 20, 1981:50–53.

————. "Never Will Our Hearts Harbor Ingratitude, Opportunism, or Treason! Fidel to the 26th Congress of the SUCP," *Bohemia*, February 27, 1981:50–51.

————. "Address by Fidel Castro at the Twentieth Anniversary of the Proclamation of the Socialist Nature of the Revolution," April 16, 1981; *Bohemia*, April 24, 1981:51–58.

————. "Address by Fidel Castro at the 20th Anniversary of the Bay of Pigs Victory," April 19, 1981; *Bohemia*, May 1, 1981:36–39.

————. "Address by Fidel Castro at the Closing of the Meeting of the Presidency of the World Peace Council," April 21, 1981; *Bohemia*, May 1, 1981:50–54.

————. "Address by Fidel Castro at the Opening of the 2d Congress of Economists of the Third World," April 26, 1981; *Granma, Resumen Semanal*, May 10, 1981:5–6.

————. "Address by Fidel Castro in the Inaugural Session of the 68th Conference of the Interparliamentary Union," September 15, 1981; *Bohemia*, September 25, 1981:51–60.

————. "Address by Fidel Castro at the Closing Session of the 2d Congress of the CDR," October 24, 1981; *Bohemia*, October 30, 1981:52–63.

————. "Address by Fidel Castro at the Opening Session of the 10th World Labor Congress," February 10, 1982; *Granma, Resumen Semanal*, February 21, 1982:2–4.

————. "Address by Fidel Castro at the Main Ceremony of the 29th Anniversary of the Attack on the Moncada Barracks," July 26, 1982; *Granma, Resumen Semanal*, August 8, 1982:2–4.

Constitution of the Republic of Cuba, *Granma*, March 7, 1976.

"Declaration of the Revolutionary Government of Cuba," *Bohemia*, September 11, 1981:49.

"Declarations of the Ministry of Foreign Relations of Cuba: Cuba Vigorously Rejects the Accusations of the Spokesmen of Yankee Imperialism and of the Rotten Colombian Oligarchy," *Bohemia*, March 27, 1981:56.

"Editorial: Denied Lies Get Answered with Ever Bigger Lies," *Bohemia*, November 13, 1981:53.

"Editorial: For Socialism," *Bohemia*, April 10, 1981:48–49.

"An Interview with Carlos Rafael Rodríguez About Statements Made by Ronald Reagan," *Granma, Resumen Semanal*, February 2, 1982:1.

"Joint Communique of the Cuban Communist Party and the FRELIMO Party of the Mozambique Popular Republic," *Granma, Resumen Semanal*, February 28, 1982:8–9.

"Joint Communique of the Cuban Communist Party and the MPLA–Work Party of Angola," *Granma, Resumen Semanal*, February 28, 1982:8.

"Joint Cuban-Congolese Communique," *Granma, Resumen Semanal*, June 25, 1982:8.

"Joint Cuban-Mozambican Communique," *Granma, Resumen Semanal*, June 13, 1982:5.

"Joint Cuban-Saharan Communique," *Granma, Resumen Semanal*, May 16, 1982:3.

"Joint Cuban-Yemenite Communique," *Granma, Resumen Semanal*, March 7, 1982:8.

Isidoro Malmierca, "Address by Isidoro Malmierca as President of the Ministerial Meeting of the Coordination Bureau of the Movement of Non-Aligned Nations," June 2, 1982; *Granma, Resumen Semanal*, June 13, 1983:3–4.

"Minrex Note," *Bohemia*, March 27, 1981:55.

Jorge Risquet, "Address by Jorge Risquet at the Third Anniversary of the Triumph of the Revolution at Granada," *Granma, Resumen Semanal*, April 4, 1982:8.

Carlos Rafael Rodríguez, "Address by Carlos Rafael Rodríguez at the 36th Session of COMECON," June 8, 1982; *Granma, Resumen Semanal*, June 20, 1982:9.

12. Authoritarian Regimes and Foreign Policy: The Case of Argentina

While I was drafting this chapter, the war in the South Atlantic assumed transcendent importance for an understanding of Argentine foreign policy. The rhetoric of the nation's leaders and the exalted quality of the national fervor that characterized public discussion of the hostilities followed closely the pattern of Argentine adherence to basic principles that I have described elsewhere.[1] The manner in which the decisions for war had been taken appeared to fit perfectly the model for military-authoritarian regimes described by Barbara and Stephen Salmore.[2] Indeed, a great deal was made in discussions during the conference at Viña del Mar in 1982 of the impact of the war on Argentine foreign policy and on domestic politics. Some observers at the conference even went so far as to insist that the war would mark a turning point in relations among Latin American states and in their relations with the United States. Although I must admit to being skeptical about the impact of the war outside of Argentina and shall come back to this point later in the chapter, I shall leave the detailed discussion of effects of the war on Argentine foreign policy to Carlos Moneta in Chapter 8. My purpose is to place the conflict in a broader context, so that we might understand it within a theoretical framework that will permit comparative analysis of the events leading up to the war, and to help us understand better the way in which the nature of a political regime influences the content and type of foreign policy.

The Argentine case is a clear demonstration of the validity and utility of the suggestion made by Alberto van Klaveren in the first chapter: to combine theoretical perspectives hitherto kept separate by the nature of the historical evolution of the study of international relations and by the organization of the formal academic study of these themes in the United States and Latin America. For the most part, all of us are captives to some degree of our academic training—tied to a specific methodology and perspective. It is extremely hard for us to force ourselves to incorporate the perspective of another scholar and to abandon or modify our own.

But in trying to study the foreign policy of Argentina, it is increasingly important to make the effort, however difficult it might be. A rapid review of the literature on Argentina, cited by van Kalveren emphasizes the virtual bankruptcy of the distinct explanatory models when applied to the study of Argentine international behavior either in the specific case of the war in the Malvinas or in a more general historical context. When I use the word *bankrupt* in reference to the theoretical models, I mean that when the various perspectives identified by van Klaveren are applied individually, each one lacks explanatory power and appears disconnected from empirical reality.

Without going into each writing systematically, I offer by way of example the observation that most of what has been written about Argentina in the field of international relations falls back lamely on the assertion that Argentine behavior was irrational or erratic and that the nation's leaders were stupid or ineffectual. It may well be in one situation or another that such was the case, but it is not a mode of analysis that holds out much value to those interested in comparative foreign-policy behavior or in the construction of explanatory models even for a single country. Can we anticipate that Argentine leaders will be dense and ill informed? Even if we could, how does that knowledge help to predict or understand the nation's behavior?

From the long series of empirical studies of Argentine foreign policy that I have conducted over the past fifteen years, covering nearly a century of Argentine history, I would suggest that, as a minimum, the analysis of Argentine foreign policy in the case of the Malvinas war must take into account internal variables and external variables, must take seriously and evaluate the relevance of the geopolitical perspective, and should include, though perhaps not rely heavily on, the method-ological approaches known as bureaucratic politics and political culture.[3] It is within this context that I should like to turn to consideration of the specific variable of political regimes and the impact of those regimes on foreign policy and to some of the assumptions that variable implies and some of the elements that I consider necessary for its systematic study in the case of Argentina. Having done that, I will offer some tentative suggestions as to how we might combine this focus with others in order to formulate an approach that will prove more fruitful and useful in studying such cases.

We can begin by referring to the most straightforward proposition by Barbara and Stephen Salmore: "We have argued that the study of the effect of regime type and regime change both within and between nations will add significantly to the explanatory power of any perspective purporting to explain variations in foreign-policy behavior. The uses made of foreign policy by the leaders of regimes, the constraints placed on foreign-policy behaviors by the nature of the regime, and the internal political system in which the regime is embedded promise to be important concepts for explaining foreign-policy behavior."[4]

Summarizing and evaluating the relevant literature, the Salmores offered a series of bivariate propositions in which they crossed five elements or dimensions of international behavior with the variable regime constraints. The results are a series of prediction dichotomies such as great constraint, less international commitment by the regime, and so on. The relationship between regime type and international behavior is disarmingly simple.

At this point, it is useful to mention that much of the writing on the phenomenon of the bureaucratic-authoritarian state (B-A state) shares, implicitly, the basic assumptions underlying the analysis offered by the Salmores. Of course, the language is different, but the points of contact between them are important. Combining the two sets of categories, or of languages, the intersection that concerns us is one that we might state in this fashion: The more responsible or more open the regime, the more constructive or more pacific its international behavior. Let me remind you of the discussion in earlier chapters concerning the Chilean case, which argued that the lack of internal dialogue—that is to say, the lack of political pluralism, to use a more general formulation— redounds to the detriment of the foreign policy of the regime by increasing both internal and external constraints.

As a subjective statement of values such a formulation is impeccable. I share it. But taken as a theoretical imperative for an explanatory model, it strikes me as an assertion that must be demonstrated. Without entering into a long and formal logical argument, I will content myself with pointing out that Argentina, Brazil, and Chile, three bureaucratic-authoritarian regimes, exhibit markedly different patterns of international behavior and that each has altered its international behavior in the course of the period during which it has been a B-A state. In other words, if we accept as a general proposition the assertion that the more closed the regime, the more restricted or inflexible its foreign policy, it does not follow that we can predict the behavior of a nation simply because we know that its political regime is a B-A state. We need to know more about it.

How, then, are we to conceptualize the study of regime types and foreign policy? I shall attempt here to indicate some elements for the study of the Argentine case, which I believe can be used in a comparative mode to study the behavior of similar regimes. These three elements are closely interrelated:

- decision making under an authoritarian regime
- the peculiar, even singular, definition of national priorities under such a regime
- the legitimacy of the regime, as defined by popular acceptance of the national priorities set by it, to defend the national interests

In the following pages, I want to describe or define each of these elements empirically in the Argentine case since 1976. Then, I want to return to the question of methodology or approach to the general question in order to identify some independent variables that I consider vital for precise, comparative study of the relationship between regime type and foreign policy.

DECISION MAKING

Although there have been few systematic studies of decision making under the Argentine military government,[5] and most of the information we have about public administration during the period 1976–1982 is anecdotal,[6] it seems to me that there are three propositions that can be made without much fear of contradiction concerning the period up to the Malvinas war. First, there was no formal political opposition to the regime, and there were no organized groups that systematically subjected the actions of the government to public discussion and whose criticism represented a factor that the government had to take into account in formulating policy. Second, there were no institutions of intermediation in the society to fulfill the role of articulating the interests of groups or sectors in the society and making them known, in a systematic fashion, to the government. Labor unions and labor centrals, such as the Confederación General de Trabajo (CGT), might be considered an exception, although their role was anything but systematic. Third, there were serious impediments to freedom of expression among the mass media. Incidents of government censorship, in the form of pulling specific issues of a periodical off the newsstands or closing down an offending news organ, together with a pervasive, deadening self-censorship, left the mass media opaque and timid from 1976 to 1981. The radio and television newscasts were anodyne, and the large circulation dailies were either sympathetic to the regime and wished to avoid public controversy or focused their critical energies on fringe issues, such as the level of tariffs or the deficits of public corporations. Only the English-language daily, the *Buenos Aires Herald,* made a practice of commenting openly on the political events of the day, and that earned for its managing editor, Robert Cox, threats against his life that drove him into exile. The combination of these three elements over a period of time had the effect of virtually eliminating any mechanisms through which the government might hear alternate scenarios or consider heterodox perceptions in the course of formulating policy.

The junta has stated repeatedly that the armed forces are united behind decisions and policies of the government, but that is not the same thing as eliminating discussion during the decision-making process. The absence of free expression, together with reiterated insistence by the junta that the armed forces are united, has led observers to assume that authoritarian regimes are monolithic and unified state actors. Nothing could be more misleading, as far as the Argentine government is concerned. The insistence on the unity of the armed forces is a reaction both to the sad history of internecine conflict among the military groups in power and to the stark fact that they took power in 1976 in the midst of chaos. Their claim of having ended that chaos and of having repaired the sociopolitical fragmentation that characterized Argentina in the years leading up to the *golpe* (coup d'état) in 1976 represents one of the principal sources of their legitimacy. To solve the nation's problems, once and for all, the junta declared their unified support for a "process" that required the faithful adherence of all groups in the society for the benefit of the nation. In the first months following the *golpe*, the process was defined largely in terms of what the military was against—anarchy, clumsy mismanagement in government, galloping inflation, economic stagnation, leftist revolutionary guerrilla movements in the city and in the countryside, and a breakdown between the civilian government and the military authorities in their efforts to wipe out the guerrillas. Once the "dirty war" against subversion had been won, definition of the process in political terms proved more difficult and subject to severe disagreement among the military leaders.

In formal or institutional terms, the unity of the armed forces translated into unity in the junta and the right of any one of the services to veto any policy with which it was not in agreement. This was known as the *veto compartido* (shared veto) and often led to situations very much like government by committee, which created massive administrative bottlenecks. To protect the junta from the appearance of disagreement, bargaining and trading off often was relegated to subordinate bodies, particularly the Comité de Acción Legislativa (CAL—Legislative Action Commission), and to a vast, shifting array of ad hoc subcommittees on which each service was represented. If disagreements could not be reconciled within any of these bodies on matters not impinging directly upon the national interest, the decision was postponed. This occurred most frequently in the discussion of personnel files. On one occasion, the nomination of a senior career diplomat to an important post ran into some unspecified difficulty in committee and never emerged. The post remained unfilled for months, until the gentleman solved the problem by withdrawing his name from consideration. Similar embarrassing impasses attended a number of staff appointments in various ministries of the government.

The insistence upon formal unity within the junta also has more deadly consequences. Once a question of policy was placed before the junta and had been decided, it was made public as an act of the state as represented by the unified armed forces. Differences of opinion within the junta sometimes were expressed after the fact by the minority service by shooting down a representative of the majority services on the streets of Buenos Aires, in broad daylight. It was as if one of the armed forces, having lost a vote in the junta, gave notice publicly that its interests had not been represented and that it was exacting a price for its continued cooperation.[7]

Bottlenecks in the decision-making process and discontinuities in the process of bureaucratic politics were made worse by the traditional military distrust of the civilian experts upon whom they had to rely for information and advice on a wide variety of policy issues. This problem was particularly acute in the Ministry of Foreign Relations where the career staff appeared often to be at odds with their military superiors. Heraldo Muñoz has suggested that this problem existed throughout the Southern Cone and was exacerbated by the Reagan administration's search for allies in the crusade against communism: "This U.S. preference for military linkage had tended to further erode the legitimacy of Foreign Ministries in the handling of external relations, which increasingly have turned, particularly in Chile and Argentina, into a business either of high military officers or economists-technocrats. The outcome of this process is that the foreign policies of Southern Cone countries have become less professional, moderate and conciliatory, and more irredentist, ideological and unpredictable."[8]

Argentina long has had the reputation of conducting its foreign affairs in an unprofessional manner and of coming to the diplomatic bargaining table ill-prepared.[9] Not too long ago, a former foreign minister told me that he had been unable to find critical background papers in the ministerial archives and that it was his common experience to attend international meetings without the benefit of briefing memoranda summarizing the historical antecedents of the issues under discussion, the sort of memoranda that dot the records of the Brazilian and Chilean foreign ministries, not to mention the National Archives of the United States and the Public Record Office of Great Britain.[10]

But the dilemma of the present military government is not a lack of professionalism among the diplomatic corps nor a lack of information. Systematic interviews among senior foreign-service officers, especially those who had held posts in the Argentine embassies in Washington, London, or Brasília, made plain that the leadership in Palacio San Martín was provided with an ample supply of information about events in other countries and perceptive reports on the attitudes of those countries toward conditions in Argentina and policies of the Argentine government.[11] The problem was the lack of channels for that information to reach the decision makers in the cabinet and the junta. Censorship in the press, the often murderous manner in which the armed services carried on their political dialogue outside the government, and the severe repression of public political activity virtually eliminated mediating mechanisms in the society and in the government bureaucracy itself through which the nation's leaders could assimilate information vital to their decision-making function. The information was there; what was lacking was the means to bring it to the attention of the decision makers and the context in which it could be evaluated to determine its consequences for the nation's policies.

DEFINITION OF NATIONAL PRIORITIES

Aside from the residual distrust of civilian politicians, the principal reason the military leaders did not listen well or often to their civilian, professional, technocratic advisers is that they came to power with a grimly determined sense of what should be the top priorities for their government and for the nation. These were set forth by the leaders of the junta in a series of public pronouncements immediately following the coup in March 1976:

- to eliminate internal subversion
- to reaffirm Argentine greatness and to restructure the society and the economy in order to make achieving that greatness a certainty
- to secure the nation's frontiers, especially in the Beagle Channel and to end the affront to Argentine sovereignty represented by continued British control over the Malvinas Islands
- to end the nation's dependence on imported energy by expanding production of petroleum products and by pushing to completion the several ambitious hydroelectric projects under discussion, including a resolution of the dispute with Brazil concerning the height of the dam at Itaipu that threatened the viability of several Argentine projects downstream of the Brazilian-Paraguayan facility about to commence construction
- to strengthen the economy by cleansing it of artificially protected, uncompetitive elements and to permit the nation to find its proper niche in the international economy

If we can say that it is logical or natural for a military regime to define its objectives in geopolitical terms, it is not at all clear why such a regime should include in its ideological baggage a free-market economic model of the Milton Friedman type. None of the military leaders was an economist; they handpicked José ("Joe") Martínez de Hoz as their economic czar to purge the economy in the same way that they were prepared to purge the society of its antinational, Marxist, subversive cancer with a powerful diuretic, at whatever cost to the body politic. The subtleties of the economic debate did not interest most of the military leadership. They associated protected industries, Keynesian pump priming, and nationalist economic policies with populist politics, Peronism, and other unnatural acts, although most of them had a keen appreciation of strategic industries. Irrespective of the inherent defects of the free-market model, a subject far from the purpose of this paper, it seems clear that the junta never contemplated the contradictions between the long-term economic and strategic requirements of a national-security regime and the painful process of reinserting the Argentine economy into the international market on the basis of a supposed comparative advantage in the production of some agricultural staples.

Uniformed officers were put in charge of all the vital state-owned entities, the deficits of which were considered by some economists to be the greatest single impediment to bringing inflation under control. Army officers were put in charge of organizations such as the Yacimientas Petrolíferos Fiscales (YPF), the state-run steel factory, and the aluminum complex in Puerto Madryn because they were considered essential to the nation's security—the job of the armed forces—and because it was believed that their deficits were more than likely the result of civilian inefficiency or corruption. Whatever the management capacity of military technocrats, in the short run most of them displayed a passion for protecting their new turf and all but denied to the new minister of economics any influence over their corporate behavior. Rather than force a confrontation, Martínez de Hoz chose to ignore the anomalous situation, but the contradictions between his noble pronouncements on the cleansing of the economy and the continued stagnation of the state sector, which some estimated to be as high as one-third of the gross domestic product, could not be ignored forever.

For their part, the military, hardly students of the finer points of monetarist policy, ceded Martínez de Hoz a certain political and chronological space to accomplish his objectives. With the hefty exception of the state-run sector, Martínez de Hoz was given a free hand to cleanse the economy so long as he accomplished the military's primary economic objective: to accumulate within twelve or twenty-four months enough foreign reserves to permit the modernization of the armed forces, now responsible not only for national security and for the bloody crusade against internal subversion but also for the realization, once and for all, of the nation's historic destiny. From our perspective, it appears obvious enough that the contradictions between the economic consequences of the military's geopolitical schemes and the implications of the regime's official economic model would reappear sooner or later. Both in the months before and after the *golpe*, to both parties to the arrangement, the potential benefits of success were considered far greater than the risks of failure. Besides, economic success would have a political multiplier effect of sorts by doing more than anything else the regime could accomplish in the short term to forge a national consensus among the fragmented groups within the society, a consensus that would legitimate the regime and its national model of reconstruction at one fell swoop.

For a time, the strategy looked as if it was right on the money. Martínez de Hoz took his after-dinner show on the road to banks and manufacturing associations throughout the developed world. Agricultural production reached levels not seen since the 1930s. Some even saw the hand of God in the fact that between 1976 and 1978 the country enjoyed three bountiful harvests in a row, a phenomenon with few precedents in the twentieth century. In the midst of this economic surge, the nation hosted and won the World Cup. For a short while at least, everyone was an Argentine. Just as predicted, the surging exports facilitated the accumulation of hard-currency reserves, which paved the way for nothing short of an orgy of shopping in the arms markets of the world, a buying spree that accelerated in the last months of 1978, as tension built between Argentina and Chile over the Beagle Channel, and extended well into 1979. Estimates of the amount spent on sophisticated hardware soared into the billions, and the wildest of them rang true as missile-firing corvettes steamed proudly into the navy base at Puerto Belgrano and wave after wave of Mirage jets were sighted entering Argentine air space.[12]

Such was the apparent success of the economic model that it contributed to the restoration, in large measure, of the international reputation of the military regime, so badly tarnished by the blood of thousands upon thousands of disappeared, tortured, and jailed citizens. As the international pressure on the regime relaxed, it opened an internal political space and accelerated the process of political accommodation, a relaxation of controls. As Argentines returned from their summer vacations in February and March 1979, the generals seemed content with their success over the subversives and with their new equipment, the people seemed content with having won the World Cup and with the increasing purchasing power of their currency abroad (middle-class Argentines flooded into Europe and the United States to buy the latest consumer durables and luxury items), and the international bankers seemed content with their great friend "Joe" Martínez de Hoz. But the aura of well-being was chimerical. The economic situation began to deteriorate almost immediately, revealing that only under ideal economic conditions could the regime manage the contradictions between its economic and its geopolitical models.

The contradictions within the regime did not have an immediate impact on its foreign policy. The absence of normal political activity and of channels through which to express dissent had created for the regime a sense of independence that led the junta to give free rein to its grand geopolitical designs without the inhibition confronting any democratic regime, of listening to dissenting voices. In fact, it appears as if the military leadership did not even bother to go through the normal exercise of listening to competing scenarios within the bureaucracy or to collect systematically information available within the bureaucracy that might affect the selection of policy options. This became painfully clear during the Malvinas crisis. As one foreign diplomat reported:

One can sympathize with Argentine frustration at negotiations with Britain. Frustration, however, is not a good counsellor. In fact, the Argentines would have come out well ahead of the game if they had had enough sense to accept a diplomatic settlement after their occupation of the islands. Unhappily they became intoxicated with their own rhetoric quite apart from the usual difficulties the military government had in making up its collective mind. Moreover, by then Argentina had accomplished the impossible. They had reawakened the British Imperial spirit. The Argentines did Mrs. Thatcher an immense political favor.[13]

REGIME LEGITIMACY

The war with Great Britain over the Malvinas Islands allows us to study in great detail the issue of the legitimacy of the military regime and how it was able to call upon the loyalty and support of the Argentine people in carrying out the government's foreign policy. One of the central questions in the literature on international relations is to what degree a nondemocratic regime can commit the resources of the society and use troops in international conflict. Certainly, it is clear that the Argentine government had no hesitation in committing the nation to the great crusade of restoring the islands to Argentine sovereignty. All the evidence suggests that it was a wildly popular policy, at least until the shooting began. Indeed for the month following the invasion of the islands by Argentine troops, it looked as if the regime's prestige among the nation's citizens had reached new heights and that success in capturing the islands might be translated into the consensus necessary to effect a smooth transition to a civilian regime. It looked as if international adventurism had won the domestic political space that the regime felt it needed to retreat from power.

But the Argentines lost the shooting war with the British, and the Argentine military government lost whatever vestige of popular support and legitimacy it had had before the hostilities. It was as if nothing they had done since 1976 counted for anything. If the military often had expressed loathing and disdain for civilian politicians, now the feeling was openly mutual. The Malvinas episode suggests a caveat or a limiting factor in the capacity of an authoritarian regime, whose control is based entirely or in large measure on repression rather than consensus, to manipulate the widely recognized symbols of national identity. It suggests that the capacity of the authoritarian regime to commit national resources, particularly troops, in support of the regime's goals must be successful and must be severely limited. As the killing spread on the island archipelago, the debate at home centered not on whether the islands were or should be Argentine, nor on whether it was worthwhile to spill the blood of young Argentine troops to reclaim the islands, but on whether that blood should be shed in the name of a blood-stained, unpopular military regime. By the end of May and the beginning of June, increasing numbers of Argentines were rooting for their troops and against their government. Therefore, we might suggest that the capacity of an authoritarian regime to commit national resources to achieve foreign-policy objectives is a function not only of the popularity of the objective but also of the success of the adventure, in the short run, and the degree of national consensus previously earned by the regime for its political and economic models. Further, it suggests that an authoritarian regime runs much greater risks than a regime based on popular support in committing those resources for international adventures. The consequences of defeat are much greater than they would be for a democratic regime.

In a pluralist or democratic society, there is internal dialogue and the likelihood of formulating a broad consensus on the basic goals of foreign policy and how that foreign policy should reflect the objectives of the nation's basic model of growth and organization. Once that internal consensus is lost or broken, the nation's foreign policy loses much of its effectiveness in projecting the influence of the nation outside its own frontiers. Once national unity is undermined, made fragile, or completely destroyed, any regime is hindered in its efforts to invoke traditional symbols of nationalism, even if it wants to use them to achieve legitimate goals defined in terms of the axiomatic principles of the nation's foreign policy. Those symbols are even harder to employ as a mechanism for whipping up popular support or to legitimate the regime in the face of internal difficulties. Thus, in the months following the coup in 1976, the military had spoken of an internal war to justify its harsh repressive conduct of the campaign against subversion. The war was necessary, they argued, to prevent a state of national chaos and conditions that would undermine the nation's respect around the world. That argument had considerable effect on public opinion and won for the regime widespread support even as thousands and thousands of citizens were added to the lists of the disappeared.

By 1980, that support had begun to evaporate because of the deterioration of the economic situation. In February and March 1982, as social tensions mounted, as organized labor took to the streets to demand a redress of its grievances, and as the leaders of the civilian political parties, long docilely quiet, spoke out against the military, the options of using force in the Malvinas must have appeared attractive to the regime as an opportunity to capture popular support. The regime assumed that the entire citizenry would support a crusade to recapture the Malvinas. They assumed further, on the basis of pathetically selective information, that the Reagan administration would support the move. One of Senator Jesse Helms's aides had said as much to Foreign Minister Nicanor Costa Méndez in February, and he took that as the official word from Washington, despite advice to the contrary from his embassies in Washington and London.

Although the regime was tragically wrong about the United States, it was correct in the short run about its own people. The popular support of the invasion reached levels near frenzy across the nation. Every ethnic group, every economic group rushed to declare its corporate support for the war effort. Popular funds sprang up all over. Even school children were dunned for their pennies. For nearly two months it was impossible to direct the attention of the public to any issue other than the war. The very unions and political parties that had taken to the streets in

March pledged their support to the government to achieve the objectives of its foreign policy. This certainly served the interests of the government, but the strategy carried enormous political risks. As the British launched their campaign to retake the islands, the negative consequences of having manipulated the symbols of national unity without consent became obvious. The political costs of defeat in the Malvinas were much greater for the authoritarian regime than they would have been for a democratic government.

IDENTIFYING VARIABLES

To sum up, how are we to understand the regime-type variable in explaining foreign-policy behavior? The answer suggested by a careful study of the Argentine case is that it is a contingent variable and never should be taken in dichotomous terms. Further, these findings suggest fundamental revisions in the international-relations literature on regime types and some minor alterations in the assumptions we make concerning the constraints under which a bureaucratic-authoritarian regime operates, the level of internal cohesion that it can impose, and the supposed degree of consensus among critical policymaking elites.

In probing the nature of the relationship between regime type and foreign-policy behavior, the study of the Argentine regime from 1976 to 1982 indicates that there is no clear causal relationship between the two variables. Indeed, the impression drawn from intensive study of Argentine foreign policy in the past century is that the relationship between regime type and foreign-policy behavior is at best contingent and nonlinear, perhaps arrayed in the form of Markoff chains. But we still must inquire as to the critical independent variable. On what is the relationship contingent? The answer is that the regime, irrespective of type, is constrained by a set of axiomatic principles of foreign policy that perdure over time, irrespective of regime changes, and to which all regimes must conform in order to earn the support of the nation's citizens for its foreign policy. Each regime emphasizes different elements of these axiomatic principles and may stress one or another of them, but cannot ignore or flout them over an extended period of time.

There is one other independent variable that we must measure, upon which the dependent variables hinge both as to their explanatory levels and as to their causal direction. That variable is the level or degree of national consensus achieved by the political regime on how to realize the set of axiomatic principles. The levels of national consensus do not vary directly with the democratic nature of the regime, nor are they reliable indicators of a regime's disposition to use force to accomplish its foreign-policy objectives. There are numerous examples in the Argentine past of regimes attempting to use bellicose or independent external behavior as a means to relegitimate the regime or consolidate its popular base. Such idiosyncratic behavior characterized the regime of Hipólito Yrigoyen from 1916 to 1922, that of Juan D. Perón from 1946 to 1955, and the recent war in the Malvinas.

If the literature on regime types offers a set of variables that has only contingent explanatory value, how are we to use the distinction among regime types, if at all, in our effort to study foreign policy in comparative perspective? The solution to this dilemma lies in combining several theoretical perspectives. For example, we can employ the geopolitical model to understand the thinking patterns of policymaking elites under authoritarian regimes; we can use the bureaucratic-politics model because of the curious internal decision-making pattern of military regimes that is far from monolithic or homogeneous; we can use the political-culture model to evaluate the importance of symbols and public opinion under the peculiar conditions of regimes in which there is a great distance between decision makers and the mass of the population. Under what circumstances can we ignore public opinion? It is assumed in the literature that authoritarian regimes pay less attention to the opinion of the public than do responsive or democratic regimes. There are many cases in which democratic regimes engage in foreign-policy behavior that is quite autonomous of public opinion of constitutionally apposite institutions, such as a congress or a parliament. And, as we have seen, there are circumstances under which an authoritarian regime is painfully dependent upon the opinion of its public and must constrain its behavior—internally as well as externally—according to limits set by the public.

To understand more fully the foreign-policy behavior of authoritarian regimes, we must turn to careful examination of four variables often held in disrepute among political scientists in Europe and the United States: political culture; mediating or articulating institutions; the historical strength and continuity of axiomatic principles of foreign policy; and the degree of national consensus within the society and the capacity of the regime to reflect that consensus both with its economic model and with its foreign-policy behavior.

NOTES

1. J. S. Tulchin, "Los raices históricos de la política exterior argentina," in Carlos J. Moneta, ed., *Geopolítica y política de poder en el Atlántico Sur* (Buenos Aires: Pleamar, 1983).

2. Barbara G. Salmore and Stephen A. Salmore, "Political Regimes and Foreign Policy," in Maurice East et al., *Why Nations Act: Theoretical Perspectives For Comparative Foreign Policy Studies* (Beverly Hills, CA: Sage, 1978).

3. See, for example, my articles "The Argentine Proposal for Non-belligerency, April 1940," *Journal of Inter-American Studies* 11, 4 (Oct. 1969); "Argentina, Gran Bretaña y Estados Unidos, 1930–1943," *Revista Argentina de Relaciones Internacionales* 2, 5 (May–Aug. 1976); and "The Impact of U.S. Human Rights Policy: Argentina," in John D. Martz and Lars Schoultz, eds., *Latin America,*

The United States, and the Inter-American System (Boulder, CO: Westview Press, 1980).

4. Salmore and Salmore, "Political Regimes and Foreign Policy," p. 121.

5. Among the most useful studies of how the present regime functions is Oscar Oszlak, "Public Policies and Political Regimes in Latin America," paper presented at the Woodrow Wilson Center for International Scholars, Washington, D.C., March 9, 1983.

6. See, for example, *Mercado*, Nov. 30, 1978, pp. 16–17; *La Opinión*, Nov. 1978, pp. 9–11; *Tribuna de la República*, Nov. 1978, pp. 8–12; *Confirmado*, Nov. 30, 1978, pp. 56–60; and *Clarín*, Apr. 9, 1983, pp. 2–3.

7. Rumor had it that the civilian editor of *Confirmado*, said to be an army spokesman, was shot down in the Barrio Norte in August 1978 by plainclothes agents of another service following a bitter debate over financial policy. Similarly, when President Jorge Rafael Videla announced that the government would crack down on paramilitary death squads acting without government authorization, uniformed troops kidnapped the head of the Department of Pediatrics of the Hospital de Niños while he was attending a clinic, as if to express their dissent from the president's decision.

8. Heraldo Muñoz, "Reflections on the Malvinas Conflict," paper presented at the Woodrow Wilson Center for International Scholars, Washington, D. C., June 10, 1982. My interviews with officials at the Foreign Ministry, October 1982, confirm this view.

9. See, for example, the laments of two former foreign ministers, separated by half a century, Estanislao S. Zeballos, *Conferencias de Williamstown* (Buenos Aires: Talleres Gráficos de la Penetencia Nacional, 1927); and Miguel A. Cárcano, *La política internacional en la historia argentina*, 2 vols. (Buenos Aires: Editorial Universitaria de Buenos Aires, 1969).

10. Interview with Miguel Ángel Cárcano, January 28, 1970.

11. Interviews I conducted during October 1980, August 1981, and October 1982.

12. A recent report by the Banco Central (*Informe Mensual*, Aug. 1983) commented dryly that the accumulated foreign debt included a "miscellaneous category of $15 billion that undoubtedly corresponds to arms transfers during this biennium."

13. Interview August 11, 1982.

13. Peru: The Military Government's Foreign Policy in Its Two Phases (1968–1980)

INTRODUCTION

Except in times of crisis or war, few countries not recognized as global or regional powers ever succeed in projecting a clear and forceful image of themselves through their foreign policy. This is particularly so in the case of Third World countries. For many nations of Asia, the Arab world, Africa, and Latin America, only events of the magnitude of border conflicts, coups d'etat, civil wars, and natural or economic disasters— events behind which superpower interference often lies concealed— eventually rescue them from anonymity.

Peru was no exception to this rule until the military regime came to power in 1968 and set in motion a revolutionary process. Before that, Peru, a middle-range power in South America, played no significant role on the international scene. Peruvian analysts of their own country's diplomatic history and foreign policy consider that, during 160 years of life as an independent republic, the country reached its highest international standing in the middle of the past century, during the successive governments of Ramón Castilla, José Balta, and Manuel Pardo (1845–1872).[1]

Following that period, the War of the Pacific and the tragic impact of Peru's defeat by Chile cast a shadow over Peru's activity on the international scene for more than fifty years, so that it took on a minor, narrow, and formal tone and essentially focused on reconstructing a sense of national unity and identity and creating a new affirmative, sovereign, and autonomous international personality.[2] Although that difficult period was left behind several decades ago, there were no new events or initiatives in the area of Peruvian foreign policy during the years that followed. For that very reason, we are struck by the emergence of Peru on the international scene, especially during the early 1970s under the military regime established by General Juan Velasco Alvarado in 1968 and continued by General Francisco Morales Bermúdez from

1975 until July 1980, when power was transferred to the civil government headed by Fernando Belaúnde.

The so-called Peruvian Experiment of the 1970s embraced such diverse and controversial elements as the reforms undertaken in the areas of agriculture, business management and ownership, education, exploitation of natural resources, and press ownership. It included as well various new ways of encouraging popular participation, a number of incentives for technological development, several attempts to incorporate marginal groups, and the adoption of an eminently growth-oriented role by the armed forces. To these elements must be added other aspects of the experiment that were directly linked to economic management: the nationalization of strategic resources, the expropriation of important transnational businesses, the creation of an autonomous sector, the partial nationalization of banking and the financial system, and the promotion of the state as active agent, producer, commercializer, and negotiator.

Also in evidence were some less attractive features: authoritarian bureaucracy, the manipulation of public opinion, corporativist affinities, manifestations of "Yugoslavian" influences or models, attempts to fit professional organizations into a popular framework, stifling centralization of the decision-making process, and statist leanings. In any case, both the positive and negative aspects of the Peruvian Experiment have resulted in analyses and evaluations of the Peruvian process that concentrate on the country's internal affairs and on the difficult relations established among the principal protagonists in the political arena: the armed forces, the political parties, the power groups, the popular organizations, the elites, and the political vanguards.[3]

It is not difficult, however, to focus on other factors that, taken together, acquire great significance. Of special note is Peru's conduct of its foreign policy, which appears relatively autonomous whether one compares it with former practices by that country or with the behavior of other nations in the area. Examples of this autonomy can be found in Peru's strained relations with the United States; its unilateral recognition of Cuba; the leadership role Peru assumed in calling for reorganization of the Organization of American States (OAS) and the Tratado Interamericano de Asistencia Recíproca (TIAR); the support it gave to Third World positions and the militance it showed in the Nonaligned Movement; the decided support it gave to the machinery of integration; its establishment of dynamic relations with socialist countries; its assumption of a leadership role in the defense of rights relating to maritime sovereignty and the exploitation of marine resources; and the diversification of markets and other actions that were of comparable importance in terms of international economics.

On the basis of this preliminary listing it is easy to see the reason for Peru's unexpected rise to international prominence. Of course, the central point to be explained is how the prime movers of this new approach to foreign relations, the individuals who debated and decided on it and then put it into effect, emerged from a military team that took power and governed the nation for twelve years as contemporaries of other military regimes in Brazil, Uruguay, Argentina, Paraguay, Chile, Bolivia, as well as Ecuador and Panama, though with undeniable and radical differences from the majority of them.

Once the Peruvian military government had unfurled the banner of structural change; had claimed the right to autonomy, national sovereignty, and nonintervention; had demanded the necessary means to put into effect an ambitious plan of development that incorporated the claims of fifty years; and had gleaned the positive aspects of its initial radicalism along with a discovery of how one negotiates from a third-way position, it pragmatically proposed to maintain in its foreign policy the predominance of certain "permanent national interests" above and beyond those espoused by the prevailing authoritarian internal order. Was this goal reached or was foreign policy subordinated to the needs of the time and to the survival of the regime? This chapter attempts to answer this crucial question.

MAIN DIRECTIONS OF FOREIGN POLICY DURING THE MILITARY REGIME

A number of studies emphasize the differences between the so-called first and second phases of the revolutionary military government of Peru, the two phases corresponding to the governments of General Velasco Alvarado (1968–1975) and of General Francisco Morales Bermúdez (1975–1980). Differences are evident as far as internal policies are concerned, especially in the measures adopted on the economic front after Velasco was replaced. The intent of the new measures was to provide a better response to the impact of the international economic crisis. They involved a reorientation of disposable resources in terms of changed priorities and a retrenchment in the reform process in line with the political and ideological decision to slow down and redirect the revolutionary process.

The picture is not the same in foreign policy. In this area, after what can be described as a virtual break with earlier practices during 1968 and 1969, there followed a period of relative continuity of thought. In this consensus on the way to approach international questions we note a linking of the military government's interest in creating a positive and acceptable image of the country on the international scene with its simultaneous desire to exercise its power and influence in a new direction. This new direction was based on certain substantive proposals that were increasingly accepted as valid by the best-informed groups in Peruvian diplomatic circles and that were intended to deal successfully with a rapidly changing and not always positive international situation.[4]

In these terms of relative continuity, four elements can be seen as characterizing the military government's foreign policy during the twelve years that government was in power:

1. It was to play a constant role in legitimating the regime and in supporting the government's policies of structural reform while these were in force.
2. It was to provide a guarantee of permanence and reenforcement for certain Peruvian diplomatic policies that had long been proposed, though not always carried out, all within a framework of cautious respect for diplomatic professionalism.
3. It was to provide explicit reenforcement for the nationalist content of the government's long-range program and to aid in the insertion of national goals into the global context of international policy and economy, especially by giving support to positions of Third World and nonaligned countries.
4. It was to derive the maximum benefit from a policy of heterodox autonomy and from a policy designed to overcome all dependency on transnational forces.

To achieve this end, the military government would resort, on the one hand, to nationalization efforts and the imposition of limitations on foreign capital and, on the other hand, to participation in collective economic-security organizations and in integration efforts.

The Legitimation Role

Throughout the twelve years, but especially during the first ten months it was in power, the military government's foreign-policy initiatives played an essential role. For the citizenry in general and especially for the politically involved among them, distrustful as they were of the presence once again of the military in government, both the goals pursued and the aggressive radicalism of the measures adopted in foreign policy were disconcerting. However, the rationale that accompanied these goals and actions had as a permanent point of reference the following concerns: the defense of national sovereignty, the recovery of national resources and property, the forging of an autonomous space in the hemisphere for Peru, the prospect of a possible leadership role throughout the region and subregion, and also the appropriateness of introducing the country into the larger community of Third World nations, with which, it was felt, there were similarities in terms of common interests and level of development.[5]

The Plan Inca (or Plan de Gobierno), which was introduced in 1974, has a section on international policy. Despite questions raised regarding the true date of its formulation, the plan is undoubtedly based on the thinking characteristic of both the government's manifesto on taking power and on the Revolutionary Government Statute of 1968. It emphasizes the country's dependence on the United States, the restriction of its foreign-policy options to relations exclusively with capitalist countries, the failure to recognize Peru as part of the Third World, the meager prestige enjoyed by Peru on the international scene, the lack of aggressiveness shown in defense of the two-hundred-mile limit, the inclination—even in commercial dealings—to yield to foreign pressures and interests, and the absence of a policy of integration and development of frontier areas. The regime's determination to establish its legitimacy through a bold foreign policy is evident in this document. It espouses an independent and nationalist foreign policy for Peru, one based on a firm and active defense of national sovereignty and dignity and one aimed at counteracting each of the positions mentioned.

Continuity with Long-Standing Peruvian Diplomatic Positions

One of the points most heavily debated is whether or not there really was a break in Peruvian foreign policy with the change of regimes in 1968. The answer is both yes and no. In terms of action, in the space of only a few months there was put into effect an aggressive foreign policy that was without precedent in Peruvian diplomacy. One need only review the period from October 1968 to July 1969 to realize the impressive array of actions, decisions, postures, speeches, and highly politicized gestures that characterized the conduct of the regime and seemed to argue for the advent of a new foreign policy. On the other hand, although it is true that the country was asked to confront a series of externally generated actions during this time, it is no less certain that, in all matters of greatest importance, the principal lines of action did no more than continue, emphasize, and eventually put into effect the very proposals that Peruvian diplomacy had been elaborating for years. As a result of this meeting of political will and existing institutional resources, the foreign-policy measures of the regime that came to power in 1968 proved to be neither mere experiments nor a smattering of spectacular measures.

In actuality—and this was characteristic of most of the period—there followed an orderly sequence of actions and speeches that issued from the Foreign Office and were then analyzed and modified by the executive branch to make certain that they met the military, political, and economic needs of the moment. Everything was carried out in an objective and consistent manner. In support of this point, it is sufficient to note that at the very beginning of the process the only change made within the Foreign Office was the replacement of the minister, the new minister bringing with him a military adviser in order to guarantee a link with the armed forces. The rest of the organizational structure remained unchanged. The first thing the new foreign minister did was to ask that the different departments bring him all previously established plans of action so that they could be studied in terms of their feasibility in the new situation. This strategy contributed to the adoption, within a few months, of a series of very concrete lines of action.

In the following years, the initiative came from the executive. Velasco and Morales each had, in his own way, a very clear idea of the measures and projects that he wanted to promote at the international level. However, both of them much preferred to see these measures carried out as a result of teamwork with the Foreign Office. It is true that Velasco often went beyond conventional statements and accepted formulas in his press conferences. Speaking in rather plain language, he frequently radicalized positions. Yet he was always careful to point out that the official version of any measure or attitude was the one issued by the Ministry of Foreign Relations.[6]

The military background of these leaders, with its respect for specialization and professionalism, had a significant influence on the relationship between the military leadership and the Foreign Office personnel. It is true that there were tensions, based on generalizations and caricatures and lack of confidence in the ambassadorial old guard. There were some unnecessary and arbitrary measures adopted at the beginning. This tension, however, did not last long.

In subsequent years a great deal of attention was given to the Diplomatic Academy and to the decision made to set its students to work on projects of various kinds having to do with the country's development.[7]

Backing the Government's Nationalist Program and Inserting National Goals into a Global Context

Actions taken on the foreign front constituted a useful support for all of the measures adopted internally in the area of reforms or structural changes. When agrarian reform was decided on, there was a clear appreciation of the control exercised over farm production by foreign landholders, transnational companies, and supranational marketing agents. As a result, measures were taken to provide foreign nations and international forums with the information needed to justify the government's actions. The same thing happened when some of the mines were nationalized and when companies were either penalized for not exploiting their concessions or were asked to return them.

Even more popular were the measures explaining and justifying Peru's declaration of sovereignty over the two hundred miles of its maritime domain and its setting of limits on the foreign fishing boats that were pillaging its national waters, threatening the extinction of species, and laying waste to nonrenewable resources. (Ironically, these same things were later done by the very same national, even state-owned, companies to which the fishing monopoly was transferred.) Note was taken of the extent of foreign penetration in areas such as educational and press reform. This penetration resulted from the activities of a variety of agencies, including monopolistic transnational consortia that controlled international systems of communication, news agencies, publishing companies, and telecommunication systems. Behind each of these stood the interests of governments engaged in protecting the interests of their own citizens.

Peruvian positions had to be made known not only through bilateral relations, but also through the Assembly of the OAS, the United Nations General Assembly, and the regional forums of various organs and agencies of the United Nations system. Given the need to seek wider support and greater coherence of purpose with nations in similar situations, it was equally important to make these positions known through the Group of 77 and especially through the Movement of Nonaligned Nations.

It was not easy, however, for a military government or an army traditionally linked to the United States and to the other industrialized countries to prove convincing. Nor was it easy for the government to be accepted in its bid to acquire a level of autonomy that would permit it to carry out successfully all these reforms and, even more, to introduce them and utilize them in the area of international negotiations.[8]

In exchange for foreign support of the internal measures adopted by the country, Peru gave its support to other equally important measures. For example, it backed the reform of the inter-American system, demanded the modification of the Inter-American Reciprocal Assistance Treaty, and offered unilateral recognition to Cuba as a country that would be part of a future Latin American system. It also went on to make commercial agreements, on a government-to-government basis, with socialist countries. This measure would not only guarantee markets for Peruvian exports but would also open important lines of credit and import markets for goods from those countries. All this had to be accomplished without forgetting the most pressing concerns of the moment, which included the maintenance of a reasonable equilibrium with neighboring countries, support for the integration movement taking shape in the Andean Pact, and the search for concrete ways to cooperate on frontier problems, including certain integration schemes that might allow for the easing of nearby conflicts on the traditionally "hot" boundaries of Peru to the north and south.

Breaking with Transnational Conditioning

The Peruvian military government showed a continuing concern, throughout the greater part of its twelve-year rule, with the problems arising from the country's dependent status and from the transnational character of its economy.[9] Consequently, measures first adopted internally, then through the mechanisms of the Andean Pact, crystallized in Decision 24 to control the influx of foreign capital and to regulate the acquisition of technology. Somewhat later, proposals regarding the mechanisms of finance would be outlined, as the problem of foreign debts reached a point of crisis. Cases involving nationalization were less important, though they received more publicity. They provide proof of the determination to avoid imbalances in both the primary resources and the productive sector, and especially in the financial system.

The support that Peru received through its participation in associations of primary-resource producing and exporting nations represents an immediate and dynamic contrast with the slower integration processes embodied in organizations like the Asociación Latinoamericana de Libre Comercio (ALALC), the Sistema Económico Latinoamericano (SELA) (newly created in 1975), and the Andean Pact. This latter organization reached its highest point of unity in 1978, when it decided to widen its institutional frame and to project itself not only commercially and industrially but also politically. This decision led to the creation of the Conference of Foreign Ministers, a coordinating agency. Moreover, since 1973 Peru has repeatedly, though unsuccessfully, presented, in the working sessions devoted to the reform of the inter-American system, a proposal regarding the need to create mechanisms to guarantee the mutual economic security of countries in the region.

THE MILITARY GOVERNMENT'S FOREIGN POLICY: RISE AND DECLINE

The Government of Velasco Alvarado

No matter how good its long-range plans might have been, the revolution of October 1968 was in immediate need of something to legitimate it. Of the various scandals that had rocked the final months of the Belaúnde administration, none semed more important to resolve than that associated with the almost century-old problem of the International Petroleum Company (IPC). By expropriating the wells of La Brea and Pariñas the armed forces set out to demonstrate to the country how decisively they could move, how much their approach contrasted with the vacillations and long-winded disquisitions that had characterized the controversies over petroleum for some twenty years. As is evident from available documents, they were not unaware that the expropriation would provoke a violent reaction in the United States and that such a reaction, added to the break in institutional order implicit in the expropriation, would undoubtedly create a difficult situation abroad for the new government. What made this situation different from others in the past was the new regime's determination to use the confrontation to vindicate its use of power before the entire country and to justify internally the array of actions that it proposed to carry out. The confrontation with the United States was not deliberately sought out. On the contrary, a great deal of emphasis was placed on the strictly limited character of the expropriation, as well as on the reasons, in terms of national sovereignty, that led to it. On the other hand, no effort was made to avoid the confrontation. When it came, and threats and pressures began to mount, the military government responded by coining a new language and adopting a line of argument that, up to that time, had seemed neither useful nor viable in dealing bilaterally with the United States. Without going into great detail or discussing the immediate causes of the events in question, it can be affirmed that the expropriation of the IPC was accompanied by a number of closely related international initiatives undertaken by the Peruvian government that were in harmony with other regional and subregional currents and even anticipated the subsequent development of the government's extracontinental interests.

Seen in perspective, the period from 1968 to 1975 laid down the norms or guidelines that governed the regime's foreign policy for all of its twelve years. These norms are well worth summarizing here in view of the fact that policies later took a different course:[10]

1. Sustained increase in the country's capacity to negotiate on an international plane, particularly in the economic, commercial, and financial spheres
2. Development of answers commensurate with the challenge posed by the country's historical and geographic position as embodied in a new policy on maritime sovereignty and the southern Pacific, a new policy of greater involvement in the Andean subregion, and a new policy of cooperation for the better utilization and development of the Amazon region
3. Consistent presence of Peru in areas of essential interest to Latin America as these related to solidarity and community interests with the Third World
4. Gradual elimination of dependence on the United States and development of ties with other developed countries of the West as well as with the socialist countries

These guidelines emerged from a reading of the country's future potential that differed from assessments made by prior generations of internationalists. It must have been difficult, to be sure, for many trained professional diplomats to admit that the military regime's program was not only appealing but also eminently realistic and feasible and that it provided a measured and viable approach to a concrete renewal of the country's permanent interests in the area of foreign policy.

It would be useful, however, to discuss in greater detail the actual historical shape taken by these general guidelines. Three issues were central to the foreign policy of the Velasco regime: relations with the United States, the effort to diversify international relations, and the challenge of resolving regional problems. Only one of these, the conflict with the United States and the search for ways to become less dependent, is discussed here in detail.

Confrontation with the United States marked the entire seven-year period during which first General Edgardo Mercado Jarrín and then General Miguel A. de la Flor Valle held the post of foreign minister. To be sure, there were variations in the intensity of the conflict; as initial aggressiveness waned, it tended to surface in new ways.

The initial conflict covered a number of issues: the expropriation of the IPC, the application of the Hickenlooper and the Pell amendments, the embargo on the sale of arms and Peru's refusal to receive the Rockefeller mission, the request by Peru to have military missions recalled, and the discussion concerning sanctions to be applied to illegal fishing in territorial waters within the two-hundred-mile limit. All of these issues were, for all practical purposes, frozen after 1969. Peru continued to feel the pressure of cuts in the sugar quota and the possibility of a surprise cut in military supplies, but the debate took a different course.

Greater importance was given not only to establishing relations with socialist countries but also to increasing commercial exchanges with these countries. Also in the limelight were Peru's support for Andean integration and its search for more effective regional integration. These positions taken by Peru went hand in hand with a systematic questioning of the entire inter-American system and its principal institutions, including the OAS, the Inter-American Reciprocal Assistance Treaty, and the Inter-American Development Bank.

Other actions taken by Peru must be seen in the same context. Tensions arose for a variety of reasons, but there was not always an open confrontation. There was some movement toward a *modus vivendi*, as in the case of the new expropriations (in agriculture, the mines, and industry). Once the objectives and the extent of these new expropriations were made known, U.S. industrialists and other business people living in Peru were quick to express their agreement and to affirm that the actions taken had no bearing on their activities and in no way endangered the influx of foreign capital into the country. The same thing happened with the negotiated nationalization of banking, the purchase of International Telephone and Telegraph (ITT) stock, and the underwriting of the contract for the expropriation of the Cuajone mines. In the latter case, as a matter of fact, the government was accused by its opposition on the left of making concessions and handing over Peru's natural resources to foreign investors. The very terms used during the presence of the Irwin Mission are proof that Velasco's verbal radicalism was often used for tactical purposes, to establish a negotiating position.

During the last two years of the first phase, the debate on the U.S. law of foreign commerce, which slighted the Latin American Organization of Petroleum Exporting Countries (OPEC) of Ecuador and Venezuela in its system of generalized preferences, offered Peru another opportunity to propose a regional thesis in opposition to U.S. policy. However, the most difficult moments of the confrontation had now been left behind. On February 19, 1974, the Agreement between the Governments of Peru and the United States, also known as the de la Flor–Greene Agreement, was signed. It put an end to discussions about compensations claimed by companies that had been expropriated by Peru and basically concerned the holdings of companies like Cerro de Pasco and Grace, as well as a number of fishing enterprises. It also affected certain claims made against a group of building enterprises and the Conchan-Chevron refinery. With these accords a chapter of open confrontation came to an end. It remained for future history to reveal whether the International Petroleum Company did or did not receive a covert payment and, if it did so, whether it was with or without the Peruvian government's approval or acquiescence.

After the de la Flor–Greene agreement there occurred only one other incident with the same aggressive character as those of the initial years, and it had a very different and less satisfactory solution than its predecessors: the expropriation of the Marcona iron mines. No less important in terms of Peruvian-U.S. relations was the repercussion of the decision to "socialize" the communications media and, in particular, the expropriation of the press in July 1974. By this time, however, it had become evident that the impact of the economic crisis was such as to counsel a reduction in this level of confrontation and to encourage the negotiation of a *modus vivendi.* Velasco repudiated this approach, and his departure from power was tied to this stand.

B. Morales Bermúdez's Government

What happened in this so-called second phase progressively reduced Peru's international image and standing, bringing them back to what they traditionally had been. President Velasco's removal from office took place during the course of the Fifth Conference of Ministers of the Nonaligned Nations in Lima. President Velasco opened the conference; President Morales closed it. In his closing remarks on August 30, 1975, he said, "The revolution which today bids you farewell is the very same revolution that welcomed you a few days ago with fraternal greetings." A few minutes later he added, "Peru's irrevocable position as a non-aligned Third World country will remain as firm as ever as we continue the struggle to which our countries are committed."[11] Apparently nothing had changed. However, at the root of this change of command in the Peruvian revolutionary process was also a foreign-policy issue: a basic disagreement with the former government's response to the growing impact of the international economic crisis.

The global context certainly had changed. Whereas events had at first moved in an apparently positive direction for the Third World, they had now reached a climax and had begun at first a slow, then a progressively faster, decline that has continued to the present. The Declaration and Plan of Action for a New International Economic Order and the declarations issued by the Seventh General Assembly of the United Nations, which were much applauded by Third World representatives, were a kind of swan song. The last months of the Velasco government had foreshadowed this crisis, and the failure of the process of nationalization of the Marcona Mining Company's iron mines when no buyer could be found demonstrates the position in which the country found itself. Peru had to choose either to deepen its commitment to the revolutionary process or to take a less haughty approach than it had been taking in its dealings with a number of countries.

Faced with these conditions, Morales Bermúdez decided to moderate the changes being made internally and, on the international plane, to reevaluate foreign-policy priorities.[12] The factors that led Morales Bermúdez to make these decisions barely six months after coming to power seem quite clear: the need to lessen, and eventually to get beyond, confrontation with the United States; the advisability of not letting the confrontation with Chile lead to war (Chile had announced its departure from the Andean Pact and there was evidence of new friction on the frontier); and no less important, the need to establish or renew cordial relations with Brazil. These represented real pressures, to which were added a certain sense of frustration with the Andean Group and, at the same time, a relative discomfort over the tensions caused in Chile and Brazil by the pact's expansion. These factors encouraged the Morales government to focus on issues closer to home and to forsake, for a time, the larger view, especially as it became evident that all the Third World countries were desperately trying to resolve very similar problems. In the regional context, the Nonaligned Movement had very little weight and in terms of the confrontation with the United States, the Nonaligned Movement was considerably less important than joint declarations and actions by the Latin American countries would be.

It was not only external factors, however, that counseled a change in Peruvian foreign policy. Also at work was a marked ideological conflict that pitted those who saw the Peruvian Experiment as a means of building a qualitatively different—i.e., "noncapitalist"—order against those who only sought a modernization of capitalism. The debate over socialism, which had practically died out during the first phase, reappeared with marked virulence. Having lost the counterpoise previously provided by the leftist Latin American governments of Chile, Bolivia, and Argentina (during the first decade these governments had made the Peruvian regime appear only moderately radical), the government could not now play the role of representing the extreme left in Latin America. With increasing frequency concessions began to be made to conservative elements within the country, precisely those elements most prone to resort to authoritarian solutions. At times there was even recourse to open repression.[13] At the same time, the region was undergoing a process of dynamic change. Right-wing military governments were looking for a possible rapprochement, but the press in countries like Brazil and Chile continued to brand the Peruvian government as "pro-Communist" or, with ironic condescension, as "Marxist-infiltrated."

Peru's relationship with the United States improved as soon as the armed forces decided that current pressures and possible future conflicts with other countries in the region made it advisable to pursue a rapid increase in the procurement of arms rather than the disarmament proposed in the Ayacucho Declaration. A high proportion of every budget from 1976 through 1979 was devoted to arms purchases.[14]

There is an important point to be made regarding these arms purchases. A vital lesson was learned during the first phase: the importance of diversification and the dangers of vulnerability and dependency. It was the armed forces themselves who opposed the purchase of arms from a single source. Although it scandalized Pentagon strategists and high-ranking officers of a number of Latin American armies, Peru continued to buy arms from a variety of sources in Western Europe as well as in the socialist countries, a practice that culminated in the acquisition from the Soviet Union of the latest model tanks and planes. This time it was not a matter of belligerence or arrogance as might have been the case in 1974 when, just as the press was being nationalized and while Raúl Castro was visiting Lima, General Velasco presided over a parade to show off the army's new Soviet tanks. The second phase was based on a rational policy by the military. Before committing themselves to the high level of investment required to guarantee national safety and sovereignty, the military leaders first made a careful study of various Middle Eastern wars, evaluated the quality and appropriateness of different types of equipment, and even went on special missions to determine the effectiveness of the sophisticated armaments being offered.

The reversal in foreign policy was to be gradual. As was said before, the change in foreign policy would be a change in emphasis more than anything else. Translated into political decisions, it would represent, for instance, a rapprochement with Brazil and especially the acceptance of a long-standing Brazilian proposal to develop a means to integrate the area of the Amazon. Conscious of the permanent interests involved and of the options that ought to be left open in any agreement at this level, Peruvian diplomacy succeeded in turning the initial proposal from an integration pact into a much less ambitious Treaty for Amazonic Coop-eration, signed in 1979. Also needing to be rescued was Peru's firm support for Panama in the negotiations that ultimately culminated in the treaty returning the canal to Panama.

The context of Peru's relationships with other Latin American countries had changed and, consequently, Peru had to adapt itself to new realities and problems. In the first place, relations with Chile had hardened in the wake of the debate over a possible solution to Bolivia's lack of access to the sea. Friction increased in 1975 as a military confrontation became more and more possible. And the situation continued to worsen as the centennial of the War of the Pacific approached. Matters finally reached a climax in 1978, when the discovery of Chilean espionage resulted in the execution of a Peruvian airman. A reduction in the level of diplomatic relations between the two countries occurred as a con-sequence of Peru's ensuing demand that Chile recall its ambassador.

Relations with Argentina remained cordial despite the fact that in the past, and especially right after the military regime came to power (March 1976), Peru served as a way station or refuge for a number of Argentine government exiles. This welcoming attitude changed, however, during the following years, and there were frequent accusations that the Peruvian police were indeed collaborating with Argentine security forces, even to the point of persecuting Argentine exiles on Peruvian soil. However, the notion of a convenient understanding between Lima, La Paz, and Buenos Aires, in the face of the rivalry with Chile, allowed relations between these countries to remain at an acceptable level.

With regard to Brazil, there was a burgeoning of exchanges and a marked improvement in the overall relationship between the two countries as a result of the meeting held by their respective presidents at their common border and of the 1979 visit of President Morales Bermúdez to Brasília. Finally, in the case of Ecuador, following the tranquil years between 1970 and 1977, there arose once again border problems, skirmishes between patrols, and other belligerent incidents that were finally resolved only through the personal efforts of the foreign minister in one case and of the president of the joint command in another.

There were four foreign ministers during the second phase. The first of these, General Miguel de la Flor, held his post only until June 1976, at which point he was effectively purged. José de la Puente, a career diplomat, was the first nonmilitary foreign minister in the regime. He remained in office until early 1979, when he was replaced by another ambassador, Carlos García Bedoya, who held his post for less than a year. He, in turn, was replaced by Arturo García García, also a professional diplomat, who remained in office until the end of the period (July 1980).

García Bedoya deserves special mention in this period. In the first place, he represented a continuation of the type of thinking and professional effort that characterized the Foreign Office even before the military came to power in 1968—a concern with tracing the broad outlines of the country's foreign policy, with focusing attention on the theory and practice to be derived from these broad outlines, and with devising a complex scheme to bring unity to the diverse directions in which foreign policy had to move.[15] It was during his brief time in office that one of the most important achievements of the period was made. The Subregional Andean Pact, in its very wording, acknowledged the advisability of superimposing a political structure on the economic scheme initially proposed. This was to place the determination of long-range and institutional-level strategy in the hands of a more authoritative body, to be composed of the foreign ministers of the Andean countries. This Peruvian proposal, which became the Cartagena Mandate,[16] was signed by the five presidents of the Andean countries. It shortly found concrete application with the intervention by the pact countries in the Nicaraguan crisis, and some months later, after Bedoya had left the foreign ministry, with the joint subregional decision condemning the coup d'etat that toppled the democratic government of Bolivia.

It is important to recall in this overview that although in 1968 the Peruvian armed forces had to find a way to legitimate at an international level the coup that ousted Belaúnde, eleven years later they give their support, at a subregional level, to the process of change leading to democracy in Peru, a process that began with the calling of the Constituent

Assembly of 1978 and culminated in the elections of 1980. In an attempt to demonstrate the viability of the new, less military administrative approach, which was intended to correct a number of the supposed shortcomings of the first phase, the carefully devised teamwork model was gradually dismantled. Professional standards changed, and there was a return to more conventional—at times apathetic—behavior that concentrated more on reacting than on initiating. In addition—and this is probably the most important factor—with structural reforms brought to a standstill and with the revolutionary process stripped of its appeal, Peruvian foreign policy had little leverage left. Nothing proved capable of rescuing Peru's foreign policy from the loss of stature it experienced.

ACKNOWLEDGEMENTS

I wish to acknowledge my special indebtedness to Jorge Morelli P. for his invaluable suggestions and revision of the text. I am equally indebted to César Arias Q. for his contributions to this chapter.

NOTES

1. See Alberto Ulloa y Sotomayor, *Posición Internacional del Perú* (Lima: Imprenta Torres Aguirre, 1977), p. 366 ff.

2. For a modern and thought-provoking version of these tendencies, see Carlos García Bedoya, *Política Exterior Peruana, Teoría y Práctica* (Lima: Mosca Azul Editores, 1981), p. 52 ff.

3. The term *Peruvian Experiment* was coined in English by Abraham Lowenthal. See his *The Peruvian Experiment* (Princeton: Princeton University Press, 1975). There is abundant literature on the Peruvian revolutionary process and especially on the so-called first phase. Probably the most exhaustive bibliography of the period is that prepared by Clemencia Galindo de Jaworski, "El Proceso Político Peruano, 1968–1977—Bibliografía," which is included in Henry Pease G., *El Ocaso del Poder Oligárquico* (Lima: Desarrollo y Comunidad [DESCO], 1977), pp. 253–310.

4. For a competent assessment of the context from which the military regime emerged, see César Arias Quincot, "Perú: Una década de política exterior independiente" (Lima, mimeographed, 1980).

5. Regarding the "move toward the Third World," see Carlos García Bedoya, "Para un esquema de la política internacional en el Perú," *Socialismo y Participación*, no. 12 (Lima: Ediciones CEDEP, 1980), pp. 33–34.

6. The official versions of the president's press conferences were edited by the Comité Asesor de la Presidencia (COAP—Advisory Committee to the President of the Republic) and by the Information Office. The discrepancy between this edited version and the recorded version was clearly evident. Harsh references to neighboring countries, to the great powers, and to international financial institutions (which Velasco never liked) were readily eliminated by this editorial process.

7. With General de la Flor Valle as minister, the process of giving greater responsibility to young diplomats and of encouraging them to participate in

projects of social mobilization and interaction with other sectors was speeded up. In addition, the importance acquired by a number of career diplomats and secretaries gave rise to quite a few resentments in an institution as rank conscious as the diplomatic service.

8. A classic text with regard to these formulations, which were new in terms of international relations but nonetheless well anchored in the thinking of the armed forces, is the book by General Edgardo Mercado Jarrín, *Seguridad, Política, Estrategia*, published in Lima in 1974 after its author had left the post of foreign minister and had become prime minister and minister of war.

9. In this connection see the speech given by President Velasco at the opening of the Thirteenth Conference of the Economic Commission for Latin America (ECLA) on April 14, 1969.

10. Lack of space has made it necessary to eliminate from this chapter a section dealing with Peruvian foreign policy from the end of World War II to 1968, a period that provides a certain background and serves as a point of reference for the years under consideration here. An excellent contribution to a much-needed comprehensive view can be found in a paper entitled "Política Internacional del Perú," which was presented by Ambassador Jorge Morelli P. at the Fourth Meeting of the Relaciones Internacionales de América Latina (RIAL) Member Centers (Caracas, October 1982). The lack of any prior studies dealing with Peruvian foreign policy of the last few decades and the marginal attention paid to the subject by political scientists is well worth noting here. In the RIAL meeting just mentioned, I critiqued Ambassador Morelli's paper and presented an initial bibliography on the subject ("Bibliografía sobre Política Internacional del Perú") consisting of fifty-one entries, of which thirty-six are books and the rest are articles and pamphlets. Given the global scope of this bibliography, none of the numerous works on border treaties and problems, which abounded in the first half of this century, were included in it.

11. *Participación*, no. 7 (Lima, September 1975), pp. 8–9.

12. *Consideraciones políticas y económicas del momento actual*, a statement issued on March 31, 1976, by the president of the Republic (Lima: Editora Perú, 1976), 43 pp.

13. For an almost chronological account of the evolution of the internal political process, the social conflicts, and the tensions that were generated, see Henry Pease G.'s useful guide, *Los Caminos del Poder* (Lima: Desarrollo y Communidad, [DESCO], 1979), 363 pp.

14. In this entire process there was an inevitable trade-off that anticipated the transfer of power to a civilian government and the need to guarantee that all branches of the military were adequately reequipped. As the resurgence of terrorism and the guerrilla movement later made clear, this concern for general armament did not include rearming the police and other auxiliary forces. The concern was limited, rather, by the military's traditional lack of confidence in the other forces.

15. The posthumously published Bedoya, *Política Exterior Peruana, Teoría y Práctica*, outlines in the second and third chapters a foreign-policy plan based on eight central themes.

16. The mandate, which contains a twenty-four-paragraph "Parte Política" and a forty-four-paragraph "Parte Económica," was signed in Cartagena on May 28, 1979.

14. Democratic Transition and Foreign Policy: The Experience of Brazil

This chapter analyzes the relationship between the internal and external factors affecting Brazilian foreign policy during the past few years. The frame of reference will be the present process of democratic transition in Brazil, beginning with the so-called phase of political distension. The initial idea is to call to mind certain moments and certain political initiatives present during the Ernesto Geisel administration in the mid-1970s and to pinpoint traces of continuity in the present administration. The central concern will be to evaluate to what extent those policies were related to the internal dynamics of the country and the degree of relative _autonomy_ from external forces.

THE PROCESS OF POLITICAL LIBERALIZATION

In devising a typology for the interpretative forms whereby recent political changes in Brazil can be accounted for, Fernando Henrique Cardoso singled out four variants. The first is defined as being _strategic and conservative_, the main concept being the need for change as a way to avoid impairment of power. What is envisaged here is the overcoming of an internal conflict among the so-called holders of power, a consequence of which would be the removal of the armed forces from the closest circles of government, without, however, challenging their power to veto and make decisions. This reasoning is justified in terms of the need to maintain power so as to ensure national development in harmony with the pattern of an "emerging world power."

The second variant is termed _structural and critical_ and is accounted for basically by the inexorable nature of the structural conditioning factors of the economic crisis. In line with this approach political liberalization is viewed as the result of pressures that have escaped the control of the regime itself.

Third comes the _liberal-democratic_ version, viewing political decompression as a crisis of the legitimacy of the state. In this case the

216

point of view—contrary to the preceding variant—is that the success of economic transformations has brought into being a new political frame of reference, broadening the spectrum of demands by civilian society.

The last line of explanation is founded on the *crisis of hegemony*. It embodies certain elements of all three foregoing models in terms of the existence of structural conditioning factors and of a crisis within the dominant sector, valorizing the articulation of autonomous political forces outside the state itself.

Based on analysis of these four views of the situation, Cardoso aimed at presenting a particular definition of the process of democratic transition in Brazil, affirming that it is

> a process of political liberalization intended to adapt the possible proposal of bourgeois domination (hegemony?) to the challenges of an extremely dynamic society. In its most expressive aspects, this liberalization is intended to create "controlled spaces" for the exercise of criticism, without giving way, on the plane of the power struggle, to pressures in the direction of democratization.[1]

It is within this framework that one should seek to understand the recent transformations of Brazil's foreign policy in two dimensions, that of time and that of the specific dynamics of the transition. In the first place, it is important to emphasize that, chronologically speaking, the changes of a *political* nature in the international action of Brazil coincide with the inauguration of an administration whose purpose was implementation of a project for distension of the Brazilian political system. These changes can be more readily perceived by briefly characterizing the foreign policies of the military governments that preceded the Geisel period.

From 1964 onward, with the inception of the military regime, Brazilian foreign policy had reverted to unrestricted alignment with the United States. That approach embodied a lack of interest in the neighboring countries on the continent and in the underdeveloped nations as a whole. During that period, commercial and political relationships with the socialist bloc were jeopardized as well, and foreign-policy makers also lost sight of any attempt at tightening of bonds with Portuguese-speaking Africa, in terms of revitalization of the bonds of friendship between Brazil and the Portuguese world.

With the inauguration of the Costa e Silva administration in 1967, that policy gradually started to be revised. Two issues stood out: questioning the concept of bipolarity and identification of Brazil with the Third World. However, there were no measures on the part of the state permitting the expansion of the process of transformation. Within that context the fragile attempts at political liberalization were frustrated and abandoned in the ensuing period of the Brazilian military regime.

The 1969–1973 period was marked not only by a hardening of the political situation but also by celebration of the so-called economic miracle. On the external plane, relationships between Brazil and the United States were envisaged in terms of friendship between "equals." The Third World was once again swept away from the international interests of Brazil, to the point of even denying its existence.

> The foreign policy of the Medici administration was thus to stem from something that the Costa e Silva administration did not have eyes to see, namely: the intuition that nothing needed to be altered in the established world order, except the relative position that Brazil held within it. [With the advent of the Medici administration in 1969,] there was a rearrangement of the relative positions occupied by the three axes around which the production process was articulated, namely: the large international companies, the public sector of the economy and non-associated national capital.[2]

It was the conjoining of these three factors that was to permit, in a subsequent period, the gradual diversification of Brazil's foreign economic relationships. That diversification, in turn, was to comprise the material basis of Brazilian foreign policy as it commenced with the Geisel administration. It was at that time that a trend toward growth got under way in the trade relationships between Brazil and the Latin American, European, African, and Asian countries and even with those of the socialist bloc.

The second dimension of Brazil's foreign-policy transformation to be emphasized is that the political changes in Brazil's international relationships are embodied within the context of the democratic transition as manifestation of a *strategic-conservative* approach on the part of the Brazilian political regime. In this respect the implementation of the foreign policy of the Geisel administration became caught up in the rearrangement of the constellation of forces within the structure of power. It was a project that looked like both cause and effect of that rearrangement, to the extent that it formed part of the group of policies that, when carried out, intensified the level of tensions within military circles themselves.

It is important to emphasize that the subject of foreign policy comprised a "matter of State" only partially linked with the overall matter of distension of the system. The way the new project was handled depended on the reformulation of political and strategic concepts in far more flexible terms, ideologically speaking, on the *external* plane. Moreover, the opening of new fields of activity within the international system was bound to valorize the operations of the Itamaraty within the system of power itself. The scenario was greatly favored by progress in the direction of distension during the Geisel administration itself. Gradual displacement of the more "hard-line" sectors during his term of office gave rise—within the circles of power themselves—to increasing support and legitimacy for the so-called pragmatic foreign policy.[3]

It should finally be borne in mind that there is a certain amount of variation as regards the intensity of the relationship between the present foreign policy of Brazil and the process of democratic transition. That relationship was a good deal more intensive in the first stages of the phase of distension, when the strategic-conservative question in the dominant sectors also affected the field of foreign policy. But as a greater and greater degree of consensus was achieved among economic, political, and military sectors—through a process that has gone even further in the present administration—the pattern of Brazilian foreign policy began to gain increasing autonomy in relation to the dynamics of the democratic transition. In that respect, the question of the "crisis of legitimacy" and the "liberal democratic" explanatory version, though present in other sectors of national life, did not make itself felt in the area of Brazil's international relationships. In other words, the problems of party representation, freedom of opinion, alternative demands and political organization, up to the present stage of the process of transition, had not yet encountered the necessary bridges of relationship with Brazil's foreign policy. The field of international relationships thus looked like an immense unknown as regards the day-to-day practices that were being deployed to pave the highways of communication between civilian society and the state.

CURRENT BRAZILIAN FOREIGN POLICY

It is important in the first place to stress that it was the changes in the economic field that established the material bases for the major redefinitions of Brazil's foreign policy. Diversification occurred in the areas of foreign trade, foreign investments, and the procurement of financial resources abroad.

To characterize Brazil's foreign policy as formulated from the 1970s onward, three fundamental variables must be observed.

Redefinition of Relationships with the United States. The primordial point here was the breaking down of the "automatic alignment" relationship. That decision represented at one and the same time a new stance in bilateral terms and a basic step in the direction of overall international involvement by Brazil.

Moreover the areas of disagreement and possible clashes with the United States expanded and became diversified with the adoption of this stand. Political redefinition of relationships with the United States was directly related to the new Brazilian profile of economic dependency. The decline in relationships with the United States in terms of foreign trade, foreign investment, and external indebtedness was progressively offset by relationships with Western Europe, Latin America, Africa, and Japan.

The Quest for Ideological Neutrality. The effort in this direction entailed an entirely different dimension in Brazilian foreign policy for the post-1964 period. On the one hand, the Brazilian government proceeded to develop relationships with countries whose internal ideologies were rejected internally by the political system in the country (one example being the diplomatic recognition of the former Portuguese colonies in Africa). On the other, an endeavor was made to achieve a stand of ideological neutrality through defense of unaligned relationships, condemnation of the policy of blocs fostered by the United States and the USSR, and condemnation of interventionist practices.

Closer Ties with the Third World. The main instrument for tightening bonds with the Third World was the replacement of a special relationship with the United States by a multilateral conflict with the advanced capitalist countries. That position was particularly reinforced by the active participation of the Brazilian government in the North-South dialogue. In that respect Brazil intensified its South-South relationships in both bilateral and multilateral terms. New political and economic relationships were formulated in regional terms with Latin America, Black Africa, and the Middle East.

Where the Middle East is concerned, the most important aspect has been the intensification in barter relationships with the petroleum-producing countries and the support for the Palestinian cause. Ever since the increase in the price of crude oil in 1973, Brazil has succeeded in enormously expanding its exports of manufactures to the Middle East.

In the case of Black Africa, Brazil has been developing quite an innovative and original policy, through diplomatic recognition and tightening of bonds with the governments of Mozambique, Angola, Cabo Verde and Guinea-Bissau and currently in championing the independence of Namibia. That policy has won for Brazil a special political dimension in its Third World relationships.

Finally, and of most importance to the analysis in this chapter, there are the relationships developed with Latin America. The main objective of that policy is recovery of the "Latin" identity of Brazil. Specifically that effort had as its starting point the Tripartite Agreement with Argentina in 1979, when the two countries reached an agreement in relation to the Itaipu and Corpus projects. The next step was the development of what has been termed presidential diplomacy (in two years, President Figueiredo visited six different countries on the continent) and the innovation of the Brazilian diplomatic discourse—through the inclusion of concepts such as democracy, regional integration, and human rights. In the economic sphere, foreign trade with Latin America has come to be of more and more significance to Brazil and has even exceeded exports to the United States in the past two years.

Relations with the United States

The redefinition of the relationships between Brazil and the United States was of extreme significance to Brazil. Ever since the end of World

War II a relationship of alignment had become consolidated through which the presence of the United States became dominant in economic, military, political, and ideological terms. That domination at some times took the form of a harmonious friendship and at others a factor of tension that had the effect of producing internal destabilization.

The declining U.S. participation in Brazil's external trade from the beginning of the 1970s created the basic conditions for transformation of that relationship. In that respect, the political revision of the relationships with the United States was directly associated with the new profile of the country's economy. Added to that situation was greater diversification in transactions in the area of purchases of military equipment, thanks to the increasing competitiveness of the European armaments industry, together with expansion of Brazil's own domestic armaments industry.[4]

These data are fundamental to an understanding of the gradual drawing apart that started between the two countries after 1976, with the reactions of the Brazilian government to the new policies of the Carter administration in relation to Latin America. What was involved were the policies on human rights, on nonproliferation of nuclear devices, and on disarmament. U.S. pressure on the Brazilian government to carry these policies forward proved ineffective and ended up by causing a cooling-off in political relationships between the two countries.

The disagreements between the Carter administration and the Geisel administration had different effects in the respective countries. On the side of the U.S. government the liberal platform championed by the Carter administration was aimed at rectifying old policies, while at the same time maintaining the nation's traditional interventionist stance in the region. Adoption of the human-rights policy as an instrument of pressure in relation to the policies of armaments sales and nonproliferation reinforced that image internally even more. But in Brazil, the internal repercussions ran counter to the expectations of the liberal Carter administration. A Brazilian newspaperman Walder de Góes commented: "Ironically, U.S. pressure may foster in the Southern Cone region political developments antagonistic to those proclaimed by President Carter, whose championing of human rights aims to assume the guise of a crusade in favor of democratic forms of political organization."[5]

The attitude of the Brazilian government in denouncing the 1952 military agreement and pursuing negotiations for the nuclear agreement with Germany put an end to U.S. pressures. That stand, which in itself comprised a redefining of political relationships with the United States, also embodied various internal implications. The cooling off of relationships with the Carter administration could be clearly associated with a closed internal policy of nationalistic tendencies, wherein the demonstration of decision-making autonomy served as a sign of internal force and cohesion. Yet at the same time it implied touching on a sensitive factor in the Brazilian political system, namely that of the presence of the United States as an element of internal instability.

Inauguration of the conservative Reagan administration tested the nonalignment relationship. The current agenda of relationships between Brazil and the United States has become a good deal more complex and conflictive than under the Carter administration. Problems have arisen that are not subject to solution on a bilateral level, including questions having to do with the crisis situation of the U.S. economy itself and the international capitalist system as well.

The same thing might be said in political and military terms. The difficulties created in this area are linked with the crisis of power in the United States itself. Inability to cope with the conflict in the Malvinas Islands will undoubtedly cause the United States to proceed with greater caution in the future. Yet to the extent that the U.S. government does not open up space within the inter-American system for some kind of participation other than that in hegemonic terms, the lines of communication between Washington and Brasília will continue to be circumscribed. The consequences of this scenario, in the event of another crisis in the inter-American systrem, may entail even more drifting apart and cooling off of relationships.

At this stage of the discussion it is worthwhile getting back to the matter of the democratic transition. The relationship between the new political stance of Brazil toward the United States and the process of internal decompression still is somewhat vague. It has, nevertheless, been possible to identify some internal sectors favorable to closer ties with the United States along the former pattern of long-standing friendship. The posture of nonalignment adopted by Brazil on specific matters is condemned as an approach distorting the traditional Western orientation of the country. During the period of the Malvinas war that position was made explicit.

At the present time this view reflects the attitude of a minority. Actually, the Malvinas conflict ended up as a bond establishing legitimacy between the internal and the external dimensions of the position of nonalignment toward the United States. Externally, it became somewhat difficult for the United States to bring pressure to bear on the Brazilian government to adopt a different position in terms of its alliance with Great Britain. And on the internal plane, a consensus arose among the Itamaraty, the armed forces, and political sectors—both incumbents and opposition—without precedent in the recent years.

It becomes a matter of importance from this time on to follow up the ability of internal political sectors directly involved in the Brazilian democratic project to find forms of articulation between external nonalignment and internal political liberalization. With the effective consolidation of such a bridge, a basic step forward will have been taken in deactivating the influence of Brazil-U.S. relationships on Brazilian political life.

Latin American Policy

One of the outstanding traits of recent Brazilian diplomacy has been the effort to deepen and improve the bases of cooperation and understanding in Latin America. The development of a more consistent relationship within the continent is not only an objective in its own right but is also intended to reinforce the position of nonalignment in relation to the United States.

In the case of Latin America as well, transformations in the economic field precede political transformations. The most significant factor in this process has been the volume of Brazilian exports to the region, which has, in the last two years, unprecedentedly exceeded sales to the United States. The bulk of these exports are of manufactures, and at the present time Latin America consumes over 30 percent of the Brazilian industrial products sold abroad. To this panorama should be added the opening of new areas of interchange and cooperation in the cultural and technological field, which form a part of the general policy of upgrading of South-South relationships.

Relationships between Brazil and Latin America have proved to be a fertile field for interaction between the external and the internal facets of the democratic transition. In the first place, it is interesting to note how the process of democratic transition in Brazil has become transformed into a component also frequently present in Brazil's diplomatic attitudes. A second relevant factor is the way in which the effects of continental crises have produced their repercussions within Brazil.

According to some authorities of the Ministry of External Relations, the internal political context in Brazil has turned into a substantial factor in the tightening of bonds between this country and its neighbors. In stressing this point one Brazilian diplomat had this to say:

> Without political liberalization in Brazil, such a process of drawing together would have been simply impossible and undoubtedly these trips would not have achieved the impact they have had, no matter how much the countries visited are capable of drawing a line of separation between foreign relations and ideological content, and no matter how authoritarian are the regimes in force in some of them.[6]

Actually, the questions of democracy, liberty, and pluralism appear frequently in the statements of the minister of foreign affairs and the Brazilian president himself. Just one instance is the recent joint declaration with Ecuador (September 2, 1982) in which the two governments "underscored the fact that one of the Latin American ideals is full democratic activity, and coincided in the view that the two governments have firm commitments towards the enhancement of democratic formulas for political existence and towards the achievement of social justice and economic development in the respective countries."[7]

As regards the situation of tension in Central America, Brazilian foreign policy has focused on four major points: (1) the general context of Latin American policy as recently developed by Brazil; (2) the differences arising among Brazil, Venezuela, Colombia, and Mexico in terms of the relative importance of their various foreign policies in the region; (3) manipulation of the region by the United States as an area of extension of the East-West conflict within the context of the hemisphere; and (4) the problem of relationships with Cuba. Of these items, only the last two entail internal political dimensions touching upon the process of political liberalization.

The Brazilian government has been endeavoring to express its disagreements with the policy adopted by the Reagan administration in Central America by reaffirming the principle of nonintervention. That approach is one of the more relevant aspects of the rejection of a return to a policy of alignment. It is a question that has aroused disagreements between certain Brazilian political sectors, some of which accuse the Itamaraty of passivity in the most acute moments of the crisis in Central America. In view of prospects of a visit by President Figueiredo to Washington, that view of the matter was spelled out in *O Estado de São Paulo* (the pro-U.S. daily São Paulo press) in a February 19, 1982 article:

> At a time when the drums of counterinsurgency are starting to beat more vigorously in the United States, while subversion makes headway in the Antilles and in Central America, the House of Rio Branco cannot remain in a posture of upholding the formulas of diplomatic action of the Fifties, without realizing that they were valid because they were backed by the machinery of collective intervention based on the Treaty of Petropolis.

The main point of the discussion here refers to the "triangulation" of the relationships between Brazil and Latin America. Two currents of thought are opposed to one another: one to the effect that Brazil ought to relate to the continent through identification of its interests with those of the United States and the other urging a Brazilian position of its own, independent of U.S. foreign policy.

It is in this respect that Brazil has sought to make quite clear the specific nature of its disagreements with the Cuban government, avoiding viewing the presence of Cuba as a focal point of trouble, whereas the United States has more and more upheld the retrograde view of contamination, seeking to expand the long-standing theory of dominion in the Caribbean and in Central America. A clear-cut instance of the difference in approach can be seen specifically in the nature of the relationships between the respective countries and Nicaragua, where Brazil has been engaged in a progressive effort at providing cooperation and assistance to the new government. Apart from the field of technical cooperation, significant steps have been taken at the level of political and diplomatic relationships.

The Malvinas conflict was one episode of importance in recovery of the Latin-American identity of Brazil. It gave priority to recognizing the historic rights of Argentina to the islands in the South Atlantic. Its understandings with the United States took place on the basis of that priority and not vice versa, as had occurred on other occasions. That position was consolidated during the Organization of American States (OAS) meeting, when Trinidad, Colombia, and Chile alone voted along with the U.S. government.

Attitudes in relation to Argentina have currently become a topic of particular interest in Brazil in terms of their political connotations. The democratic approach has become instrumentalized as an argument for discrediting the action of the Argentine government, involving criticism of any Brazilian manifestations of solidarity toward the neighboring country. Not only has the lack of legitimacy of the Argentine regime been denounced in terms of the political nature of the latter, but there has been a trend toward a return to the position of antagonism between Brazil and Argentina as a guiding principle of Brazilian foreign policy on the continent. Pursuant to this line of reasoning, a cry of alert has been raised in the following terms: "What will happen to South America if an Argentina armed to the teeth and ostensively or covertly backed up by the USSR were disposed to revise frontiers by force?"[8]

Others upheld the need for supporting Argentina, as a mechanism for fortifying the Latin American system itself. Hence the national and regional questions turned into conditioning factors in the formulation of Brazilian foreign policy.[9]

In more immediate political terms, the repercussions of the Malvinas war occurred mainly within the restricted environment of the decision-making circles of the Brazilian regime. The geostrategic questions involved implied the need for close articulation between the armed forces and the Itamaraty in handling Brazilian foreign policy during the entire conflict. On the internal political scene, moreover, the episode fostered discussion of the question of nationalism, regionalism, and democracy within the Latin American area. The minor extent to which these subjects have been capitalized on by political figures and organizations, however, bears out the difficulty of converting external affairs into internal issues, even at times when international crises arise almost on the country's very borders.

Brazil and Black Africa

Relationships with the new nations of Black Africa involved an important step in the reformulation of Brazil's foreign policy. Although the fundamental political axis was the anticolonial stance, the strengthening of bonds came to have specific political implications in terms of the ideological options prevailing in the struggle for national liberation in those countries. Those options in many cases meant external alignments that, for the Brazilian state, would be inconceivable in terms of its "Western-leaning" vocation.[10]

The strengthening of relationships between the Brazilian government and southern Africa have involved quite a shift in the orientation of Brazil's foreign policy in relation to its geopolitical concepts. The long-standing idea of a South Atlantic Treaty aimed at uniting within a single security pact Brazil, Argentina, Uruguay, and South Africa was automatically done away with. But the decision in favor of a "new" African policy had been preceded by certain concrete events during the Medici administration. An example is the trip by Minister of Foreign Affairs Gibson Barbosa to nine different countries on the west coast of Africa toward the end of 1972 and its consequences on the plane of trade relationships, plus the establishment in São Paulo in 1973 of the Afro-Brazilian Chamber of Commerce. The year 1974 saw the commencement of the Geisel administration, the victory of the anti-Salazarian revolution in Portugal, and the inauguration of the process of Portuguese decolonization.

The implementation of a policy of support for the new African nations was faced at the outset by internal and external resistance. Internally, it was a matter of displacing those forces that traditionally upheld close ties with the dictatorship of Salazar and its colonial possessions. The very marked ideological bias of those groups, in both military and civilian circles, gave rise to an attitude even more hostile to the liberation of the Portuguese colonies in terms of the definitely leftist orientation of the African movements. In describing this confrontation Hugo de Abreu, head of the civil household of the Geisel administration, commented:

> We have referred to the lack of comprehension on the part of radical sectors in Brazil. Actually, after the semi-Fascist dictatorship of Salazar and Marcelo Caetano, it was only natural that the Portuguese should lean towards the other side and tend, at least at the outset, towards Communism. By the same token, while oppressed and massacred by the former Portuguese regime, the former African colonies were supported almost alone by the Communist countries, so it was only natural that their greatest heroes at the time of liberation should be those same Communist leaders that had struggled against the oppression of the Metropolis. And it was with those leaders that our diplomats would have to negotiate. Agostinho Neto, Samora Machel, Luís Cabral, amongst others, were the true leaders of the new African countries. Some people in Brazil actually censured the Itamaraty for engaging in negotiations with Communist leaders, overlooking the fact that although they really were Communists, they were first of all the national leaders of greatest prestige in their own countries.[11]

The other front of resistance occurred among the African leaders themselves, who found it hard to credit the new posture of the Brazilian government. The distrust of the Africans was explicitly demonstrated to the Brazilian diplomatic missions. In bureaucratic terms, it is interesting to note the specific activity of the staff of the Ministry of Foreign Relations, the main actors in the process of external liberalization, the decisions for which were taken in the National Security Council. Three years later it became quite evident that that policy had given rise to serious tension in military circles. On his dismissal from the post of minister of war, General Sílvio Frota mentioned as one of his points of disagreement with the Geisel administration the hasty recognition of the communist government of Angola.

Yet the new African policy has had only limited impact on the democratic question in Brazil itself. The initial moments of tension within the Brazilian state were undoubtedly associated with broader difficulties of implementation of a project of political distension. Although the conditions necessary for making progress have been established within the state, significant bonds between that policy and the civilian society have not been fostered. That articulation will become feasible only when the banner of racial equality has been taken up as a topic in the path of democracy.

EXPANDING NATIONAL INTERESTS

Analysis of specific instances of the international action of Brazil has borne out the number of new questions that have come to be involved in the list of national interests. The emergence of these questions within a situation of political revitalization in itself stands for a new potential of action and thought on the part of both the state and of Brazilian society. Added to the diversity of external fronts is the need for expanding the spectrum of political representation reflecting the range of internal demands. What exists at the present time is a hiatus between the action of the state and the mechanisms of participation of the actors in society and the political organizations.

It is worthwhile at this point to go back to the following comments by Cardoso:

> Unless there is a continuing critique in the interstices of society—the microphysics of politics—and unless there is a new proposal aimed at a symbiosis between society and state, leading to the actual socialization of the state and to its being brought under democratic control, and at the same time valorization of Power and of state authority, as an objective to be achieved (at all levels and not just that of the central authority), then the opposition runs the risk of facing a dilemma: either it repeats in power the Panopticon proposal or it is generously inoperative, if it merely turns its back on the state.[12]

That position is especially true in the case of foreign policy, as the recent activities of Brazil on the international scene inexorably lead to strengthening of the state and of the national interests.

Besides being a factor in the official foreign-policy stance, the question of democracy has also come to be incorporated into the "rendering of accounts" by the Itamaraty to sectors of the power structure of the internal political system. Of particular relevance in this respect was the lecture delivered at the Superior War College, in which the internal and the external dimensions of liberalization (*abertura*) were linked. In his final remarks, the Brazilian chancellor affirmed that "the coordination observed at a government level, the solidity of the consensus that is backed up by society, the certainty that it contributes to the building of a Brazil that will be better, and be both just and democratic, are the other essential ingredients that render foreign policy trustworthy."[13]

When dealing with party organizations, it is worthwhile mentioning a document produced by the Partido de Movimiento Democrático Brasileiro (PMDB—Brazilian Democratic Movement party), the strongest opposition party in the country, in which the question of foreign policy was taken up. In general terms, the principles upheld were closely in agreement with the ideas expressed by the Itamaraty itself. The only specific demand alluded to in the text had to do with the inclusion of Cuba within the framework of relationships with Latin America. Another particular feature of the text was the emphasis on the relationship between self-determination and democracy, with practices of destabilization and external interference being condemned.[14]

There is also a broad field of interests not directly channeled by the state and by the political groups, but present in the definitions of Brazil's international activity. One of the most expressive social sectors in this respect is the entrepreneurial class. And one of the important topics in internal political discussions has been the demand by that sector for greater participation in the process of decision making on economic policy in Brazil. That demand relates to both internal and external space in relation to economic activities.

In an interview on this question, the president of the Rio de Janeiro Commercial Association upheld the need for establishment of representative mechanisms on democratic lines, permitting expanded participation of the parliamentary system in formulation of economic policies. That participation is perceived as a basic datum for the upholding of national industry and the creation of better conditions for competing abroad. In line with that approach, internal stability is a decisive factor in attracting foreign capital and in expanding the international market.[15]

It is worthwhile, in conclusion, to mention the question of procedure in the overall dynamics of the democratic transition. In a recent presentation at an academic venue, one Brazilian diplomat upheld the need for recovering space for negotiation, on the international plane, as an instrument for transformation and innovation of the existing order. The internal political moment is in turn showing that the question of negotiation has become a vital factor in the process of "decompression." That tactical coincidence permits the conclusion that democratic strategy will be enhanced to the extent that the internal and external demands and interests of Brazilian society coincide.

NOTES

1. Fernando Henrique Cardoso, "Regime Político e Mudança Social," *Revista de Cultura & Política*, no. 3, 1981, p. 22.

2. Carlos Estevam Martins, *Capitalismo de Estado e Modelo Político no Brasil* (Rio de Janeiro: Graal, 1977), pp. 394–409.

3. In October 1977 General Sílvio Frota was relieved of his post as minister of war. At the time, a note was released in which he criticized a number of measures adopted by the Geisel administration. Foreign policy stood out as an area of strong disagreement. Specifically censured were the decisions to establish diplomatic relationships with the People's Republic of China, abstain from the vote in the Organization of American States on admission of Cuba, grant recognition to the government of Angola, and vote in favor of anti-Zionism at the United Nations General Assembly.

4. Hugo Abreu, *O outro lado do Poder* (Rio de Janeiro: Nova Fronteira, 1979), p. 58.

5. Walder de Góes, *O Brasil do Governo Geisel* (Rio de Janeiro: Nova Fronteira, 1978), p. 160. Exactly the same point with reference to Argentina is made in Joseph S. Tulchin, "The Impact of U.S. Human Rights Policy: Argentina," in John D. Martz and Lars Schoultz, eds., *Latin America, the United States, and the Inter-American System* (Boulder, Colo.: Westview Press, 1980).

6. *Jornal do Brasil*, August 28, 1981.

7. Brazilian-Ecuadorian Joint Declaration, September 2, 1982, Ministry of External Relations, Brasília.

8. *Jornal do Brasil*, May 17, 1982.

9. Hélio Jaguaribe, "Malvinas: Urgência de Paz," *Jornal do Brasil*, December 5, 1982.

10. José Maria Nunes Pereira, "Relações Brasil-África: Problemas e Perspectivas," paper presented at seminar "La Política Internacional a Comienzos de los años 80," Quito, November 1981.

11. Abreu, "O outro lado do Poder," p. 54.

12. Cardoso, "Regime Político e Mudança Social," p. 24.

13. Paper presented by His Excellency Minister of State for External Relations Ambassador Ramiro Saraíva Guerreiro at the Superior War College, Ministry of Foreign Relations, Rio de Janeiro, March 9, 1982.

14. "Esperança e mudança," *Revista do PMDB*, no. 4 (Brasília: Fundação Pedroso Horta, August 1982), pp. 117–119.

15. Personal interview, September 9, 1982.

15. The Foreign Policy Implications of the International System

CONCEPTUAL FRAMEWORK OF AN EVOLUTIONARY PROCESS

Presently there is an intense debate in Latin America about the need to coordinate foreign policies in the economic and political spheres. Various initiatives already have been launched in this sense, both at the regional and subregional levels as well as in relation to the reform of the inter-American system.[1] It is interesting to observe that the preoccupation with coordination is as old as the very history of independent Latin America. This chapter will examine key periods of this historical evolution, trying to identify the principal models of coordination that have prevailed in each of these stages and formulating conclusions that are of importance to the present efforts.

This analysis rests on five central hypotheses.

- The fundamental purposes of all the initiatives of coordination have been the attainment of a regional identity and the consequent autonomous management of the respective foreign policies.
- The evolution that the general international system has gone through in each stage has determined the feasibility or modalities of those Latin American efforts.
- The conditions of political maturity prevailing in the region or in given countries of special significance, with particular reference to the exercise of democracy and the institutionalization of political power, have been another determinate factor of that feasibility and its alternatives.
- International political pluralism and consensual processes are also factors affecting the success of these efforts.
- Regional crises, including some of an internal nature, have led to a resurgence of these efforts at coordination.

These factors can explain the evolution that the foreign policy of Latin America has experienced and its insertion into the international system over a prolonged period.

Independence and the Global Bolivarian Model

The struggle for independence gave rise to the first type of model, characterized by its formality and all-comprehensive scope. The projects of Bolivarian federation or confederation, with a strong emphasis on the coordination or fusion of foreign and defense policies, were the preferred schemes in this first stage.[2] The need to maintain the unity of the new republics was the declared objective of all these Bolivarian and other similar projects, seeing in unity an essential condition for the consolidation of the recently won independence. The preoccupation with regional identity and its external autonomy appeared in regional policy from the first moment. The intense resistance that the idea of Latin American dismemberment awoke in the leaders of the time represented a true expression of this purpose.

The relation between this Latin American phenomenon and the international system of the time was particularly close. Of course, independence of the Latin American countries could only be attained after the violent convulsion that shook the European system as a consequence of the Napoleonic wars. But the greater degree of permissibility that the system had at that moment threatened to be of short duration. The danger of the Holy Alliance and of a Spanish reconquest served as a powerful factor of cohesion for Bolivarian projects. It should be noted that this danger was avoided, not by a Latin American disposition coordinated through the projects in question, but by continuing differences among European powers, with special reference to England and, very particularly, by the Monroe Doctrine, as the first formal expression of the interest of the United States regarding the exercise of its influence in regional affairs.

This already marked a clear conditioning of Latin American autonomy and its limits within the international system, establishing at the same time a pattern of insertion subordinated to the interests of other principal powers. This risk did not go unnoticed by some statesmen of the period, who perceived the emerging interest of the United States and correctly concluded that the relative weight of Latin America in the international arena depended on the preservation of its identity and autonomy.[3] On the other hand, it is necessary to keep in mind that the very characteristics of the internal politics of Latin American countries undermined the Bolivarian plans. The more Latin America turned *caudillista* (leadership by *caudillos*), the more unstable its institutions and governments became. As a result the presence of external influences was greatly facilitated. Regional identity and autonomy thus became illusory concepts.

Though the Bolivarian model was nominally consensual, in that it started on the basis of freely negotiated federations, in fact it was an agreement among powerful military statesmen who did not discard the use of arms to realize their plans. This factor led to a growing distrust among the countries of the region; each country began to fear the expansive purposes of the others. With this the Bolivarian dream became nothing but a utopian and idealistic conception.

A dominant international system, domestic anarchy, and the lack of consensus were thus the factors that ultimately led to a total crisis in Latin American identity and its regional autonomy within a few years of independence. Latin America remained politically fragmented and inserted dependently into an international system that completely escaped its influence.

Emergence of the Functional-Formalist Model

As the Bolivarian ideal appeared unattainable, the countries of Latin America tried more flexible modalities that could lead to the same objective. Thus a functional model began to emerge, with nonspecific and frequently conjunctural goals that maintained a strong inclination toward the creation of formal structures. The majority of the alliance treaties issued by South American congresses, above all starting around the middle of the nineteenth century, correspond to this other model.[4]

The central purposes of a regional identity and autonomous management of foreign policies also were maintained unaltered in this case, particularly because this model found its principal stimulus in external threats to the region, as occurred with the Bolivarian model. The war against Spain was an especially illustrative situation of this phenomenon, motivating reactions of solidarity of the countries on the Pacific, expressed through this functional-formalist approach.

But Latin American behavior continued to be subordinated to the prevailing international system, without succeeding in influencing or in altering it in Latin America's favor. From this point of view, usefulness of the behavior would turn out to be highly limited, at times being reduced to a merely symbolic expression of intentions. Moreover, with only very specific exceptions, the period did not coincide with an especially auspicious stage with regard to political institutionalization and the stability of governments involved in the model. Thus, despite the fact that consensualism was preserved in the search for appropriate forms of coordination, in the end the model had no significant success and had to be abandoned.

Coercive Models

Parallel to the developments that have been explained, determined in good measure by events external to the region, Latin America was initiating the formation of its regional political system on the basis of its own internal dynamics. In this process the predominance of a coercive model could be observed, a model that attempted to impose the will of one or several states in the conduct of the international affairs of other countries or, on the contrary, to impede the materialization of that intention. This third model was of a noncooperative nature and was strongly influenced by the tendencies toward balance of power and the consequent attitudes of confrontation.

The formation of one subsystem in the Pacific and of another in the Atlantic, the first expressions of this phenomenon, later led to the overlapping interests between both and still later to their expansion from the Southern Cone to envelop the whole of South America. Thus, one closely bound regional political system gradually began to operate. In spite of the predominance of confrontation, the system started to respond to the interests and viewpoints of the region itself or of some of its principal units. In this way one can observe the evolution of the system as a whole toward new forms of regional identity, which for the first time acquired a certain configuration of its own.[5]

Two factors seem to have had a decisive influence on this process. The first is that this period coincided with some alterations of importance in the general international system. Continued European rivalries, the social effervescence that affected that continent, and the development of colonial struggles in other places in the world perhaps explain a greater degree of permissibility of the system in regard to policy alternatives in Latin America. At the same time, the Civil War in the United States signified a transitory absence of the interests of that country in Latin American affairs. In this way Latin America was able to attain a certain relative autonomy in the management of its regional and foreign policies, advancing in the formation of its own regional political system.

The second factor that becomes evident during the period is that of the greater institutionalization of the national political system of the principal countries of the region, with which the correlation among identity, autonomy, and political institutionalization acquired a new shape, this time of a positive nature.[6]

It should also be kept in mind that not all forms of coordination or unification had a coercive character during this period. There were interesting examples of effective consensual mechanisms, with particular reference to economic integration and foreign trade. One very relevant case in this sense was that of the Bello Clause, through which a Latin American preferential margin was created, establishing a regional exception to the most-favored-nation clause then prevailing in world trade. This first scheme of the coordination of commercial policies would reemerge one century later.[7]

The Beginning of Pan-Americanism: The Disintegrative Model

The autonomist pause would be of short duration. The renewed interest of U.S. policy in the region began to be strongly felt around the 1880s; the more intensely it was manifested, the greater was the weakening and deterioration that it caused to the objectives of Latin American identity and autonomy. At the end of the last century perhaps only the countries of the Southern Cone maintained a certain relative autonomy, taking advantage of their geographic distance from the United States and their greater historical association with Europe.

Thus, a disintegrative political model began to emerge, one that would make impossible the desired coordination in terms of the objectives of identity and autonomy. The formal expression of this model was Pan-Americanism. The implantation of this model coincided with important changes in the international system, which transferred the axis of international policy from the European continent to the United States. What had formerly been an insertion of a Latin America dependent on a Eurocentric system now moved to one dependent on a system centered on the United States.

This reality seems to contradict the thesis of a "consented dependency" in the Latin American case, since there was no other available option for the policy of this region than that of following the path determined by the international system. Perhaps at some time an option could have been made for an alignment with Europe or the United States, but it was not possible to do without one or another power center. A shift of this type made famous the diplomacy of the baron of Rio Branco, which at an opportune time separated from the traditional European framework to identify the foreign policy of Brazil with that of the United States. But even this option later became limited.[8]

Even though formally this model was based on a consensualism expressed within the confines of conferences and Pan-American mechanisms, in fact it was a highly coercive scheme. The war between the United States and Spain and the consequent situation of Cuba and Puerto Rico; the policy of intervention in Mexico, Central America, the Caribbean, and other latitudes; and the "big stick" policy are all evidence of the coercive character of the system. On the other hand, the schemes oriented to establish an inter-American customs union—which awoke an intense resistance in Argentina and Chile—expressed the intention of attaining an important degree of economic fusion, which obviously would have benefited only the dominant power within the system.

The disintegrative model and its coercive modality were accompanied also by a deterioration in the nature of political regimes in Latin America, which in many places fell into a phase of decomposition, loss of authority, and decline of all democratic principles of government. This scenario had few exceptions at the beginning of the century, principally in the Southern Cone. It was no accident that the countries of the Southern Cone were the ones most opposed to the new Pan-Americanism. This political decomposition served as a cause for the model, in that it facilitated its application; it also constituted a consequence of the same, since many times the establishment of governments subordinated to the interests prevalent in the region was deliberately sought.

However, these same negative characteristics of the disintegrative model would determine the birth of a renewed current aimed at reconstituting the framework of the action peculiar to Latin America as a unit. From a general point of view, this tendency aspired to Latin American reintegration and would express itself cyclically from the beginning of the century to the present. In a more specific sense, this movement was seen in the continuous search for lost autonomy, trying to eliminate the manifestations that were most adverse to this objective.

Changing Interventional Conditions: The Vindicative Model

The inter-American system consolidated gradually and adequately served the interests of the United States during more than six decades. The resistance that this traditionally produced in the countries of the Southern Cone—principally Argentina and Chile—was not sufficient to generate a reaction that would permit a reversal of that tendency. However, gradually efforts of this type appeared through which some initial forms of foreign-policy coordination were produced. They can be grouped under a vindicative-type model, which aspired to retake for Latin America the conduct of certain basic policies, always maintaining in the background the objectives of regional identity and autonomy, even when that occurred unconsciously.

This model had political and economic expressions. The principle of nonintervention was typically found among the first of these expressions, along with other associated principles such as the Calvo Clause, the prohibition of compulsory collection of international debts, or the peaceful solution of controversies. On the economic plane, efforts could be observed in the direction of modalities of integration in the years immediately following World War I and in other initiatives that eventually would be particular to the second postwar period. Above all, the first demands began to be manifested on the international trade level, with particular reference to the prices of raw materials and to tariffs and other situations. This picture would become typical of the decade of the 1950s, but has a great deal of past history.[9]

The emergence of this model is tied closely to the changing international conditions of the decades of the 1930s and 1940s, particularly with respect to World War II. Already with the occasion of the war of 1914, a limited opening of the international system and its conditions of permissibility could be observed, a moment in which Latin American demands intensified in some matters. However, in spite of the creation of the League of Nations and the participation of Latin America in it, the countries of the region did not succeed in attaining a dimension properly international in their foreign policies, maintaining themselves within an inter-American sphere.

The context of World War II was more decisive even in this sense. The first great Latin American demand—that related to nonintervention—materialized in 1936. This is explained, in the first place, by the fact that the United States no longer had a priority need for the policy instrument regarding intervention and, afterward, by the fact that the United States required an understanding with Latin America to facilitate

U.S. participation in the European problem. The Good Neighbor Policy had a greater relationship with Europe than with the interests of Latin America. In this way, the functioning of the general international system continued to be a determinant of the alternatives of regional policy. When the Bogotá Charter was signed in 1948, with all its solemn political and juridical principles, the United States had already moved on to be the principal world power, with interests that were very different from those of the region.

A similar phenomenon occurred with the economic demands. The United States acceded to them only in the reforms of the charter of the Organization of American States (OAS) in 1967, two decades after Latin America had proposed them in a more systematic manner. This occurred in a moment in which the United States had changed its regional interests for others of a global nature, thereby undermining the reforms. Also, some partial exceptions, such as the Alliance for Progress, are explained in the light of these global interests.

This period demonstrates well how the feasibility of those foreign policies and their specific coordination depended upon the evolution of the international system. Just as the change of the system from its Eurocentric nature to another centered on the United States had generated conditions of permissibility in the latter part of the nineteenth century, so the changes associated with World War II also produced a similar effect for Latin America. However, this experience also demonstrated that the Latin American policy was in general outdated in respect to the direction of the changes. In fact, its objectives had only been achieved when the interest in the respective matters had already changed from the point of view of the principal actors, being, as a consequence, concessions of little importance. In this sense, it was a question of demands that were met too late when the concern of the system was no longer the same, rather than being opportune and anticipated policies.

Also this period was relevant from the viewpoint of the association that existed between the coordination of foreign policies and the degree of internal political institutionalization in the region, which already in this century appeared closely related to the exercise of democracy. The succession of military governments that emerged in the decade of the 1930s as a consequence of the economic crisis, as well as the typical dictatorships of the 1950s, mark perhaps a low period for the purpose of coordinating such foreign policies. On the other hand, the greater normality that is observed before that crisis, and afterwards in the 1940s, coincided with a situation more favorable to that end, as evidenced by the proposals of concrete initiatives and the attainment of some results. The low period was characterized as well by a smaller degree of pluralism and consensualism than in the case of the high period.

Restructuring of the International System: The Reintegrative Model

Starting with World War II, the important restructuring of the international system began that is currently in force, with its principal characteristics of globalization and multipolarity. The emergence of the two superpowers and of other principal centers of power determined that the attention of each of those actors would be concentrated more specifically on the global level than on more limited regional affairs. It also meant that a greater degree of options and alternatives for the foreign policy of every state, including developing countries, had to be introduced. As in each point of historical change of the system, new conditions of relative permissibility emerged.

These were effectively exploited by Latin American countries in the search for the purposes of regional identity that had been frustrated for a period lasting almost a century. Thus, a reintegrative model that characterized Latin America was born starting in the 1960s; the clearest expression of this model is that of successive processes of economic integration and the concurrent policies of other organisms, such as the Inter-American Development Bank. That regional identity began to acquire a structured and institutionalized nature.[10]

At the same time, the region effectively developed a greater autonomy at the level of individual foreign policies of each country. This was clearest in the case of the countries with greater scope, such as Argentina, Brazil, and Mexico. Subjects such as the policy on raw materials, foreign trade, nuclear development, maritime rights, and many others began to materialize in Latin America as a consequence of this relative autonomy. It was during this period that a new form of functional coordination of foreign policies, within the reintegrative model, also began. In the framework of the processes of integration one could observe the concern for advancing toward the coordination of foreign-trade policies and, in some cases, of sectoral policies or of the general economic policy, even when this did not produce very important results.

A similar phenomenon began to occur within other international organisms, principally in the United Nations and its specialized organizations and bargaining conferences, where the Latin American group acquired for the first time an expression of weight and coherence. The Latin American initiatives regarding economic cooperation, law of the sea, or international economic negotiations are relevant examples. This same phenomenon began to expand toward an even more universal dimension seeking the coordination of policies with other developing nations, as was attested by the Latin American participation in the Group of 77 or the movement of nonaligned countries.

The most important expression of this tendency was undoubtedly the creation f the Special Commission of Latin American Coordination (CECLA), that for the first time established a stable mechanism for the purposes of that coordination and the unification of the bargaining capability of Latin America regarding the principal external actors. Even though CECLA mainly limited its work to economic and commercial subjects, taking into consideration the conditions and concerns of the period, it marked the creation of a precedent that had the greatest significance.

If the relationship of this process with the evolution of the international system is clear, its relationship with the democratization of Latin American politics is even more apparent. The decade of the 1960s coincided with an exceptional period of dominance of democratic governments in Latin America. It is no accident that at the same time important achievements occurred regarding regional integration, identity, development, and autonomy. Moreover, it must be observed that important exceptions, such as that of Brazil starting in 1964, confirmed that relationship, since Brazil's military government had a rather passive attitude toward regional affairs during this period.

Likewise, it must be kept in mind that in this stage important regional manifestations of political pluralism appeared, which gave the entire model an essentially consensual nature. Some specific problems, such as the exclusion of Cuba from the inter-American system, were due not to a Latin American policy but to a regional expression of struggle by the superpowers at a global level. In this sense, they constituted part of the limits of autonomy derived from the international system itself.

THE AUTHORITARIAN PHASE AND DECLINE OF THE RESTRICTIVE MODELS

Beginning in the middle of the 1960s, the rebirth of authoritarian military governments began in Latin America, a phenomenon that to an important degree was generalized during the 1970s. As is well known, this process is not independent of the evolution and characteristics of the international system and its cult of violence.[11] What is important to point out is the effect of this period on the problem of the coordination of external Latin American policies.

The conceptions of extreme nationalism and certain geopolitical views on which several of these governments have relied obviously could not facilitate the purposes of regional identity. On the contrary, the progress of integration suffered a serious paralysis, as shown by the still existing crises of the economic organisms of the cooperation schemes. Antagonism, rivalry, and conflict became again a common scene in Latin America. Perhaps the very conditions of permissibility of the international system facilitated this phenomenon, as a negative by-product.[12]

For this reason, although the degree of autonomy that was developing in the foreign policies of the Latin American countries was maintained in various cases, in general it was in a manner disassociated from regional concerns; to that same degree, it also became weakened. In fact, all the Latin American countries had to reevaluate the regional political space, after having found serious limitations in the management of their disassociated foreign policies.

On several occasions during this period attempts were made to structure modalities for the coordination of foreign policies, both on the part of authoritarian governments and others. All of them could be grouped under the common denominator of a restrictive, nonpluralistic model. They would be translated likewise into an important failure. The following experiences can be mentioned in this sense:

- The policy of ideological frontiers that Brazil attempted after the election of President Salvador Allende in Chile. This scheme did not generate followers, except in certain aspects, and determined as a reaction the thesis of ideological pluralism in Latin American policy. Even though the latter was formally adopted by the OAS in 1972 and in diverse bilateral declarations, it was never effectively fulfilled.
- The diplomacy of national security, which implicitly sought the coordination among the regimes of the Southern Cone but never succeeded because of the intrinsic climate of rivalry that affected those governments. Even though this modality—called in journalistic versions the Holy Alliance of the Southern Cone—was repeatedly denied, its implicit character was evident.
- The incursion of the Andean Group in foreign-policy matters, with particular reference to Panama, Nicaragua, and Bolivia. This initiative also had a restrictive ideological nature, even though contrary to former ones, and led to failure as a consequence of the disagreements among member countries, above all over the attempted exclusion of the Bolivian government.
- The first Mexican-Venezuelan initiatives for the creation of the Sistema Económico Latinoamericano (SELA), which had also a strong ideological context. Its implicit restrictive nature motivated a strong opposition from the military governments of the Southern Cone and the later compromise that led to a highly limited constitutive agreement.

It can be seen that the essence of the failure of this nonpluralistic model was not so much in the characteristics of the prevailing international system, which continued to maintain its general conditions of permissibility. Instead it was in factors internal to the region, particularly the authoritarian nature of its governments and the nonpluralist character of their external coordination schemes, a mistake committed by both military governments and established democracies. This situation explains the paradox that while certain forms of foreign-policy autonomy were developed under one or another type of government, taking advantage of those conditions of permissibility, the conflicts within the region and their lack of pluralism impeded the materialization of any useful form of coordination. This definitely ended up affecting the very identity and autonomy and destroyed all the forms that had emerged in former decades, such as the mechanisms of integration, CECLA, and other modalities. It is how in some cases national-security governments ended up unconsciously working against the security of Latin America and their own national unities.

THE CRISIS OF THE INTERNATIONAL SYSTEM AND THE
SEARCH FOR THE RECONSTITUTIVE MODEL

The international system has entered again into a phase of conflictive polarization between the superpowers, with certain direct repercussions in the case of Latin America. The proliferation of authoritarian regimes, the crisis of regional cooperation that has been discussed, and the tendencies toward the use of force represent a reflection of that world situation. The British-Argentine conflict of the South Atlantic could not be explained except in the light of this complex international picture.

This most recent conflict, as in all great historical crises in the region, has led to the emergence of new concerns over the problem of Latin American identity and autonomy, with particular reference to the coordination of foreign policies oriented toward determining forms of insertion into the international system and especially with the great powers. Initiatives geared toward assembling foreign ministers and presidents, reforming institutions, or institutionalizing procedures have proliferated in recent months.

In contrast to former historical experiences, the model now emerging is one that will reconstitute the being of Latin America. It has a strong emphasis on the political end, intending to that extent to have a more global reach. The preoccupation for Latin American participation in the international political and economic system is today evident. In this way, for the first time the perception clearly emerges that only a united Latin America will be able to have a role to perform in the framework of that system.[13]

Even though it is not relevant to examine the actual initiatives, it is fitting to wonder about their feasibility in the light of the long historical experience already mentioned and to use that experience to identify criteria by which they can be evaluated.

1. Even if the international system still keeps certain features of permissibility, these will become more limited to the degree to which the system polarizes. This will not facilitate the purpose of Latin American identity and autonomy. But for precisely that reason, instead of returning to the traditional disintegration of the past, the Latin American countries today must accentuate their process of cooperation, coordination, and integration. This implies making the effort to come collectively to an understanding with the system and the dominant powers, instead of maintaining the individual and bilateral scheme that has prevailed at this level until now. Perhaps it should be kept in mind that the best opportunities have been presented historically for Latin America when the system came to a phase of change, as would appear to be the case again today. This change will not necessarily have the negative character of polarization, since symptoms of progress toward a more cooperative scheme in some areas are also observed.

2. The success of these contemporary experiences of coordination will depend on the capacity that Latin America has to overcome its

internal rivalries. The conflictive signs of disintegration in the last ten years should be replaced by positive manifestations of cooperation. In order for this to be possible, the region and its principal units must return to the path of exercise of democracy. Almost two centuries of experience show that the authoritarian model is incapable of generating by itself the currents of coordination that the region needs. From this point of view, the actual transition processes represent a hope for breaking the vicious circle that definitely has determined the international marginality of the region.[14]

3. Only a model based on pluralism and consensualism will be capable of materializing effectively. It is not feasible to hope that the entire region, at the same time, will coincide in the characteristics of its political regimes. Diversity will always be part of Latin America and must be respected and reflected in actual initiatives. To intend the contrary is to incur in the error that all the principal ideological experiments in the region have already committed in the past. Any exclusion will work against the purposes that are pursued.

4. Finally, the historical experience also strongly suggests that all-comprehensive and superstructured models should be avoided. Consensus can only be built upon the basis of functional schemes, which may successively confront the whole of priority concerns. Furthermore, formal structures do not favor the necessary pluralism already mentioned. Functionalism and pragmatism will be two pillars of a new Latin American system of coordination of foreign policies.

NOTES

1. For various articles on this subject, see *Estudios Internacionales*, no. 60, October–December 1982.

2. Raymundo Barros, *Consideraciones sobre la integración latinoamericana en el siglo XIX con particular referencia a la política chilena*, Serie de Publicaciones Especiales, no. 8 (Santiago: Instituto de Estudios Internacionales, Universidad de Chile, 1975).

3. Diego Portales, in a letter to S. M. Cea from Lima in March 1822, wrote about the Monroe Doctrine: "Beware about the danger of escaping one domination in order to fall into another. . . . I believe that all this is due to a previously prepared plan . . . to conquer America not by arms but by influence in all spheres. This will happen maybe not today; but tomorrow. . . ." Cited in Raúl Silva Castro, *Ideas y Confesiones de Portales* (Santiago: Editora del Pacífico, 1954), p. 61.

4. For the documentation of South American congresses, *Archivo Diplomático del Perú*, vol. 2, in *Congresos Americanos de Lima* (Lima: Ministerio de relaciones exteriores en Lima, 1938).

5. For an interesting analysis of the formation of the Latin American political system, see Robert N. Burr, *By Reason or Force: Chile and the Balancing of Power in South America, 1830–1905* (Berkeley and Los Angeles: University of California Press, 1967).

6. For an analysis of the whole of Latin American politics in the nineteenth and twentieth centuries, see Claudio Véliz, *The Centralist Tradition of Latin America* (Princeton: Princeton University Press, 1980).

7. Francisco Orrego Vicuña, "Estudio sobre la Cláusula Bello y la crisis de la solidaridad latinoamericana en el siglo XIX," in *Derecho Internacional Económico*, vol. 1 (México, D.F.: Fondo de Cultura Económica, 1973).

8. Félix Peña, "Argentina en América Latina," *Revista Criterio*, December 1970; and Celso Lafer, "Una interpretación del sistema de las relaciones internacionales del Brasil," *Foro Internacional* 9, no. 3 (January–March 1969), pp. 298–318.

9. For a summary of the period, see Instituto Interamericano de Estudios Jurídicos Internacionales, *Derecho de la Integración Latinoamericana* (Buenos Aires: Depalma, 1969).

10. Francisco Orrego Vicuña, "El elusivo entendimiento entre América Latina y los Estados Unidos," discussion document presented to the Interamerican Dialogue, organized by The Wilson Center, Smithsonian Institution, October 15–16, 1982.

11. Kevin J. Middlebrook, "Notes on Transitions from Authoritarian Rule in Latin America and Latin Europe," Working Paper no. 82, Latin American Program, The Wilson Center, Washington, D.C., 1981.

12. Francisco Orrego Vicuña, "La crisis del Atlántico Sur y sus afectos en el sistema regional," *Estudios Internacionales*, no. 60, October–December 1982.

13. See, for example, Sistema Económico Latino Americano (SELA), *Bases para una estrategia de seguridad e independencia de América Latina* (Caracas: SELA, August 3, 1982).

14. For an analysis of the relationship between democracy and the South Atlantic case, see Heraldo Muñoz, "Lecciones y experiencias del conflicto de las Malvinas," *Estudios Internacionales*, no. 60, October–December 1982.

16. The Soviet Union in the Foreign Relations of the Southern Cone

The role of the Soviet Union in the foreign relations of Latin American countries has been characterized by a tendency to stay within the limits of what is tolerable for the United States. The three cases analyzed below show how the USSR promotes a certain type of development strategy in Latin American countries, irrespective of the nature of their governments. That same regional strategy has led the USSR to emphasize a different facet of its relations with each of these nations—the political-ideological plane in Chile, the economic dimension in Argentina, and the political-international level in Brazil. This Soviet adaptability makes it difficult for Latin American states to define in an autonomous and comprehensive fashion the way in which they need to relate with the USSR.

SOME BACKGROUND OBSERVATIONS ON SOVIET LATIN AMERICA POLICY

The policy of the Soviet Union toward Latin America since the October Revolution[1] has been conducted through two fundamental channels: first, interstate relations with the various governments; second, relations between the Soviet Communist party (SCP) and the Communist parties of the region. In effect, until the First Latin American Communist Congress (Buenos Aires, June 1929), USSR–Latin American relations had been determined fundamentally by the Soviet interest in incorporating part of the Latin American left into the Communist International (CI); hence the Soviet efforts to establish diplomatic relations with Mexico and the support for the creation of a Mexican Communist party. However, Latin America was seen by the Soviet leaders as an area of unchallengeable influence of the United States, as a group of countries that had to move from agrarian structures toward more developed forms of capitalism so as to be able to undergo socialist revolution.

243

An Era of Fluctuating Policies: 1929–1964

The Soviet initiative to coordinate the action of existing Latin American Communist parties and to create new ones materialized in 1929 when the South American Secretariat of the Comintern was created. The policy of the secretariat originated in the Sixth Congress of the Comintern (1928), in which a policy was formulated for the CPs of Latin America that consisted in the projection of the Bolshevik strategy toward the region: the creation of committees (soviets) of peasants, soldiers, and workers and the expropriation of all activities centered around private capital.

This policy coexisted with weak interstate relations, as the subversive character of the policies emanating both from the Comintern and from the South American Secretariat made relations with official groups difficult. Noted politicians such as Victor Raúl Haya de la Torre of the Alianza Popular Revolucionaria Americana (APRA) ceased to maintain relations with the CI for these reasons. The political failures in Colombia, the difficulties with César Augusto Sandino, the frustrated Socialist Republic in Chile, and the repression in El Salvador were all factors that led the CI to recognize in the Seventh Congress of the Comintern the growing isolation of the CPs of the area and the impossibility of carrying out their revolutionary strategies.

A new policy of the Popular Fronts ended the Communist parties' isolation, directing them into institutional channels existing in each country. This change of the CI policy toward Latin America can be explained fundamentally by the Nazi danger at that moment. For the USSR the danger of a new armed intervention made it necessary to bring all its international political resources to its defense.

The policy of the Popular Fronts rescued the CPs from their isolation in the respective local politics. Thanks to that policy the USSR experienced a diversification of its diplomatic relations with the Latin American governments and states. The Soviet success in diversifying its diplomatic relations during the period led Stalin to dissolve the Comintern in 1943, before the end of World War II, in order to facilitate the negotiations with Roosevelt and Churchill. It seemed that a new stage was about to materialize in the foreign relations of the USSR.

East-West tensions and their crystallization in the cold war put an end to such expectations. The effect of Latin American alignment in the perimeter of military and political defense of the hemisphere, established in 1947 through the Inter-American Treaty of Reciprocal Assistance (TIAR), meant that the formerly positive political and diplomatic ties were abruptly altered when the majority of the governments of the region broke relations with the USSR or suspended them for a short time. This phase of deterioration of political-diplomatic relations coincided with the difficulties that the CPs of the area confronted in their respective local political arenas. Along with the suspension and rupture of diplomatic relations with the USSR, the CPs of the region were the object of strong repression. In almost all countries of the continent they were outlawed.

Despite this situation, the policies of the CPs in Latin America did not vary substantially: The thesis of the Popular Fronts was recycled in terms of Democratic Governments of National Liberation in which were to be included all the antiimperialist and anti-*latifundist* forces. This formulation was based on the belief that the principal obstacles to the development of Latin American countries were rooted in the dominance of *latifundist* forces (those favoring large land units) and of U.S. capital, both of which limited national capitalist development. In this way, the cold war situation found an internal correlate to the extent that the USSR countered the U.S. position in each country of the area with internal political forces that attempted to include themselves within the wide range of National Liberation.

The policy of National Liberation brought about the coincidence, in emergency conditions, of political and diplomatic objectives, internal purposes of the CPs, and the international interests of the USSR. This policy would have its greatest expression during the administration of Nikita Khrushchev (1958–1964), even though it had begun with the Twentieth Congress of the SCP (1956). Nevertheless, the strong tensions between the USSR and the United States during the entire period of the Khrushchev administration impeded the possibility of expressing the policies of wide-ranging alliances of the local CPs in a greater diversification and presence of the Soviet State in Latin America.

The Brezhnev Model

The substitution of Alexei Kosygin and Leonid Brezhnev for Khrushchev in 1964 initiated a new phase in the relations between the USSR and Latin America. This new phase incorporated elements of former policies, but at the same time placed them in a more comprehensive and coherent framework, giving them a symmetry and stability that has permitted them to continue for almost two decades.

Different reasons led the Soviet leadership to replace the prime minister and secretary general of the SCP. Among these were tension with the Chinese Communist party, problems in the CMEA (Council of Mutual Economic Assistance) with Romania, tension with Yugoslavia, agricultural crisis, failure of the five-year plan, and insufficient achievements of central planning that under Khrushchev had been relatively decentralized. For this reason, the Kosygin-Brezhnev policy was oriented toward overcoming international tensions, attempting a dialogue with the Chinese Communist party, initiating negotiations with the United States, reducing the 1965 military budget, and liberalizing the activity of enterprises at the same time that the formulation and control of the plan became centralized. All these factors led to a détente in East-West relations that culminated in the 1974 Strategic Arms Limitation Talks (SALT I) agreements.

The Latin American policy of the Kosygin-Brezhnev administration tended to emphasize a greater development of economic, commercial, and technical-cooperation relations with the Latin American states independent of the orientations of their various governments. Thus, emphasis was placed on exchange of Soviet merchandise for Latin American raw materials, programs of medium- and long-term commercial exchange in terms favorable to Latin America; and technical-assistance projects oriented toward developing a long-term state industrial infrastructure in areas in which Latin American countries showed abundant mineral, hydroelectric, and fishing resources.

The previously created Institute of Latin America of the Academy of Sciences of the USSR (1961), the product of the impact of the Cuban Revolution, initiated its editorial activities in 1969 by publishing the journal *América Latina*. Although this systematic interest for Latin America was no greater than that demonstrated for the Middle East, Asia, or Africa, it showed that Soviet leadership required greater knowledge on Latin America in order to be able to act more technically in hemispheric affairs. Following the experience of the special relation with Cuba, the USSR emphasized that the Soviet model of development was "a guide for action more than an inexhaustible source of resolution of the principal economic financial problems of the countries of the area, including the new revolutionary processes."[2] In this way, the Soviet orientation in interstate relations was to be centered on the "activation of the national economy, preparation of technical cadres, and struggle against neo-colonialism."[3]

This policy toward the countries of the region respected the general framework in détente and cooperation with the United States. For that reason diplomatic relations of the USSR with the Latin American countries would never surpass the limits of what was tolerable for the United States in the hemisphere. Even in the present Central American crisis, the USSR has maintained a policy mediated by Cuba, but has never become directly involved. Still more recently, the position that the USSR took regarding the British-Argentine conflict over the Malvinas, which could have been much more active, was mostly rhetorical, consistent with the patterns of not taking advantage of the reduced U.S. position in that zone. The USSR would hardly become involved again in Latin America as did Khrushchev in 1962 during the Cuban missile crisis.

The policy of aid and cooperation in the development of the economic infrastructure of Latin American countries implies political elements. Through this form of cooperation, the USSR established or intended to establish the necessary, although not sufficient, conditions for a process of national liberation.

This policy is symmetrical with that pursued by the SCP in its relations with the CPs of the region. Thus, in the World Conference of Communist and Workers' Parties of 1969, Brezhnev insisted that the popular struggle in Latin America was bound up with the struggle for democracy, against imperialism and its internal allies. To achieve the goal of democracy, the USSR called for support from a wide spectrum of forces, not exclusively workers. This policy would eventually be strengthened by the electoral victory of the Popular Unity in Chile in 1970, which the SCP highly emphasized in its Twenty-Fourth Congress in 1971.

In the framework of the ideological discussion of the Latin American left, the policy of the USSR led to the introductory steps of a socialist revolution, emphasizing in these countries the development of state capitalism, a position fully congruent with the policy observed at the level of interstate relations. These orientations allowed the USSR to renew diplomatic relations with almost all the countries with which it had maintained ties previously and to develop new ties. At the end of the 1970s the USSR could witness a noticeable diversification of its diplomatic relations in the region, and its commerce with the region increased to more than one billion dollars. The USSR also strengthened its military linkages with Cuba and maintained them with Peru. Likewise, it deepened its political relations with Brazil, Argentina, and—more recently—Nicaragua. In this way, the policy of the Brezhnev administration utilized all of its possibilities to stabilize the relations between the USSR and Latin America.

These characteristics of Soviet policy toward Latin America, which apparently continued following the death of Brezhnev and the emergence of Andropov (although it is too soon to tell the intentions of Chernenko following Andropov's death), allowed some countries of the area to define their foreign relations by contemplating this new actor in their international environment. However, not all Latin American countries that may establish closer relationships with the USSR would assign it the same role. On the contrary, the role that the USSR may play in the foreign policy of some countries of the region will depend upon their internal political conditions, as well as on the specific interests that the USSR could have in each of them.

THE ROLE OF THE USSR IN LATIN AMERICAN FOREIGN POLICY

Soviet relations with Latin American countries have been varied. The distinct character of interstate ties is determined by the internal political realities and the interests that, from the point of view of the USSR, predominate. In this way, though the framework of the Latin American policy of Brezhnev made such relations possible, it did not determine to any extent the particularities of the relationship between the parts involved. Within this foreign-policy framework interstate relations and ties can be observed that are as diverse as those that the USSR had with Chile between 1970 and 1973 or the relations that presently exist with Argentina, Brazil, or Peru.

Chile: 1970–1973

The political process that Chile lived through between 1970 and 1973 acquired such importance in the Soviet foreign policy toward Latin America because the attempt to implement a "peaceful road to socialism" represented the optimization of the Brezhnev model. According to a Soviet specialist, Chile had reached a level of development that enabled it to initiate "national-democratic, anti-imperialist, anti-feudal, anti-monopolic [transformations] and the direct preparation for the transition from a democratic stage to a socialist revolutionary stage." Later, the Soviet evaluation of the three years of Popular Unity indicated that given the "medium level of capitalist development" of Chile the definition advanced by the Chilean CP about the character of the revolution was correct: "anti-imperialist and anti-oligarchic," and a "democratic process whose successful development would open the road to socialism."[4]

Given "the central position in the social structure of the working class," this "democratic" process seemed assured, since that class was the "basis of the anti-imperialist popular movement." Even the Popular Unity was criticized for not having achieved an agreement with the Christian Democracy and for not having had an explicit policy toward the middle sectors on the level of class relations. A similar criticism was made by some Soviet analysts of the "revolutionarism" and precipitousness of some reforms.[5]

Relations between Chile and the USSR were established, then, at the level of what was *desirable* for the USSR, which implied that these ties were to be determined by the nature and projection of the Chilean political process. To the extent that the internal political events went in the direction expected by the USSR, Chile could count on a solid base for its relations with Moscow. The Chilean political process, upon constituting itself in a "referential optimum" for the rest of the Latin American countries and the Third World, had to maintain the parameters on which this relationship was based, such as the internal political capacity to carry out the process without resorting to its financing by the USSR. In this way, the USSR would be willing to deepen its relations on the political and military level provided that the direction of the internal political process was maintained in the mainstream of the peaceful transition to socialism. As a consequence, the government of the Popular Unity was not in any position to define the preferred role that—from its own perspective—the USSR should play. Rather the situation was defined in the opposite way: To the extent that the Chilean political process would adjust to Soviet expectations, Chile could aspire to a consolidation of its relations with the USSR.

During the three years of government of the Popular Unity, its relations with the USSR were inhibited by the uncertain course of the internal political process. Consequently, the role expected by the executive for the USSR never materialized. In effect, the economic relations in which the assistance in convertible currency was an affair of vital importance for the survival of the Popular Unity government not only never reached the levels desired by the Chilean government, but moreover did not represent a contribution of significant importance. The problem was that, to the extent that the internal political price that the government had to pay for this relationship was disproportionately high in relation to the economic assistance received, the role ultimately performed by the USSR in Chilean internal and external politics could be qualified as a "boomerang."

An analysis of Soviet aid to Chile during the period shows us a reality different from that hoped for by the executive. Even though there has been no estimate of the total amount of aid to Chile from the Soviet Union and the rest of the socialist countries, the sum reaches nearly $350 million, of which the majority was destined for projects such as fishing and construction of popular housing and the minor part for the purchase of foodstuffs.[6]

In May 1971, as a conclusion to the visit of Minister of Foreign Relations Clodomiro Almeyda, an agreement was signed with the Soviet minister of foreign trade, Nikolai Patolichev. It included technical assistance for the construction of an industrial oil refinery and a factory producing prefabricated houses, the increase of a credit previously granted to the Frei government for the purchase of Soviet equipment, and the establishment of a Soviet trade agency in Santiago and a Chilean commercial office in Moscow. The USSR complemented such agreements with various technical-assistance projects: Soviet specialists for the copper industry, aid for the fishing industry, and construction of ports and fishing vessels.[7]

In June 1972 Chile was granted a $50-million credit, and in July of the same year the president of the Central Bank obtained credit for $260 million to buy machinery. In December 1972, on the occasion of Allende's trip to the USSR, various agreements for cooperation and economic assistance were signed. As a result of these, at the end of December the USSR granted credit amounting to $335 million. It was to be given in two parts: one for the purchase of Soviet products and the other in hard currency, $185 million for machinery and $30 million for foodstuffs.[8]

Given the financial necessities resulting from the reduction in Western foreign aid to the Allende government, that small contribution in convertible and immediately usable currency for the purchase of foodstuffs lacked global impact. To the degree that the internal political crisis deepened and the need for economic aid in hard currency for immediate purchases increased, the USSR saw that the role of the Chilean political process as model was being called into question. As this situation worsened, the USSR increased its distance from the Chilean process on the political, economic, and ideological planes.

This situation became clear during the visit of the commander-in-chief of the army to the socialist countries when the possibility of a military-assistance agreement was explored. According to some sources, this could not materialize because of the developments that the Soviets perceived within the Chilean armed forces.[9] The positive evaluation of the Chilean political process on the part of the Soviets had been based partly on the assumption of eventual support that the armed institutions would give to the program of changes in the country. Thus, according to Boris Ponomariev, "the simplist anti-militarism that visualizes the military as a mere instrument of the dominant class was condemned and the fact that the military is a part of society and consequently able to be affected by social-political developments was recognized."[10] To the degree that this expectation, founded in the experience of the Velasco Alvarado government in Peru, was not realized in the Chilean case, military and economic support were not forthcoming to the extent hoped for. As expressed in *Tiempos Nuevos*, "money for Popular Unity reforms would have to come from the nationalization of the copper industry, the banks, and foreign companies."[11]

This definition of the role of the USSR in the internal and foreign policy of the Popular Unity was not due to the lack of a mutually beneficial economic interest. Nor did it result from the remoteness of Chile as an area of strategic interest for the USSR, from the Soviet interest in détente, from the minority position of the Chilean CP within the Popular Unity, from the economic ineptitude of its administration, or, lastly, from U.S. efforts to destabilize the government. All of those causes would have stemmed from the assumption that the role of the USSR in the Chilean political process and consequently in the foreign policy of Chile, especially in relation to the United States, had to be determined by a congruence of interests.

The problem arose when it became evident that the definition made by the USSR of the events in Chile *did not imply* such congruence. On the contrary, the role of the USSR in that context could not go beyond the frameworks defined by the Brezhnev model. Consequently, the significance of the Chilean political process did not mean that the USSR had to take advantage of the United States in the latter's own area of influence. On the contrary, the significance of the Chilean process was basically ideological; it constituted a point of reference for the rest of the Latin American countries in terms of indicating that the Cuban model was not favored by the USSR in this period for economic reasons as well as for political and military reasons having to do with the United States. As a consequence, it is not that the role of Chile may have been politically and militarily insignificant to the USSR. Rather, what occurred was that the USSR never defined its relationship with Chile in such terms. Its definition of the situation was of another kind, in which ideological elements, synthesized in what we have characterized as the Brezhnev model, prevailed.

If it is possible to talk of errors in these matters, it could be affirmed that the mistake on the part of the Popular Unity government, as well as many of its components, was to think that the USSR would support a process such as that in Chile in the framework of its confrontation with the United States. On the contrary, what most interested the USSR in the Chilean political process was to show how a policy of making the economy state owned could be carried out with broad political and class support and with the support of the armed forces, without altering relations with the United States. To the degree that this dimension was lost, the role that the USSR could play in Chilean foreign relations was altered.

The lack of a precise analysis of the role and possible function that the USSR could perform in the internal political process and in the foreign policy of the country had serious consequences. I agree that the political and military defeat of the Popular Unity was not a consequence of the lack of USSR support, of the role that the latter played in the internal ideological struggle, or of the function that it did not play in international terms, but I do insist that such defeat could have had other characteristics and that other resources could have been mobilized provided that the definition of the role of the USSR in the internal political process had been better adjusted to reality.

The most important element in the USSR-Chilean military junta confrontation was provided by the latter with the launching of an anticommunist crusade that created a new situation for the Brezhnev policy. This action, unprecedented since the emergence of the Brezhnev model, meant that the Chilean military junta represented the USSR as exactly the opposite of how it wanted to appear or act. The anti-Soviet rhetoric turned into a new and unexpected danger for the stabilization of the Brezhnev model in the relations between the USSR and the rest of the Latin American countries. The subversive role that the military wanted to assign to the behavior of the USSR during the three years of the Popular Unity meant an ideological threat to the USSR, which—compared to the definition of the Chilean political process as a reference point for the rest of the countries of the area—demanded the suppression of that danger with all available force.

Chile's experience was unlike the Argentine case, in which even the harshest repression was not justified in the same terms and in which the attitude of the USSR could keep to its permanent interests of bilateral trade relations. In the Chilean case such relations did not exist. For that reason, along with the solidarity with the proscribed sectors, it is to be expected that the USSR should hold on to a policy of confrontation with the Chilean military government so long as the characteristics that define the latter's foreign policy remain unchanged.

Argentina During the 1970s

USSR trade relations with Argentina date back quite some time. Between 1920 and 1925 the Commercial Office of the USSR located in Montevideo carried out a grain purchase of 125,000 tons of wheat. However, it was

not until the beginning of the 1970s, and in the framework of USSR–
Latin American relations implemented by the Brezhnev administration,
that these relations began to reach increasingly higher exchange levels
and to be accompanied by a small exchange in the military area.

In the Argentine case a new specificity of the relations between the
USSR and Latin American countries can be detected, in which more
permanent and reciprocal economic interests prevail. To the degree that
one of the principal problems of the USSR was its deficit in cereal
production, and considering that Argentina had exportable surpluses,
commercial ties for both states meant the alleviation of tensions and
bottlenecks that both could experience in determined periods. From the
Argentine viewpoint, the trade relation with the USSR implied an
unfavorable trade balance for the latter; Argentine sales of wheat, furs,
leather, wool, and meat had never been accompanied by Soviet sales
to Argentina of great significance. Thus, Argentine imports of machinery,
hydraulic and crane equipment, transport equipment, ferrous metals and
chemical products, and iron and steel did not amount to a significant
portion of the total bilateral trade.[12] These mutually beneficial trade
relations were unique in Latin America and symbolized the evolution
of the ties that began to deepen in the earlier years of the 1970s during
the Lanusse administration. The later Perónist government, as well as
that of Videla and Viola, maintained the growing pace of exchange.

This reciprocal interest in trade matters, developed through such
diverse governments, reveals an ample consensus among the various
internal sectors in favor of advancing ties with the USSR. Thus in 1979
the Argentine secretary of agriculture refused to support the cereal
embargo proposed by the United States, pointing out that "the market
forces will decide the final destiny of Argentine grains."[13] The director
of the Argentine grains organization, Federico Lacroze, indicated in
Washington in that same period that the affirmations of the United
States on Afghanistan did not reflect the true situation. At the end of
January 1979 President Videla rejected the arguments about the embargo
presented by President Carter's special envoy, General Andrew Jackson.
Along with indicating that the Argentine government "will not take
commercial advantage of the situation," at the end of the same month
Argentina opened up without restrictions to Soviet grain requirements.
Later, in 1981, a new trade agreement was signed with the USSR for
the period 1981–1985, including nearly 100,000 tons of meat. Although
Argentine grain exports represented 80 percent of its wheat surpluses,
and it was hoped that they would reach 85 percent in 1982, with this
contract the possible exchange levels were increased to incorporate into
this flow other items that had not received the same Soviet attention.
Likewise, from a sociopolitical viewpoint, this diversification permitted
the broadening of internal entrepreneurial support of the ties with the
USSR, integrating the farmers into these relationships as well as in their
projections.

The importance to Argentina of this exchange is evident. In 1981, 33.7 percent of the USSR's total purchases came from Argentina. The contrast becomes clearer when comparing the $2.91 billion exported to the USSR in 1981 with the $8.8 million in imports from the latter in the same year. Such a situation derived from two relatively independent situations. For one thing, the trade-relations model between the USSR and the Latin American countries contemplated favorable conditions for the exports of the continent as a result of competitive prices and stable purchase programs. In the Argentine case, the payments were not subordinated to purchases of Soviet export products. This led to a deficit trade balance for the USSR, which did not attempt to counterbalance it. For another thing, the USSR was a safe and stable market in terms of Argentine political contingencies. In effect, as pointed out by former Secretary of Commerce Alberto E. de las Carreras, "it is precisely in 1980, when protectionism sharpened in Western Europe, that Argentina because of the cereal embargo found in the Soviet Union a new market that absorbed, since then, around 35 percent of its exports."[14]

In this way, Argentina showed a trade balance in its favor that increased from $771 million between 1972 and 1976 to $1 billion in 1980, which almost equaled the deficit in its exchange with the United States.[15] This tripartite aspect of Argentine foreign trade became one of the principal characteristics of its international exchange, which went on to determine the nature of its political and military relations with the USSR. To the degree that Argentina showed growing imports from and decreasing exports to the United States and that it maintained its trade deficit with the European Economic Community (EEC), the compatibility of trade interests between Argentina and the USSR could only increase and become more stable. An agricultural recuperation in the USSR in the near future is not likely, nor is a dynamic recuperation of Argentine exports to the EEC or the United States.

This structural characteristic of the commercial ties with Argentina allowed Moscow to attempt to project these ties to military spheres with evident political implications. In 1979 a military delegation led by General José Montes, who directed the army training program and whose brother was military attaché until that date, traveled to the USSR. There it visited the principal military schools in Moscow, Leningrad, and Kiev and held conversations with high Soviet officials. The visit was to reciprocate one made a month before by a Soviet delegation headed by General Ivan Jacovik Braiko. In 1980 a mission of the Argentine Atomic Energy Commission visited Moscow, apparently as a reaction to the difficulties posed by the United States for an Argentine-German nuclear agreement. This mission succeeded in obtaining from the USSR the shipment of five tons of heavy water to Buenos Aires in January 1981.[16] Later, in 1982, three additional contracts were signed for the provision of various services and nuclear supplies. The deliveries were to be used in the RA-3 and RA-6 reactors and in the Nuclear Center of Atucha.[17] Soviet nuclear cooperation allowed Argentina to operate in Latin America with a technical-assistance policy in nuclear matters. For instance, Argentina furnished Peru with uranium enriched to 20 percent for the Nuclear Center of Huarangal.

The aloof posture of the USSR in the conflict of the Malvinas did not necessarily imply that its role in Argentine foreign policy lacked significance. Rather, that role was not played directly, as could be expected within an analytical framework of bipolarity. On the contrary, the USSR performed a political, economic, and military role in the region but *through* Argentina and *within* these parameters. For such reasons, even though there may be political and ideological changes in Argentina, they would not necessarily imply that the actual ties with the Eastern bloc would be realigned. In this way, without intervening directly in the region, the USSR has cooperated in fragmenting the framework of U.S. alliances in the continent, supporting Latin American nations in confronting the United States by their own means.

From this point of view it is possible to consider that for the USSR, Argentina was a good example of how first a commercial and eventually a politico-military relationship could be developed despite ideological differences. In this way, directly and indirectly, the USSR showed how unrealistic it is to define its role as subversive. This nonideological, political pragmatism, which can be observed also in Soviet relations with Uruguay, Bolivia, and other Latin American states, maintained the basic Soviet orientations toward the region: to support the creation of a solid state economic infrastructure (for instance, by means of the fourteen turbines for the Salto Grande dam, feasibility studies for the Paraná Medio, and proposals for turbines for Yaciretá); to continue ties with the armed institutions that serve as an available market for arms when conditions so permit; and to reciprocate commercial interests even though this might imply an imbalance and international tripartite merchandise flows.

Brazil as a New Center of Regional Power

As in the case of the rest of the Latin American countries, the relations of the USSR with Brazil have been the result of a growing trade link that culminates in a specific type of interstate tie. This specificity of Soviet-Brazilian relations was determined by the political alliances that became possible through some kind of joint action in Third World countries, both in Africa and in Latin America.

Soon after diplomatic relations were established between the USSR and Brazil in 1945, the TIAR cut short those relations. Later, within the framework of the cold war, the recuperation of these relations was slow and difficult, being achieved in 1961. However, relatively modest exchanges had been carried out some years earlier. It could be said that during the governments of Kubitschek, Quadros, and Goulart the relations with the USSR did not suffer great changes. Nevertheless, after 1964 and as a result of the anticommunism of Brazilian president Castelo Branco, such trade ties were suspended until 1966.[18]

Then with the political turnabout of Soviet posture toward Latin America and within the framework of the military governments in Brazil, these trade relations began to grow, especially when Moscow granted a credit to Brazil in 1969 for $100 million. Already in 1969 Brazil had created a commission for relations with Eastern bloc nations, COLESTE. The USSR had committed itself to utilize 25 percent of the hard currency obtained in its exports to Brazil in the purchase of Brazilian manufactured or semimanufactured products. In 1973, following the rapid rhythm of Brazilian industrial growth, the minister of planning, Reis Velloso, traveled to Moscow. His trip led to the expansion of the agreement, and the USSR provided turbine equipment for the Capivari dam. In this way, the trade between Brazil and the USSR rose from $25 million in 1970 to $145 million in 1974.[19]

The acceleration of Brazilian industrial development led the South American country to seek in the USSR resources that could be delivered under better conditions than could be provided by other suppliers and/ or buyers. This new stage in USSR-Brazil relations started in 1974 during the Organization of Petroleum Exporting Countries (OPEC) oil embargo, leading to the Brazilian acquisition of 31.5 million barrels of petroleum from the USSR. Along with these oil purchases, the USSR sent turbines, and it purchased Brazilian manufactured products such as shoes, textiles, and electrical articles. These relations were further consolidated in 1975 with the agreement signed during March that guaranteed an expansion of the bilateral trade, which soon reached $548.9 million.

Even though this exchange never equaled the Soviet-Argentine trade flow, it represented the third in importance in Latin America (that with Cuba was second) and was more balanced than that with Argentina. Exports were not primary goods, as in the Argentine case, but reflected the level of development that Brazil had achieved. Despite a deficit trade balance for the USSR, following the oil crisis of 1974 the political possibilities and projections of this exchange had a broader international meaning than links with Argentina.

From the Brazilian viewpoint, the role that the USSR could play in Brazil's international economic expansion as much as in its foreign policy was more important than the relatively modest figures of its trade exchanges. In July 1981 a trade mission headed by the minister of planning, Delfín Netto, accompanied by 150 business people, functionaries, and entrepreneurs, traveled to Moscow. They came to an agreement with their Soviet counterparts on a number of accords that would amplify the Soviet-Brazilian economic exchange. The so-called Red Package contemplated construction of two hydroelectric plants on the Amazon and Paraná rivers, technical assistance for the exploitation of gas and petroleum in various states, and purchases of Brazilian raw materials. Although this "package" suffered certain reversals when the Soviets rejected a Brazilian effort to increase the quota of Soviet purchases of manufactured products from 30 percent to 65 percent, it did not fundamentally alter their bilateral relations.[20]

When the first negotiations in 1981 were concluded, the minister of planning declared that "we have great hope that closer economic and political contacts between the two countries will permit Brazil to benefit from the influence of Soviet banks on the European banking sector. The USSR will strengthen our credibility in the international financial community." These assertions had several implications that are worth noting. In the first place, they tended to moderate the position of the hard-line military sectors, which was reinforced by the Argentine-Brazilian rapprochement of 1981. In the second place, according to declarations made by a functionary who participated in the Red Package negotiations, Minister Delfín Netto deliberately exaggerated the potential of USSR-Brazil relations with the purpose of demonstrating to the international commercial banks that Brazil had other options available. Finally, and most important, this credibility necessarily meant that Brazil had to become a force for cooperation with the Soviets in the Third World. Thus, Brazilian construction companies began to explore the possibilities of subcontracts granted by the USSR for the carrying out of projects in African countries with close relations to the USSR.[21]

This new form of economic association between Brazil and the Soviet Union was oriented by the strategic interests of the former regarding its expansion beyond the continent. Brazilian foreign policy has had as one of its principal recourses the ability to diversify its ties with the Third World. Armament exports reaching one billion dollars in 1981 have had special importance, mostly being directed to the countries of the South. Equal importance has been given to the exportation of petroleum technology, which has even been sold to OPEC countries. The same occurred with the export of technology to take advantage of sugarcane as fuel (gasohol). However, it is in the African countries of the sub-Sahara, in particular the former Portuguese colonies, that Brazil has placed a major emphasis for reasons of greater linguistic and ethnic affinity. Consequently, this new kind of trade relation—subcontracting with the USSR in areas of the sub-Sahara where Moscow or Havana had a presence of political importance—considerably reinforced the Brazilian presence in Africa.

Something similar also began to be perceived in joint Soviet-Brazilian activity in the Latin American region. For instance, the USSR—in order to carry out engineering works in a hydroelectric project developed by the USSR in Peru—created a Soviet-Brazilian Consortium. All later developments could be framed in this same pattern: increase in bilateral trade, greater purchases of Brazilian manufactured goods, exports of agricultural products to the USSR, and purchase of Soviet technology and subcontracting. The agreements signed during 1981 only diversified the Brazilian export items.

In this way, Soviet-Brazilian relations showed that the level of development achieved by Brazil found in the USSR a point of support important enough to resolve specific problems as well as to support its strategy of a power base in Latin America and the Third World. As a consequence, it was not strange that these relations contemplated questions of international politics of importance, such as the Palestinian problem and nuclear nonproliferation. The permanent Brazilian refusal to join a South Atlantic pact (a question in some ways important to the United States) and more recent reactions, especially on the part of the Brazilian military regarding the presence of North Atlantic Treaty Organization (NATO) members—which propelled them into a new armament phase—presented to the USSR political opportunities of which it would not fail to take advantage. Again it became clear that the factor that the USSR valued as central in its ties with Latin America was the actual capacity of each country to adopt and maintain policies independent of the United States, even though Moscow would not be the one to finance or promote directly such autonomous policies.

CONTINUITY OR CHANGE?

If the conclusions in these case studies are valid, we find ourselves in the presence of a number of effects of the Brezhnev model that merit closer analysis.

In the first place, this strong deemphasis of ideology in the relations between the USSR and Latin American countries ends up burying any attempt to vindicate a "proletarian internationalism." The situation becomes clearer through the words of the director of the Institute of Latin America, Victor Volski, who affirmed that

> the Latin American people themselves recognize and increasingly verify that the Soviet Union does not mingle in their internal affairs. The best proof of this is our relations with two countries that nobody, perhaps, dares to call communist or pro-communist, which are Argentina and Brazil. It is evident to the entire world that these governments are not so progressive. But they themselves recognize that the Soviet Union does not interfere in their internal affairs. Although it is clear not only from the ideological, but also the human, point of view, we cannot in any way sympathize with regimes that crush and liquidate democratic institutions or that antagonize those who think differently than they do. But we can neither send out troops nor stimulate some movement against those regimes.[22]

This clear state policy has ended up subordinating policies directed to the Communist parties, leaving the latter in an increasingly more isolated position in the respective internal politics. Such a situation is evident in each of the three cases just analyzed.

In the second place, these consequences of the Brezhnev model created some controversy within the Soviet government. Thus, there is sufficient information to conjecture with good reason that regarding the effects of such a policy, those sectors that put more emphasis on violent revolution reemerged. This has been reinforced by the revolutionary success in Nicaragua and the struggles in El Salvador and Guatemala, none of which have been led by the respective CPs. As a consequence, it is possible to sustain the argument that, along with the failure of the Chilean experience and the developments recently observed in the Caribbean, the policy of the USSR toward Latin America—and consequently the Soviet role in the foreign policy of the actual states of the area—could be modified in the future.[23]

Thus we have an eventual contradiction between a model of relations that gave a very pragmatic and instrumental role to the USSR in relation to the objectives, needs, and capacities of the Latin American countries and another conception of the relations between both regions that could begin to put a stronger emphasis on the internal political consequences of such aid. As a result, in the face of this analytical euphoria, it would not be strange if the most orthodox positions regarding the problem of revolution in Latin America were again to emerge in the Soviet decision-making process.

Such developments would not be impossible, even when great variations cannot be expected in the short range given the rigidities and slowness of the process of internal change in the USSR. However, in the face of the crisis of internal direction within the socialist bloc— Poland and others—as well as with regard to the results of Soviet policies during the Brezhnev period in Latin America, a recuperation from both failures could imply a significant change in the future role of the USSR in Latin American foreign policies.

Finally, as a derivation of this analysis, we can at least conclude that the external context of Latin American foreign policies presents potentials that can be utilized provided that the optimization of such recourses is carried out jointly by the countries of the area. In the specific case of the USSR, the ability of Argentina to put manufactured products on the Soviet market and the materialization of the desired contracts or subcontracts that Brazil expects in Africa and Latin America basically depend upon the capacity of the countries that presently have ties with the USSR to formulate a common policy toward Moscow. Only in this way could the Soviet Union, as an available resource for development policies that consider state action as basic, find effective support.

NOTES

1. For background see S. Clissold, *Soviet Relations with Latin America: 1918–1969* (New York: Oxford University Press, 1970); F. Claudin, *The Communist Movement* (London: Penguin, 1975), p. 75; and "América Latina y la Unión Soviética: Relaciones interestatales y vínculos políticos," CIDE, *Cuadernos Semestrales*, no. 12, 1982.

2. L. Brezhnev, quoted by E. K. Valkenier, "The USSR, the Third World, and the Global Economy," *Problems of Communism* 28 (July–August 1979), pp. 17–33.

3. *23rd Congreso del PCUS* (Santiago: Horizonte, n. d.).

4. Quoted in J. L. Nogee and J. W. Sloan, "Allende's Chile and the Soviet Union: A Policy Lesson for Latin American Nations Seeking Autonomy," *Journal of Interamerican Studies and World Affairs* 21, no. 3 (August 1979), p. 351.

5. *América Latina*, no. 7, 1980.

6. See Nogee and Sloan, "Allende's Chile and the Soviet Union"; also see P. Sigmund, "The USSR, Cuba, and the Revolution in Chile," in R. H. Donaldson (ed.), *The Soviet Union in the Third World: Successes and Failures* (Boulder, Colo.: Westview Press, 1981); and L. Goure and M. Rothemberg, "Latin America," in K. London (ed.), *The Soviet Union in World Politics* (Boulder, Colo.: Westview Press, 1980).

7. *Keesing's Report*, June 5–12, 1971, p. 24652; and Nogee and Sloan, "Allende's Chile and the Soviet Union," p. 354.

8. *Keesing's Report*, August 12–19, 1972, p. 25417, and April 9–15, 1973, p. 25825.

9. Nogee and Sloan, "Allende's Chile and the Soviet Union," p. 365, note 8.

10. Cited in Goure and Rothemberg, "Latin America," p. 237.

11. Cited in Nogee and Sloan, "Allende's Chile and the Soviet Union," p. 356.

12. See R. G. Tomberg, "Relaciones económicas de la Unión Soviética con paises de América Latina," E/CEPAL/Proy. 4/R. (Santiago, United Nations), November 12, 1979. Also see G. Fichet, "Tres decenios de relaciones entre América Latina y la Unión Soviética," *Comercio Exterior* 31, no. 2 (February 1981), pp. 160–169.

13. *Keesing's Report*, May 9, 1980, p. 30235.

14. Ministry of Economy, *Informe económico de la Argentina*, no. 122 (Buenos Aires: Imprenta Oficial, January–April 1982).

15. *Latin American Weekly Report*, May 29, 1981, p. 2; and *Latin American Commodities Report*, May 5, 1982, p. 5.

16. *Latin American Political Report*, September 21, 1972, p. 293. Also see *Testimonio Latinoamericano*, no. 11, December 1981.

17. *La Prensa*, April 6, 1982.

18. See W. Perry, *Contemporary Brazilian Foreign Policy: The International Strategy of an Emerging Power* (Beverly Hills, Calif.: Sage Publications, 1976); and R. Schneider, *Brazil: Foreign Policy of a Future World Power* (Boulder, Colo.: Westview Press, 1976).

19. C. Pérez Llana, "La política exterior de Argentina, Brasil, y México," in L. Tomassini (ed.), *Relaciones Internacionales de América Latina* (Mexico City: Fondo de Cultura Económica, 1981).

20. *Latin American Weekly Report*, July 23, 1982.

21. Ibid.

22. *Testimonio Latinoamericano*, April 1982, pp. 14, 15.

23. M. Rothemberg, "The Soviet Union in Latin America Since Reagan," *The Washington Quarterly*, Spring 1982.

Acronyms

ABC	Argentina-Brazil-Chile
ACHIP	Asociación Chilena de Investigaciones para la Paz
AD	Acción Democrática
AFL-CIO	American Federation of Labor–Congress of Industrial Organizations
ALALC	Asociación Latinoamericana de Libre Comercio
APRA	Alianza Popular Revolucionaria Americana
B-A	bureaucratic-authoritarian state
BID	Banco Interamericano de Desarrollo; Inter-American Development Bank
CACEX	Export Office of the Central Bank of Brazil
CAL	Comité de Acción Legislativa; Legislative Action Committee
CARICOM	Caribbean Commercial
CCP	Cuban Communist party
CDC	Comunidad Democrática Centroamericana; Central American Democratic Community
CDR	Comité de Defensa de la Revolución
CECLA	Comité Especial de Coordinación Latinoamericana; Special Commission of Latin American Coordination
CEPAL	Comisión Económica para América Latina
CGT	Confederación General de Trabajo
CI	Communist International
CIPEC	Comisión Internacional de Paises Exportadores de Cobre; Association of Copper Producing Nations
CMEA	Council of Mutual Economic Assistance
COAP	Comité Asesor de la Presidencia; Advisory Committee to the President of the Republic
COAS	Comité Asesor; Advisory Committee of the Military Junta
COBEC	Corporaçâo Brasileira de Exportaçâo-Comercio
COMECON	East European Common Market
Comintern	Communist International
COPEI	Christian Democratic party of Venezuela

COPPAL	Conferencia Permanente de Partidos Políticos Latinoamericanos
CORFO	Corporación de Fomento
CP	Communist party (in Chile)
CPs	Communist parties (in Latin America)
DASP	Departamento de Servicio Público
DGI	Directorio General de Inteligencia
DPC	Departamento de Promociones Comerciales; Department of Commercial Promotions
ECLA	Economic Commission for Latin America
EEC	European Economic Community
Embraer	Empresas Militares Brasileiras Aéreas
Fedecamáras	Federación de Cámaras de Comercio
FND	Frente Nacional Democrático
GATT	General Agreement on Tariffs and Trade
GDP	gross domestic product
GNP	gross national product
ICJ	International Court of Justice
IMF	International Monetary Fund
INBEL	Industrias Belicas
Interbrás	Brazilian National Telephone Company
IPC	International Petroleum Company
ITT	International Telephone and Telegraph
JLP	Jamaica Labour party
LAFTA	Latin American Free Trade Association
MID	Movimiento de Integración y Desarrollo
MIR	Movimiento de Izquierda Revolucionaria
MPLA	Movimiento para la Liberación de Angola
NAM	Movement of Nonaligned Nations
NATO	North Atlantic Treaty Organization
NIC	New Industrializing Country
NIEO	New International Economic Order
NPT	Nonproliferation Treaty
Nuclebrás	Brazilian Nuclear Authority
OAPEP	Organization of Arabian Petroleum Producing Countries
OAS	Organization of American States
ODCA	Organización Demócrata Cristiana de América
ODEPLAN	Oficina de Planeamiento; Office of National Planning
OPEC	Organization of Petroleum Exporting Countries
OLAS	Organización Latinoamericana de Sindicatos
OSPAAAL	Organisation de Solidarité des Peuples d'Afrique, d'Asie et d'Amerique Latina
Petrobrás	Brazilian Petroleum Corporation
PLN	Partido de Liberación Nacional
PLO	Palestine Liberation Organization

PMDB	Partido de Movimiento Democrático Brasileiro; Brazilian Democrátic Movement party
PNP	People's National party
PRA	Partido Revolucionario Auténtico
PRI	Partido Revolucionario Institucional
PRO	Public Record Office (Great Britain)
RIAL	Relaciones Internacionales de América Latina
SALT	Strategic Arms Limitation Talks
SATO	South Atlantic Treaty Organization
SCP	Soviet Communist party
SELA	Sistema Económico Latinoamericano
SEREX	Services Economico del Relaciones Exteriores
SP	Socialist party (in Chile)
SWAPO	Southwest African Peoples Organization
TIAR	Tratado Interamericano de Asistencia Recíproca
UN	United Nations
UNCTAD	United Nations Commission on Trade and Development
UNITAS	Inter-American Defense Exercises
UPI	United Press International
UP	Unidad Popular
URD	Unión Republicana Democrática
WPJ	Workers Party of Jamaica
YPF	Yacimientos Petrolíferos Fiscales

Research Bibliography

DESCRIPTIVE CASE STUDIES

The following works on the foreign policies of Brazil and Chile are examples of the case studies mentioned in the Preface.

Brazil

Hayes, Margaret Daly. *Brazil and the South Atlantic.* Occasional Papers Series no. 7. Washington, D.C.: Center of Brazilian Studies, School for Advanced International Studies, Johns Hopkins University (SAIS), 1980.

Jaguaribe, Hélio. "Brasil y la América Latina." *Estudios Internacionales*, no. 29 (January–March 1975).

————. *Relações Internacionais do Brasil: Perspectives para o fim de século.* Occasional Papers Series no. 6. Washington, D.C.: Center of Brazilian Studies, SAIS, 1979.

Lafer, Celso. "La Política Exterior Brasileña: Balance y perspectivas." *Estudios Internacionales*, no. 51 (July–September 1980).

Malan, Pedro Sampaio. "Las Relaciones económicas internacionales de Brasil." *Estudios Internacionales*, no. 41 (January–March 1978).

Pérez Llana, Carlos. "¿Potencias intermedias o paises mayores? La política exterior de Argentina, Brasil y México." *Estudios Internacionales*, no. 29 (January–March 1975).

Perry, William. *Contemporary Brazilian Foreign Policy.* Beverly Hills, Calif.: Sage Foreign Policy Papers, 1976.

Schneider, Ronald. *Brazil: Foreign Policy of a Future World Power.* Boulder, Colo.: Westview Press, 1977.

Selcher, Wayne. *Brazil's Multilateral Relations.* Boulder, Colo.: Westview Press, 1978.

Chile

Fortín, Carlos. "Principled Pragmatism in the Face of External Pressure: The Foreign Policy of the Allende Government." In Ronald Hellman and H. Jon Rosenbaum (eds.), *Latin America: The Search for a New International Role.* New York: John Wiley & Sons, 1975.

Kaufman, Edy. "La Política Exterior de la Unidad Popular Chilena," *Foro Internacional*, no. 66 (October–December 1976).

Muñoz, Heraldo. *The International Relations of the Chilean Military Government: Elements for a Systematic Analysis.* Working Papers Series. Washington, D.C.: Latin American Program, The Woodrow Wilson Center, 1980.

Orrego Vicuña, Francisco. *La Participación de Chile en el Sistema Internacional.* Santiago: Editora Gabriela Mistral, 1972.

————. "Trayectoria y Orientaciones de la Política Exterior de Chile." *Seguridad Nacional* (September–October 1976).

Sánchez, Walter, and Teresa Pereira (eds). *150 Años de Política Exterior Chilena.* Santiago: Editorial Universitaria, 1977.

Wilhelmy, Manfred. "La Política Exterior Chilena en el Grupo Andino." *Estudios Internacionales*, no. 38 (April–June 1977).

————. "Hacia un Análisis de la Política Exterior Chilena Contemporánea." *Estudios Internacionales*, no. 48 (October–December 1979).

DIPLOMATIC HISTORIES

The publications listed here are among those mentioned in the Preface.

Barros Borgoño, Luis. *Las Primeras Relaciones Diplomáticas de las Naciones Americanas.* Buenos Aires: J. Peuser, 1938.

Barros, Mario. *Historia Diplomática de Chile.* Barcelona: Ariel, 1970.

Davis, Harold, John Finan, and Taylor Peck. *Latin American Diplomatic History.* Baton Rouge: Louisiana State University Press, 1977.

Eyzaguirre, Jaime. *Chile y Bolivia, Esquema de un Proceso Diplomático.* Santiago: Zig-Zig, 1963.

García Salazar, Arturo. *Historia Diplomática del Perú.* Lima: A. J. Rivas Berrío, 1930.

Pérez Concha, Jorge. *Ensayo Histórico-Crítico de las Relaciones Diplomáticas del Ecuador con los Estados Limítrofes.* 2 vols. Quito: Editorial Casa de la Cultura Ecuatoriana, 1961–1964.

Peterson, Harold. *Argentina and the United States, 1810–1960.* Albany: State University of New York, 1964.

Pike, Frederick. *Chile and the United States: 1880–1962.* Notre Dame, Ind.: University of Notre Dame Press, 1963.

Quesada, Vicente. *Historia Diplomática Hispanoamericana.* 3 vols. Buenos Aires: La Cultura Argentina, 1918–1920.

Rivas, Raimundo. *Historia Diplomática de Colombia: 1810–1834.* Bogotá: Imprenta Nacional, 1961.

Rodríguez Larretta, A. *Orientación de la Política Internacional de América Latina.* Montevideo: Peña, 1938.

Ruiz Moreno, Isidoro. *Historia de las Relaciones Exteriores Argentina, 1810–1955.* Buenos Aires: Ed. Perrot, 1961.

Vianna, Hélio. *Historia Diplomática do Brazil.* São Paulo: Edicoes Melhoramentos, 1958.

INTERNATIONAL RELATIONS STUDIES

These are among the most recent works of the type described in the Preface.

Atkins, G. Pope. *Latin America in the International Political System.* New York: The Free Press, 1977.

Fontaine, Roger, and James Theberge (eds.). *Latin America's Internationalism.* New York: Praeger, 1976.

Grunwald, Joseph (ed.). *Latin America and World Economy.* Beverly Hills, Calif.: Sage, 1978.

Hellman, Ronald G., and H. Jon Rosenbaum (eds.). *Latin America: The Search for a New International Role*. New York: John Wiley & Sons, 1975.

Kinson, F. Par. *Latin America, the Cold War, and the World Powers, 1945–1973*. Beverly Hills, Calif.: Sage, 1974.

Lagos, Gustavo (ed.). *Las Relaciones entre América Latina, Estados Unidos y Europa Occidental*. Santiago: Editorial Universitaria, 1980.

Martz, John D., and Lars Schoultz (eds.). *Latin America, the United States, and the Inter-American System*. Boulder, Colo.: Westview Press, 1980.

Orrego Vicuña, Francisco (ed.). *¿América Latina: Clase Media de las Naciones?* Santiago: Talleres Gráficos Corporación, 1979.

Urquidi, Victor, and Rosemary Thorp (eds.). *Latin America in the International Economy*. New York: John Wiley & Sons, 1973.

Titles in This Series

The Exclusive Economic Zone: A Latin American Perspective, edited by Francisco Orrego Vicuña

†*The Third World Coalition in International Politics,* Second, Updated Edition, Robert A. Mortimer

Militarization and the International Arms Race in Latin America, Augusto Varas

†*Latin American Nations in World Politics,* edited by Heraldo Muñoz and Joseph S. Tulchin

Other Titles of Interest from Westview Press

Change in Central America: Internal and External Dimensions, edited by Wolf Grabendorff, Heinrich-W. Krumwiede, and Jörg Todt

†*FOREIGN POLICY on Latin America, 1970–1980,* edited by the staff of *Foreign Policy*

†*Latin American Foreign Policies: Global and Regional Dimensions,* edited by Elizabeth G. Ferris and Jennie K. Lincoln

†*The New Cuban Presence in the Caribbean,* edited by Barry B. Levine

Colossus Challenged: The Struggle for Caribbean Influence, edited by H. Michael Erisman and John D. Martz

Brazil in the International System: The Rise of a Middle Power, edited by Wayne A. Selcher

Sovereignty in Dispute: The Falklands/Malvinas, 1493–1982, Fritz L. Hoffman and Olga Mingo Hoffman

†*Latin America and the U.S. National Interest: A Basis for U.S. Foreign Policy,* Margaret Daly Hayes

†*The Caribbean Challenge: U.S. Policy in a Volatile Region,* edited by H. Michael Erisman

†Available in hardcover or paperback.

About the Book and Editors

Latin American Nations in World Politics
edited by Heraldo Muñoz and Joseph S. Tulchin

This unique volume of essays adds to the subject of international relations a new Latin American perspective. Distinguished scholars from Latin America, the United States, and Europe analyze foreign policies and international behaviors of major Latin American nations and, using a comparative framework, explore the role of the individual countries in world politics. The authors systematically test a variety of theoretical models from the Latin American perspective to evaluate the utility of the tests for the analysis of North-South relations. This approach makes the book especially useful to professors and students of international politics and Latin American studies.

Heraldo Muñoz is professor and research associate at the Institute of International Studies, University of Chile, and is associated with CERC–Academia de Humanismo Cristiano. **Joseph S. Tulchin** is professor of history and director of the Office of International Programs at the University of North Carolina at Chapel Hill.

Index